KB002625

박문각 공무원

기출문제

브랜드만족 1위 박문각

2025

수석합격 2연속 배출

진가영 영어

진가영 편저

New Trend
단기합격 길라잡이

- 2025 출제 기조 전환 1차, 2차 예시 문제 반영
- 국가직과 지방직 및 기타 9급 핵심 기출 반영
- 기출 독해 유형별 문제 풀이 전략 수록
- 9급 기출 핵심 어휘 총정리 자료 수록

반한다 기출 독해

동영상 강의 www.pmg.co.kr

박문각

PREFACE

머리말

수험생들에게 최고의 문법 학습서가 될
합격까지, 반드시 한 번에 다잡는다!
New Trend 진가영 영어 반한다 기출 독해를 펴내며...

안녕하세요. 여러분들의 단기합격 길라잡이 진가영입니다. 모든 수험생이 알고 있듯이 공무원 시험에서 기출문제의 중요성은 아무리 강조해도 지나치지 않습니다. 하지만 기출문제를 반드시 한 번에 다잡아 합격까지 이어지게 하기 위해서는 기출문제를 푸는 데서 그치는 것이 아니라 기출을 통해서 배운 이론을 다시 한 번 정리하고 실전 문제에 이론을 적용하는 훈련을 하는 것이 중요합니다. 또한 실전 기출문제 풀이를 통해서 앞으로 출제 가능성이 있는 문제들의 유형과 패턴을 분석하여 출제 알고리즘을 파악해서 다음 시험을 대비하시는 것이 매우 중요합니다. 즉, 기출문제는 단순히 문제를 풀고 분석해서 내용 아는 것을 넘어서 기출되는 문제의 유형과 답이 되는 패턴 등을 배울 수 있고 알게 해주는 소중한 자료이므로 문제만 풀고 넘기는 것이 아니라 반드시 출제 경향을 파악하고 출제 알고리즘을 익혀야 합니다. 여러분들의 이러한 중요한 학습 과정을 돕기 위해서 나온 교재가 바로 "박문각 공무원 New Trend 진가영 영어 반한다 기출 독해"입니다.

이 교재가 가진 장점은 다음과 같습니다.

- 독해 기출문제는 영역별로 구분하여 학습자가 배운 이론을 체계적으로 문제에 적용해 볼 수 있도록 구성하였다.
- 독해 기출문제를 풀기 전에 영역별 핵심 정리를 할 수 있도록 하는 별도의 장을 마련하여 해당 영역에 대한 확실한 정리가 가능하도록 구성하였다.
- 독해 기출 어휘 중에서 핵심 어휘들을 제시하고 복습테스트를 제공함으로써 독해를 위한 기본 토대를 탄탄히 할 수 있도록 구성하였다.
- 독해 기출 문제를 풀고 틀린 문제들은 다시 풀어 볼 수 있도록 해설지에 기출 문제를 추가함으로써 복습을 제대로 할 수 있도록 구성하였다.
- 해설지에 지문에서 답이 되는 단서를 표시해 놓음으로써 감으로 독해를 하는 것이 아니라 정확한 독해를 할 수 있도록 구성하였다.

이 교재의 좋은 장점들을 잘 활용하신다면 방대한 영어 기출문제들에서 벗어나 시험에서 적용되는 출제 알고리즘을 확실하게 배워, 감으로 문제를 찍는 것이 아니라 단서를 통해 확신을 가지고 문제를 풀 수 있게 될 것입니다. 또한 저자 직강을 통해 여러분들이 이 교재를 효율적으로 활용하신다면 합격까지 한 번에 다게 될 것입니다. 결국 이 교재를 선택하는 순간 여러분들은 시험에 최적화된 공무원 영어 기출 문제집을 선택하신 것이니 반드시 합격에 이를 것입니다. 매일 조금씩 합격하는 길로 나아가고 있으니 매일 자신의 공부 상태와 내용을 잘 점검하여 원하시는 바를 이루시길 바랍니다. 이 "박문각 공무원 진가영 영어 반한다 기출 독해"에 진심으로 반하셔서 꼭 빠른 합격을 이루시길 항상 응원합니다!

Dreams come true!
꿈은 반드시 이루어진다!

진심을 다해 가르치는 영어 - 진가영

2025 출제 기조 전환

① 2025년도 출제 기조 전환 "핵심 내용"

"지식암기 위주에서 현장 직무 중심으로 9급 공무원 시험의 출제 기조가 바뀐다"

인사혁신처가 출제하는 9급 공무원 시험 국어·영어 과목의 출제 기조가 2025년부터 전면 전환됩니다. 인사혁신처 처장은 '2023년 업무보고'에서 발표했던 인사처가 출제하는 9급 공무원 시험의 '출제 기조 전환'을 2025년부터 본격 추진한다고 밝혔습니다.

'출제 기조 전환'의 핵심내용은 지식암기 위주로 출제되고 있는 현행 9급 공무원 시험 국어·영어 과목의 출제 기조를 직무능력 중심으로 바꾸고, 민간 채용과의 호환성을 강화하는 것입니다. 현장 직무 중심의 평가를 위해 영어 과목에서는 실제 업무수행에 필요한 실용적인 영어능력을 검증하고자 합니다. 특히 영어 과목에서는 실제 활용도가 높은 어휘를 주로 물어보고 어법의 암기를 덜 요구하는 방식이고, 전자메일과 안내문 등 업무 현장에서 접할 수 있는 소재와 형식을 적극 활용한 문제들로 구성될 것으로 보입니다.

이를 바탕으로 인사혁신처는 종합적 사고력과 실용적 능력을 평가하게 되는 출제 기조 전환으로 공직에 더 적합한 인재를 선발할 수 있고, 공무원과 민간부문 채용시험 간 호환성 제고로 청년들의 시험 준비 부담이 감소되고 우수한 인재가 공직에 보다 더 지원할 것으로 기대하고 있습니다.

② 2025년 "현명한" 신경향 공무원 영어 학습 전략

신경향 어휘 학습

출제 기조 전환 전에는 유의어 유형을 많이 물어보고 단순 암기로 인하여 문제 푸는 시간 또한 절약할 수 있었습니다. 하지만 2025년 출제 기조 전환 예시문제를 보면 어휘는 빈칸 유형으로만 구성된 것으로 보아 **제시문의 맥락을 고려하고 정확한 단서를 찾은 후에 빈칸 안에 어떤 어휘가 적절한 것인지 찾는 훈련과 연습**이 반드시 필요합니다.

신경향 문법 학습

출제 기조 전환 전에는 문법 문제들이 박스형, 문장형, 영작형으로만 구성되었지만 출제 기조 전환 발표 중 일부인 민간 채용과의 호환성을 강화하는 취지로 **TOEIC, TEPS 시험에서 잘 나오는 빈칸 유형이 문법 문제로 새로 추가되었습니다.** 이런 유형들은 기존의 유형들과 확실하게 다른 접근법으로 문제를 풀어야 하므로 **문법 파트별로 체계적인 이론 정리와 더불어 다양한 문제들을 많이 풀어보고 문제 풀이 전략을 정확하고 확실하게 배워야 합니다.**

신경향 독해 학습

출제 기조 전환 전에는 1지문 1문제로 구성되고 각 선지들이 지문에 맞는지, 안 맞는지만 판단하기만 하면 되었지만 **2025년 출제 기조 전환 예시문제를 보면 독해 유형에 세트형이 2문제**로 구성되어 있습니다. 세트형이라고 난도가 더 올라갔다고 보기는 어렵지만 **다소 생소한 형식의 문제 유형이 출제되면 수험생들이 당황하기가 쉬우므로 신유형 독해 문제인 전자메일과 안내문, 홈페이지 게시글 등의 형식들에 대한 체계적인 학습을 통해 빠르고 정확하게 푸는 전략을 체화시켜야 합니다.** 이와 같은 형식으로 단일 지문으로 구성되기도 하니 특히 많은 훈련이 필요한 영역입니다.

구성과 특징

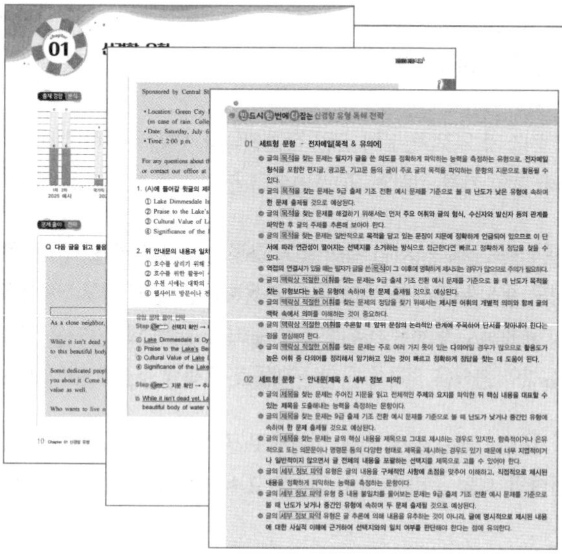

독해 기출문제를 풀기 전에 영역별 핵심 정리를 할 수 있도록 하는 별도의 장을 마련하여 해당 영역에 대한 확실한 정리가 가능하도록 구성하였다.

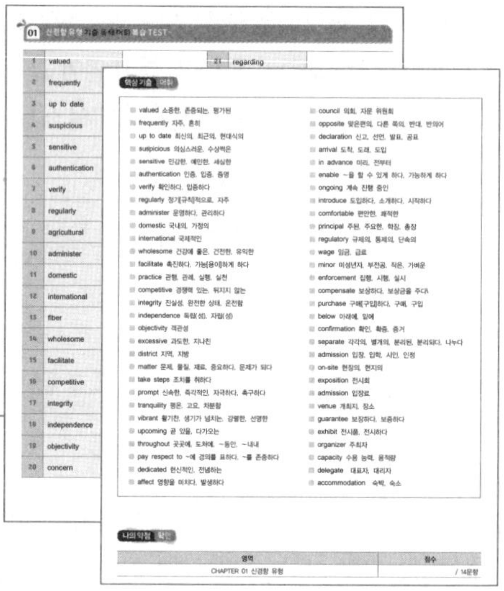

독해 기출 어휘 중에서 핵심 어휘들을 제시하고 복습테스트를 제공함으로써 독해를 위한 기본 토대를 탄탄히 할 수 있도록 구성하였다.

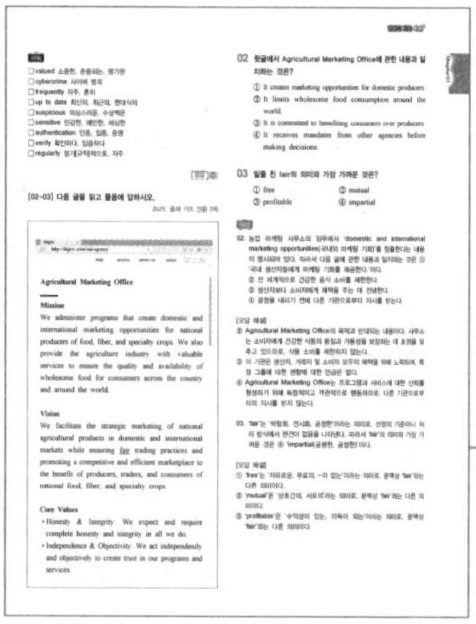

독해 기출문제를 풀고 틀린 문제들은 다시 풀어 볼 수 있도록 해설지에 기출문제를 추가함으로써 복습을 제대로 할 수 있도록 구성하였다.

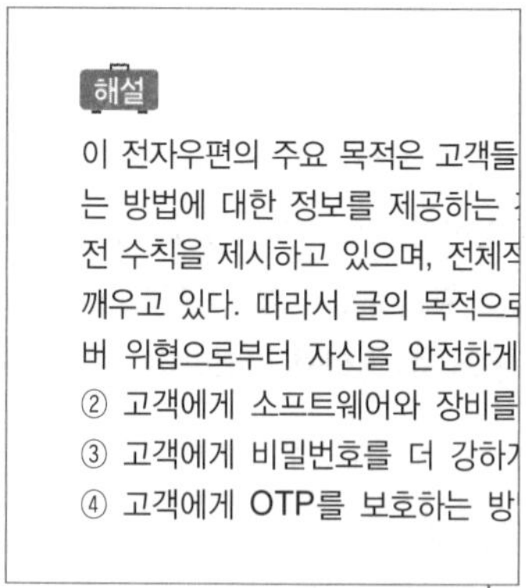

해설지에 지문에서 답이 되는 단서를 표시해 놓음으로써 감으로 독해를 하는 것이 아니라 정확한 독해를 할 수 있도록 구성하였다.

후기

가영쌤과 점수 수직 상승을 만들어 낸 "생생한" 수강후기

★★★★★ 충남 교행 수석 영어 100점 김**

가영쌤의 커리는 기본적으로 반복을 거듭해서 확실하게 기억하고 또 여러 방향으로 적용하면서 어떤 식으로 문제로 변형되어 나와도 확실하게 캐치할 수 있게 만드는 방향으로 진행됩니다. 특히 여러 번 강조해서 배우는, 자주 출제되는 중요한 내용들은 계속 따로 자료를 만들고, 또 특강으로도 계속 또 반복해서 빠짐없이 떠 먹여 주기까지 합니다. 따라 가려고 노력만 하면 보상을 받을 수 있는 그런 시간을 보낼 수 있는 강의라고 생각합니다. 가영쌤은 또, 더 재밌는 강의를 위해 매번 좀 웃긴 거를 많이 준비해 오시는 것 같은 모습이 보이는데 많은 정성과 노력을 기울이고 계시다는 걸 느낄 수 있는 시간들이었습니다.

★★★★★ 우정직 수석 합격 영어 85점 박*태

영어 선생님을 고를 때 가영쌤을 추천하는 이유는 먼저 탄탄한 커리큘럼과 숙제 관리, 그리고 문법 교재가 너무너무 좋습니다! 콤팩트한 책에 있을 내용 다 있고, 문판왕이나 동형모의고사 등 문풀 수업과의 연계도 잘 되어있습니다. 그리고 매주 실강 수업 때 나오는 ox 숙제를 계속 반복해야 문법 출제 포인트가 무엇인지 익숙해집니다. 또한, 가영쌤의 어휘책 구성도 좋았고, 매 수업 전에 테스트를 하기 때문에 미리 공부해가야 하는 게 실력 향상에 도움이 되었습니다. 덕분에 이번 문제 풀이 소요시간, 24분, 동형 때는 달성해보지 못했던 최고기록입니다. 가영쌤 I cannot thank you enough!!

★★★★★ 2024 일반행정직 영어 100점 **선

영어 100점은 진짜 운이라고 생각했는데 선생님 만나고 나서 이게 진짜 실력으로 된다는 걸 알았어요. 단어 미친 반복으로 겨우 다 외우고 문법도 단판승 3시간 너무 좋았고 독해는 그 200제가 정말 좋았어요. 제가 국가직 영어 35분 걸려서 정말 선생님도 찾아뵈고 걱정 많이 했는데 이번 지방직은 20분 컷해서 정말 좋았어요. 언제나 감사합니다!!

★★★★★ 2024 일반행정직 영어 95점 **경

공시 시작하고 가영쌤을 만나서 영어 공부도 즐겁게 할 수 있었고 95점이라는 고득점도 해볼 수 있었고 항상 최선을 다하시는 모습을 보면서 많이 본받아야겠다 생각했습니다. 나태해질 때마다 쌤을 보면서 힘을 얻었고 앞으로도 제가 많이 존경하고 진심으로 응원할 영원한 제 1타 강사 가영쌤♥ 건강 잘 챙기시고 곧 태어날 아이와 가족들 또 주변 사람들과 행복한 순간만 앞으로 더 가득하시면 좋겠어요♥ 서울 가게 되면 인사드리러 꼭 갈게요!! 쌤이랑 함께한 시간들 항상 소중했어요♥ I cannot thank you enough♥

★★★★★ 2024년 사회복지직 영어 95점 **화

I cannot thank you enough♥시험을 준비하면서 나름의 소소한 목표 중 하나가 영어 시험을 잘 봐서 가영쌤한테 제가 먼저 올해 영어 잘 봤다고 연락드리는 거였는데, 드디어 그 목표를 이룰 수 있게 되어서 너무 기뻐요! 처음 박문각 와서 하프 들었을 때 3,4개 맞기도 하고 그랬던 적이 있었는데~ 쌤과 열심히 함께 달렸더니 95점이라는 이런 좋은 점수를 받았습니다. 영어는 제 발목을 잡는 과목 중 하나여서 처음부터 끝까지 긴장을 놓지 않고 제일 큰 비중을 두고 공부한 과목이었습니다. 이번 지방직에서 단어, 문법, 생활영어까지 쌤과 함께 공부했던 범위 내에서 계속 반복하며 공부했던 부분들이라 신속하고 정확하게 풀 수 있어시간 절약을 했던 것 같아요! 다 가영쌤과 함께한 덕분이에요!

CURRICULUM

커리큘럼

2025 출제 기조 전환 대비 단기합격 커리큘럼 영상

2025년
신경향(New Trend)
정규 커리큘럼

합격을 위한 필수 과정

1단계 — 이론 완성
New Trend
단기합격 All In One 시리즈
(문법, 독해)

2단계 — 기출 분석
New Trend
반한다 기출 분석 시리즈
(문법 · 어휘 & 생활영어, 독해)

3단계 — 문제 풀이
New Trend
끝판왕 문제 풀이 시리즈
(문법, 어휘, 독해)

4단계 — 최종 정리
New Trend
만점 동형 모의고사
시리즈

Daily Training
- New Trend 단기합격 VOCA
- New Trend 올타임 레전드 하프 모의고사
- New Trend 스파르타 일일 모의고사
- New Trend 단판승 문법 적중 포인트 100

2025년
신경향(New Trend)
보완 커리큘럼

합격을 위한 선택 과정

기초 이론	공무원 영어 시작, 입문
구문 독해	진(Real) 독해 기초 체력 다지기 / 신경향 독해 기본 실력 다지기
문풀 N제	신경향 마스터 시리즈 (독해, 문법, 어휘)
적중 특강	진(眞) 족보 마무리 특강 시리즈 (독해, 문법, 어휘, 생활영어)

CONTENTS

차례

반한다 독해

정답 및 해설

진가영 영어
반한다 기출
독해

진가영 영어연구소 | cafe.naver.com/easyenglish7

Chapter

01

신경향 유형

chapter 01

신경향 유형

출제 경향 분석

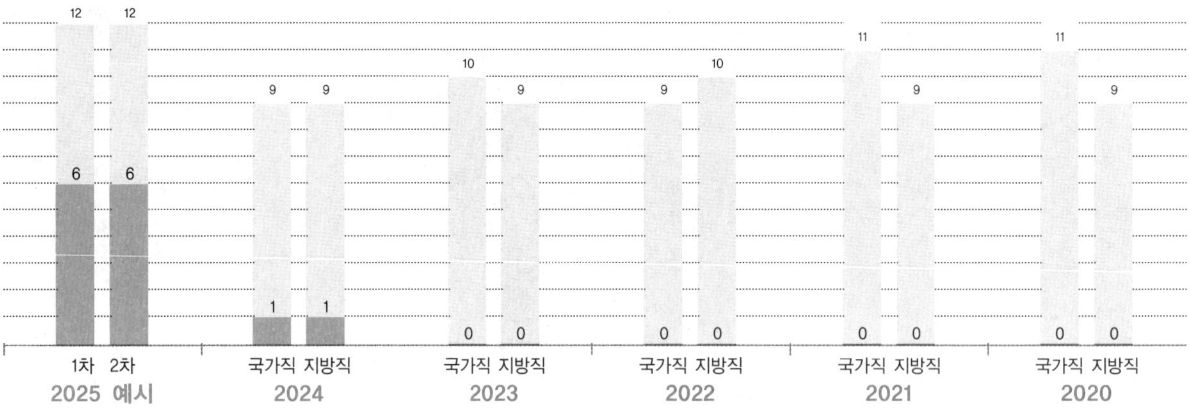

문제풀이 전략

Q 다음 글을 읽고 물음에 답하시오. 2025. 출제 기조 전환 2차

(A)

As a close neighbor, you will want to learn how to save your lake.

While it isn't dead yet, Lake Dimmesdale is heading toward this end. So pay your respects to this beautiful body of water while it is still alive.

Some dedicated people are working to save it now. They are having a special meeting to tell you about it. Come learn what is being done and how you can help. This affects your property value as well.

Who wants to live near a dead lake?

Sponsored by Central State Regional Planning Council

•Location: Green City Park Opposite Southern State College
(in case of rain: College Library Room 203)
•Date: Saturday, July 6, 2024
•Time: 2:00 p.m.

For any questions about the meeting, please visit our website at www.planningcouncilsavelake.org or contact our office at (432) 345-6789.

1. (A)**에 들어갈 윗글의 제목으로 가장 적절한 것은**?

① Lake Dimmesdale Is Dying
② Praise to the Lake's Beauty
③ Cultural Value of Lake Dimmesdale
④ Significance of the Lake to the College

2. **위 안내문의 내용과 일치하지 않는 것은**?

① 호수를 살리기 위해 노력하는 사람들이 있다.
② 호수를 위한 활동이 주민들의 재산에 영향을 미친다.
③ 우천 시에는 대학의 구내식당에서 회의가 열린다.
④ 웹사이트 방문이나 전화로 회의에 관해 질문할 수 있다.

유형 문제 풀이 전략

Step 1 선택지 확인 → 내용 예측하기

① Lake Dimmesdale Is Dying
② Praise to the Lake's Beauty
③ Cultural Value of Lake Dimmesdale
④ Significance of the Lake to the College

Step 2 지문 확인 → 주제 문장 찾기

☑ While it isn't dead yet, Lake Dimmesdale is heading toward this end. So pay your respects to this beautiful body of water while it is still alive.

Step ③ 단서 확인 후 선택지 분석하기 → 오답 소거 후 정답 도출

단서	While it isn't dead yet, Lake Dimmesdale is heading toward this end. 아직 호수가 죽지는 않았지만, 딤즈데일 호수는 그 방향으로 나아가고 있습니다.
선택지	✓① 딤즈데일 호수가 죽어가고 있다 ② 호수의 아름다움에 대한 찬사 ③ 딤즈데일 호수의 문화적 가치 ④ 대학에 대한 호수의 중요성

'세부 정보 파악' 유형 문제 풀이 전략

Step ① 선택지 확인 → 고유한 어휘를 확인하기

① 호수를 살리기 위해 노력하는 사람들이 있다.
② 호수를 위한 활동이 주민들의 재산에 영향을 미친다.
③ 우천 시에는 대학의 구내식당에서 회의가 열린다.
④ 웹사이트 방문이나 전화로 회의에 관해 질문할 수 있다.

● 고유한 어휘란 다른 선택지에는 없고 하나의 선택지에만 존재하는 단어를 의미한다.

Step ② 지문 확인 → 고유한 어휘를 기준으로 선택지에 해당하는 정보를 지문에서 찾기

● 하나의 선택지만 먼저 읽고 지문으로 바로 가서 내용을 확인한다.

Step ③ 선택지 분석 → 오답 소거 후 정답 도출

선택지	지문
① 호수를 살리기 위해 노력하는 사람들이 있다.	Some dedicated people are working to save it now.
② 호수를 위한 활동이 주민들의 재산에 영향을 미친다.	This affects your property value as well.
✓③ 우천 시에는 대학의 구내식당에서 회의가 열린다.	(in case of rain: College Library Room 203)
④ 웹사이트 방문이나 전화로 회의에 관해 질문할 수 있다.	For any questions about the meeting, please visit our website at www.planningcouncilsavelake.org or contact our office at (432) 345-6789.

핵심 기출 어휘

- valued 소중한, 존중되는, 평가된
- frequently 자주, 흔히
- up to date 최신의, 최근의, 현대식의
- suspicious 의심스러운, 수상쩍은
- sensitive 민감한, 예민한, 세심한
- authentication 인증, 입증, 증명
- verify 확인하다, 입증하다
- regularly 정기[규칙]적으로, 자주
- administer 운영하다, 관리하다
- domestic 국내의, 가정의
- international 국제적인
- wholesome 건강에 좋은, 건전한, 유익한
- facilitate 촉진하다, 가능[용이]하게 하다
- practice 관행, 관례, 실행, 실천
- competitive 경쟁력 있는, 뒤지지 않는
- integrity 진실성, 완전한 상태, 온전함
- independence 독립(성), 자립(성)
- objectivity 객관성
- excessive 과도한, 지나친
- district 지역, 지방
- matter 문제, 물질, 재료, 중요하다, 문제가 되다
- take steps 조치를 취하다
- prompt 신속한, 즉각적인, 자극하다, 촉구하다
- tranquility 평온, 고요, 차분함
- vibrant 활기찬, 생기가 넘치는, 강렬한, 선명한
- upcoming 곧 있을, 다가오는
- throughout 곳곳에, 도처에, ~동안, ~내내
- pay respect to ~에 경의를 표하다, ~를 존중하다
- dedicated 헌신적인, 전념하는
- affect 영향을 미치다, 발생하다
- council 의회, 자문 위원회
- opposite 맞은편의, 다른 쪽의, 반대, 반의어
- declaration 신고, 선언, 발표, 공표
- arrival 도착, 도래, 도입
- in advance 미리, 전부터
- enable ~을 할 수 있게 하다, 가능하게 하다
- ongoing 계속 진행 중인
- introduce 도입하다, 소개하다, 시작하다
- comfortable 편안한, 쾌적한
- principal 주된, 주요한, 학장, 총장
- regulatory 규제의, 통제의, 단속의
- wage 임금, 급료
- minor 미성년자, 부전공, 작은, 가벼운
- enforcement 집행, 시행, 실시
- compensate 보상하다, 보상금을 주다\
- purchase 구매[구입]하다, 구매, 구입
- below 아래에, 밑에
- confirmation 확인, 확증, 증거
- separate 각각의, 별개의, 분리된, 분리되다, 나누다
- admission 입장, 입학, 시인, 인정
- on-site 현장의, 현지의
- exposition 전시회
- admission 입장료
- venue 개최지, 장소
- guarantee 보장하다, 보증하다
- exhibit 전시품, 전시하다
- organizer 주최자
- capacity 수용 능력, 용적량
- delegate 대표자, 대리자
- accommodation 숙박, 숙소

나의 약점 확인

영역	점수
CHAPTER 01 신경향 유형	/ 14문항

반드시 한 번에 다 잡는 '신경향 유형' 독해 전략

01 세트형 문항 - 전자메일[목적 & 유의어]

- 글의 목적을 찾는 문제는 **필자가 글을 쓴 의도**를 정확하게 파악하는 능력을 측정하는 유형으로, **전자메일 형식**을 포함한 편지글, 광고문, 기고문 등의 글이 주로 글의 목적을 파악하는 문항의 지문으로 활용될 수 있다.
- 글의 목적을 찾는 문제는 9급 출제 기조 전환 예시 문제를 기준으로 볼 때 **난도가 낮은 유형**에 속하며 **한 문제** 출제될 것으로 예상된다.
- 글의 목적을 찾는 문제를 해결하기 위해서는 먼저 **주요 어휘와 글의 형식, 수신자와 발신자 등의 관계를 파악**한 후 글의 주제를 추론해 보아야 한다.
- 글의 목적을 찾는 문제는 일반적으로 **목적을 담고 있는 문장이 지문에 정확하게 언급되어 있으므로 이 단서에 따라 연관성이 떨어지는 선택지를 소거하는 방식**으로 접근한다면 빠르고 정확하게 정답을 찾을 수 있다.
- **역접의 연결사**가 있을 때는 필자가 글을 쓴 목적이 **그 이후**에 명확하게 제시되는 경우가 많으므로 주의가 필요하다.
- 글의 맥락상 적절한 어휘를 찾는 문제는 9급 출제 기조 전환 예시 문제를 기준으로 볼 때 **난도가 목적을 찾는 유형보다는 높은 유형**에 속하며 **한 문제** 출제될 것으로 예상된다.
- 글의 맥락상 적절한 어휘를 찾는 문제의 정답을 찾기 위해서는 **제시된 어휘의 개별적 의미와 함께 글의 맥락 속에서 의미**를 이해하는 것이 중요하다.
- 글의 맥락상 적절한 어휘를 추론할 때 **앞뒤 문장의 논리적인 관계에 주목하여 단서를 찾아내야 한다**는 점을 명심해야 한다.
- 글의 맥락상 적절한 어휘를 찾는 문제는 주로 여러 가지 뜻이 있는 **다의어**일 경우가 많으므로 **활용도가 높은 어휘 중 다의어를 정리해서 암기하고 있는 것이 빠르고 정확하게 정답을 찾는 데 도움이 된다.**

02 세트형 문항 - 안내문[제목 & 세부 정보 파악]

- 글의 제목을 찾는 문제는 주어진 지문을 읽고 전체적인 **주제**와 **요지**를 파악한 뒤 **핵심 내용을 대표할 수 있는 제목**을 도출해내는 능력을 측정하는 문항이다.
- 글의 제목을 찾는 문제는 9급 출제 기조 전환 예시 문제를 기준으로 볼 때 **난도가 낮거나 중간인 유형**에 속하며 **한 문제** 출제될 것으로 예상된다.
- 글의 제목을 찾는 문제는 글의 핵심 내용을 제목으로 그대로 제시하는 경우도 있지만, 함축적이거나 은유적으로 또는 의문문이나 명령문 등의 다양한 형태로 제목을 제시하는 경우도 있기 때문에 **너무 지엽적이거나 일반적이지 않으면서 글 전체의 내용을 포괄하는 선택지**를 제목으로 고를 수 있어야 한다.
- 글의 세부 정보 파악 유형은 글의 내용을 **구체적인 사항에 초점**을 맞추어 이해하고, **직접적으로 제시된 내용**을 정확하게 파악하는 능력을 측정하는 문항이다.
- 글의 세부 정보 파악 유형 중 내용 불일치를 물어보는 문제는 9급 출제 기조 전환 예시 문제를 기준으로 볼 때 **난도가 낮거나 중간인 유형**에 속하며 **두 문제** 출제될 것으로 예상된다.
- 글의 세부 정보 파악 유형은 글 추론에 의해 내용을 유추하는 것이 아니라, **글에 명시적으로 제시된 내용에 대한 사실적 이해에 근거하여 선택지와의 일치 여부를 판단**해야 한다는 점에 유의한다.

반드시 한 번에 다 잡는 '신경향 유형' 독해 전략

03 단일형 문항 - 홈페이지 게시글[세부 정보 파악(내용 일치·불일치)]

- 글의 세부 정보 파악 유형은 담화나 글에 제시된 **특정 정보**를 사실적이고 **정확하게 이해하는 능력**을 측정하는 문항이다.
- 글의 세부 정보 파악 유형 중 **내용 불일치**를 물어보는 문제는 9급 출제 기조 전환 예시 문제를 기준으로 볼 때 **난도가 낮은 유형**에 속하며 **두 문제** 출제될 것으로 예상된다.
- 글의 세부 정보 파악 유형은 글의 내용을 **구체적인 사항에 초점**을 맞추어 이해하고, **직접적으로 제시된 내용**을 정확하게 파악하는 연습을 필요로 한다.
- 글의 세부 정보 파악 유형은 글 추론에 의해 내용을 유추하는 것이 아니라, **글에 명시적으로 제시된 내용에 대한 사실적 이해에 근거하여 선택지와의 일치 여부를 판단**해야 한다는 점에 유의한다.
- 글의 세부 정보 파악 유형을 시간 이내에 정확하게 풀기 위해서는 미리 어떻게 시험에서 내용 일치 또는 불일치 선택지를 만드는지 **함정 포인트**를 잘 알고 주의해야 한다.
- 글의 세부 정보 파악 유형은 다른 유형과 달리 특히 **부사 표현, 형용사, 특정 명사, 수치와 부정어** 등 말 그대로 세부 정보를 표시하기 위해서 사용되는 표현들에 주의해야 한다.

꿀팁 선택지에 자주 등장하는 함정 포인트

- 부정부사 또는 부정의 의미를 내포하는 단어들은 주의한다.
- 시간부사나 장소부사 등 여러 가지 부사 표현들은 주의한다.
- 숫자에 관련된 정보는 주의한다.
- 반의어를 가질 수 있는 어휘는 주의한다.
- 비교급과 최상급 표현은 주의한다.
- 2가지 이상의 대상이 나오는 경우 주의한다.
- 인명이나 지명과 같은 고유명사는 주의한다.

01 다음 글의 목적으로 가장 적절한 것은?

2025. 출제 기조 전환 2차

Send Preview Save

To cbsclients@calbank.com
From calbanks@calmail.com
Date May 7, 2024
Subject Important notice

My PC Browse

Times New 10pt

Dear Valued Clients,

In today's world, cybercrime poses a serious threat to your security. As your trusted partner, we want to help you protect your personal and business information. Here are five easy ways to safeguard yourself from cyber threats:

1. Use strong passwords and change them frequently.
2. Keep your software and devices up to date.
3. Be wary of suspicious emails, links, or telephone calls that pressure you to act quickly or give out sensitive information.
4. Enable Two Factor authentication and use it whenever possible. When contacting California Bank & Savings, you will be asked to use a One Time Passcode (OTP) to verify your identity.
5. Back up your data regularly.

Visit our Security Center to learn more about how you can stay safe online. Remember, cybersecurity is a team effort. By working together, we can build a safer online environment for ourselves and the world.

Sincerely,

California Bank & Savings

① to inform clients of how to keep themselves safe from cyber threats
② to inform clients of how to update their software and devices
③ to inform clients of how to make their passwords stronger
④ to inform clients of how to safeguard their OTPs

[02-03] 다음 글을 읽고 물음에 답하시오.

2025. 출제 기조 전환 2차

dagov ×

http://dagov.com/our-agency

HOME ABOUT US CONTACT US SEARCH

Agricultural Marketing Office

Mission

We administer programs that create domestic and international marketing opportunities for national producers of food, fiber, and specialty crops. We also provide the agriculture industry with valuable services to ensure the quality and availability of wholesome food for consumers across the country and around the world.

Vision

We facilitate the strategic marketing of national agricultural products in domestic and international markets while ensuring <u>fair</u> trading practices and promoting a competitive and efficient marketplace to the benefit of producers, traders, and consumers of national food, fiber, and specialty crops.

Core Values

- Honesty & Integrity: We expect and require complete honesty and integrity in all we do.
- Independence & Objectivity: We act independently and objectively to create trust in our programs and services.

02 윗글에서 Agricultural Marketing Office에 관한 내용과 일치하는 것은?

① It creates marketing opportunities for domestic producers.
② It limits wholesome food consumption around the world.
③ It is committed to benefiting consumers over producers.
④ It receives mandates from other agencies before making decisions.

03 밑줄 친 fair의 의미와 가장 가까운 것은?

① free
② mutual
③ profitable
④ impartial

[04-05] 다음 글을 읽고 물음에 답하시오.

2025. 출제 기조 전환 2차

(A)

As a close neighbor, you will want to learn how to save your lake.

While it isn't dead yet, Lake Dimmesdale is heading toward this end. So pay your respects to this beautiful body of water while it is still alive.

Some dedicated people are working to save it now. They are having a special meeting to tell you about it. Come learn what is being done and how you can help. This affects your property value as well.

Who wants to live near a dead lake?

Sponsored by Central State Regional Planning Council

•Location: Green City Park Opposite Southern State College
(in case of rain: College Library Room 203)
•Date: Saturday, July 6, 2024
•Time: 2:00 p.m.

For any questions about the meeting, please visit our website at www.planningcouncilsavelake.org or contact our office at (432) 345-6789.

04 (A)에 들어갈 윗글의 제목으로 가장 적절한 것은?

① Lake Dimmesdale Is Dying
② Praise to the Lake's Beauty
③ Cultural Value of Lake Dimmesdale
④ Significance of the Lake to the College

05 위 안내문의 내용과 일치하지 않는 것은?

① 호수를 살리기 위해 노력하는 사람들이 있다.
② 호수를 위한 활동이 주민들의 재산에 영향을 미친다.
③ 우천 시에는 대학의 구내식당에서 회의가 열린다.
④ 웹사이트 방문이나 전화로 회의에 관해 질문할 수 있다.

06 다음 글의 내용과 일치하지 않는 것은?

2025. 출제 기조 전환 2차

> The David Williams Library and Museum is open 7 days a week, from 9:00 a.m. to 5:00 p.m. (NOV－MAR) and 9:00 a.m. to 6:00 p.m. (APR－OCT). Online tickets may be purchased at the link below. You will receive an email confirmation after making a purchase (be sure to check your SPAM folder). Bring this confirmation — printed or on smart device — as proof of purchase.
>
> ■ **Online tickets**: buy.davidwilliams.com/events
>
> The David Williams Library and Museum and the Home of David Williams (operated by the National Heritage Service) offer separate $10.00 adult admission tickets. Tickets for tours of the Home may be purchased on-site during normal business hours.
>
> ■ **CLOSED**: Thanksgiving, Christmas and New Year's Day
>
> There is no charge for conducting research in the David Williams Library research room.
>
> For additional information, call 1 (800) 333-7777.

① The Library and Museum closes at 5:00 p.m. in December.
② Visitors can buy tour tickets for the Home on-site.
③ The Home of David Williams is open all year round.
④ One can do research in the Library research room for free.

07 Enter-K 앱에 관한 다음 글의 내용과 일치하지 않는 것은?

2025. 출제 기조 전환 1차

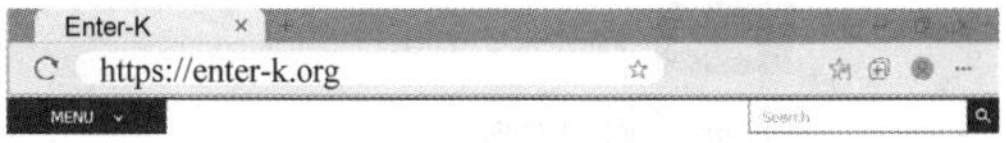

> **Use the new Enter-K app for your customs declaration.**
>
> Use the new Enter-K app upon your arrival at the airport. One notable feature offered by Enter-K is the Advance Declaration, which allows travellers the option to submit their customs declaration in advance, enabling them to save time at all our international airports. As part of the ongoing Traveller Modernization initiative, Enter-K will continue to introduce additional border-related features in the future, further improving the overall border experience. Simply download the latest version of the app from the online store before your arrival. There is also a web version of the app for those who are not comfortable using mobile devices.

① It allows travellers to declare customs in advance.
② More features will be added later.
③ Travellers can download it from the online store.
④ It only works on personal mobile devices.

[08-09] 다음 글을 읽고 물음에 답하시오.

2025. 출제 기조 전환 1차

Send Preview Save

To	Clifton District Office
From	Rachael Beasly
Date	June 7
Subject	Excessive Noise in the Neighborhood

My PC Browse

Times New 10pt

To whom it may concern,

I hope this email finds you well. I am writing to express my concern and frustration regarding the excessive noise levels in our neighborhood, specifically coming from the new sports field.

As a resident of Clifton district, I have always appreciated the peace of our community. However, the ongoing noise disturbances have significantly impacted my family's well-being and our overall quality of life. The sources of the noise include crowds cheering, players shouting, whistles, and ball impacts.

I kindly request that you look into this matter and take appropriate <u>steps</u> to address the noise disturbances. Thank you for your attention to this matter, and I appreciate your prompt response to help restore the tranquility in our neighborhood.

Sincerely,
Rachael Beasley

08 윗글의 목적으로 가장 적절한 것은?

① 체육대회 소음에 대해 주민들의 양해를 구하려고
② 새로 이사 온 이웃 주민의 소음에 대해 항의하려고
③ 인근 스포츠 시설의 소음에 대한 조치를 요청하려고
④ 늦은 시간 악기 연주와 같은 소음의 차단을 부탁하려고

09 밑줄 친 "steps"의 의미와 가장 가까운 것은?

① movements
② actions
③ levels
④ stairs

[10-11] 다음 글을 읽고 물음에 답하시오.

2025. 출제 기조 전환 1차

(A) ________

We're pleased to announce the upcoming City Harbour Festival, an annual event that brings our diverse community together to celebrate our shared heritage, culture, and local talent. Mark your calendars and join us for an exciting weekend!

Details

- **Dates** : Friday, June 16 – Sunday, June 18
- **Times** : 10 : 00 a.m. – 8 : 00 p.m. (Friday & Saturday)
  10 : 00 a.m. – 6 : 00 p.m. (Sunday)
- **Location** : City Harbour Park, Main Street, and surrounding areas

Highlights

- **Live Performances**
  Enjoy a variety of live music, dance, and theatrical performances on multiple stages throughout the festival grounds.
- **Food Trucks**
  Have a feast with a wide selection of food trucks offering diverse and delicious cuisines, as well as free sample tastings.

For the full schedule of events and activities, please visit our website at www.cityharbourfestival.org or contact the Festival Office at (552) 234-5678.

10 (A)에 들어갈 윗글의 제목으로 가장 적절한 것은?

① Make Safety Regulations for Your Community
② Celebrate Our Vibrant Community Events
③ Plan Your Exciting Maritime Experience
④ Recreate Our City's Heritage

11 City Harbour Festival에 관한 윗글의 내용과 일치하지 않는 것은?

① 일 년에 한 번 개최된다.
② 일요일에는 오후 6시까지 열린다.
③ 주요 행사로 무료 요리 강습이 진행된다.
④ 웹사이트나 전화 문의를 통해 행사 일정을 알 수 있다.

12 **Office of the Labor Commissioner에 관한 다음 글의 내용과 일치하는 것은?**

2025. 출제 기조 전환 1차

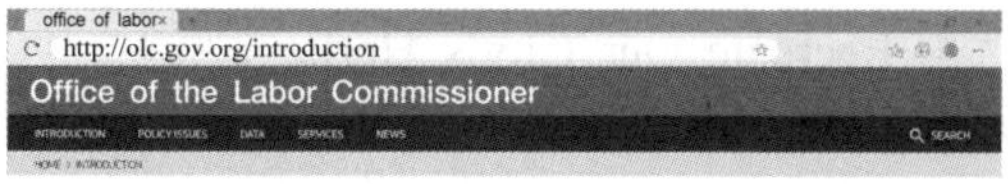

Office of the Labor Commissioner(OLC) Responsibilities

The OLC is the principal labor regulatory agency for the state. The OLC is responsible for ensuring that minimum wage, prevailing wage, and overtime are paid to employees, and that employee break and lunch periods are provided. In addition, the OLC has authority over the employment of minors. It is the vision and mission of this office to resolve labor-related problems in an efficient, professional, and effective manner. This includes educating employers and employees regarding their rights and responsibilities under the law. The OLC takes enforcement action when necessary to ensure that workers are treated fairly and compensated for all time worked.

① It ensures that employees pay taxes properly.
② It has authority over employment of adult workers only.
③ It promotes employers' business opportunities.
④ It takes action when employees are unfairly treated.

13 **Northeastern Wildlife Exposition에 관한 다음 글의 내용과 일치하는 것은?**

2024. 국가직 9급

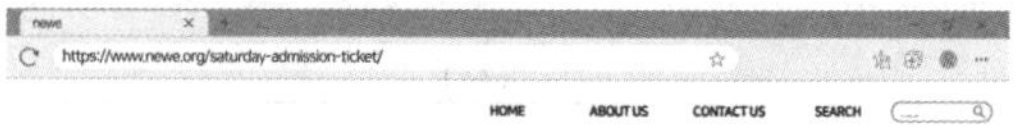

NORTHEASTERN WILDLIFE EXPOSITION (NEWE)

Admission ticket for Saturday, March 30th, 2024

•**Price** : $40.00
•**Opening hours** : 10 : 00 a.m. − 6 : 00 p.m.

Kids 10 and under are free. Entry to shows and lectures are first-come, first-served. All venues open rain or shine.

March 20th is the last day to buy tickets online for the 2024 Northeastern Wildlife Exposition.

Please note : Purchasing NEWE tickets in advance is the best way to guarantee entry into all exhibits. NEWE organizers may discontinue in-person ticket sales should any venue reach capacity.

① 10세 어린이는 입장료 40불을 지불해야 한다.
② 공연과 강연의 입장은 선착순이다.
③ 비가 올 경우에는 행사장을 닫는다.
④ 입장권은 온라인으로만 구매할 수 있다.

14 다음 이메일의 내용과 일치하지 않는 것은?

2024. 지방직 9급

To	reserve@metropolitan.com
From	BruceTaylor@westcity.com
Date	June 22, 2024
Subject	Venue facilities

Dear Sir,

I am writing to ask for information about Metropolitan Conference Center.

We are looking for a venue for a three-day conference in September this year. We need to have enough room for over 200 delegates in your main conference room, and we would also like three small conference rooms for meetings. Each conference room needs wi-fi as well. We need to have coffee available mid-morning and mid-afternoon, and we would also like to book your restaurant for lunch on all three days.

In addition, could you please let me know if there are any local hotels with discount rates for Metropolitan clients or large groups? We will need accommodations for over 100 delegates each night.

I look forward to hearing from you.

Best regards,
Bruce Taylor, Event Manager

① 주 회의실은 200명 이상의 대표자를 수용할 수 있어야 한다.
② wi-fi가 있는 작은 회의실 3개가 필요하다.
③ 3일간의 저녁 식사를 위한 식당 예약이 필요하다.
④ 매일 밤 100명 이상의 대표자를 위한 숙박시설이 필요하다.

01 신경향 유형 기출 독해 어휘 복습 TEST

1	valued		21	regarding	
2	frequently		22	excessive	
3	up to date		23	district	
4	suspicious		24	look into	
5	sensitive		25	matter	
6	authentication		26	take steps	
7	verify		27	address	
8	regularly		28	prompt	
9	agricultural		29	tranquility	
10	administer		30	vibrant	
11	domestic		31	upcoming	
12	international		32	heritage	
13	fiber		33	a variety of	
14	wholesome		34	throughout	
15	facilitate		35	feast	
16	competitive		36	cuisine	
17	integrity		37	pay respect to	
18	independence		38	dedicated	
19	objectivity		39	affect	
20	concern		40	property	

01 신경향 유형 기출 독해 어휘 복습 TEST

41	sponsor		61	compensate	
42	council		62	purchase	
43	opposite		63	below	
44	in case of		64	confirmation	
45	customs		65	be sure to	
46	declaration		66	separate	
47	arrival		67	admission	
48	in advance		68	on-site	
49	enable		69	charge	
50	ongoing		70	exposition	
51	introduce		71	admission	
52	comfortable		72	first-come, first-served	
53	principal		73	venue	
54	regulatory		74	in advance	
55	minimum		75	guarantee	
56	wage		76	organizer	
57	employee		77	capacity	
58	minor		78	delegate	
59	employer		79	discount	
60	enforcement		80	accommodation	

진가영 영어
반한다 기출
독해

Chapter

02

중심 내용 파악 유형

chapter 02

중심 내용 파악 유형

출제경향 분석

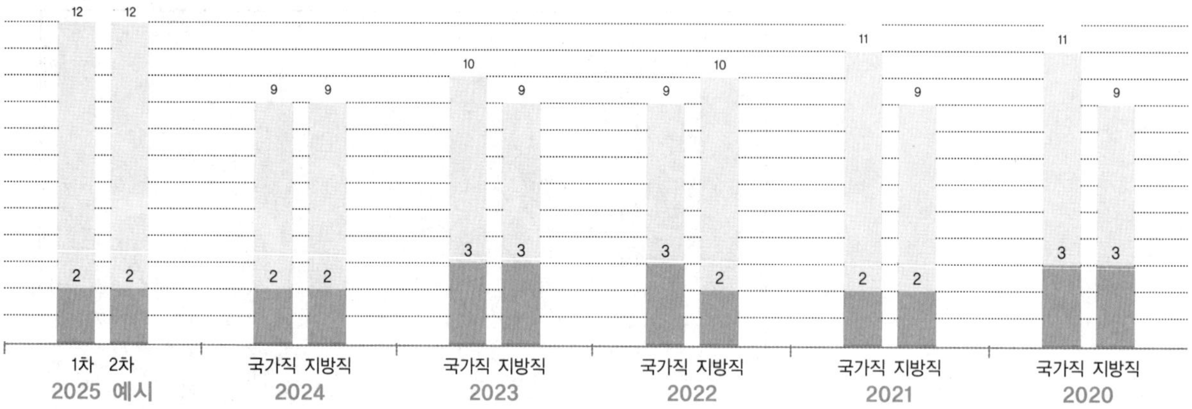

문제풀이 전략

Q 다음 글의 주제로 가장 적절한 것은? 2025. 출제 기조 전환 2차

The International Space Station, orbiting some 240 miles above the planet, is about to join the effort to monitor the world's wildlife — and to revolutionize the science of animal tracking. A large antenna and other equipment aboard the orbiting outpost, installed by spacewalking Russian astronauts in 2018, are being tested and will become fully operational this summer. The system will relay a much wider range of data than previous tracking technologies, logging not just an animal's location but also its physiology and environment. This will assist scientists, conservationists and others whose work requires close monitoring of wildlife on the move and provide much more detailed information on the health of the world's ecosystems.

① evaluation of sustainability of global ecosystems
② successful training projects of Russian astronauts
③ animal experiments conducted in the orbiting outpost
④ innovative wildlife monitoring from the space station

Step ① 선택지 확인 → 어휘 확인하고 내용 예측하기

① evaluation of sustainability of global ecosystems
② successful training projects of Russian astronauts
③ animal experiments conducted in the orbiting outpost
④ innovative wildlife monitoring from the space station

- 공통 어휘가 없는 경우에는 바로 지문으로 들어가서 글에서 반복되는 어휘를 확인하기
- 선택지에 반의어 관계의 어휘가 나오면 두 개 선택지 중 하나가 답이 되는 경우가 많으므로 주의하기

Step ② 지문 확인 → 단서(주제를 나타내는 문장) 찾기

Step ③ 단서 확인 후 선택지 분석하기 → 오답 소거 후 정답 도출

단서	<u>The International Space Station</u>, orbiting some 240 miles above the planet, is about to join the effort to monitor the world's wildlife—and to revolutionize the science of animal tracking. 국제 우주 정거장이 지구에서 약 240마일 상공을 돌며 세계의 야생 동물을 모니터링하고 동물 추적 과학에 혁신을 일으킬 준비를 하고 있다. This will assist scientists, conservationists and others whose work requires close monitoring of wildlife on the move and provide much more detailed information on the health of the world's ecosystems. 이는 야생 동물의 이동을 밀접하게 모니터링을 해야 하는 과학자, 환경 보호 활동가 및 기타 연구자들에게 도움을 주며, 세계 생태계의 건강에 대한 보다 자세한 정보를 제공할 것이다.
선택지	① evaluation of sustainability of global ecosystems 지구 생태계의 지속 가능성 평가 ② successful training projects of Russian astronauts 러시아 우주비행사들의 성공적인 훈련 프로젝트 ③ animal experiments conducted in the orbiting outpost 궤도 전초기지에서 행해진 동물 실험 ④✓ innovative wildlife monitoring from the space station 우주 정거장에서 혁신적인 야생 동물 모니터링

핵심 기출 어휘

- install 설치하다, 설비하다
- previous 이전의, 바로 앞의
- outbreak 발생, 발발
- extensive 아주 넓은, 대규모의, 광범위한
- diagnose 진단하다
- temperature 온도, 기온, 체온
- optimal 최적의, 최선의
- infection 감염, 전염병
- disparity 격차, 차이
- persistent 끊임없이 지속되는, 끈질긴, 집요한
- vulnerable 취약한, 연약한
- emphasize 강조하다
- incredible 믿기 어려운, 놀라운
- excavate 발굴하다
- volatile 변덕스러운, 불안한, 휘발성의
- dilute 희석하다, 약화시키다
- replenish 보충하다, 채우다
- encounter 만나다, 직면하다
- nonverbal 비언어적인
- means 수단, 방법, 수입
- relieve 완화하다, 줄이다
- surround 둘러싸다, 에워싸다
- possession 소유물, 소지품
- attribute ~의 탓으로 보다, 속성, 특성, 특질
- dedicate 바치다, 전념하다
- deliberate 고의의, 의도적인, 신중한, 사려 깊은
- interpret 해석하다, 이해하다
- cultivate 양성하다, 경작하다, 재배하다
- excessive 과도한, 지나친
- incumbent 의무적인, 재임 중인
- intervene 개입하다, 간섭하다
- intact 그대로의, 온전한, 손상되지 않은
- anonymity 익명성
- authenticity 진실성
- obsession 강박, 집착, 사로잡힘
- flexibility 유연성
- meditation 명상
- prosperity 번영, 번성, 번창
- reward 보상, 보상하다
- injection 주입
- perception 인지, 자각
- assume 추정하다, 알다, 띠다
- sustain 유지하다, 지속시키다
- commitment 헌신, 전념, 약속
- exploit 착취하다, 이용하다
- voluntary 자발적인, 임의적인
- interest 이해관계, 이익, 관심, 흥미
- merit 받을 만하다[자격/가치가 있다], 가치, 장점
- perspective 관점, 시각
- artificial 인공의, 인위적인
- realm 영역, 범위
- sanction 제재, 허가, 제재를 가하다, 허가하다
- lay off 해고하다
- explicit 분명한, 명백한, 노골적인
- transformation 변화, 변신
- hierarchy 계층, 계급
- attain 이루다, 달성하다
- striking 인상적인, 현저한, 두드러진

나의 약점 확인

영역	점수
CHAPTER 02 중심 내용 파악 유형	/ 37문항

반드시 한번에 다잡는 '중심 내용 파악 유형' 독해 전략

- 글의 중심 내용 파악 유형은 주어진 지문을 읽고 전체적인 **주제**와 **요지**를 파악한 뒤 **핵심 내용을 대표할 수 있는 제목**을 도출해내는 능력을 측정하는 문항이다.
- 글의 중심 내용 파악 유형은 9급 출제 기조 전환 예시 문제를 기준으로 볼 때 **난도가 낮거나 중간인 유형**에 속하며 **한 문제** 출제될 것으로 예상된다.
- 글의 중심 내용 파악을 위해서는 **글의 첫 문장**과 **마지막 문장**, 또는 **역접의 연결사**(예: however)가 제시된 경우 그 이후 부분을 중심으로 지문에서 제시되는 **반복적인 어구** 또는 **특정 개념**과 관련된 표현을 주의 깊게 살펴 보아야 한다.
- 글의 중심 내용 파악 유형은 선택지에서 정답을 찾을 때 오답이 가진 특징을 잘 파악해야 한다. **오답은 주로 지문의 일부 내용 요소를 다루지만, 지문의 내용과 무관한 것을 언급하거나 중심 소재나 내용 요소를 언급하지 않는 특징**을 가졌다는 점에 주목해야 한다.

찐팁 글의 논리 구조에 따른 주제문

- 예시와 열거 - 예시와 열거가 시작되기 전 또는 끝난 이후에 주제문이 제시된다.
  - ★ for example, for instance, for an illustration, to illustrate, to be specific, let's take an example, suppose, imagine
- 통념과 반박/진실 - 반박이나 진실이 주제문이다.
- 실험 또는 연구 인용 전문가의 견해 인용
  - 실험이나 연구의 절차나 과정을 설명하고 그에 관한 결과를 제시하거나 권위 있는 전문가의 의견이 제시된다.
- 문제점과 해결책 또는 질문과 답변 - 해결책이나 답변은 주로 주제문이다.
- 비교와 대조 - 공통점 또는 차이점이 주로 주제문이다.
- 순서 - 시간적 순서 또는 절차적 순서가 시작되기 전이나 후에 주로 주제문이 제시된다.
- 기타 주제문을 알려주는 표현
  - ★ Should, must, have to, need to 등 "~해야 한다"라는 표현을 담고 있는 문장
  - ★ So, thus, therefore와 같은 결론을 나타내는 문장
  - ★ I believe, I think, I argue 등과 같은 필자의 견해를 나타내는 표현을 담고 있는 문장
  - ★ 최상급, 비교급을 담고 있는 문장

01 다음 글의 주제로 가장 적절한 것은?

2025. 출제 기조 전환 2차

The International Space Station, orbiting some 240 miles above the planet, is about to join the effort to monitor the world's wildlife — and to revolutionize the science of animal tracking. A large antenna and other equipment aboard the orbiting outpost, installed by spacewalking Russian astronauts in 2018, are being tested and will become fully operational this summer. The system will relay a much wider range of data than previous tracking technologies, logging not just an animal's location but also its physiology and environment. This will assist scientists, conservationists and others whose work requires close monitoring of wildlife on the move and provide much more detailed information on the health of the world's ecosystems.

① evaluation of sustainability of global ecosystems
② successful training projects of Russian astronauts
③ animal experiments conducted in the orbiting outpost
④ innovative wildlife monitoring from the space station

02 다음 글의 요지로 가장 적절한 것은?

2025. 출제 기조 전환 2차

Animal Health Emergencies

Preparedness for animal disease outbreaks has been a top priority for the Board of Animal Health (BOAH) for decades. A highly contagious animal disease event may have economically devastating effects as well as public health or food safety and security consequences.

Foreign Animal Diseases

A foreign animal disease (FAD) is a disease that is not currently found in the country, and could cause significant illness or death in animals or cause extensive economic harm by eliminating trading opportunities with other countries and states.

Several BOAH veterinarians who are trained in diagnosing FADs are available 24 hours a day to investigate suspected cases of a FAD. An investigation is triggered when report of animals with clinical signs indicative of a FAD is received or when diagnostic laboratory identifies a suspicious test result.

① BOAH focuses on training veterinarians for FADs.
② BOAH's main goal is to repsond to animal disease epidemic.
③ BOAH actively promotes international trade opportunities.
④ BOAH aims to lead laboratory research on the causes of FADs.

03 다음 글의 주제로 가장 적절한 것은?

2025. 출제 기조 전환 1차

The Ministry of Food and Drug Safety warned that cases of food poisoning have occurred as a result of cross-contamination, where people touch eggs and neglect to wash their hands before preparing food or using utensils. To mitigate such risks, the ministry advised refrigerating eggs and ensuring they are thoroughly cooked until both the yolk and white are firm. Over the past five years, a staggering 7,400 people experienced food poisoning caused by Salmonella bacteria. Salmonella thrives in warm temperatures, with approximately 37 degrees Celsius being the optimal growth condition. Consuming raw or undercooked eggs and failing to separate raw and cooked foods were identified as the most common causes of Salmonella infection. It is crucial to prioritize food safety measures and adhere to proper cooking practices to minimize the risk of Salmonella-related illnesses.

① Benefits of consuming eggs to the immune system
② Different types of treatments for Salmonella infection
③ Life span of Salmonella bacteria in warm temperatures
④ Safe handling of eggs for the prevention of Salmonella infection

04 다음 글의 요지로 가장 적절한 것은?

2025. 출제 기조 전환 1차

Despite ongoing efforts to address educational disparities, the persistent achievement gap among students continues to highlight significant inequities in the education system. Recent data reveal that marginalized students, including those from low-income back grounds and vulnerable groups, continue to lag behind their peers in academic performance. The gap poses a challenge to achieving educational equity and social mobility. Experts emphasize the need for targeted interventions, equitable resource allocation, and inclusive policies to bridge this gap and ensure equal opportunities for all students, irrespective of their socioeconomic status or background. The issue of continued educational divide should be addressed at all levels of education system in an effort to find a solution.

① We should deal with persistent educational inequities.
② Educational experts need to focus on new school policies.
③ New teaching methods are necessary to bridge the achievement gap.
④ Family income should not be considered in the discussion of education.

05 다음 글의 주제로 적절한 것은?

2024. 국가직 9급

It seems incredible that one man could be responsible for opening our eyes to an entire culture, but until British archaeologist Arthur Evans successfully excavated the ruins of the palace of Knossos on the island of Crete, the great Minoan culture of the Mediterranean was more legend than fact. Indeed its most famed resident was a creature of mythology: the half-man, half-bull Minotaur, said to have lived under the palace of mythical King Minos. But as Evans proved, this realm was no myth. In a series of excavations in the early years of the 20th century, Evans found a trove of artifacts from the Minoan age, which reached its height from 1900 to 1450 B.C.: jewelry, carvings, pottery, altars shaped like bull's horns, and wall paintings showing Minoan life.

① King Minos' successful excavations
② Appreciating artifacts from the Minoan age
③ Magnificence of the palace on the island of Crete
④ Bringing the Minoan culture to the realm of reality

06 다음 글의 제목으로 적절한 것은?

2024. 국가직 9급

Currency debasement of a good money by a bad money version occurred via coins of a high percentage of precious metal, reissued at lower percentages of gold or silver diluted with a lower value metal. This adulteration drove out the good coin for the bad coin. No one spent the good coin, they kept it, hence the good coin was driven out of circulation and into a hoard. Meanwhile the issuer, normally a king who had lost his treasure on interminable warfare and other such dissolute living, was behind the move. They collected all the good old coins they could, melted them down and reissued them at lower purity and pocketed the balance. It was often illegal to keep the old stuff back but people did, while the king replenished his treasury, at least for a time.

① How Bad Money Replaces Good
② Elements of Good Coins
③ Why Not Melt Coins?
④ What Is Bad Money?

07 다음 글의 주제로 적절한 것은?

2024. 지방직 9급

In recent years Latin America has made huge strides in exploiting its incredible wind, solar, geothermal and biofuel energy resources. Latin America's electricity sector has already begun to gradually decrease its dependence on oil. Latin America is expected to almost double its electricity output between 2015 and 2040. Practically none of Latin America's new large-scale power plants will be oil-fueled, which opens up the field for different technologies. Countries in Central America and the Caribbean, which traditionally imported oil, were the first to move away from oil-based power plants, after suffering a decade of high and volatile prices at the start of the century.

① booming oil industry in Latin America
② declining electricity business in Latin America
③ advancement of renewable energy in Latin America
④ aggressive exploitation of oil-based resources in Latin America

08 다음 글의 제목으로 적절한 것은?

2024. 지방직 9급

Every organization has resources that it can use to perform its mission. How well your organization does its job is partly a function of how many of those resources you have, but mostly it is a function of how well you use the resources you have, such as people and money. You as the organization's leader can always make the use of those resources more efficient and effective, provided that you have control of the organization's personnel and agenda, a condition that does not occur automatically. By managing your people and your money carefully, by treating the most important things as the most important, by making good decisions, and by solving the problems that you encounter, you can get the most out of what you have available to you.

① Exchanging Resources in an Organization
② Leaders' Ability to Set up External Control
③ Making the Most of the Resources: A Leader's Way
④ Technical Capacity of an Organization: A Barrier to Its Success

09 다음 글의 제목으로 알맞은 것은? 2023. 국가직 9급

The feeling of being loved and the biological response it stimulates is triggered by nonverbal cues: the tone in a voice, the expression on a face, or the touch that feels just right. Nonverbal cues — rather than spoken words — make us feel that the person we are with is interested in, understands, and values us. When we're with them, we feel safe. We even see the power of nonverbal cues in the wild. After evading the chase of predators, animals often nuzzle each other as a means of stress relief. This bodily contact provides reassurance of safety and relieves stress.

① How Do Wild Animals Think and Feel?
② Communicating Effectively Is the Secret to Success
③ Nonverbal Communication Speaks Louder than Words
④ Verbal Cues: The Primary Tools for Expressing Feelings

10 다음 글의 주제로 알맞은 것은? 2023. 국가직 9급

There are times, like holidays and birthdays, when toys and gifts accumulate in a child's life. You can use these times to teach a healthy nondependency on things. Don't surround your child with toys. Instead, arrange them in baskets, have one basket out at a time, and rotate baskets occasionally. If a cherished object is put away for a time, bringing it out creates a delightful remembering and freshness of outlook. Suppose your child asks for a toy that has been put away for a while. You can direct attention toward an object or experience that is already in the environment. If you lose or break a possession, try to model a good attitude ("I appreciated it while I had it!") so that your child can begin to develop an attitude of nonattachment. If a toy of hers is broken or lost, help her to say, "I had fun with that."

① building a healthy attitude toward possessions
② learning the value of sharing toys with others
③ teaching how to arrange toys in an orderly manner
④ accepting responsibility for behaving in undesirable ways

11 다음 글의 요지로 알맞은 것은?

2023. 국가직 9급

Many parents have been misguided by the "self-esteem movement," which has told them that the way to build their children's self-esteem is to tell them how good they are at things. Unfortunately, trying to convince your children of their competence will likely fail because life has a way of telling them unequivocally how capable or incapable they really are through success and failure. Research has shown that how you praise your children has a powerful influence on their development. Some researchers found that children who were praised for their intelligence, as compared to their effort, became overly focused on results. Following a failure, these same children persisted less, showed less enjoyment, attributed their failure to a lack of ability, and performed poorly in future achievement efforts. Praising children for intelligence made them fear difficulty because they began to equate failure with stupidity.

① Frequent praises increase self-esteem of children.
② Compliments on intelligence bring about negative effect.
③ A child should overcome fear of failure through success.
④ Parents should focus on the outcome rather than the process.

12 다음 글의 제목으로 가장 적절한 것은?

2023. 지방직 9급

Well-known author Daniel Goleman has dedicated his life to the science of human relationships. In his book *Social Intelligence* he discusses results from neuro-sociology to explain how sociable our brains are. According to Goleman, we are drawn to other people's brains whenever we engage with another person. The human need for meaningful connectivity with others, in order to deepen out relationships, is what we all crave, and yet there are countless articles and studies suggesting that we are lonelier than we ever have been and loneliness is now a world health epidemic. Specifically, in Australia, according to a national Lifeline survey, more than 80% of those surveyed believe our society is becoming a lonelier place. Yet, our brains crave human interaction.

① Lonely People
② Sociable Brains
③ Need for Mental Health Survey
④ Dangers of Human Connectivity

13 다음 글의 주제로 가장 적절한 것은?

2023. 지방직 9급

Certainly some people are born with advantages (e.g., physical size for jockeys, height for basketball players, an "ear" for music for musicians). Yet only dedication to mindful, deliberate practice over many years can turn those advantages into talents and those talents into successes. Through the same kind of dedicated practice, people who are not born with such advantages can develop talents that nature put a little farther from their reach. For example, even though you may feel that you weren't born with a talent for math, you can significantly increase your mathematical abilities through mindful, deliberate practice. Or, if you consider yourself "naturally" shy, putting in the time and effort to develop your social skills can enable you to interact with people at social occasions with energy, grace, and ease.

① advantages some people have over others
② importance of constant efforts to cultivate talents
③ difficulties shy people have in social interactions
④ need to understand own strengths and weaknesses

14 다음 글의 요지로 가장 적절한 것은?

2023. 지방직 9급

Dr. Roossinck and her colleagues found by chance that a virus increased resistance to drought on a plant that is widely used in botanical experiments. Their further experiments with a related virus showed that was true of 15 other plant species, too. Dr. Roossinck is now doing experiments to study another type of virus that increases heat tolerance in a range of plants. She hopes to extend her research to have a deeper understanding of the advantages that different sorts of viruses give to their hosts. That would help to support a view which is held by an increasing number of biologists, that many creatures rely on symbiosis, rather than being self-sufficient.

① Viruses demonstrate self-sufficiency of biological beings.
② Biologists should do everything to keep plants virus-free.
③ The principle of symbiosis cannot be applied to infected plants.
④ Viruses sometimes do their hosts good, rather than harming them.

15 다음 글의 주제로 가장 적절한 것은?

2023. 법원직 9급

Do you want to be a successful anchor? If so, keep this in mind. As an anchor, the individual will be called upon to communicate news and information to viewer during newscasts, special reports and other types of news programs. This will include interpreting news events, adlibbing, and communicating breaking news effectively when scripts are not available. Anchoring duties also involve gathering and writing stories. The anchor must be able to deliver scripts clearly and effectively. Strong writing skills, solid news judgement and a strong sense of visual storytelling are essential skills. This individual must be a self-starter who cultivates sources and finds new information as a regular part of job. Live reporting skills are important, as well as the ability to adlib and describe breaking news as it takes place.

① difficulties of producing live news
② qualifications to become a news anchor
③ the importance of the social role of journalists
④ the importance of forming the right public opinion

16 다음 글의 주제로 가장 적절한 것은?

2023. 법원직 9급

Cosmetics became so closely associated with portraiture that some photography handbooks included recipes for them. American photographers also, at times, used cosmetics to retouch negatives and prints, enlivening women's faces with traces of rouge. Some customers with dark skin requested photographs that would make them look lighter. A skin lightener advertisement that appeared in an African American newspaper in 1935 referenced this practice by promising that its product could achieve the same look produced by photographers: a lighter skin Cop free of blemishes. By drawing attention to the face and encouraging cosmetics use, portrait photography heightened the aesthetic valuation of smooth and often light-colored skin.

* blemish (피부 등의) 티

① side effects of excessive use of cosmetics
② overuse of cosmetics promoted by photographers
③ active use of cosmetics to make the face look better
④ decreased use of cosmetics due to advances in photography

17 다음 글의 제목으로 가장 적절한 것은?

2022. 국가직 9급

Lasers are possible because of the way light interacts with electrons. Electrons exist at specific energy levels or states characteristic of that particular atom or molecule. The energy levels can be imagined as rings or orbits around a nucleus. Electrons in outer rings are at higher energy levels than those in inner rings. Electrons can be bumped up to higher energy levels by the injection of energy — for example, by a flash of light. When an electron drops from an outer to an inner level, "excess" energy is given off as light. The wavelength or color of the emitted light is precisely related to the amount of energy released. Depending on the particular lasing material being used, specific wavelengths of light are absorbed (to energize or excite the electrons) and specific wavelengths are emitted (when the electrons fall back to their initial level).

① How Is Laser Produced?
② When Was Laser Invented?
③ What Electrons Does Laser Emit?
④ Why Do Electrons Reflect Light?

18 다음 글의 제목으로 가장 적절한 것은?

2022. 국가직 9급

Do people from different cultures view the world differently? A psychologist presented realistic animated scenes of fish and other underwater objects to Japanese and American students and asked them to report what they had seen. Americans and Japanese made about an equal number of references to the focal fish, but the Japanese made more than 60 percent more references to background elements, including the water, rocks, bubbles, and inert plants and animals. In addition, whereas Japanese and American participants made about equal numbers of references to movement involving active animals, the Japanese participants made almost twice as many references to relationships involving inert, background objects. Perhaps most tellingly, the very first sentence from the Japanese participants was likely to be one referring to the environment, whereas the first sentence from Americans was three times as likely to be one referring to the focal fish.

① Language Barrier Between Japanese and Americans
② Associations of Objects and Backgrounds in the Brain
③ Cultural Differences in Perception
④ Superiority of Detail-oriented People

19 다음 글의 요지로 가장 적절한 것은?

2022. 국가직 9급

If someone makes you an offer and you're legitimately concerned about parts of it, you're usually better off proposing all your changes at once. Don't say, "The salary is a bit low. Could you do something about it?" and then, once she's worked on it, come back with "Thanks. Now here are two other things I'd like..." If you ask for only one thing initially, she may assume that getting it will make you ready to accept the offer (or at least to make a decision). If you keep saying "and one more thing...," she is unlikely to remain in a generous or understanding mood. Furthermore, if you have more than one request, don't simply mention all the things you want — A, B, C, and D; also signal the relative importance of each to you. Otherwise, she may pick the two things you value least, because they're pretty easy to give you, and feel she's met you halfway.

① Negotiate multiple issues simultaneously, not serially.
② Avoid sensitive topics for a successful negotiation.
③ Choose the right time for your negotiation.
④ Don't be too direct when negotiating salary.

20 다음 글의 제목으로 가장 적절한 것은?

2022. 지방직 9급

One of the areas where efficiency can be optimized is the work force, through increasing individual productivity — defined as the amount of work (products produced, customers served) an employee handles in a given time. In addition to making sure you have invested in the right equipment, environment, and training to ensure optimal performance, you can increase productivity by encouraging staffers to put an end to a modern-day energy drain: multitasking. Studies show it takes 25 to 40 percent longer to get a job done when you're simultaneously trying to work on other projects. To be more productive, says Andrew Deutscher, vice president of business development at consulting firm The Energy Project, "do one thing, uninterrupted, for a sustained period of time."

① How to Create More Options in Life
② How to Enhance Daily Physical Performance
③ Multitasking is the Answer for Better Efficiency
④ Do One Thing at a Time for Greater Efficiency

21 다음 글의 요지로 가장 적절한 것은?

2022. 지방직 9급

In one study, done in the early 1970s when young people tended to dress in either "hippie" or "straight" fashion, experimenters donned hippie or straight attire and asked college students on campus for a dime to make a phone call. When the experimenter was dressed in the same way as the student, the request was granted in more than two-thirds of the instances; when the student and requester were dissimilarly dressed, the dime was provided less than half the time. Another experiment showed how automatic our positive response to similar others can be. Marchers in an antiwar demonstration were found to be more likely to sign the petition of a similarly dressed requester and to do so without bothering to read it first.

① People are more likely to help those who dress like themselves.
② Dressing up formally increases the chance of signing the petition.
③ Making a phone call is an efficient way to socialize with other students.
④ Some college students in the early 1970s were admired for their unique fashion.

22 다음 글의 주제로 가장 적절한 것은?

2022. 법원직 9급

Daily training creates special nutritional needs for an athlete, particularly the elite athlete whose training commitment is almost a fulltime job. But even recreational sport will create nutritional challenges. And whatever your level of involvement in sport, you must meet these challenges if you're to achieve the maximum return from training. Without sound eating, much of the purpose of your training might be lost. In the worst-case scenario, dietary problems and deficiencies may directly impair training performance. In other situations, you might improve, but at a rate that is below your potential or slower than your competitors. However, on the positive side, with the right everyday eating plan your commitment to training will be fully rewarded.

① how to improve body flexibility
② importance of eating well in exercise
③ health problems caused by excessive diet
④ improving skills through continuous training

23 다음 글의 제목으로 가장 적절한 것은?

2021. 국가직 9급

Warming temperatures and loss of oxygen in the sea will shrink hundreds of fish species — from tunas and groupers to salmon, thresher sharks, haddock and cod — even more than previously thought, a new study concludes. Because warmer seas speed up their metabolisms, fish, squid and other water-breathing creatures will need to draw more oxygen from the ocean. At the same time, warming seas are already reducing the availability of oxygen in many parts of the sea. A pair of University of British Columbia scientists argue that since the bodies of fish grow faster than their gills, these animals eventually will reach a point where they can't get enough oxygen to sustain normal growth. "What we found was that the body size of fish decreases by 20 to 30 percent for every 1 degree Celsius increase in water temperature," says author William Cheung.

① Fish Now Grow Faster than Ever
② Oxygen's Impact on Ocean Temperatures
③ Climate Change May Shrink the World's Fish
④ How Sea Creatures Survive with Low Metabolism

24 다음 글의 주제로 가장 적절한 것은?

2021. 국가직 9급

During the late twentieth century socialism was on the retreat both in the West and in large areas of the developing world. During this new phase in the evolution of market capitalism, global trading patterns became increasingly interlinked, and advances in information technology meant that deregulated financial markets could shift massive flows of capital across national boundaries within seconds. 'Globalization' boosted trade, encouraged productivity gains and lowered prices, but critics alleged that it exploited the low-paid, was indifferent to environmental concerns and subjected the Third World to a monopolistic form of capitalism. Many radicals within Western societies who wished to protest against this process joined voluntary bodies, charities and other non-governmental organizations, rather than the marginalized political parties of the left. The environmental movement itself grew out of the recognition that the world was interconnected, and an angry, if diffuse, international coalition of interests emerged.

① The affirmative phenomena of globalization in the developing world in the past
② The decline of socialism and the emergence of capitalism in the twentieth century
③ The conflict between the global capital market and the political organizations of the left
④ The exploitative characteristics of global capitalism and diverse social reactions against it

25 다음 글의 제목으로 가장 적절한 것은?

2021. 지방직 9급

The definition of 'turn' casts the digital turn as an analytical strategy which enables us to focus on the role of digitalization within social reality. As an analytical perspective, the digital turn makes it possible to analyze and discuss the societal meaning of digitalization. The term 'digital turn' thus signifies an analytical approach which centers on the role of digitalization within a society. If the linguistic turn is defined by the epistemological assumption that reality is constructed through language, the digital turn is based on the assumption that social reality is increasingly defined by digitalization. Social media symbolize the digitalization of social relations. Individuals increasingly engage in identity management on social networking sites(SNS). SNS are polydirectional, meaning that users can connect to each other and share information.

※ epistemological 인식론의

① Remaking Identities on SNS
② Linguistic Turn Versus Digital Turn
③ How to Share Information in the Digital Age
④ Digitalization Within the Context of Social Reality

26 다음 글의 요지로 가장 적절한 것은?

2021. 지방직 9급

"In Judaism, we're largely defined by our actions," says Lisa Grushcow, the senior rabbi at Temple Emanu-El-Beth Sholom in Montreal. "You can't really be an armchair do-gooder." This concept relates to the Jewish notion of tikkun olam, which translates as "to repair the world." Our job as human beings, she says, "is to mend what's been broken. It's incumbent on us to not only take care of ourselves and each other but also to build a better world around us." This philosophy conceptualizes goodness as something based in service. Instead of asking "Am I a good person?" you may want to ask "What good do I do in the world?" Grushcow's temple puts these beliefs into action inside and outside their community. For instance, they sponsored two refugee families from Vietnam to come to Canada in the 1970s.

① We should work to heal the world.
② Community should function as a shelter.
③ We should conceptualize goodness as beliefs.
④ Temples should contribute to the community.

27 다음 글의 요지로 가장 알맞은 것은?

2021. 법원직 9급

If your kids fight every time they play video games, make sure you're close enough to be able to hear them when they sit down to play. Listen for the particular words or tones of voice they are using that are aggressive, and try to intervene before it develops. Once tempers have settled, try to sit your kids down and discuss the problem without blaming or accusing. Give each kid a chance to talk, uninterrupted, and have them try to come up with solutions to the problem themselves. By the time kids are elementary-school age, they can evaluate which of those solutions are win-win solutions and which ones are most likely to work and satisfy each other over time. They should also learn to revisit problems when solutions are no longer working.

① Ask your kids to evaluate their test.
② Make your kids compete each other.
③ Help your kids learn to resolve conflict.
④ Teach your kids how to win an argument.

28 다음 글의 요지로 가장 적절한 것은?

2020. 국가직 9급

Listening to somebody else's ideas is the one way to know whether the story you believe about the world — as well as about yourself and your place in it — remains intact. We all need to examine our beliefs, air them out and let them breathe. Hearing what other people have to say, especially about concepts we regard as foundational, is like opening a window in our minds and in our hearts. Speaking up is important. Yet to speak up without listening is like banging pots and pans together: even if it gets you attention, it's not going to get you respect. There are three prerequisites for conversation to be meaningful: 1. You have to know what you're talking about, meaning that you have an original point and are not echoing a worn-out, hand-me-down or pre-fab argument; 2. You respect the people with whom you're speaking and are authentically willing to treat them courteously even if you disagree with their positions; 3. You have to be both smart and informed enough to listen to what the opposition says while handling your own perspective on the topic with uninterrupted good humor and discernment.

① We should be more determined to persuade others.
② We need to listen and speak up in order to communicate well.
③ We are reluctant to change our beliefs about the world we see.
④ We hear only what we choose and attempt to ignore different opinions.

29 다음 글의 제목으로 가장 적절한 것은?

2020. 국가직 9급

The future may be uncertain, but some things are undeniable: climate change, shifting demographics, geopolitics. The only guarantee is that there will be changes, both wonderful and terrible. It's worth considering how artists will respond to these changes, as well as what purpose art serves, now and in the future. Reports suggest that by 2040 the impacts of human-caused climate change will be inescapable, making it the big issue at the centre of art and life in 20 years' time. Artists in the future will wrestle with the possibilities of the post-human and post-Anthropocene — artificial intelligence, human colonies in outer space and potential doom. The identity politics seen in art around the #MeToo and Black Lives Matter movements will grow as environmentalism, border politics and migration come even more sharply into focus. Art will become increasingly diverse and might not 'look like art' as we expect. In the future, once we've become weary of our lives being visible online for all to see and our privacy has been all but lost, anonymity may be more desirable than fame. Instead of thousands, or millions, of likes and followers, we will be starved for authenticity and connection. Art could, in turn, become more collective and experiential, rather than individual.

① What will art look like in the future?
② How will global warming affect our lives?
③ How will artificial intelligence influence the environment?
④ What changes will be made because of political movements?

30 다음 글의 주제로 가장 적절한 것은?

2020. 국가직 9급

For many people, work has become an obsession. It has caused burnout, unhappiness and gender inequity, as people struggle to find time for children or passions or pets or any sort of life besides what they do for a paycheck. But increasingly, younger workers are pushing back. More of them expect and demand flexibility — paid leave for a new baby, say, and generous vacation time, along with daily things, like the ability to work remotely, come in late or leave early, or make time for exercise or meditation. The rest of their lives happens on their phones, not tied to a certain place or time — why should work be any different?

① ways to increase your paycheck
② obsession for reducing inequity
③ increasing call for flexibility at work
④ advantages of a life with long vacations

31 다음 글의 주제로 가장 적절한 것은?

2020. 지방직 9급

The e-book applications available on tablet computers employ touchscreen technology. Some touchscreens feature a glass panel covering two electronically-charged metallic surfaces lying face-to-face. When the screen is touched, the two metallic surfaces feel the pressure and make contact. This pressure sends an electrical signal to the computer, which translates the touch into a command. This version of the touchscreen is known as a resistive screen because the screen reacts to pressure from the finger. Other tablet computers feature a single electrified metallic layer under the glass panel. When the user touches the screen, some of the current passes through the glass into the user's finger. When the charge is transferred, the computer interprets the loss in power as a command and carries out the function the user desires. This type of screen is known as a capacitive screen.

① how users learn new technology
② how e-books work on tablet computers
③ how touchscreen technology works
④ how touchscreens have evolved

32 다음 글의 제목으로 가장 적절한 것은?

2020. 지방직 9급

Louis XIV needed a palace worthy of his greatness, so he decided to build a huge new house at Versailles, where a tiny hunting lodge stood. After almost fifty years of labor, this tiny hunting lodge had been transformed into an enormous palace, a quarter of a mile long. Canals were dug to bring water from the river and to drain the marshland. Versailles was full of elaborate rooms like the famous Hall of Mirrors, where seventeen huge mirrors stood across from seventeen large windows, and the Salon of Apollo, where a solid silver throne stood. Hundreds of statues of Greek gods such as Apollo, Jupiter, and Neptune stood in the gardens; each god had Louis's face!

① True Face of Greek Gods
② The Hall of Mirrors vs. the Salon of Apollo
③ Did the Canal Bring More Than Just Water to Versailles?
④ Versailles: From a Humble Lodge to a Great Palace

33 다음 글의 요지로 가장 적절한 것은?

2020. 지방직 9급

Evolutionarily, any species that hopes to stay alive has to manage its resources carefully. That means that first call on food and other goodies goes to the breeders and warriors and hunters and planters and builders and, certainly, the children, with not much left over for the seniors, who may be seen as consuming more than they're contributing. But even before modern medicine extended life expectancies, ordinary families were including grandparents and even great-grandparents. That's because what old folk consume materially, they give back behaviorally—providing a leveling, reasoning center to the tumult that often swirls around them.

① Seniors have been making contributions to the family.
② Modern medicine has brought focus to the role of old folk.
③ Allocating resources well in a family determines its prosperity.
④ The extended family comes at a cost of limited resources.

34 다음 글의 제목으로 가장 적절한 것은?

2019. 국가직 9급

Mapping technologies are being used in many new applications. Biological researchers are exploring the molecular structure of DNA ("mapping the genome"), geophysicists are mapping the structure of the Earth's core, and oceanographers are mapping the ocean floor. Computer games have various imaginary "lands" or levels where rules, hazards, and rewards change. Computerization now challenges reality with "virtual reality," artificial environments that stimulate special situations, which may be useful in training and entertainment. Mapping techniques are being used also in the realm of ideas. For example, relationships between ideas can be shown using what are called concept maps. Starting from a general or "central" idea, related ideas can be connected, building a web around the main concept. This is not a map by any traditional definition, but the tools and techniques of cartography are employed to produce it, and in some ways it resembles a map.

① Computerized Maps vs. Traditional Maps
② Where Does Cartography Begin?
③ Finding Ways to DNA Secrets
④ Mapping New Frontiers

35 다음 글의 요지로 가장 적절한 것은?

2019. 국가직 9급

When giving performance feedback, you should consider the recipient's past performance and your estimate of his or her future potential in designing its frequency, amount, and content. For high performers with potential for growth, feedback should be frequent enough to prod them into taking corrective action, but not so frequent that it is experienced as controlling and saps their initiative. For adequate performers who have settled into their jobs and have limited potential for advancement, very little feedback is needed because they have displayed reliable and steady behavior in the past, knowing their tasks and realizing what needs to be done. For poor performers — that is, people who will need to be removed from their jobs if their performance doesn't improve — feedback should be frequent and very specific, and the connection between acting on the feedback and negative sanctions such as being laid off or fired should be made explicit.

① Time your feedback well.
② Customize negative feedback.
③ Tailor feedback to the person.
④ Avoid goal-oriented feedback.

36 다음 글의 주제로 가장 적절한 것은?

2019. 국가직 9급

Imagine that two people are starting work at a law firm on the same day. One person has a very simple name. The other person has a very complex name. We've got pretty good evidence that over the course of their next 16 plus years of their career, the person with the simpler name will rise up the legal hierarchy more quickly. They will attain partnership more quickly in the middle parts of their career. And by about the eighth or ninth year after graduating from law school the people with simpler names are about seven to ten percent more likely to be partners — which is a striking effect. We try to eliminate all sorts of other alternative explanations. For example, we try to show that it's not about foreignness because foreign names tend to be harder to pronounce. But even if you look at just white males with Anglo-American names. so really the true in-group, you find that among those white males with Anglo names they are more likely to rise up if their names happen to be simpler. So simplicity is one key feature in names that determines various outcomes.

① the development of legal names
② the concept of attractive names
③ the benefit of simple names
④ the roots of foreign names

37 다음 글의 주제로 가장 적절한 것은?

2019. 지방직 9급

As the digital revolution upends newsrooms across the country, here's my advice for all the reporters. I've been a reporter for more than 25 years, so I have lived through a half dozen technological life cycles. The most dramatic transformations have come in the last half dozen years. That means I am, with increasing frequency, making stuff up as I go along. Much of the time in the news business, we have no idea what we are doing. We show up in the morning and someone says, "Can you write a story about (pick one) tax policy/immigration/climate change?" When newspapers had once-a-day deadlines, we said a reporter would learn in the morning and teach at night — write a story that could inform tomorrow's readers on a topic the reporter knew nothing about 24 hours earlier. Now it is more like learning at the top of the hour and teaching at the bottom of the same hour. I'm also running a political podcast, for example, and during the presidential conventions, we should be able to use it to do real-time interviews anywhere. I am just increasingly working without a script.

① a reporter as a teacher
② a reporter and improvisation
③ technology in politics
④ fields of journalism and technology

02 중심 내용 파악 유형 기출 독해 어휘 복습 TEST

1	contagious		21	crave	
2	eliminate		22	countless	
3	ministry		23	deliberate	
4	infection		24	resistance	
5	install		25	further	
6	disparity		26	extend	
7	emphasize		27	interpret	
8	excavate		28	solid	
9	exploit		29	cultivate	
10	dilute		30	negative	
11	replenish		31	excessive	
12	organization		32	overuse	
13	means		33	give off	
14	relieve		34	emit	
15	cherish		35	excite	
16	competence		36	focal	
17	attribute		37	inert	
18	equate		38	perception	
19	dedicate		39	concerned	
20	discuss		40	assume	

02 중심 내용 파악 유형 기출 독해 어휘 복습 TEST

41	meet halfway		61	uninterrupted	
42	optimize		62	intact	
43	simultaneously		63	courteously	
44	sustain		64	discernment	
45	attire		65	migration	
46	petition		66	anonymity	
47	flexibility		67	obsession	
48	shrink		68	generous	
49	allege		69	meditation	
50	subject		70	pressure	
51	diffuse		71	palace	
52	merit		72	statue	
53	perspective		73	leveling	
54	assumption		74	tumult	
55	construct		75	prosperity	
56	signify		76	artificial	
57	identity		77	sanction	
58	mend		78	striking	
59	incumbent		79	transformation	
60	intervene		80	inform	

MEMO

진가영 영어
반한다 기출
독해

진가영 영어연구소 | cafe.naver.com/easyenglish7

Chapter

03

문장 제거 유형

chapter

03 문장 제거 유형

출제경향 분석

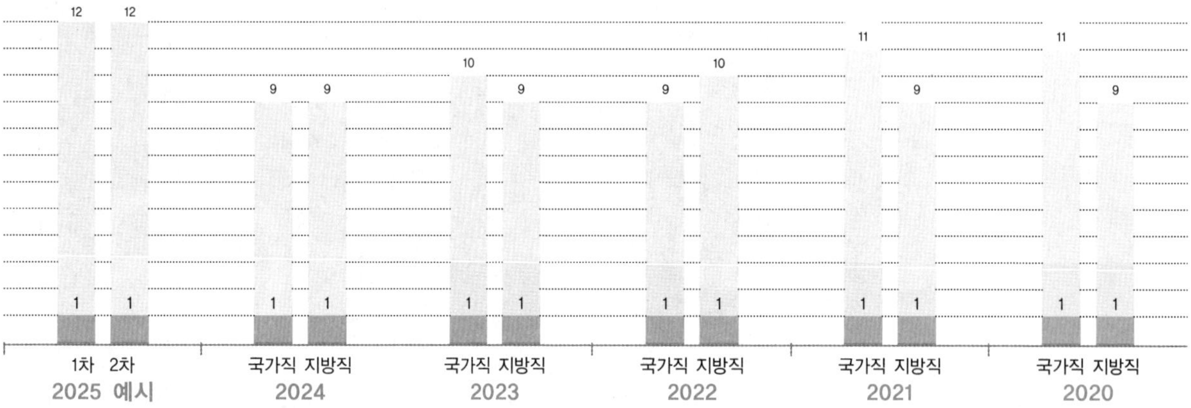

문제풀이 전략

Q 다음 글의 흐름상 어색한 문장은? 2025. 출제 기조 전환 2차

A very common type of writing task — one that appears in every academic discipline — is a reaction or response. ① In a reaction essay, the writer is usually given a "prompt" — a visual or written stimulus — to think about and then respond to. ② It is very important to gather reliable facts so that you can defend your argument effectively. ③ Common prompts or stimuli for this type of writing include quotes, pieces of literature, photos, paintings, multimedia presentations, and news events. ④ A reaction focuses on the writer's feelings, opinions, and personal observations about the particular prompt. Your task in writing a reaction essay is twofold: to briefly summarize the prompt and to give your personal reaction to it.

Step ① 글 초반에 언급되는 주제 확인하기

- 주로 글 초반에 제시되는 주제문을 찾고 그 뒤에 이어질 글의 내용을 예상하며 읽기

Step ② 문장과 문장의 연결 확인하기

- ①번, ②번, ③번 그리고 ④번 문장의 내용이 글의 전체 주제와 부합한지 확인하며 앞 뒤 문장과도 흐름이 잘 이어지는지 확인하기

Step ③ 지문 검토하기

- 글의 흐름상 어색한 문장을 제외하고 문장과 문장이 잘 연결되는지 확인하기

글 초반	A very common type of writing task— one that appears in every academic discipline — is a reaction or response. 매우 일반적인 종류의 글쓰기 과제는 모든 학문 분야에서 나타나는 반응 또는 응답이다.
①	In a reaction essay, the writer is usually given a “prompt” — a visual or written stimulus — to think about and then respond to. 반응 에세이에서는 보통 “프롬프트” — 시각적이거나 서면 자극 — 가 제공되어 이에 대해 생각하고 응답하는 방식이다.
✓②	It is very important to gather reliable facts so that you can defend your argument effectively. 당신의 주장을 효과적으로 방어하기 위해 신뢰할 수 있는 사실을 모으는 것이 매우 중요하다.
③	Common prompts or stimuli for this type of writing include quotes, pieces of literature, photos, paintings, multimedia presentations, and news events. 이 유형의 글쓰기를 위한 일반적인 프롬프트나 자극에는 인용문, 문학 작품, 사진, 그림, 멀티미디어 프레젠테이션, 뉴스 사건 등이 포함된다.
④	A reaction focuses on the writer’s feelings, opinions, and personal observations about the particular prompt. 반응은 특정 프롬프트에 대한 작가의 감정, 의견 및 개인적인 관찰에 중점을 둔다.
글 후반	Your task in writing a reaction essay is twofold: to briefly summarize the prompt and to give your personal reaction to it. 반응 에세이를 작성할 때의 작업은 두 가지이다: 프롬프트를 간결하게 요약하고 이에 대한 개인적인 반응을 제시하는 것이다.

핵심 기출 어휘

- reliable 신뢰할[믿을] 수 있는
- quote 인용문, 인용하다
- summarize 요약하다
- desperate 필사적인, 절망적인
- urge 충동, 욕구, 충고하다, 권고하다
- conspiracy 음모
- advocate 옹호하다, 지지하다
- passionate 열정적인, 열렬한
- contradict 모순되다, 부정하다, 반박하다
- convincing 설득력 있는, 확실한
- shift 전환, 전환하다
- hybrid 잡종의, 혼혈의
- renowned 유명한, 명성 있는
- conclude 끝내다, 결론을 내리다
- reckless 무분별한, 무모한, 신중하지 못한
- disagreement 불일치, 의견차이
- tension 긴장, 긴장감
- stressor 스트레스를 유발하는 요인
- fatigued 피로한, 지친
- metaphysics 형이상학
- meteorology 기상학
- transmission 전염, 전파, 전달
- practice 관행, 관례, 실행, 실천
- a string of 일련의, 연속적인
- chemical 화학적인
- anthropology 인류학
- contemporary 현대의, 동시대의
- illustrate 설명하다, 실증하다
- wilderness 황야, 황무지
- spontaneous 자발적인, 즉흥적인
- sedentary 정적인, 주로 앉아서 하는
- assemble 조립하다, 모으다
- metaphor 은유, 비유
- association 연관, 연상
- remarkable 놀라운, 주목할 만한
- presence 있음, 존재, 참석
- flamboyant 이색적인, 화려한
- attachment 부착
- submerge 물속에 잠기다, 잠수하다
- susceptible 취약한, 민감한, 영향을 받기 쉬운
- incur 유발하다, 초래하다
- urbanization 도시화
- inclined ~을 하고 싶은, ~할 것 같은
- tolerate 용인하다, 참다, 견디다
- elaborate 정교한, 정성을 들인
- banquet 연회, 만찬
- supervise 감독하다, 지휘하다
- proliferate 급증하다, 확산되다
- put on hold 연기하다, 보류하다
- cutting edge 최첨단
- isolated 고립된, 외딴
- astonish 깜짝 놀라게 하다

나의 약점 확인

영역	점수
CHAPTER 03 문장 제거 유형	/ 29문항

반드시 한번에 다 잡는 '문장 제거 유형' 독해 전략

- 문장 제거 유형은 쓰기 능력을 간접적으로 평가하기 위한 유형 중 하나로 **좋은 글쓰기를 위해 필요한 통일성**(하나의 단락에 하나의 주제), **일관성**(문장이나 내용이 서로 긴밀하게 구성되어야 한다는 원리), **그리고 응집성**(문장과 문장 사이를 구성하는 여러 요소들 사이의 표면적인 연결 관계)**에 대한 이해도를 평가**한다.
- 문장 제거 유형은 9급 출제 기조 전환 예시 문제를 기준으로 볼 때 **난도가 낮거나 중간인 유형**에 속하며 **한 문제** 출제될 것으로 예상된다.
- 문장 제거 유형 문제에서 **글의 초반부에 언급된 주제(topic)를 포함하고 있는지를 확인**하는 것이 중요하다.
- 문장 제거 유형에서 **글의 초반부에 언급된 주제(topic)가 없다면 흐름상 어색한 문장일 가능성이 높다.** 이때 주의할 점은 **주제(topic)는 같은 단어로 표현되지 않을 수도 있기 때문에** 지문의 단어나 표현들을 맥락 속에서 파악하면서 각 문장에 주제(topic)가 존재하는지 확인해야 한다.
- 문장 제거 유형 문제에서 **바로 앞 문장에 언급된 특정 단어를 설명하는 문장**은 흐름상 어색한 문장일 가능성이 높기 때문에 주의한다.
- 문장 제거 유형 문제에서 **주제와 정반대되는 내용의 문장이 갑자기 나온다면** 흐름상 어색한 문장일 가능성이 높기 때문에 주의한다.

01 다음 글의 흐름상 어색한 문장은?

2025. 출제 기조 전환 2차

A very common type of writing task — one that appears in every academic discipline — is a reaction or response. ① In a reaction essay, the writer is usually given a "prompt" — a visual or written stimulus — to think about and then respond to. ② It is very important to gather reliable facts so that you can defend your argument effectively. ③ Common prompts or stimuli for this type of writing include quotes, pieces of literature, photos, paintings, multimedia presentations, and news events. ④ A reaction focuses on the writer's feelings, opinions, and personal observations about the particular prompt. Your task in writing a reaction essay is twofold: to briefly summarize the prompt and to give your personal reaction to it.

02 다음 글의 흐름상 어색한 문장은?

2025. 출제 기조 전환 1차

Every parent or guardian of small children will have experienced the desperate urge to get out of the house and the magical restorative effect of even a short trip to the local park. ① There is probably more going on here than just letting off steam. ② The benefits for kids of getting into nature are huge, ranging from better academic performance to improved mood and focus. ③ Outdoor activities make it difficult for them to spend quality time with their family. ④ Childhood experiences of nature can also boost environmentalism in adulthood. Having access to urban green spaces can play a role in children's social networks and friendships.

03 다음 글의 흐름상 어색한 문장은?

2024. 국가직 9급

In spite of all evidence to the contrary, there are people who seriously believe that NASA's Apollo space program never really landed men on the moon. These people claim that the moon landings were nothing more than a huge conspiracy, perpetuated by a government desperately in competition with the Russians and fearful of losing face. ① These conspiracy theorists claim that the United States knew it couldn't compete with the Russians in the space race and was therefore forced to fake a series of successful moon landings. ② Advocates of a conspiracy cite several pieces of what they consider evidence. ③ Crucial to their case is the claim that astronauts never could have safely passed through the Van Allen belt, a region of radiation trapped in Earth's magnetic field. ④ They also point to the fact that the metal coverings of the spaceship were designed to block radiation. If the astronauts had truly gone through the belt, say conspiracy theorists, they would have died.

04 다음 글의 흐름상 어색한 문장은?

2024. 지방직 9급

Critical thinking sounds like an unemotional process but it can engage emotions and even passionate responses. In particular, we may not like evidence that contradicts our own opinions or beliefs. ① If the evidence points in a direction that is challenging, that can rouse unexpected feelings of anger, frustration or anxiety. ② The academic world traditionally likes to consider itself as logical and free of emotions, so if feelings do emerge, this can be especially difficult. ③ For example, looking at the same information from several points of view is not important. ④ Being able to manage your emotions under such circumstances is a useful skill. If you can remain calm, and present your reasons logically, you will be better able to argue your point of view in a convincing way.

05 다음 글의 흐름상 어색한 문장은?

2023. 국가직 9급

In our monthly surveys of 5,000 American workers and 500 U.S. employers, a huge shift to hybrid work is abundantly clear for office and knowledge workers. ① An emerging norm is three days a week in the office and two at home, cutting days on site by 30% or more. You might think this cutback would bring a huge drop in the demand for office space. ② But our survey data suggests cuts in office space of 1% to 2% on average, implying big reductions in density not space. We can understand why. High density at the office is uncomfortable and many workers dislike crowds around their desks. ③ Most employees want to work from home on Mondays and Fridays. Discomfort with density extends to lobbies, kitchens, and especially elevators. ④ The only sure-fire way to reduce density is to cut days on site without cutting square footage as much. Discomfort with density is here to stay according to our survey evidence.

06 다음 글의 흐름상 어색한 문장은?

2023. 지방직 9급

I once took a course in short-story writing and during that course a renowned editor of a leading magazine talked to our class. ① He said he could pick up any one of the dozens of stories that came to his desk every day and after reading a few paragraphs he could feel whether or not the author liked people. ② "If the author doesn't like people," he said, "people won't like his or her stories." ③ The editor kept stressing the importance of being interested in people during his talk on fiction writing. ④ Thurston, a great magician, said that every time he went on stage he said to himself, "I am grateful because I'm successful." At the end of the talk, he concluded, "Let me tell you again. You have to be interested in people if you want to be successful writer of stories."

07 다음 글에서 전체 흐름과 가장 관계 없는 문장은?

2023. 법원직 9급

One of the most interesting discoveries in the field of new sources of sustainable energy is bio-solar energy from jellyfish. Scientists have discovered that the fluorescent protein in this animal can be used to generate solar energy in a more sustainable way than current photovoltaic energy. How is this energy generated? ① The process involves converting the jellyfish's fluorescent protein into a solar cell that is capable of generating energy and transferring it to small devices. ② There has been constant criticism that the natural environment is being damaged by reckless solar power generation. ③ The main advantage of using these living beings as a natural energy source is that they are a clean alternative that does not use fossil fuels or require the use of limited resources. ④ Although this project is still currently in the trial phase, the expectation is that this source of energy will be able to be expanded and become a green alternative for powering the type of small electronic devices that are becoming more and more common.

* photovoltaic 광전기성의

08 다음 글에서 전체 흐름과 가장 관계 없는 문장은?

2023. 법원직 9급

Fast fashion is a method of producing inexpensive clothing at a rapid pace to respond to the latest fashion trends. With shopping evolving into a form of entertainment in the age of fast fashion, customers are contributing to what sustainability experts refer to as a throwaway culture. This means customers simply discard products once they are deemed useless rather than recycling or donating them. ① The consumers are generally satisfied with the quality of fast fashion brand clothing. ② As a result, these discarded items add a huge burden to the environment. ③ To resolve the throwaway culture and fast fashion crisis, the concept of sustainability in fashion is brought to the spotlight. ④ Sustainable fashion involves apparel, footwear, and accessories that are produced, distributed, and utilized as sustainably as possible while taking into account socio-economic and environmental concerns.

09 글의 흐름상 가장 어색한 문장은? 2022. 지방직 9급

The skill to have a good argument is critical in life. But it's one that few parents teach to their children. ① We want to give kids a stable home, so we stop siblings from quarreling and we have our own arguments behind closed doors. ② Yet if kids never get exposed to disagreement, we may eventually limit their creativity. ③ Children are most creative when they are free to brainstorm with lots of praise and encouragement in a peaceful environment. ④ It turns out that highly creative people often grow up in families full of tension. They are not surrounded by fistfights or personal insults, but real disagreements. When adults in their early 30s were asked to write imaginative stories, the most creative ones came from those whose parents had the most conflict a quarter-century earlier.

10 다음 글의 흐름상 가장 어색한 문장은?

2021. 국가직 9급

The term burnout refers to a "wearing out" from the pressures of work. Burnout is a chronic condition that results as daily work stressors take their toll on employees. ① The most widely adopted conceptualization of burnout has been developed by Maslach and her colleagues in their studies of human service workers. Maslach sees burnout as consisting of three interrelated dimensions. The first dimension—emotional exhaustion—is really the core of the burnout phenomenon. ② Workers suffer from emotional exhaustion when they feel fatigued, frustrated, used up, or unable to face another day on the job. The second dimension of burnout is a lack of personal accomplishment. ③ This aspect of the burnout phenomenon refers to workers who see themselves as failures, incapable of effectively accomplishing job requirements. ④ Emotional labor workers enter their occupation highly motivated although they are physically exhausted. The third dimension of burnout is depersonalization. This dimension is relevant only to workers who must communicate interpersonally with others (e.g. clients, patients, students) as part of the job.

11 다음 글의 흐름상 적절하지 않은 문장은?

2021. 지방직 9급

There was no divide between science, philosophy, and magic in the 15th century. All three came under the general heading of 'natural philosophy'. ① Central to the development of natural philosophy was the recovery of classical authors, most importantly the work of Aristotle. ② Humanists quickly realized the power of the printing press for spreading their knowledge. ③ At the beginning of the 15th century Aristotle remained the basis for all scholastic speculation on philosophy and science. ④ Kept alive in the Arabic translations and commentaries of Averroes and Avicenna, Aristotle provided a systematic perspective on mankind's relationship with the natural world. Surviving texts like his *Physics, Metaphysics*, and *Meteorology* provided scholars with the logical tools to understand the forces that created the natural world.

12 글의 흐름상 가장 어색한 문장은?

2021. 법원직 9급

Fiction has many uses and one of them is to build empathy. When you watch TV or see a film, you are looking at things happening to other people. Prose fiction is something you build up from 26 letters and a handful of punctuation marks, and you, and you alone, using your imagination, create a world and live there and look out through other eyes. ① You get to feel things, and visit places and worlds you would never otherwise know. ② Fortunately, in the last decade, many of the world's most beautiful and unknown places have been put in the spotlight. ③ You learn that everyone else out there is a me, as well. ④ You're being someone else, and when youreturn to your own world, you're going to be slightly changed.

13 다음 글에서 전체 흐름과 관계없는 문장은?

2021. 법원직 9급

Medical anthropologists with extensive training in human biology and physiology study disease transmission patterns and how particular groups adapt to the presence of diseases like malaria and sleeping sickness. ① Because the transmission of viruses and bacteria is strongly influenced by people's diets, sanitation, and other behaviors, many medical anthropologists work as a team with epidemiologists to identify cultural practices that affect the spread of disease. ② Though it may be a commonly held belief that most students enter medicine for humanitarian reasons rather than for the financial rewards of a successful medical career, in developed nations the prospect of status and rewards is probably one incentive. ③ Different cultures have different ideas about the causes and symptoms of disease, how best to treat illnesses, the abilities of traditional healers and doctors, and the importance of community involvement in the healing process. ④ By studying how a human communityperceives such things, medical anthropologists help hospitals and other agencies deliver health care services more effectively.

* epidemiologist 유행[전염]병학자

14 다음 글의 흐름상 가장 어색한 문장은?

2020. 국가직 9급

When the brain perceives a threat in the immediate surroundings, it initiates a complex string of events in the body. It sends electrical messages to various glands, organs that release chemical hormones into the bloodstream. Blood quickly carries these hormones to other organs that are then prompted to do various things. ① The adrenal glands above the kidneys, for example, pump out adrenaline, the body's stress hormone. ② Adrenaline travels all over the body doing things such as widening the eyes to be on the lookout for signs of danger, pumping the heart faster to keep blood and extra hormones flowing, and tensing the skeletal muscles so they are ready to lash out at or run from the threat. ③ The whole process is called the fight-or-flight response, because it prepares the body to either battle or run for its life. ④ Humans consciously control their glands to regulate the release of various hormones. Once the response is initiated, ignoring it is impossible, because hormones cannot be reasoned with.

15 글의 흐름상 가장 어색한 문장은?

2020. 지방직 9급

Philosophers have not been as concerned with anthropology as anthropologists have with philosophy. ① Few influential contemporary philosophers take anthropological studies into account in their work. ② Those who specialize in philosophy of social science may consider or analyze examples from anthropological research, but do this mostly to illustrate conceptual points or epistemological distinctions or to criticize epistemological or ethical implications. ③ In fact, the great philosophers of our time often drew inspiration from other fields such as anthropology and psychology. ④ Philosophy students seldom study or show serious interest in anthropology. They may learn about experimental methods in science, but rarely about anthropological fieldwork.

16 밑줄 친 부분 중 글의 흐름상 가장 어색한 것은?

2019. 국가직 9급

In 2007, our biggest concern was "too big to fail." Wall Street banks had grown to such staggering sizes, and had become so central to the health of the financial system, that no rational government could ever let them fail. ① Aware of their protected status, banks made excessively risky bets on housing markets and invented ever more complicated derivatives. ② New virtual currencies such as bitcoin and ethereum have radically changed our understanding of how money can and should work. ③ The result was the worst financial crisis since the breakdown of our economy in 1929. ④ In the years since 2007, we have made great progress in addressing the too-big- to-fail dilemma. Our banks are better capitalized than ever. Our regulators conduct regular stress tests of large institutions.

17 글의 흐름상 가장 어색한 문장은?

2019. 지방직 9급

Children's playgrounds throughout history were the wilderness, fields, streams, and hills of the country and the roads, streets, and vacant places of villages, towns, and cities. ① The term playground refers to all those places where children gather to play their free, spontaneous games. ② Only during the past few decades have children vacated these natural playgrounds for their growing love affair with video games, texting, and social networking. ③ Even in rural America few children are still roaming in a free- ranging manner, unaccompanied by adults. ④ When out of school, they are commonly found in neighborhoods digging in sand, building forts, playing traditional games, climbing, or playing ball games. They are rapidly disappearing from the natural terrain of creeks, hills, and fields, and like their urban counterparts, are turning to their indoor, sedentary cyber toys for entertainment.

18 글의 흐름상 가장 적절하지 않은 문장은?

2019. 서울시 9급

It seems to me possible to name four kinds of reading, each with a characteristic manner and purpose. The first is reading for information —reading to learn about a trade, or politics, or how to accomplish something. ① We read a newspaper this way, or most textbooks, or directions on how to assemble a bicycle. ②With most of this material, the reader can learn to scan the page quickly, coming up with what he needs and ignoring what is irrelevant to him, like the rhythm of the sentence, or the play of metaphor. ③ We also register a track of feeling through the metaphors and associations of words. ④ Courses in speed reading can help us read for this purpose, training the eye to jump quickly across the page.

19 다음 글에서 전체의 흐름과 가장 관계없는 문장은?

2019. 법원직 9급

The immortal operatically styled single Bohemian Rhapsody by Queen was released in 1975 and proceeded to the top of the UK charts for 9 weeks. ① A song that was nearly never released due to its length and unusual style but which Freddie insisted would be played became the instantly recognizable hit. ② By this time Freddie's unique talents were becoming clear, a voice with a remarkable range and a stage presence that gave Queen its colorful, unpredictable and flamboyant personality. ③ The son of Bomi and Jer Bulsara, Freddie spent the bulk of his childhood in India where he attended St. Peter's boarding school. ④ Very soon Queen's popularity extended beyond the shores of the UK as they charted and triumphed around Europe, Japan and the USA where in 1979 they topped the charts with Freddie's song Crazy Little thing Called Love.

20 다음 글에서 전체 흐름과 관계없는 문장은?

2019. 소방직 9급

Gum disease is frequently to blame for bad breath. In fact, bad breath is a warning sign for gum disease. ① This issue occurs initially as a result of plaque buildup on the teeth. ② Bacteria in the plaque irritate the gums and cause them to become tender, swollen and prone to bleeding. ③ Foul-smelling gases emitted by the bacteria can also cause bad breath. ④ Smoking damages your gum tissue by affecting the attachment of bone and soft tissue to your teeth. If you pay attention when you notice that bacteria-induced bad breath, though, you could catch gum disease before it gets to its more advanced stages.

21 다음 글의 흐름상 가장 어색한 문장은?

2018. 국가직 9급

Biologists have identified a gene that will allow rice plants to survive being submerged in water for up to two weeks — over a week longer than at present. Plants under water for longer than a week are deprived of oxygen and wither and perish. ① The scientists hope their discovery will prolong the harvests of crops in regions that are susceptible to flooding. ② Rice growers in these flood-prone areas of Asia lose an estimated one billion dollars annually to excessively waterlogged rice paddies. ③ They hope the new gene will lead to a hardier rice strain that will reduce the financial damage incurred in typhoon and monsoon seasons and lead to bumper harvests. ④ This is dreadful news for people in these vulnerable regions, who are victims of urbanization and have a shortage of crops. Rice yields must increase by 30 percent over the next 20 years to ensure a billion people can receive their staple diet.

22 밑줄 친 부분 중 글의 흐름상 가장 어색한 것은?

2018. 국가직 9급

Most people like to talk, but few people like to listen, yet listening well is a ① rare talent that everyone should treasure. Because they hear more, good listeners tend to know more and to be more sensitive to what is going on around them than most people. In addition, good listeners are inclined to accept or tolerate rather than to judge and criticize. Therefore, they have ② fewer enemies than most people. In fact, they are probably the most beloved of people. However, there are ③ exceptions to that generality. For example, John Steinbeck is said to have been an excellent listener, yet he was hated by some of the people he wrote about. No doubt his ability to listen contributed to his capacity to write. Nevertheless, the result of his listening didn't make him ④ unpopular.

23 다음 글의 흐름상 가장 어색한 문장은?

2018. 지방직 9급

The Renaissance kitchen had a definite hierarchy of help who worked together to produce the elaborate banquets. ① At the top, as we have seen, was the scalco, or steward, who was in charge of not only the kitchen, but also the dining room. ② The dining room was supervised by the butler, who was in charge of the silverware and linen and also served the dishes that began and ended the banquet — the cold dishes, salads, cheeses, and fruit at the beginning and the sweets and confections at the end of the meal. ③ This elaborate decoration and serving was what in restaurants is called "the front of the house." ④ The kitchen was supervised by the head cook, who directed the undercooks, pastry cooks, and kitchen help.

24 글의 흐름상 가장 어색한 문장은?

2017. 국가직 9급

Children's book awards have proliferated in recent years; today, there are well over 100 different awards and prizes by a variety of organizations. ① The awards may be given for books of a specific genre or simply for the best of all children's books published within a given time period. An award may honor a particular book or an author for a lifetime contribution to the world of children's literature. ② Most children's book awards are chosen by adults, but now a growing number of children's choice book awards exist. The larger national awards given in most countries are the most influential and have helped considerably to raise public awareness about the fine books being published for young readers. ③ An award ceremony for outstanding services to the publishing industry is put on hold. ④ Of course, readers are wise not to put too much faith in award-winning books. An award doesn't necessarily mean a good reading experience, but it does provide a starting place when choosing books.

25 다음 글의 흐름상 가장 어색한 문장은?

2017. 국가직 9급 하반기

Researchers have developed a new model that they said will provide better estimates about the North Atlantic right whale population, and the news isn't good. ① The model could be critically important to efforts to save the endangered species, which is in the midst of a year of high mortality, said Peter Corkeron, who leads the large whale team for the National Oceanic and Atmospheric Administration's Northeast Fisheries Science Center. ② The agency said the analysis shows the probability the population has declined since 2010 is nearly 100 percent. ③ "One problem was, are they really going down or are we not seeing them? They really have gone down, and that's the bottom line," Corkeron said. ④ The new research model has successfully demonstrated that the number of right whales has remained intact despite the worrisome, widening population gap between whale males and females.

26 다음 글의 흐름상 가장 어색한 문장은?

2017. 지방직 9급

Whether you've been traveling, focusing on your family, or going through a busy season at work, 14 days out of the gym takes its toll — not just on your muscles, but your performance, brain, and sleep, too. ① Most experts agree that after two weeks, you're in trouble if you don't get back in the gym. "At the two week point without exercising, there are a multitude of physiological markers that naturally reveal a reduction of fitness level," says Scott Weiss, a New York-based exercise physiologist and trainer who works with elite athletes. ② After all, despite all of its abilities, the human body (even the fit human body) is a very sensitive system and physiological changes (muscle strength or a greater aerobic base) that come about through training will simply disappear if your training load dwindles, he notes. Since the demand of training isn't present, your body simply slinks back toward baseline. ③ More protein is required to build more muscles at a rapid pace in your body. ④ Of course, how much and how quickly you'll decondition depends on a slew of factors like how fit you are, your age, and how long sweating has been a habit. "Two to eight months of not exercising at all will reduce your fitness level to as if you never exercised before," Weiss notes.

27 글의 흐름상 가장 어색한 것은?

2017. 지방직 9급 하반기

A story that is on the cutting edge of modern science began in an isolated part of northern Sweden in the 19th century. ① This area of the country had unpredictable harvests through the first half of the century. In years that the harvest failed, the population went hungry. However, the good years were very good. ② The same people who went hungry during bad harvests overate significantly during the good years. A Swedish scientist wondered about the long-term effects of these eating patterns. He studied the harvest and health records of the area. He was astonished by what he found. ③ Boys who overate during the good years produced children and grandchildren who died about six years earlier than the children and grandchildren of those who had very little to eat. Other scientists found the same result for girls. ④ Both boys and girls benefited greatly from the harvests of the good years. The scientists were forced to conclude that just one reason of overeating could have a negative impact that continued for generations.

28 글의 흐름상 가장 어색한 문장은?

2016. 국가직 9급

One of the largest celebrations of the passage of young girls into womanhood occurs in Latin American and Hispanic cultures. This event is called La Quinceañera, or the fifteenth year. ① It acknowledges that a young woman is now of marriageable age. The day usually begins with a Mass of Thanksgiving. ② By comparing the rites of passage of one culture with those of another, we can assess differences in class status. The young woman wears a full- length white or pastel-colored dress and is attended by fourteen friends and relatives who serve as maids of honor and male escorts. ③ Her parents and godparents surround her at the foot of the altar. When the Mass ends, other young relatives give small gifts to those who attended, while the Quinceañera herself places a bouquet of flowers on the altar of the Virgin. ④ Following the Mass is an elaborate party, with dancing, cake, and toasts. Finally, to end the evening, the young woman dances a waltz with her favorite escort.

29 글의 흐름상 가장 어색한 문장은?

2016. 지방직 9급

Progress is gradually being made in the fight against cancer. ① In the early 1900s, few cancer patients had any hope of long-term survival. ② But because of advances in medical technology, progress has been made so that currently four in ten cancer patients survive. ③ It has been proven that smoking is a direct cause of lung cancer. ④ However, the battle has not yet been won. Although cures for some forms of cancer have been discovered, other forms of cancer are still increasing.

03 문장 제거 유형 기출 독해 어휘 복습 TEST

1	discipline		21	reckless	
2	quote		22	limited	
3	summarize		23	argument	
4	briefly		24	quarrel	
5	desperate		25	insult	
6	urge		26	exposure	
7	get out of		27	toll	
8	let off steam		28	fatigued	
9	conspiracy		29	incapable	
10	advocate		30	depersonalization	
11	trapped		31	speculation	
12	contradict		32	metaphysics	
13	rouse		33	meteorology	
14	anxiety		34	empathy	
15	norm		35	slightly	
16	density		36	transmission	
17	reduce		37	practice	
18	renowned		38	involvement	
19	paragraph		39	initiate	
20	conclude		40	a string of	

03 문장 제거 유형 기출 독해 어휘 복습 TEST

41	chemical		61	irritate	
42	widen		62	tender	
43	lash out		63	submerge	
44	anthropology		64	deprive of	
45	contemporary		65	prolong	
46	illustrate		66	incur	
47	implication		67	urbanization	
48	progress		68	inclined	
49	spontaneous		69	tolerate	
50	sedentary		70	no doubt	
51	direction		71	hierarchy	
52	assemble		72	supervise	
53	irrelevant		73	proliferate	
54	metaphor		74	outstanding	
55	register		75	put on hold	
56	association		76	intact	
57	remarkable		77	dwindle	
58	presence		78	isolated	
59	flamboyant		79	astonish	
60	triumph		80	status	

진가영 영어
반한다 기출
독해

진가영 영어연구소 | cafe.naver.com/easyenglish7

Chapter

04

문장 삽입 유형

chapter 04 문장 삽입 유형

출제경향 분석

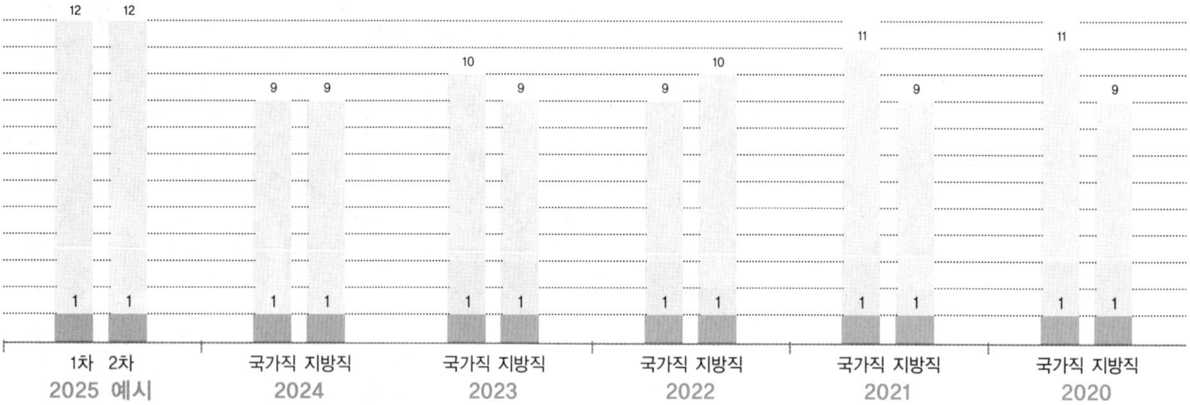

문제풀이 전략

Q 주어진 문장이 들어갈 위치로 가장 적절한 것은? 2025. 출제 기조 전환 2차

For others, activism is controversial and disruptive; after all, it often manifests as confrontational activity that directly challenges the order of things.

Activism is frequently defined as intentional, vigorous or energetic action that individuals and groups practice to bring about a desired goal. (①) For some, activism is a theoretically or ideologically focused project intended to effect a perceived need for political or social change. (②) Activism is uncomfortable, sometimes messy, and almost always strenuous. (③) In addition, it does not occur without the presence and commitment of activists, that is, folks who develop workable strategies, focus a collective spotlight onto particular issues, and ultimately move people into action. (④) As a noted scholar suggests, effective activists also make noise, sometimes loudly.

Step ① 주어진 문장 확인 & 맥락 예측하기

주어진 보기 문장을 먼저 읽고 무엇에 관한 내용인지를 확인하고 주어진 문장 앞 또는 뒤에 나올 내용을 예측하기

Step ② 문장과 문장 사이의 연결 관계를 확인하고 논리적 단절 찾기

문장 간 연결 여부를 확인할 때는 세부정보, 연결사, 지시사, 대명사를 활용한다.

주어진 문장	For others, activism is controversial and disruptive; after all, it often manifests as confrontational activity that directly challenges the order of things. 다른 사람들에게 행동주의는 논란이 많고 파괴적이다; 결국에는, 그것은 종종 사물의 질서에 직접적으로 도전하는 대립적인 활동으로 나타난다.

Activism is frequently defined as intentional, vigorous or energetic action that individuals and groups practice to bring about a desired goal.
행동주의는 종종 개인과 집단이 원하는 목표를 달성하기 위해 연습하는 의도적이고, 격렬하거나 에너지가 넘치는 행동으로 정의된다.
(①) For some, activism is a theoretically or ideologically focused project intended to effect a perceived need for political or social change.
어떤 사람들에게 행동주의는 정치적 또는 사회적 변화에 대한 인식된 필요에 영향을 미치기 위한 이론적 또는 이념적으로 집중된 프로젝트이다.
(②) Activism is uncomfortable, sometimes messy, and almost always strenuous.
행동주의는 불편하고, 때로는 지저분하며, 거의 항상 격렬하다.
(③) In addition, it does not occur without the presence and commitment of activists, that is, folks who develop workable strategies, focus a collective spotlight onto particular issues, and ultimately move people into action.
게다가, 행동주의자들, 즉 실행 가능한 전략을 개발하고, 특정 문제에 집단적인 스포트라이트를 집중하고, 궁극적으로 사람들을 행동으로 옮기는 사람들의 존재와 헌신 없이는 발생하지 않는다.
(④) As a noted scholar suggests, effective activists also make noise, sometimes loudly.
저명한 학자가 시사하듯이, 효과적인 활동가들은 또한 때때로 큰 소리로 소음을 낸다.

Step ③ 지문 검토하기

주어진 문장을 삽입한 후 글의 흐름이 자연스러운지 확인하기

핵심 기출 어휘

- controversial 논란이 많은
- define 정의하다, 규정하다
- vigorous 격렬한, 활발한, 건강한
- operate 가동[작동]하다, 작용하다, 수술하다
- suspend 부유시키다, 매달다, 중지하다, 연기하다
- amendment 개정, 수정
- peninsula 반도
- inhabit 거주하다
- feed 먹이다, 먹이, 자료, 원료
- command 명령하다, 지시하다, 지휘하다
- resolve 결의, 결심, 결심하다, 해결하다
- novel 소설, 새로운, 기발한
- deputy 대리인, 의원, 보안관
- come by 잠깐 들르다, 얻다
- objective 목적, 목표, 객관적인
- outlook 관점, 전망
- variability 가변성, 변동성
- circulate 순환하다, 유포하다
- gravitational force 중력
- tolerable 견딜 수 있는
- resistance 저항, 저항력
- analogy 비유, 유추
- disparate 서로 전혀 다른, 이질적인
- apparatus 기구, 장치
- reverse (정)반대, 뒤바꾸다
- archive 기록 보관소
- material 재료, 자료
- indispensable 없어서는 안 될, 필수적인
- legislature 입법부, 의회
- application 응용, 적용, 지원서, 신청서
- compulsive 강박적인, 강제적인
- residue 나머지, 잔여물
- complicate 복잡하게 하다, 복잡한
- inspiration 영감
- make sense 이해하다, 타당하다
- integral 필수적인, 완전한
- nausea 메스꺼움
- increment 임금 인상, 증가
- overwhelm 압도하다
- make a living 생계를 꾸리다
- contradict 반박하다, 부인하다, 모순되다
- accommodate 적응하다, 조정하다, 수용하다
- distribution 분배, 분포, 유통
- substantially 상당히, 실질적으로
- drowsy 졸리는, 나른하게 만드는
- interruption 방해
- look up 찾아보다
- confusion 혼란
- exert 발휘하다, 가하다, 힘쓰다
- sincerity 진심, 진실성

나의 약점 확인

영역	점수
CHAPTER 04 문장 삽입 유형	/ 29문항

반드시 한 번에 다 잡는 '문장 삽입 유형' 독해 전략

- 문장 삽입 유형은 쓰기 능력을 간접적으로 평가하기 위한 유형 중 하나로 **좋은 글쓰기를 위해 필요한 통일성**(하나의 단락에 하나의 주제), **일관성**(문장이나 내용이 서로 긴밀하게 구성되어야 한다는 원리), **그리고 응집성**(문장과 문장 사이를 구성하는 여러 요소들 사이의 표면적인 연결 관계)**에 대한 이해도를 평가**한다.
- 문장 삽입 유형은 9급 출제 기조 전환 예시 문제를 기준으로 볼 때 **난도가 중간이거나 높은 유형**에 속하며 **한 문제** 출제될 것으로 예상된다.
- 문장 삽입 유형 문제는 **주어진 글을 신속히 읽고 글의 소재 및 중심 내용을 파악**한 후, **문장 간의 논리적 관계와 단서들(세부 정보, 연결사, 지시사 등)을 활용**하여 주어진 글이 들어갈 알맞은 위치를 찾는 훈련이 중요하다.
- 문장 삽입 유형은 반드시 글의 논리적 구성을 위해 사용되는 **대명사, 지시사, 연결사 등의 단서들에 대한 학습**이 필요하다.
- 문장 삽입 유형은 지문 안에 **논리적 단절**이 있는 곳이 주어진 문장이 들어갈 적절한 위치일 가능성이 높으므로 주의한다.

꿀팁 문장 삽입 유형 문제를 효율적으로 풀기 위한 추가 전략

- 주어진 문장을 읽을 때 도움되는 전략 3가지
  - 반드시 이 글이 무슨 내용인지 예측하려고 노력하며 읽는다.
  - 연결어가 있으면 연결어의 기능을 상기시켜 주며 논리적 관계를 생각하며 앞뒤에 올 내용을 예측한다.
  - 지시사나 대명사가 있는 경우 지칭하는 대상을 확인한다.
- 주어진 문장에 단서가 없는 경우에는 최대한 무엇에 관한 내용인지만 파악하고 지문을 확인하면서 주어진 내용과 비슷한 어휘가 나오는 부분에 주의하면서 읽는다.
- 지문을 직독직해로 꼼꼼하게 해석하기보다는 처음부터 빠르게 읽어가면서 주어진 문장과 비슷한 내용이 자연스럽게 연결되어있는지 확인한다.
  (긍정 + 긍정 / 부정 + 부정)
- 주어진 문장과 비슷한 어휘가 나온다면 그때부터는 주의해서 읽는다.
- 주어진 문장을 기준 삼아서 문장과 문장 사이를 읽어 주며 해당 문장이 들어가도 되는지를 확인한다.

01 주어진 문장이 들어갈 위치로 가장 적절한 것은?

2025. 출제 기조 전환 2차

For others, activism is controversial and disruptive; after all, it often manifests as confrontational activity that directly challenges the order of things.

Activism is frequently defined as intentional, vigorous or energetic action that individuals and groups practice to bring about a desired goal. (①) For some, activism is a theoretically or ideologically focused project intended to effect a perceived need for political or social change. (②) Activism is uncomfortable, sometimes messy, and almost always strenuous. (③) In addition, it does not occur without the presence and commitment of activists, that is, folks who develop workable strategies, focus a collective spotlight onto particular issues, and ultimately move people into action. (④) As a noted scholar suggests, effective activists also make noise, sometimes loudly.

02 주어진 문장이 들어갈 위치로 가장 적절한 것은?

2025. 출제 기조 전환 1차

In particular, in many urban counties, air pollution, as measured by the amount of total suspended particles, had reached dangerous levels.

Economists Chay and Greenstone evaluated the value of cleaning up of air pollution after the Clean Air Act of 1970. (①) Before 1970, there was little federal regulation of air pollution, and the issue was not high on the agenda of state legislators. (②) As a result, many counties allowed factories to operate without any regulation on their pollution, and in several heavily industrialized counties, pollution had reached very high levels. (③) The Clean Air Act established guidelines for what constituted excessively high levels of five particularly dangerous pollutants. (④) Following the Act in 1970 and the 1977 amendment, there were improvements in air quality.

03 주어진 문장이 들어갈 위치로 적절한 것은?

2024. 국가직 9급

Tribal oral history and archaeological evidence suggest that sometime between 1500 and 1700 a mudslide destroyed part of the village, covering several longhouses and sealing in their contents.

From the village of Ozette on the westernmost point of Washington's Olympic Peninsula, members of the Makah tribe hunted whales. (①) They smoked their catch on racks and in smokehouses and traded with neighboring groups from around the Puget Sound and nearby Vancouver Island. (②) Ozette was one of five main villages inhabited by the Makah, an Indigenous people who have been based in the region for millennia. (③) Thousands of artifacts that would not otherwise have survived, including baskets, clothing, sleeping mats, and whaling tools, were preserved under the mud. (④) In 1970, a storm caused coastal erosion that revealed the remains of these longhouses and artifacts.

04 주어진 문장이 들어갈 위치로 적절한 것은?

2024. 지방직 9급

But she quickly popped her head out again.

The little mermaid swam right up to the small window of the cabin, and every time a wave lifted her up, she could see a crowd of well-dressed people through the clear glass. Among them was a young prince, the handsomest person there, with large dark eyes. (①) It was his birthday, and that's why there was so much excitement. (②) When the young prince came out on the deck, where the sailors were dancing, more than a hundred rockets went up into the sky and broke into a glitter, making the sky as bright as day. (③) The little mermaid was so startled that she dove down under the water. (④) And look! It was just as if all the stars up in heaven were falling down on her. Never had she seen such fireworks.

05 주어진 문장이 들어갈 위치로 알맞은 것은?

2023. 국가직 9급

> They installed video cameras at places known for illegal crossings, and put live video feeds from the cameras on a Web site.

Immigration reform is a political minefield. (①) About the only aspect of immigration policy that commands broad political support is the resolve to secure the U. S. border with Mexico to limit the flow of illegal immigrants. (②) Texas sheriffs recently developed a novel use of the Internet to help them keep watch on the border. (③) Citizens who want to help monitor the border can go online and serve as "virtual Texas deputies." (④) If they see anyone trying to cross the border, they send a report to the sheriff's office, which follows up, sometimes with the help of the U. S. Border Patrol.

06 주어진 문장이 들어갈 위치로 가장 적절한 것은?

2023. 지방직 9급

> Yet, requests for such self-assessments are pervasive throughout one's Career.

The fiscal quarter just ended. Your boss comes by to ask you how well you performed in terms of sales this quarter. How do you describe your performance? As excellent? Good? Terrible? (①) Unlike when someone asks you about an objective performance metric (e.g., how many dollars in sales you brought in this quarter), how to subjectively describe your performance is often unclear. There is no right answer. (②) you are asked to subjectively describe your own performance in school applications, in job applications, in interviews, in performance reviews, in meetings—the list goes on. (③) How you describe your performance is what we call your level of self-promotion. (④) Since self-promotion is a pervasive part of work, people who do more self-promotion may have better chances of being hired, being promoted, and getting a raise or a bonus.

07 글의 흐름으로 보아, 주어진 문장이 들어가기에 가장 적절한 곳은? 2023. 법원직 9급

> Healthcare chatbots have been purposed to solve this problem and ensure proper diagnosis and advice for people from the comfort of their homes.

People have grown hesitant to approach hospitals or health centers due to the fear of contracting a disease or the heavy sum of consultation fees. (①) This leads them to self-diagnose themselves based upon unverified information sources on the Internet. (②) This often proves harmful effects on the person's mental and physical health if misdiagnosed and improper medicines are consumed. (③) Based upon the severity of the diagnosis, the chatbot prescribes over the counter treatment or escalates the diagnosis to a verified healthcare professional. (④) Interactive chatbots that have been trained on a large and wide variety of symptoms, risk factors, and treatment can handle user health queries with ease, especially in the case of COVID-19.

08 글의 흐름으로 보아, 주어진 문장이 들어가기에 가장 적절한 곳은? 2023. 법원직 9급

> But here it's worth noting that more than half the workforce has little or no opportunity for remote work.

COVID-19's spread flattened the cultural and technological barriers standing in the way of remote work. One analysis of the potential for remote work to persist showed that 20 to 25 percent of workforces in advanced economies could work from home in the range of three to five days a week. (①) This is four to five times more remote work than pre-COVID-19. (②) Moreover, not all work that can be done remotely should be; for example, negotiations, brainstorming, and providing sensitive feedback are activities that may be less effective when done remotely. (③) The outlook for remote work, then, depends on the work environment, job, and the tasks at hand, so *hybrid work setups, where some work happens on-site and some remotely, are likely to persist. (④) To unlock sustainable performance and well-being in a hybrid world, the leading driver of performance and productivity should be the sense of purpose work provides to employees, not compensation.

* hybrid 혼합체

09 글의 흐름으로 보아, 주어진 문장이 들어가기에 가장 적절한 곳은?

2023. 법원직 9급

These may appear as challenges which may be impossible to address because of the uncertainty in our ability to predict future climate.

Global warming is a reality man has to live with. (①) This is a very important issue to recognize, because, of all the parameters that affect human existence, on planet earth, it is the food security that is of paramount importance to life on earth and which is most threatened by global warming. (②) Future food security will be dependent on a combination of the stresses, both biotic and *abiotic, imposed by climate change, variability of weather within the growing season, development of **cultivars more suited to different ***ambient conditions, and, the ability to develop effective adaptation strategies which allow these cultivars to express their genetic potential under the changing climate conditions. (③) However, these challenges also provide us the opportunities to enhance our understanding of soil-plant-atmosphere interaction and how one could utilize this knowledge to enable us achieve the ultimate goal of enhanced food security across all areas of the globe. (④)

* abiotic 비생물적인
** cultivar 품종
*** ambient 주변의

10 주어진 문장이 들어갈 위치로 가장 적절한 곳은?

2022. 국가직 9급

Thus, blood, and life-giving oxygen, are easier for the heart to circulate to the brain.

People can be exposed to gravitational force, or g-force, in different ways. It can be localized, affecting only a portion of the body, as in getting slapped on the back. It can also be momentary, such as hard forces endured in a car crash. A third type of g-force is sustained, or lasting for at least several seconds. (①) Sustained, body-wide g-forces are the most dangerous to people. (②) The body usually withstands localized or momentary g-force better than sustained g-force, which can be deadly because blood is forced into the legs, depriving the rest of the body of oxygen. (③) Sustained g-force applied while the body is horizontal, or lying down, instead of sitting or standing tends to be more tolerable to people, because blood pools in the back and not the legs. (④) Some people, such as astronauts and fighter jet pilots, undergo special training exercises to increase their bodies' resistance to g-force.

11 주어진 문장이 들어갈 위치로 가장 적절한 곳은?

2022. 지방직 9급

The comparison of the heart to a pump, however, is a genuine analogy.

An analogy is a figure of speech in which two things are asserted to be alike in many respects that are quite fundamental. Their structure, the relationships of their parts, or the essential purposes they serve are similar, although the two things are also greatly dissimilar. Roses and carnations are not analogous. (①) They both have stems and leaves and may both be red in color. (②) But they exhibit these qualities in the same way; they are of the same genus. (③) These are disparate things, but they share important qualities: mechanical apparatus, possession of valves, ability to increase and decrease pressures, and capacity to move fluids. (④) And the heart and the pump exhibit these qualities in different ways and in different contexts.

12 글의 흐름으로 보아, 주어진 문장이 들어가기에 가장 적절한 곳은?

2022. 법원직 9급

The effect, however, was just the reverse.

How we dress for work has taken on a new element of choice, and with it, new anxieties. (①) The practice of having a "dress-down day" or "casual day," which began to emerge a decade or so ago, was intended to make life easier for employees, to enable them to save money and feel more relaxed at the office. (②) In addition to the normal workplace wardrobe, employees had to create a "workplace casual" wardrobe. (③) It couldn't really be the sweats and T-shirts you wore around the house on the weekend. (④) It had to be a selection of clothing that sustained a certain image — relaxed, but also serious.

* wardrobe 옷, 의류

13 글의 흐름으로 보아, 주어진 문장이 들어가기에 가장 적절한 곳은? 2022. 법원직 9급

But the demand for food isn't *elastic; people don't eat more just because food is cheap.

The free market has never worked in agriculture and it never will. (①) The economics of a family farm are very different than a firm's: When prices fall, the firm can lay off people and idle factories. (②) Eventually the market finds a new balance between supply and demand. (③) And laying off farmers doesn't help to reduce supply. (④) You can fire me, but you can't fire my land, because some other farmer who needs more cash flow or thinks he's more efficient than I am will come in and farm it.

* elastic 탄력성 있는

14 주어진 문장이 들어갈 위치로 가장 적절한 것은? 2021. 국가직 9급

For example, the state archives of New Jersey hold more than 30,000 cubic feet of paper and 25,000 reels of microfilm.

Archives are a treasure trove of material: from audio to video to newspapers, magazines and printed material — which makes them indispensable to any History Detective investigation. While libraries and archives may appear the same, the differences are important. (①) An archive collection is almost always made up of primary sources, while a library contains secondary sources. (②) To learn more about the Korean War, you'd go to a library for a history book. If you wanted to read the government papers, or letters written by Korean War soldiers, you'd go to an archive. (③) If you're searching for information, chances are there's an archive out there for you. Many state and local archives store public records — which are an amazing, diverse resource. (④) An online search of your state's archives will quickly show you they contain much more than just the minutes of the legislature — there are detailed land grant information to be found, old town maps, criminal records and oddities such as peddler license applications.

* treasure trove 귀중한 발굴물(수집물)
* land grant (대학 · 철도 등을 위해) 정부가 주는

15 주어진 문장이 들어갈 위치로 가장 적절한 것은?

2021. 지방직 9급

And working offers more than financial security.

Why do workaholics enjoy their jobs so much? Mostly because working offers some important advantages. (①) It provides people with paychecks — a way to earn a living. (②) It provides people with self-confidence; they have a feeling of satisfaction when they've produced a challenging piece of work and are able to say, "I made that". (③) Psychologists claim that work also gives people an identity; they work so that they can get a sense of self and individualism. (④) In addition, most jobs provide people with a socially acceptable way to meet others. It could be said that working is a positive addiction; maybe workaholics are compulsive about their work, but their addiction seems to be a safe — even an advantageous — one.

16 주어진 문장이 들어갈 위치로 가장 적절한 것은?

2020. 국가직 9급

It was then he remembered his experience with the glass flask, and just as quickly, he imagined that a special coating might be applied to a glass windshield to keep it from shattering.

In 1903 the French chemist, Edouard Benedictus, dropped a glass flask one day on a hard floor and broke it. (①) However, to the astonishment of the chemist, the flask did not shatter, but still retained most of its original shape. (②) When he examined the flask he found that it contained a film coating inside, a residue remaining from a solution of collodion that the flask had contained. (③) He made a note of this unusual phenomenon, but thought no more of it until several weeks later when he read stories in the newspapers about people in automobile accidents who were badly hurt by flying windshield glass. (④) Not long thereafter, he succeeded in producing the world's first sheet of safety glass.

17 주어진 문장이 들어갈 위치로 가장 적절한 것은?

2020. 지방직 9급

> But there is also clear evidence that millennials, born between 1981 and 1996, are saving more aggressively for retirement than Generation X did at the same ages, 22~37.

Millennials are often labeled the poorest, most financially burdened generation in modern times. Many of them graduated from college into one of the worst labor markets the United States has ever seen, with a staggering load of student debt to boot. (①) Not surprisingly, millennials have accumulated less wealth than Generation X did at a similar stage in life, primarily because fewer of them own homes. (②) But newly available data providing the most detailed picture to date about what Americans of different generations save complicates that assessment. (③) Yes, Gen Xers, those born between 1965 and 1980, have a higher net worth. (④) And that might put them in better financial shape than many assume.

18 글의 흐름으로 보아 아래 문장이 들어가기에 가장 적절한 곳은?

2020. 법원직 9급

> The great news is that this is true whether or not we remember our dreams.

Some believe there is no value to dreams, but it is wrong to dismiss these nocturnal dramas as irrelevant. There is something to be gained in remembering. (①) We can feel more connected, more complete, and more on track. We can receive inspiration, information, and comfort. Albert Einstein stated that his theory of relativity was inspired by a dream. (②) In fact, he claimed that dreams were responsible for many of his discoveries. (③) Asking why we dream makes as much sense as questioning why we breathe. Dreaming is an integral part of a healthy life. (④) Many people report being inspired with a new approach for a problem upon awakening, even though they don't remember the specific dream.

19 주어진 문장이 들어갈 위치로 가장 적절한 것은?

2019. 국가직 9급

Some of these ailments are short-lived; others may be long-lasting.

For centuries, humans have looked up at the sky and wondered what exists beyond the realm of our planet. (①) Ancient astronomers examined the night sky hoping to learn more about the universe. More recently, some movies explored the possibility of sustaining human life in outer space, while other films have questioned whether extraterrestrial life forms may have visited our planet. (②) Since astronaut Yuri Gagarin became the first man to travel in space in 1961, scientists have researched what conditions are like beyond the Earth's atmosphere, and what effects space travel has on the human body. (③) Although most astronauts do not spend more than a few months in space, many experience physiological and psychological problems when they return to the Earth. (④) More than two-thirds of all astronauts suffer from motion sickness while traveling in space. In the gravity-free environment, the body cannot differentiate up from down. The body's internal balance system sends confusing signals to the brain, which can result in nausea lasting as long as a few days.

20 주어진 문장이 들어갈 위치로 가장 적절한 것은?

2019. 지방직 9급

The same thinking can be applied to any number of goals, like improving performance at work.

The happy brain tends to focus on the short term. (①) That being the case, it's a good idea to consider what short-term goals we can accomplish that will eventually lead to accomplishing long-term goals. (②) For instance, if you want to lose thirty pounds in six months, what short-term goals can you associate with losing the smaller increments of weight that will get you there? (③) Maybe it's something as simple as rewarding yourself each week that you lose two pounds. (④) By breaking the overall goal into smaller, shorter-term parts, we can focus on incremental accomplishments instead of being overwhelmed by the enormity of the goal in our profession.

21 〈보기〉의 문장이 들어갈 위치로 가장 적절한 것은?

2019. 서울시 9급

| 보 기 |

In this situation, we would expect to find less movement of individuals from one job to another because of the individual's social obligations toward the work organization to which he or she belongs and to the people comprising that organization.

Cultural differences in the meaning of work can manifest themselves in other aspects as well. (①) For example, in American culture, it is easy to think of work simply as a means to accumulate money and make a living. (②) In other cultures, especially collectivistic ones, work may be seen more as fulfilling an obligation to a larger group. (③) In individualistic cultures, it is easier to consider leaving one job and going to another because it is easier to separate jobs from the self. (④) A different job will just as easily accomplish the same goals.

22 글의 흐름으로 보아, 주어진 문장이 들어가기에 가장 적절한 곳은?

2019. 법원직 9급

"Soft power" on the contrary is "the ability to achieve goals through attraction and persuasion, rather than coercion or fee."

The concept of "soft power" was formed in the early 1990s by the American political scientist, deputy defense of the Clinton's administration, Joseph Nye, Jr. The ideas of the American Professor J. Nye allowed to take a fresh look at the interpretation of the concept of "power," provoked scientific debate and stimulated the practical side of international politics. (①) In his works he identifies two types of power: "hard power" and "soft power." (②) He defines "hard power" as "the ability to get others to act in ways that contradict their initial preferences and strategies." (③) The "soft power" of the state is its ability to "charm" other participants in the world political process, to demonstrate the attractiveness of its own culture (in a context it is attractive to others), political values and foreign policy (if considered legitimate and morally justified). (④) The main components of "soft power" are culture, political values and foreign policy.

* contradict 부인하다, 모순되다

23 주어진 문장이 들어갈 위치로 가장 적절한 것은?

2018. 국가직 9급

Some remain intensely proud of their original accent and dialect words, phrases and gestures, while others accommodate rapidly to a new environment by changing their speech habits, so that they no longer "stand out in the crowd."

Our perceptions and production of speech change with time. (①) If we were to leave our native place for an extended period, our perception that the new accents around us were strange would only be temporary. (②) Gradually, we will lose the sense that others have an accent and we will begin to fit in to accommodate our speech patterns to the new norm. (③) Not all people do this to the same degree. (④) Whether they do this consciously or not is open to debate and may differ from individual to individual, but like most processes that have to do with language, the change probably happens before we are aware of it and probably couldn't happen if we were.

24 주어진 문장이 들어갈 위치로 가장 적절한 것은?

2018. 지방직 9급

If neither surrendered, the two exchanged blows until one was knocked out.

The ancient Olympics provided athletes an opportunity to prove their fitness and superiority, just like our modern games. (①) The ancient Olympic events were designed to eliminate the weak and glorify the strong. Winners were pushed to the brink. (②) Just as in modern times, people loved extreme sports. One of the favorite events was added in the 33rd Olympiad. This was the pankration, or an extreme mix of wrestling and boxing. The Greek word pankration means "total power." The men wore leather straps with metal studs, which could make a terrible mess of their opponents. (③) The dangerous form of wrestling had no time or weight limits. In this event, only two rules applied. First, wrestlers were not allowed to gouge eyes with their thumbs. Secondly, they could not bite. Anything else was considered fair play. The contest was decided in the same manner as a boxing match. Contenders continued until one of the two collapsed. (④) Only the strongest and most determined athletes attempted this event. Imagine wrestling "Mr. Fingertips," who earned his nickname by breaking his opponents' fingers!

25 주어진 문장이 들어갈 위치로 가장 적절한 곳은?

2017. 국가직 9급

This inequality is corrected by their getting in their turn better portions from kills by other people.

Let us examine a situation of simple distribution such as occurs when an animal is killed in a hunt. One might expect to find the animal portioned out according to the amount of work done by each hunter to obtain it. (①) To some extent this principle is followed, but other people have their rights as well. (②) Each person in the camp gets a share depending upon his or her relation to the hunters. (③) When a kangaroo is killed, for example, the hunters have to give its main parts to their kinfolk and the worst parts may even be kept by the hunters themselves. (④) The net result in the long run is substantially the same to each person, but through this system the principles of kinship obligation and the morality of sharing food have been emphasized.

26 주어진 문장이 들어갈 위치로 가장 적절한 곳은?

2017. 국가직 9급 하반기

Only New Zealand, New Caledonia and a few small islands peek above the waves.

Lurking beneath New Zealand is a long-hidden continent called Zealandia, geologists say. But since nobody is in charge of officially designating a new continent, individual scientists will ultimately have to judge for themselves. (①) A team of geologists pitches the scientific case for the new continent, arguing that Zealandia is a continuous expanse of continental crust covering around 4.9 million square kilometers. (②) That's about the size of the Indian subcontinent. Unlike the other mostly dry continents, around 94 percent of Zealandia hides beneath the ocean. (③) Except those tiny areas, all parts of Zealandia submerge under the ocean. "If we could pull the plug on the world's oceans, it would be quite clear that Zealandia stands out about 3,000 meters above the surrounding ocean crust," says a geologist. (④) "If it wasn't for the ocean level, long ago we'd have recognized Zealandia for what it was—a continent."

27 주어진 문장이 들어갈 위치로 가장 적절한 것은?

2017. 지방직 9급

Fortunately, however, the heavy supper she had eaten caused her to become tired and ready to fall asleep.

Various duties awaited me on my arrival. I had to sit with the girls during their hour of study. (①) Then it was my turn to read prayers; to see them to bed. Afterwards I ate with the other teachers. (②) Even when we finally retired for the night, the inevitable Miss Gryce was still my companion. We had only a short end of candle in our candlestick, and I dreaded lest she should talk till it was all burnt out. (③) She was already snoring before I had finished undressing. There still remained an inch of candle. (④) I now took out my letter; the seal was an initial F. I broke it; the contents were brief.

28 주어진 문장이 들어갈 위치로 가장 적절한 곳은?

2017. 지방직 9급 하반기

However, should understanding not occur, you will find yourself soon becoming drowsy.

Dictionaries are your most reliable resources for the study of words. Yet the habit of using them needs to be cultivated. Of course, it can feel like an annoying interruption to stop your reading and look up a word. You might tell yourself that if you keep going, you would eventually understand it from the context. (①) Indeed, reading study guides often advise just that. (②) Often it's not the need for sleep that is occurring but a gradual loss of consciousness. (③) The knack here is to recognize the early signs of word confusion before drowsiness takes over when it is easier to exert sufficient willpower to grab a dictionary for word study. (④) Although this special effort is needed, once the meaning is clarified, the perceptible sense of relief makes the effort worthwhile.

29 다음 주어진 문장이 들어갈 가장 적절한 곳은?

2017. 서울시 9급

Instead, these employees spoke first of the sincerity of the relationships at work, that their work culture felt like an extension of home, and that their colleagues were supportive.

(①) There is a clear link between job satisfaction and productivity. However, job satisfaction also depends on the service culture of an organization. (②) This culture comprises the things that make a business distinctive and make the people who work there proud to do so. (③) When employees of the Top 10 Best Companies to Work For were asked by Fortune magazine why they loved working for these companies, it was notable that they didn't mention pay, reward schemes, or advancing to a more senior position. (④)

04 문장 삽입 유형 기출 독해 어휘 복습 TEST

1	controversial		21	negotiation	
2	messy		22	outlook	
3	strenuous		23	variability	
4	commitment		24	ultimate	
5	federal		25	circulate	
6	suspend		26	localized	
7	amendment		27	momentary	
8	inhabit		28	horizontal	
9	preserve		29	analogy	
10	reveal		30	structure	
11	cabin		31	dissimilar	
12	startle		32	reverse	
13	reform		33	relaxed	
14	resolve		34	lay off	
15	deputy		35	material	
16	come by		36	application	
17	objective		37	indispensable	
18	subjectively		38	peddler	
19	unverified		39	financial	
20	escalate		40	satisfaction	

04 문장 삽입 유형 기출 독해 어휘 복습 TEST

41	addiction		61	coercion	
42	compulsive		62	dialect	
43	advantageous		63	fit in	
44	shatter		64	be open to	
45	retain		65	debate	
46	residue		66	superiority	
47	retirement		67	glorify	
48	staggering		68	contender	
49	inspiration		69	distribution	
50	integral		70	portion	
51	realm		71	kinfolk	
52	astronomer		72	beneath	
53	result in		73	continent	
54	lasting		74	stand out	
55	accomplish		75	afterward	
56	incremental		76	companion	
57	overwhelm		77	brief	
58	obligation		78	drowsy	
59	on the contrary		79	worthwhile	
60	persuasion		80	sincerity	

MEMO

진가영 영어
반한다 기출
독해

Chapter

05

순서 배열 유형

chapter 05 순서 배열 유형

출제경향 분석

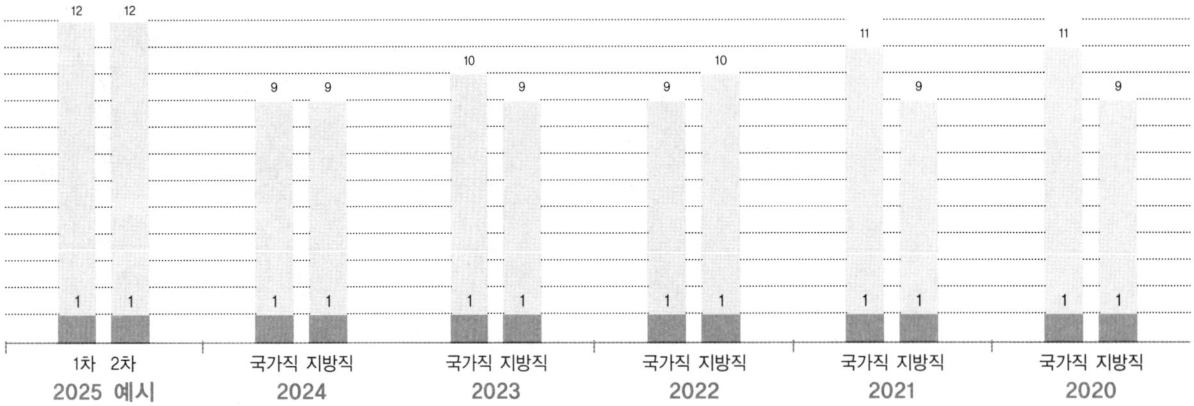

문제풀이 전략

Q 주어진 글 다음에 이어질 글의 순서로 가장 적절한 것은? 2025. 출제 기조 전환 2차

Nick started a fire with some chunks of pine he got with the ax from a stump. Over the fire he stuck a wire grill, pushing the four legs down into the ground with his boot.

(A) They began to bubble, making little bubbles that rose with difficulty to the surface. There was a good smell. Nick got out a bottle of tomato ketchup and cut four slices of bread.

(B) The little bubbles were coming faster now. Nick sat down beside the fire and lifted the frying pan off.

(C) Nick put the frying pan on the grill over the flames. He was hungrier. The beans and spaghetti warmed. He stirred them and mixed them together.

① (B) − (A) − (C)
② (B) − (C) − (A)
③ (C) − (A) − (B)
④ (C) − (B) − (A)

Step 1 선택지 확인 & 주어진 문장 확인하기

- 주어진 보기 문장을 먼저 읽고 무엇에 관한 내용인지 확인하기
- 주어진 명사에 특히 강조점을 두고 뒤에 이어질 내용을 예측하기

Step 2 [A], [B], [C] 첫 문장 확인 후 주어진 문장과 연결 여부 확인하기

- 문장 간 연결 여부를 확인할 때는 세부 정보, 연결사, 지시사, 대명사를 활용하기

Step 3 지문 검토하기(하나의 순서가 결정된 이후 끝 문장에 집중하며 다음 순서 정하기)

주어진 문장	Nick started a fire with some chunks of pine he got with the ax from a stump. Over the fire he stuck a wire grill, pushing the four legs down into the ground with his boot. Nick은 그루터기에서 도끼로 얻은 소나무 조각으로 불을 피우기 시작했다. 그는 불 위에 철망 그릴을 얹고, 네 개의 다리를 부츠로 땅에 눌러 고정했다.
(C)	Nick put the frying pan on the grill over the flames. He was hungrier. The beans and spaghetti warmed. He stirred them and mixed them together. Nick은 불꽃 위에 그릴에 프라이팬을 올렸다. 그는 더 배가 고팠다. 콩과 스파게티가 데워졌다. 그는 그것들을 저어 섞었다.
(A)	They began to bubble, making little bubbles that rose with difficulty to the surface. There was a good smell. Nick got out a bottle of tomato ketchup and cut four slices of bread. 그것들은 기포가 생기기 시작했고, 작은 기포들이 힘겹게 표면으로 올라왔다. 좋은 냄새가 났다. Nick은 토마토케첩 병을 꺼내고 빵 네 조각을 잘랐다.
(B)	The little bubbles were coming faster now. Nick sat down beside the fire and lifted the frying pan off. 작은 기포들이 이제 더 빨리 올라오고 있었다. Nick은 불 옆에 앉아 프라이팬을 들어 올렸다.

핵심 기출 어휘

- surface 표면, 지면
- witness 목격하다, 목격자, 증인
- hearty 푸짐한, 원기 왕성한, 애정어린, 친절한
- promote 촉진하다, 홍보하다
- expand 확장하다, 넓히다
- fundamental 기본적인, 근본적인
- authentic 진정한, 진짜의
- renew 갱신하다, 새롭게 하다
- complex 복잡한
- administration 행정, 관리, 집행
- apocalyptic 종말론적, 세상에 종말이 온 듯한
- summon 불러내다, 소환하다
- avid 열심인
- scrutiny 정밀 조사, 철저한 검토
- transformation 변화, 변신
- alchemy 연금술
- indulge 충족시키다, 채우다
- exert 행사하다, 가하다, 분투하다
- inheritance 유전, 상속
- offspring 자손, 자식
- sort 종류, 유형, 분류하다, 구분하다
- primate 영장류
- ambiguity 애매모호함
- stand out 눈에 띄다, 뚜렷하게 나타나다
- vocalization 발성
- rudimentary 기본적인, 기초적인
- renewable 재생 가능한
- deplete 고갈시키다, 대폭 감소시키다
- emission 배출, 방출
- deforestation 산림 파괴
- prestigious 훌륭한, 명성 있는
- vicinity 주변, 근처
- real estate 부동산
- cardiovascular 심혈관의
- refer to 언급하다, 참고하다
- executive 경영진, 임원
- surrender 항복하다, 포기하다
- cease 그치다, 중단되다
- prone to ~하는 경향이 있는, ~하기 쉬운
- exhaustion 피로, 고갈
- embrace 받아들이다
- obsessed 빠져 있는, 집착하는
- make sense of 이해하다, 의미를 파악하다
- weigh down 무겁게 누르다, 짓누르다
- causal 인과의
- leading 주요한, 선도적인
- alien 상반되는, 이질적인
- solitary 유일한, 고독한
- empathic 감정이입의
- impulse 자극, 욕망
- capacity 공간, 능력
- propositional 명제적인

나의 약점 확인

영역	점수
CHAPTER 05 순서 배열 유형	/ 34문항

반드시 한번에 다 잡는 '순서 배열 유형' 독해 전략

- 순서 배열 유형은 쓰기 능력을 간접적으로 평가하기 위한 유형 중 하나로 **좋은 글쓰기를 위해 필요한 통일성**(하나의 단락에 하나의 주제), **일관성**(문장이나 내용이 서로 긴밀하게 구성되어야 한다는 원리), **그리고 응집성**(문장과 문장 사이를 구성하는 여러 요소들 사이의 표면적인 연결 관계)**에 대한 이해도를 평가**한다.
- 순서 배열 유형은 9급 출제 기조 전환 예시 문제를 기준으로 볼 때 **난도가 중간이거나 높은 유형**에 속하며 **한 문제** 출제될 것으로 예상된다.
- 순서 배열 유형은 **예시, 나열, 비교와 대조, 원인과 결과 등 글쓰기에서 사용되는 보편적 글의 구조**를 이해하는 것을 통해 문제 풀이의 속도와 정확성을 키워야 한다.
- 순서 배열 유형은 **주어진 글을 신속히 읽고 글의 소재 및 중심 내용을 파악**한 후, **문장 간의 논리적 관계와 단서들(세부 정보, 연결사, 지시사 등)을 활용**하여 글의 적절한 순서를 고르는 연습을 해야 한다.

꿀팁 순서 배열 유형 문제를 효율적으로 풀기 위한 명시적 단서

대명사, 지시사	성과 수가 일치하는 명사가 있는 문장 뒤에 위치
지시 형용사	this 명사, these 명사, that 명사, such 명사 → 앞에 언급하는 명사 확인
역접	but, however, still, yet, nevertheless, even so, rather, instead
대조	on the other hand, in contrast, by contrast
예시	for example, for instance
추가	also, moreover, in addtion, furthermore
비교	likewise, similarly, in the same way
인과	so, therefore, thus, as a result, consequently, hence
기타	일반적인 진술 → 구체적인 진술 / '이름 + 성' → '성' 또는 '이름' some, others → 주로 some이 먼저 언급되고 other가 그 이후 before, after, then, finally, last → 순서 표현

01 주어진 글 다음에 이어질 글의 순서로 가장 적절한 것은? 2025. 출제 기조 전환 2차

Nick started a fire with some chunks of pine he got with the ax from a stump. Over the fire he stuck a wire grill, pushing the four legs down into the ground with his boot.

(A) They began to bubble, making little bubbles that rose with difficulty to the surface. There was a good smell. Nick got out a bottle of tomato ketchup and cut four slices of bread.
(B) The little bubbles were coming faster now. Nick sat down beside the fire and lifted the frying pan off.
(C) Nick put the frying pan on the grill over the flames. He was hungrier. The beans and spaghetti warmed. He stirred them and mixed them together.

① (B) − (A) − (C)
② (B) − (C) − (A)
③ (C) − (A) − (B)
④ (C) − (B) − (A)

02 주어진 글 다음에 이어질 글의 순서로 가장 적절한 것은? 2025. 출제 기조 전환 1차

Before anyone could witness what had happened, I shoved the loaves of bread up under my shirt, wrapped the hunting jacket tightly about me, and walked swiftly away.

(A) When I dropped them on the table, my sister's hands reached to tear off a chunk, but I made her sit, forced my mother to join us at the table, and poured warm tea.
(B) The heat of the bread burned into my skin, but I clutched it tighter, clinging to life. By the time I reached home, the loaves had cooled somewhat, but the insides were still warm.
(C) I sliced the bread. We ate an entire loaf, slice by slice. It was good hearty bread, filled with raisins and nuts.

① (A) − (B) − (C)
② (B) − (A) − (C)
③ (B) − (C) − (A)
④ (C) − (A) − (B)

03 주어진 글 다음에 이어질 글의 순서로 적절한 것은?

2024. 국가직 9급

Interest in movie and sports stars goes beyond their performances on the screen and in the arena.

(A) The doings of skilled baseball, football, and basketball players out of uniform similarly attract public attention.

(B) Newspaper columns, specialized magazines, television programs, and Web sites record the personal lives of celebrated Hollywood actors, sometimes accurately.

(C) Both industries actively promote such attention, which expands audiences and thus increases revenues. But a fundamental difference divides them: What sports stars do for a living is authentic in a way that what movie stars do is not.

① (A) − (C) − (B)
② (B) − (A) − (C)
③ (B) − (C) − (A)
④ (C) − (A) − (B)

04 주어진 글 다음에 이어질 글의 순서로 적절한 것은?

2024. 지방직 9급

Computer assisted language learning (CALL) is both exciting and frustrating as a field of research and practice.

(A) Yet the technology changes so rapidly that CALL knowledge and skills must be constantly renewed to stay apace of the field.

(B) It is exciting because it is complex, dynamic and quickly changing — and it is frustrating for the same reasons.

(C) Technology adds dimensions to the domain of language learning, requiring new knowledge and skills for those who wish to apply it into their professional practice.

① (A) − (C) − (B)
② (B) − (A) − (C)
③ (B) − (C) − (A)
④ (C) − (B) − (A)

05 **주어진 글 다음에 이어질 글의 순서로 알맞은 것은?**

2023. 국가직 9급

All civilizations rely on government administration. Perhaps no civilization better exemplifies this than ancient Rome.

(A) To rule an area that large, the Romans, based in what is now central Italy, needed an effective system of government administration.
(B) Actually, the word "civilization" itself comes from the Latin word civis, meaning "citizen."
(C) Latin was the language of ancient Rome, whose territory stretched from the Mediterranean basin all the way to parts of Great Britain in the north and the Black Sea to the east.

① (A) − (B) − (C)
② (B) − (A) − (C)
③ (B) − (C) − (A)
④ (C) − (A) − (B)

06 **주어진 글 다음에 이어질 글의 순서로 가장 적절한 것은?**

2023. 지방직 9급

Just a few years ago, every conversation about artificial intelligence (AI) seemed to end with an apocalyptic prediction.

(A) More recently, however, Things have begun to change. AI has gone from being a scary black box to something people can use for a variety of use cases.
(B) In 2014, an expert in the field said that, with AI, we are summoning the demon, while a Nobel Prize winning physicist said that AI could spell the end of the human race.
(C) This shift is because these technologies are finally being explored at scale in the industry, particularly for market opportunities.

① (A) − (B) − (C)
② (B) − (A) − (C)
③ (B) − (C) − (A)
④ (C) − (A) − (B)

07 주어진 글 다음에 이어질 글의 순서로 가장 적절한 것은?

2023. 법원직 9급

Sports fan depression is a real phenomenon that affects many avid sports fans, especially during times of disappointment or defeat.

(A) Fans may experience a decrease in mood, appetite, and sleep quality, as well as an increase in stress levels and a heightened risk of developing anxiety or depression. There are many factors that can contribute to sports fan depression, including personal investment in a team's success, social pressures to support a particular team, and the intense media coverage and scrutiny that often accompanies high-profile sports events.

(B) For many fans, their emotional investment in their favorite teams or athletes can be so intense that losing or failing to meet expectations can lead to feelings of sadness, frustration, and even depression. Research has shown that sports fan depression can have a range of negative effects on both mental and physical health.

(C) To mitigate the negative effects of sports fan depression, it's important for fans to maintain a healthy perspective on sports and remember that they are ultimately just games. Engaging in self-care activities such as exercise, spending time with loved ones, and seeking support from a mental health professional can also be helpful.

* avid 열심인

① (A) − (C) − (B)
② (B) − (A) − (C)
③ (B) − (C) − (A)
④ (C) − (B) − (A)

08 주어진 글 다음에 이어질 글의 순서로 가장 적절한 것은?

2023. 법원직 9급

On the human level, a cow seems simple. You feed it grass, and it pays you back with milk. It's a trick whose secret is limited to cows and a few other mammals (most can't digest grass).

(A) A cow's complexity is even greater. In particular, a cow (plus a bull) can make a new generation of baby cows. This is a simple thing on a human level, but inexpressibly complex on a microscopic level.

(B) Seen through a microscope, though, it all gets more complicated. And the closer you look, the more complicated it gets. Milk is not a single substance, but a mixture of many. Grass is so complex that we still don't fully understand it.

(C) You don't need to understand the details to exploit the process: it's a straightforward transformation from grass into milk, more like chemistry—or alchemy—than biology. It is, in its way, magic, but it's rational magic that works reliably. All you need is some grass, a cow and several generations of practical knowhow.

* alchemy 연금술

① (B) − (A) − (C)
② (B) − (C) − (A)
③ (C) − (A) − (B)
④ (C) − (B) − (A)

09 주어진 글 다음에 이어질 글의 순서로 가장 적절한 것은? 2023. 법원직 9급

At the level of lawmaking, there is no reason why tech giants should have such an ironclad grip on technological resources and innovation.

(A) As the Daily Wire's Matt Walsh has pointed out, for example, if you don't buy your kid a smartphone, he won't have one. There is no need to put in his hand a device that enables him to indulge his every impulse without supervision.
(B) At the private and personal level, there's no reason why they should have control of your life, either. In policy, politics, and our personal lives, it should not be taken as "inevitable" that our data will be sold to the highest bidder, our children will be addicted to online games, and our lives will be lived in the metaverse.
(C) As a free people, we are entitled to exert absolute control over which kinds of digital products we consume, and in what quantities. Most especially, parents should control what tech products go to their kids.

① (B) – (A) – (C)
② (B) – (C) – (A)
③ (C) – (A) – (B)
④ (C) – (B) – (A)

10 주어진 글 다음에 이어질 글의 순서로 가장 적절한 것은? 2022. 국가직 9급

Today, Lamarck is unfairly remembered in large part for his mistaken explanation of how adaptations evolve. He proposed that by using or not using certain body parts, an organism develops certain characteristics.

(A) There is no evidence that this happens. Still, it is important to note that Lamarck proposed that evolution occurs when organisms adapt to their environments. This idea helped set the stage for Darwin.
(B) Lamarck thought that these characteristics would be passed on to the offspring. Lamarck called this idea *inheritance of acquired characteristics*.
(C) For example, Lamarck might explain that a kangaroo's powerful hind legs were the result of ancestors strengthening their legs by jumping and then passing that acquired leg strength on to the offspring. However, an acquired characteristic would have to somehow modify the DNA of specific genes in order to be inherited.

① (A) – (C) – (B)
② (B) – (A) – (C)
③ (B) – (C) – (A)
④ (C) – (A) – (B)

11 주어진 글 다음에 이어질 글의 순서로 가장 적절한 것은? 2022. 지방직 9급

For people who are blind, everyday tasks such as sorting through the mail or doing a load of laundry present a challenge.

(A) That's the thinking behind Aira, a new service that enables its thousands of users to stream live video of their surroundings to an on-demand agent, using either a smartphone or Aira's proprietary glasses.
(B) But what if they could "borrow" the eyes of someone who could see?
(C) The Aira agents, who are available 24/7, can then answer questions, describe objects or guide users through a location.

① (A) − (B) − (C)
② (A) − (C) − (B)
③ (B) − (A) − (C)
④ (C) − (A) − (B)

12 주어진 글 다음에 이어질 글의 순서로 가장 적절한 것은? 2022. 법원직 9급

Once they leave their mother, primates have to keep on making decisions about whether new foods they encounter are safe and worth collecting.

(A) By the same token, if the sampler feels fine, it will reenter the tree in a few days, eat a little more, then wait again, building up to a large dose slowly. Finally, if the monkey remains healthy, the other members figure this is OK, and they adopt the new food.
(B) If the plant harbors a particularly strong toxin, the sampler's system will try to break it down, usually making the monkey sick in the process. "I've seen this happen," says Glander. "The other members of the troop are watching with great interest — if the animal gets sick, no other animal will go into that tree. There's a cue being given — a social cue."
(C) Using themselves as experiment tools is one option, but social primates have found a better way. Kenneth Glander calls it "sampling." When howler monkeys move into a new habitat, one member of the troop will go to a tree, eat a few leaves, then wait a day.

① (A) − (B) − (C)
② (B) − (A) − (C)
③ (C) − (B) − (A)
④ (C) − (A) − (B)

13 주어진 글 다음에 이어질 글의 순서로 가장 적절한 것은? 2022. 법원직 9급

The historical evolution of Conflict Resolution gained momentum in the 1950s and 1960s, at the height of the Cold War, when the development of nuclear weapons and conflict between the superpowers seemed to threaten human survival.

(A) The combination of analysis and practice implicit in the new ideas was not easy to reconcile with traditional scholarly institutions or the traditions of practitioners such as diplomats and politicians.
(B) However, they were not taken seriously by some. The international relations profession had its own understanding of international conflict and did not see value in the new approaches as proposed.
(C) A group of pioneers from different disciplines saw the value of studying conflict as a general phenomenon, with similar properties, whether it occurs in international relations, domestic politics, industrial relations, communities, or between individuals.

① (B) − (A) − (C)
② (B) − (C) − (A)
③ (C) − (A) − (B)
④ (C) − (B) − (A)

14 주어진 글 다음에 이어질 글의 순서로 가장 적절한 것은? 2022. 법원직 9급

Ambiguity is so uncomfortable that it can even turn good news into bad. You go to your doctor with a persistent stomachache. Your doctor can't figure out what the reason is, so she sends you to the lab for tests.

(A) And what happens? Your immediate relief may be replaced by a weird sense of discomfort. You still don't know what the pain was! There's got to be an explanation somewhere.
(B) A week later you're called back to hear the results. When you finally get into her office, your doctor smiles and tells you the tests were all negative.
(C) Maybe it is cancer and they've just missed it. Maybe it's worse. Surely they should be able to find a cause. You feel frustrated by the lack of a definitive answer.

① (B) − (A) − (C)
② (B) − (C) − (A)
③ (C) − (A) − (B)
④ (C) − (B) − (A)

15 주어진 글 다음에 이어질 글의 순서로 가장 적절한 것은?

2021. 국가직 9급

To be sure, human language stands out from the decidedly restricted vocalizations of monkeys and apes. Moreover, it exhibits a degree of sophistication that far exceeds any other form of animal communication.

(A) That said, many species, while falling far short of human language, do nevertheless exhibit impressively complex communication systems in natural settings.

(B) And they can be taught far more complex systems in artificial contexts, as when raised alongside humans.

(C) Even our closest primate cousins seem incapable of acquiring anything more than a rudimentary communicative system, even after intensive training over several years. The complexity that is language is surely a species-specific trait.

① (A) − (B) − (C)
② (B) − (C) − (A)
③ (C) − (A) − (B)
④ (C) − (B) − (A)

16 주어진 글 다음에 이어질 글의 순서로 가장 적절한 것은?

2021. 지방직 9급

Growing concern about global climate change has motivated activists to organize not only campaigns against fossil fuel extraction consumption, but also campaigns to support renewable energy.

(A) This solar cooperative produces enough energy to power 1,400 homes, making it the first large-scale solar farm cooperative in the country and, in the words of its members, a visible reminder that solar power represents "a new era of sustainable and 'democratic' energy supply that enables ordinary people to produce clean power, not only on their rooftops, but also at utility scale."

(B) Similarly, renewable energy enthusiasts from the United States have founded the Clean Energy Collective, a company that has pioneered "the model of delivering clean power-generation through medium-scale facilities that are collectively owned by participating utility customers."

(C) Environmental activists frustrated with the UK government's inability to rapidly accelerate the growth of renewable energy industries have formed the Westmill Wind Farm Co-operative, a community-owned organization with more than 2,000 members who own an onshore wind farm estimated to produce as much electricity in a year as that used by 2,500 homes. The Westmill Wind Farm Co-operative has inspired local citizens to form the Westmill Solar Co-operative.

① (C) − (A) − (B)　② (A) − (C) − (B)
③ (B) − (C) − (A)　④ (C) − (B) − (A)

17 **주어진 글 다음에 이어질 글의 순서로 가장 적절한 것은?** 2021. 법원직 9급

Religion can certainly bring out the best in a person, but it is not the only phenomenon with that property.

(A) People who would otherwise be self-absorbed or shallow or crude or simply quitters are often ennobled by their religion, given a perspective on life that helps them make the hard decisions that we all would be proud to make.

(B) Having a child often has a wonderfully maturing effect on a person. Wartime, famously, gives people an abundance of occasions to rise to, as do natural disasters like floods and hurricanes.

(C) But for day-in, day-out lifelong bracing, there is probably nothing so effective as religion: it makes powerful and talented people more humble and patient, it makes average people rise above themselves, it provides sturdy support for many people who desperately need help staying away from drink or drugs or crime.

① (B) − (A) − (C)
② (B) − (C) − (A)
③ (C) − (A) − (B)
④ (C) − (B) − (A)

18 **주어진 글 다음에 이어질 글의 순서로 가장 적절한 것은?** 2021. 법원직 9급

More people require more resources, which means that as the population increases, the Earth's resources deplete more rapidly.

(A) Population growth also results in increased greenhouse gases, mostly from CO_2 emissions. For visualization, during that same 20th century that saw fourfold population growth, CO_2 emissions increased twelvefold.

(B) The result of this depletion is deforestation and loss of biodiversity as humans strip the Earth of resources to accommodate rising population numbers.

(C) As greenhouse gases increase, so do climate patterns, ultimately resulting in the long-term pattern called climate change.

* deplete 고갈시키다, 대폭 감소시키다

① (A) − (B) − (C)
② (B) − (A) − (C)
③ (B) − (C) − (A)
④ (C) − (A) − (B)

19 주어진 글 다음에 이어질 글의 순서로 가장 적절한 것은? 2021. 법원직 9급

Sequoya (1760?-1843) was born in eastern Tennessee, into a prestigious family that was highly regarded for its knowledge of Cherokee tribal traditions and religion.

(A) Recognizing the possibilities writing had for his people, Sequoya invented a Cherokee alphabet in 1821. With this system of writing, Sequoya was able to record ancient tribal customs.

(B) More important, his alphabet helped the Cherokee nation develop a publishing industry so that newspapers and books could be printed. School-age children were thus able to learn about Cherokee culture and traditions in their own language.

(C) As a child, Sequoya learned the Cherokee oral tradition; then, as an adult, he was introduced to Euro-American culture. In his letters, Sequoya mentions how he became fascinated with the writing methods European Americans used to communicate.

① (B) − (A) − (C)
② (B) − (C) − (A)
③ (C) − (A) − (B)
④ (C) − (B) − (A)

20 주어진 글 다음에 이어질 글의 순서로 가장 적절한 것은? 2021. 소방직 9급

There are hundreds of gas stations around San Francisco in the California Bay Area. One might think that gas stations would spread out to serve local neighborhoods.

(A) The phenomenon is partly due to population clustering. Gas stations will be more common where demand is high, like in a city, rather than in sparsely populated areas like cornfields.

(B) But this idea is contradicted by a common observation. Whenever you visit a gas station, there is almost always another in the vicinity, often just across the street. In general, gas stations are highly clustered.

(C) Moreover, there are many factors at play. Locating a gas station is an optimization problem involving demand, real estate prices, estimates of population growth, and supply considerations such as the ease of refueling.

① (A) − (C) − (B)
② (B) − (A) − (C)
③ (C) − (A) − (B)
④ (C) − (B) − (A)

21 주어진 글 다음에 이어질 글의 순서로 가장 적절한 것은? 2020. 국가직 9급

Past research has shown that experiencing frequent psychological stress can be a significant risk factor for cardiovascular disease, a condition that affects almost half of those aged 20 years and older in the United States.

(A) Does this mean, though, that people who drive on a daily basis are set to develop heart problems, or is there a simple way of easing the stress of driving?
(B) According to a new study, there is. The researchers noted that listening to music while driving helps relieve the stress that affects heart health.
(C) One source of frequent stress is driving, either due to the stressors associated with heavy traffic or the anxiety that often accompanies inexperienced drivers.

① (A) − (C) − (B)
② (B) − (A) − (C)
③ (C) − (A) − (B)
④ (C) − (B) − (A)

22 주어진 글 다음에 이어질 글의 순서로 가장 적절한 것은? 2020. 지방직 9급

Nowadays the clock dominates our lives so much that it is hard to imagine life without it. Before industrialization, most societies used the sun or the moon to tell the time.

(A) For the growing network of railroads, the fact that there were no time standards was a disaster. Often, stations just some miles apart set their clocks at different times. There was a lot of confusion for travelers.
(B) When mechanical clocks first appeared, they were immediately popular. It was fashionable to have a clock or a watch. People invented the expression "of the clock" or "o'clock" to refer to this new way to tell the time.
(C) These clocks were decorative, but not always useful. This was because towns, provinces, and even neighboring villages had different ways to tell the time. Travelers had to reset their clocks repeatedly when they moved from one place to another. In the United States, there were about 70 different time zones in the 1860s.

① (A) − (B) − (C)
② (B) − (A) − (C)
③ (B) − (C) − (A)
④ (C) − (A) − (B)

23 주어진 글 다음에 이어질 글의 순서로 가장 적절한 것은? 2020. 법원직 9급

As cars are becoming less dependent on people, the means and circumstances in which the product is used by consumers are also likely to undergo significant changes, with higher rates of participation in car sharing and short-term leasing programs.

(A) In the not-too-distant future, a driverless car could come to you when you need it, and when you are done with it, it could then drive away without any need for a parking space. Increases in car sharing and short-term leasing are also likely to be associated with a corresponding decrease in the importance of exterior car design.

(B) As a result, the symbolic meanings derived from cars and their relationship to consumer self-identity and status are likely to change in turn.

(C) Rather than serving as a medium for personalization and self-identity, car exteriors might increasingly come to represent a channel for advertising and other promotional activities, including brand ambassador programs, such as those offered by Free Car Media.

① (A) − (C) − (B)
② (B) − (C) − (A)
③ (C) − (A) − (B)
④ (C) − (B) − (A)

24 주어진 글 다음에 이어질 글의 순서로 가장 적절한 것은? 2020. 법원직 9급

There is a wonderful story of a group of American car executives who went to Japan to see a Japanese assembly line. At the end of the line, the doors were put on the hinges, the same as in America.

(A) But something was missing. In the United States, a line worker would take a rubber mallet and tap the edges of the door to ensure that it fit perfectly. In Japan, that job didn't seem to exist.

(B) Confused, the American auto executives asked at what point they made sure the door fit perfectly. Their Japanese guide looked at them and smiled sheepishly. "We make sure it fits when we design it."

(C) In the Japanese auto plant, they didn't examine the problem and accumulate data to figure out the best solution — they engineered the outcome they wanted from the beginning. If they didn't achieve their desired outcome, they understood it was because of a decision they made at the start of the process.

① (A) − (B) − (C)
② (A) − (C) − (B)
③ (B) − (A) − (C)
④ (B) − (C) − (A)

25 주어진 글 다음에 이어질 글의 순서로 가장 적절한 것은? 2020. 소방직 9급

In World War II, Japan joined forces with Germany and Italy. So there were now two fronts, the European battle zone and the islands in the Pacific Ocean.

(A) Three days later, the United States dropped bombs on another city of Nagasaki. Japan soon surrendered, and World War II finally ended.
(B) In late 1941, the United States, Britain and France participated in a fight against Germany and Japan; the U.S. troops were sent to both battlefronts.
(C) At 8:15 a.m. on August 6, 1945, a U.S. military plane dropped an atomic bomb over Hiroshima, Japan. In an instant, 80,000 people were killed. Hiroshima simply ceased to exist. The people at the center of the explosion evaporated. All that remained was their charred shadows on the walls of buildings.

① (A) − (B) − (C)
② (B) − (A) − (C)
③ (B) − (C) − (A)
④ (C) − (A) − (B)

26 주어진 글 다음에 이어질 글의 순서로 가장 적절한 것은? 2020. 소방직 9급

Trivial things such as air conditioners or coolers with fresh water, flexible schedules and good relationships with colleagues, as well as many other factors, impact employees' productivity and quality of work.

(A) At the same time, there are many bosses who not only manage to maintain their staff's productivity at high levels, but also treat them nicely and are pleasant to work with.
(B) In this regard, one of the most important factors is the manager, or the boss, who directs the working process.
(C) It is not a secret that bosses are often a category of people difficult to deal with: many of them are unfairly demanding, prone to shifting their responsibilities to other workers, and so on.

① (A) − (B) − (C)
② (B) − (A) − (C)
③ (B) − (C) − (A)
④ (C) − (B) − (A)

27 주어진 문장 다음에 이어질 글의 순서로 가장 적절한 것은? 2019. 국가직 9급

South Korea boasts of being the most wired nation on earth.

(A) This addiction has become a national issue in Korea in recent years, as users started dropping dead from exhaustion after playing online games for days on end. A growing number of students have skipped school to stay online, shockingly self-destructive behavior in this intensely competitive society.
(B) In fact, perhaps no other country has so fully embraced the Internet.
(C) But such ready access to the Web has come at a price as legions of obsessed users find that they cannot tear themselves away from their computer screens.

① (A) − (B) − (C)
② (A) − (C) − (B)
③ (B) − (A) − (C)
④ (B) − (C) − (A)

28 주어진 글 다음에 이어질 글의 순서로 가장 적절한 것은? 2019. 지방직 9급

There is a thought that can haunt us: since everything probably affects everything else, how can we ever make sense of the social world? If we are weighed down by that worry, though, we won't ever make progress.

(A) Every discipline that I am familiar with draws caricatures of the world in order to make sense of it. The modern economist does this by building models, which are deliberately stripped down representations of the phenomena out there.
(B) The economist John Maynard Keynes described our subject thus: "Economics is a science of thinking in terms of models joined to the art of choosing models which are relevant to the contemporary world."
(C) When I say "stripped down," I really mean stripped down. It isn't uncommon among us economists to focus on one or two causal factors, exclude everything else, hoping that this will enable us to understand how just those aspects of reality work and interact.

① (A) − (B) − (C)
② (A) − (C) − (B)
③ (B) − (C) − (A)
④ (B) − (A) − (C)

29 주어진 문장 다음에 이어질 글의 순서로 가장 적절한 것은? 2018. 국가직 9급

A technique that enables an individual to gain some voluntary control over autonomic, or involuntary, body functions by observing electronic measurements of those functions is known as biofeedback.

(A) When such a variable moves in the desired direction (for example, blood pressure down), it triggers visual or audible displays feedback on equipment such as television sets, gauges, or lights.
(B) Electronic sensors are attached to various parts of the body to measure such variables as heart rate, blood pressure, and skin temperature.
(C) Biofeedback training teaches one to produce a desired response by reproducing thought patterns or actions that triggered the displays.

① (A) − (B) − (C)
② (B) − (C) − (A)
③ (B) − (A) − (C)
④ (C) − (A) − (B)

30 주어진 문장 다음에 이어질 글의 순서로 가장 적절한 것은? 2018. 지방직 9급

Devices that monitor and track your health are becoming more popular among all age populations.

(A) For example, falls are a leading cause of death for adults 65 and older. Fall alerts are a popular gerotechnology that has been around for many years but have now improved.
(B) However, for seniors aging in place, especially those without a caretaker in the home, these technologies can be lifesaving.
(C) This simple technology can automatically alert 911 of a close family member the moment a senior has fallen.

① (B) − (C) − (A)
② (B) − (A) − (C)
③ (C) − (A) − (B)
④ (C) − (B) − (A)

31 주어진 글 다음에 이어질 글의 순서로 가장 적절한 것은? 2017. 국가직 9급

The most innovative of the group therapy approaches was psychodrama, the brainchild of Jacob L. Moreno. Psychodrama as a form of group therapy started with premises that were quite alien to the Freudian worldview that mental illness essentially occurs within the psyche or mind.

(A) But he also believed that creativity is rarely a solitary process but something brought out by social interactions. He relied heavily on theatrical techniques, including role-playing and improvisation, as a means to promote creativity and general social trust.

(B) Despite his theoretical difference from the mainstream viewpoint, Moreno's influence in shaping psychological consciousness in the twentieth century was considerable. He believed that the nature of human beings is to be creative and that living a creative life is the key to human health and well-being.

(C) His most important theatrical tool was what he called role reversal—asking participants to take on another's persona. The act of pretending "as if" one were in another's skin was designed to help bring out the empathic impulse and to develop it to higher levels of expression.

① (A) − (C) − (B)
② (B) − (A) − (C)
③ (B) − (C) − (A)
④ (C) − (B) − (A)

32 주어진 글 다음에 이어질 글의 순서로 가장 적절한 것은? 2017. 국가직 9급 하반기

Through the ages, industrious individuals have continuously created conveniences to make life easier. From the invention of the wheel to the lightbulb, inventions have propelled society forward.

(A) In addition, interactive media can be used to question a lecturer or exchange opinions with other students via e-mail. Such computerized lectures give students access to knowledge that was previously unavailable.

(B) One recent modern invention is the computer, which has improved many aspects of people's lives. This is especially true in the field of education. One important effect of computer technology on higher education is the availability of lectures.

(C) As a result of the development of computer networks, students can obtain lectures from many universities in real time. They are now able to sit down in front of a digital screen and listen to a lecture being given at another university.

① (A) − (B) − (C)
② (B) − (C) − (A)
③ (C) − (A) − (B)
④ (C) − (B) − (A)

33 주어진 글 다음에 이어질 글의 순서로 가장 적절한 것은? 2017. 지방직 9급

I remember the day Lewis discovered the falls. They left their camp at sunrise and a few hours later they came upon a beautiful plain and on the plain were more buffalo than they had ever seen before in one place.

(A) A nice thing happened that afternoon, they went fishing below the falls and caught half a dozen trout, good ones, too, from sixteen to twenty-three inches long.
(B) After a while the sound was tremendous and they were at the great falls of the Missouri River. It was about noon when they got there.
(C) They kept on going until they heard the faraway sound of a waterfall and saw a distant column of spray rising and disappearing. They followed the sound as it got louder and louder.

① (A) – (B) – (C)
② (B) – (C) – (A)
③ (C) – (A) – (B)
④ (C) – (B) – (A)

34 주어진 글 다음에 이어질 글의 순서로 가장 적절한 것은? 2016. 국가직 9급

All animals have the same kind of brain activation during sleep as humans. Whether or not they dream is another question, which can be answered only by posing another one: Do animals have consciousness?

(A) These are three of the key aspects of consciousness, and they could be experienced whether or not an animal had verbal language as we do. When the animal's brain is activated during sleep, why not assume that the animal has some sort of perceptual, emotional, and memory experience?
(B) Many scientists today feel that animals probably do have a limited form of consciousness, quite different from ours in that it lacks language and the capacity for propositional or symbolic thought.
(C) Animals certainly can't report dreams even if they do have them. But which pet owner would doubt that his or her favourite animal friend has perception, memory, and emotion

① (A) – (B) – (C)
② (A) – (C) – (B)
③ (B) – (C) – (A)
④ (C) – (B) – (A)

05 순서 배열 유형 기출 독해 어휘 복습 TEST

1	surface		21	rational	
2	beside		22	practical	
3	stir		23	indulge	
4	witness		24	exert	
5	tear off		25	evolve	
6	hearty		26	inheritance	
7	promote		27	offspring	
8	expand		28	mistaken	
9	authentic		29	surroundings	
10	renew		30	proprietary	
11	dimension		31	breakdown	
12	administration		32	adopt	
13	exemplify		33	harbor	
14	territory		34	reconcile	
15	prediction		35	institution	
16	summon		36	diplomat	
17	depression		37	property	
18	scrutiny		38	immediate	
19	mitigate		39	weird	
20	mammal		40	definitive	

05 순서 배열 유형 기출 독해 어휘 복습 TEST

41	fall short		61	executive	
42	rudimentary		62	assembly	
43	intensive		63	outcome	
44	utility		64	surrender	
45	medium		65	participate	
46	abundance		66	cease	
47	humble		67	evaporate	
48	sturdy		68	flexible	
49	deplete		69	demanding	
50	accommodate		70	prone to	
51	prestigious		71	exhaustion	
52	tribal		72	days on end	
53	sparsely		73	obsessed	
54	cardiovascular		74	make sense of	
55	confusion		75	representation	
56	refer to		76	attach	
57	province		77	variable	
58	exterior		78	solitary	
59	represent		79	pretend	
60	promotional		80	tremendous	

MEMO

진가영 영어
반한다 기출
독해

진가영 영어연구소 | cafe.naver.com/easyenglish7

Chapter

06

빈칸 추론 유형

chapter 06

빈칸 추론 유형

출제경향 분석

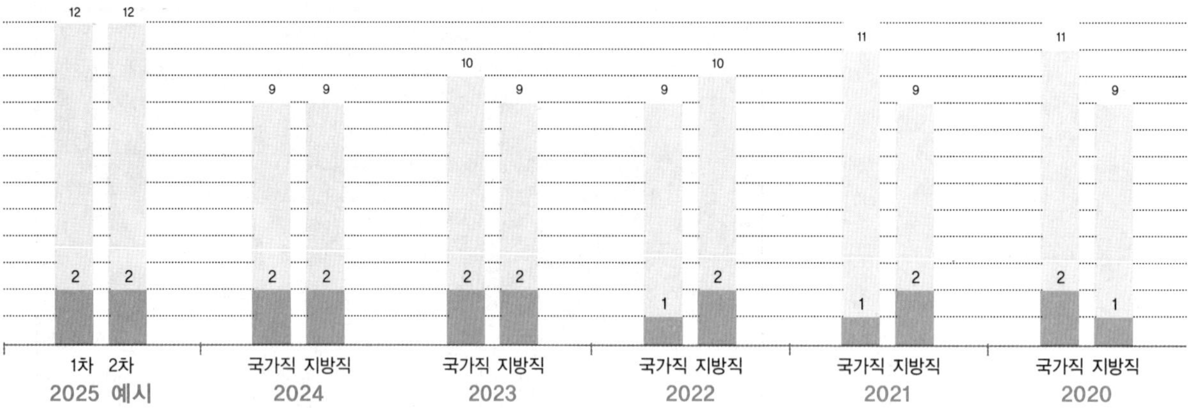

문제풀이 전략

Q 밑줄 친 부분에 들어갈 말로 가장 적절한 것은? 2025. 출제 기조 전환 2차

Technological progress can destroy jobs in a single industry such as textiles. However, historical evidence shows that technological progress does not produce unemployment in a country as a whole. Technological progress increases productivity and incomes in the overall economy, and higher incomes lead to higher demand for goods and thus ___________________. As a result, workers who lose jobs in one industry will be able to find jobs in others, although for many of them this might take time and some of them, like the Luddites, will end up with lower wages in their new jobs.

① increased job losses
② delayed promotion at work
③ greater work satisfaction
④ higher demand for labor

Step 1 지문을 빠르게 읽으며 주제문 확인하기

주제문	However, historical evidence shows that technological progress does not produce unemployment in a country as a whole. 그러나, 역사적 증거는 기술 발전이 국가 전체에서 실업을 초래하지 않는다는 것을 보여준다.

Step 2 빈칸에서 요구하는 정보 확인하고 빈칸 전과 후의 내용 확인하기

✔ 빈칸 위치에 따른 단서 문장 확인하기

빈칸 전	However, historical evidence shows that technological progress does not produce unemployment in a country as a whole. 그러나, 역사적 증거는 기술 발전이 국가 전체에서 실업을 초래하지 않는다는 것을 보여준다.
빈칸 문장	Technological progress increases productivity and incomes in the overall economy, and higher incomes lead to higher demand for goods and thus <u>higher demand for labor</u>. 기술 발전은 전체 경제의 생산성과 소득을 증가시키며, 높은 소득은 상품에 대한 수요를 증가시키고, 따라서 <u>노동력에 대한 더 높은 수요</u>도 증가한다.
빈칸 후	As a result, workers who lose jobs in one industry will be able to find jobs in others, although for many of them this might take time and some of them, like the Luddites, will end up with lower wages in their new jobs. 결과적으로 한 산업에서 일자리를 잃은 근로자들은 다른 산업에서 일자리를 찾을 수 있을 거지만, 그들 중 많은 사람들은 이것이 시간이 걸릴 수 있고, 러다이트(the Luddites)와 같은 그들 중 일부는 그들의 새로운 일자리에서 결국 더 낮은 임금을 받게 될 것이다.

Step 3 단서 확인 후 소거법으로 선택지에서 정답 선택하기

선택지 분석	① increased job losses 증가하는 실직 ② delayed promotion at work 직장에서의 승진 지연 ③ greater work satisfaction 직장의 만족도 향상 ④✔ higher demand for labor 노동력에 대한 높은 수요

Chapter 06

핵심 기출 어휘

- overall 전체의, 종합[전반]적인
- price 가격, 값, 물가, 가격을 정하다
- population 인구, 주민
- predict 예측하다, 예견하다
- mitigate 완화하다, 진정시키다
- inattention 부주의, 태만, 무관심
- conclusion 결론, 판단, 결말
- persuasion 설득, 강요
- verbal 말로 된, 언어의
- equivalent 동등한, 상당한
- devote 헌신하다, 전념하다
- paradoxical 역설적인, 자기모순의
- standardization 표준화, 규격화, 통일, 획일
- coordinate 조정[조화]하다, 동등하게 하다
- uniform 획일적인, 균일한
- disparate 서로 전혀 다른, 이질적인
- integrate 통합하다
- unified 통합된, 통일된
- resort to 의지하다, 의존하다
- distraction 주의 산만, 방해
- persist 지속되다, 집요하게 계속하다
- urgent 긴급한, 시급한
- plain 평범한, 보통의, 평원, 평지
- authority 권위, 권한
- bombard 쏟아 붓다, 퍼붓다
- prerequisite 전제 조건
- discriminate 구분하다, 식별하다, 차별하다
- scattered 산발적인, 흩어져 있는, 드문드문 있는
- empower 권한을 부여하다
- autonomy 자율성, 자주성
- tangible 유형의, 만질[감지할] 수 있는
- monetary 금전의, 통화의
- subconscious 잠재의식적인, 무의식적인
- odds 가능성, 역경, 곤란
- property 재산, 자산, 토지, 특성, 속성
- famine 기근
- dialect 방언, 사투리
- discipline 훈육, 훈련, 학과
- intuition 직관, 직감
- holistic 전체적인, 종합적인
- conscientious 양심적인, 성실한
- setback 차질, 방해
- hygiene 위생
- plummet 급락하다, 곤두박질치다
- vacant 비어 있는, 점령되지 않은
- institute 기관, 단체, 협회
- feature 특징, 특성
- matter 문제, 상황, 중요하다, 문제되다
- impede 방해하다, 지연시키다
- alert 기민한, 경계하는, (위험 등을) 알리다
- disseminate 퍼뜨리다, 전파하다
- altruism 이타주의, 이타심
- nasty 끔찍한, 형편없는, 못된
- blind spot 맹점, 약점
- streamline 간소화하다, 능률화하다
- undertake 착수하다, 떠맡다, ~할 의무를 지다

나의 약점 확인

영역	점수
CHAPTER 06 빈칸 추론 유형	/ 48문항

반드시 한 번에 다 잡는 '빈칸 추론 유형' 독해 전략

- 빈칸 추론 유형은 글의 **중심 내용**과 글의 **논리적 흐름**을 고려하여 문맥상 빈칸에 들어갈 가장 적절한 표현을 추론하는 능력을 측정하는 문항이다.
- 빈칸 추론 유형은 9급 출제 기조 전환 예시 문제를 기준으로 볼 때 **난도가 중간 또는 높은 유형**에 속하며 **두 문제** 출제될 것으로 예상된다.
- 빈칸 추론 유형은 지문을 빠르고 정확하게 읽으면서 **지문의 중심 소재 및 주제문을 찾고,** 이를 바탕으로 **빈칸에 들어갈 적절한 내용을 추론**하는 훈련이 필요하다.
- 빈칸 추론 유형은 해당 지문에 **정답과 밀접하게 관련된 단서가 되는 부분이 존재**하는 것이 일반적이므로 글을 읽어 나가면서 빈칸의 **단서가 되는 부분을 찾아 표시**하며 빠르고 정확하게 푸는 연습이 필요하다.

꿀팁 빈칸의 위치에 따른 빈칸 단서의 위치

초반 빈칸	중반 빈칸	후반 빈칸

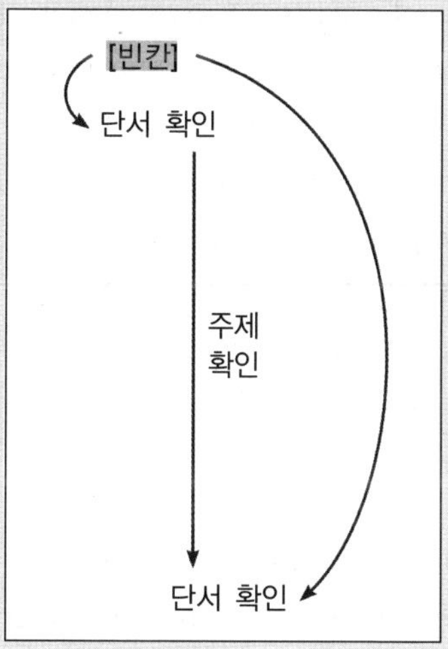

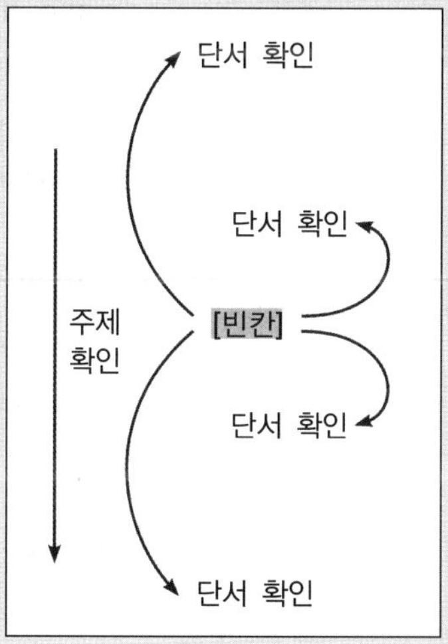

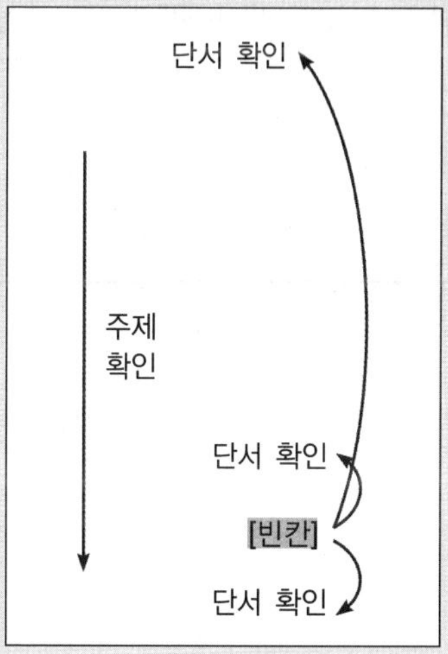

01 밑줄 친 부분에 들어갈 말로 가장 적절한 것은?

2025. 출제 기조 전환 2차

Technological progress can destroy jobs in a single industry such as textiles. However, historical evidence shows that technological progress does not produce unemployment in a country as a whole. Technological progress increases productivity and incomes in the overall economy, and higher incomes lead to higher demand for goods and thus ____________________. As a result, workers who lose jobs in one industry will be able to find jobs in others, although for many of them this might take time and some of them, like the Luddites, will end up with lower wages in their new jobs.

① increased job losses
② delayed promotion at work
③ greater work satisfaction
④ higher demand for labor

02 밑줄 친 부분에 들어갈 말로 가장 적절한 것은?

2025. 출제 기조 전환 2차

There is no substitute for oil, which is one reason ____________________, taking the global economy along with it. While we can generate electricity through coal or natural gas, nuclear or renewables — switching from source to source, according to price — oil remains by far the predominant fuel for transportation. When the global economy heats up, demand for oil rises, boosting the price and encouraging producers to pump more. Inevitably, those high prices eat into economic growth and reduce demand just as suppliers are overproducing. Prices crash, and the cycle starts all over again. That's bad for producers, who can be left holding the bag when prices plummet, and it hurts consumers and industries uncertain about future energy prices. Low oil prices in the 1990s lulled U.S. auto companies into disastrous complacency; they had few efficient models available when oil turned expensive.

① the automobile industry thrives
② it creates disruptions between borders
③ it is prone to big booms and deep busts
④ the research on renewable energy is limited

03 밑줄 친 부분에 들어갈 말로 가장 적절한 것은?

2025. 출제 기조 전환 1차

Falling fertility rates are projected to result in shrinking populations for nearly every country by the end of the century. The global fertility rate was 4.7 in 1950, but it dropped by nearly half to 2.4 in 2017. It is expected to fall below 1.7 by 2100. As a result, some researchers predict that the number of people on the planet would peak at 9.7 billion around 2064 before falling down to 8.8 billion by the century's end. This transition will also lead to a significant aging of populations, with as many people reaching 80 years old as there are being born. Such a demographic shift ___________________, including taxation, healthcare for the elderly, caregiving responsibilities, and retirement. To ensure a "soft landing" into a new demographic landscape, researchers emphasize the need for careful management of the transition.

① raises concerns about future challenges
② mitigates the inverted age structure phenomenon
③ compensates for the reduced marriage rate issue
④ provides immediate solutions to resolve the problems

04 밑줄 친 부분에 들어갈 말로 가장 적절한 것은?

2025. 출제 기조 전환 1차

Many listeners blame a speaker for their inattention by thinking to themselves: "Who could listen to such a character? Will he ever stop reading from his notes?" The good listener reacts differently. He may well look at the speaker and think, "This man is incompetent. Seems like almost anyone would be able to talk better than that." But from this initial similarity he moves on to a different conclusion, thinking "But wait a minute. I'm not interested in his personality or delivery. I want to find out what he knows. Does this man know some things that I need to know?" Essentially, we "listen with our own experience." Is the speaker to be held responsible because we are poorly equipped to comprehend his message? We cannot understand everything we hear, but one sure way to raise the level of our understanding is to ___________________.

① ignore what the speaker knows
② analyze the character of a speaker
③ assume the responsibility which is inherently ours
④ focus on the speaker's competency of speech delivery

05 밑줄 친 부분에 들어갈 말로 적절한 것은?

2024. 국가직 9급

____. Nearly every major politician hires media consultants and political experts to provide advice on how to appeal to the public. Virtually every major business and special-interest group has hired a lobbyist to take its concerns to Congress or to state and local governments. In nearly every community, activists try to persuade their fellow citizens on important policy issues. The workplace, too, has always been fertile ground for office politics and persuasion. One study estimates that general managers spend upwards of 80 % of their time in verbal communication — most of it with the intent of persuading their fellow employees. With the advent of the photocopying machine, a whole new medium for office persuasion was invented — the photocopied memo. The Pentagon alone copies an average of 350,000 pages a day, the equivalent of 1,000 novels.

① Business people should have good persuasion skills
② Persuasion shows up in almost every walk of life
③ You will encounter countless billboards and posters
④ Mass media campaigns are useful for the government

06 밑줄 친 부분에 들어갈 말로 적절한 것은?

2024. 국가직 9급

It is important to note that for adults, social interaction mainly occurs through the medium of language. Few native-speaker adults are willing to devote time to interacting with someone who does not speak the language, with the result that the adult foreigner will have little opportunity to engage in meaningful and extended language exchanges. In contrast, the young child is often readily accepted by other children, and even adults. For young children, language is not as essential to social interaction. So-called ‘parallel play’, for example, is common among young children. They can be content just to sit in each other's company speaking only occasionally and playing on their own. Adults rarely find themselves in situations where ____.

① language does not play a crucial role in social interaction
② their opinions are readily accepted by their colleagues
③ they are asked to speak another language
④ communication skills are highly required

07 밑줄 친 부분에 들어갈 말로 적절한 것은?

2024. 지방직 9급

Javelin Research noticed that not all Millennials are currently in the same stage of life. While all Millennials were born around the turn of the century, some of them are still in early adulthood, wrestling with new careers and settling down. On the other hand, the older Millennials have a home and are building a family. You can imagine how having a child might change your interests and priorities, so for marketing purposes, it's useful to split this generation into Gen Y.1 and Gen Y.2. Not only are the two groups culturally different, but they're in vastly different phases of their financial life. The younger group is financial beginners, just starting to show their buying power. The latter group has a credit history, may have their first mortgage and is raising young children. The __________ in priorities and needs between Gen Y.1 and Gen Y.2 is vast.

① contrast
② reduction
③ repetition
④ ability

08 밑줄 친 부분에 들어갈 말로 적절한 것은?

2024. 지방직 9급

Cost pressures in liberalized markets have different effects on existing and future hydropower schemes. Because of the cost structure, existing hydropower plants will always be able to earn a profit. Because the planning and construction of future hydropower schemes is not a short-term process, it is not a popular investment, in spite of low electricity generation costs. Most private investors would prefer to finance ______________________________, leading to the paradoxical situation that although an existing hydropower plant seems to be a cash cow, nobody wants to invest in a new one. Where public shareholders/owners (states, cities, municipalities) are involved, the situation looks very different because they can see the importance of the security of supply and also appreciate long-term investments.

① more short-term technologies
② all high technology industries
③ the promotion of the public interest
④ the enhancement of electricity supply

09 밑줄 친 부분에 들어갈 말로 알맞은 것은?

2023. 국가직 9급

In recent years, the increased popularity of online marketing and social media sharing has boosted the need for advertising standardization for global brands. Most big marketing and advertising campaigns include a large online presence. Connected consumers can now zip easily across borders via the internet and social media, making it difficult for advertisers to roll out adapted campaigns in a controlled,orderly fashion. As a result, most global consumer brands coordinate their digital sites internationally. For example, Coca-Cola web and social media sites around the world, from Australia and Argentina to France, Romania, and Russia, are surprisingly ____________. All feature splashes of familiar Coke red, iconic Coke bottle shapes, and Coca-Cola's music and "Taste the Feeling" themes.

① experimental
② uniform
③ localized
④ diverse

10 밑줄 친 부분에 들어갈 말로 알맞은 것은?

2023. 국가직 9급

Over the last fifty years, all major subdisciplines in psychology have become more and more isolated from each other as training becomes increasingly specialized and narrow in focus. As some psychologists have long argued, if the field of psychology is to mature and advance scientifically, its disparate parts (for example, neuroscience, developmental, cognitive, personality, and social) must become whole and integrated again. Science advances when distinct topics become theoretically and empirically integrated under simplifying theoretical frameworks. Psychology of science will encourage collaboration among psychologists from various sub-areas, helping the field achieve coherence rather than continued fragmentation. In this way, psychology of science might act as a template for psychology as a whole by integrating under one discipline all of the major fractions/factions within the field. It would be no small feat and of no small import if the psychology of science could become a model for the parent discipline on how to combine resources and study science ______________________________.

① from a unified perspective
② in dynamic aspects
③ throughout history
④ with accurate evidence

11 밑줄 친 부분에 들어갈 말로 가장 적절한 것은?

2023. 지방직 9급

We live in the age of anxiety. Because being anxious can be an uncomfortable and scary experience, we resort to conscious or unconscious strategies that help reduce anxiety in the moment — watching a movie or TV show, eating, video-game playing, and overworking. In addition, smartphones also provide a distraction any time of the day or night. Psychological research has shown that distractions serve as a common anxiety avoidance strategy. ____________, however, these avoidance strategies make anxiety worse in the long run. Being anxious is like getting into quicksand — the more you fight it, the deeper you sink. Indeed, research strongly supports a well-known phase that "what you resist, persists."

① Paradoxically
② Fortunately
③ Neutrally
④ Creatively

12 밑줄 친 부분에 들어갈 말로 가장 적절한 것은?

2023. 지방직 9급

How many different ways do you get information? Some people might have six different kinds of communications to answer — test messages, voice mails, paper documents, regular mail, blog posts, messages on different online services. Each of these is type of in-box, and each must be processed on a continuous basis. It's an endless process, but it doesn't have to be exhausting or stressful. Getting your information management down to a more manageable level and into a productive zone starts by ______________________________. Every place you have to go to check your messages or to read your incoming information is an in-box, and the more you have, the harder it is to manage everything. Cut the number of in-boxes you have down to the smallest number possible for you still to function in the ways you need to.

① setting several goals at once
② immersing yourself in incoming information
③ minimizing the number of in-boxes you have
④ choosing information you are passionate about

13 다음 빈칸에 들어갈 말로 가장 적절한 것은?

2023. 법원직 9급

As global temperatures rise, so do sea levels, threatening coastal communities around the world. Surprisingly, even small organisms like oysters ______________________________. Oysters are keystone species with *ripple effects on the health of their ecosystems and its inhabitants. Just one adult oyster can filter up to fifty gallons of water in a single day, making waterways cleaner. Healthy oyster reefs also provide a home for hundreds of other marine organisms, promoting biodiversity and ecosystem balance. As rising sea levels lead to pervasive flooding, oyster reefs act as walls to buffer storms and protect against further coastal erosion.

* ripple effect 파급효과

① can come to our defense
② can be the food for emergency
③ may be contaminated by microplastics
④ can increase the income of local residents

14 다음 빈칸에 들어갈 말로 가장 적절한 것은?

2023. 법원직 9급

Lewis Pugh is a British endurance swimmer, who is best known for his long-distance swims in cold and open waters. He swims in cold places as a way to draw attention to the urgent need to protect the world's oceans and waterways from the effects of climate change and pollution. In 2019, Pugh decided to swim in Lake Imja, which is located in the Khumbu region of Nepal, near Mount Everest. After a failed first attempt, Lewis had a *debrief to discuss the best way to swim at 5,300 meters above sea level. He is usually very aggressive when he swims because he wants to finish quickly and get out of the cold water. But this time he showed ______________ and swam slowly.

* debrief 평가회의

① grief
② anger
③ humility
④ confidence

15 밑줄 친 부분에 들어갈 말로 가장 적절한 것은?

2022. 국가직 9급

Scientists have long known that higher air temperatures are contributing to the surface melting on Greenland's ice sheet. But a new study has found another threat that has begun attacking the ice from below: Warm ocean water moving underneath the vast glaciers is causing them to melt even more quickly. The findings were published in the journal Nature Geoscience by researchers who studied one of the many "ice tongues" of the Nioghalvfjerdsfjorden Glacier in northeast Greenland. An ice tongue is a strip of ice that floats on the water without breaking off from the ice on land. The massive one these scientists studied is nearly 50 miles long. The survey revealed an underwater current more than a mile wide where warm water from the Atlantic Ocean is able to flow directly towards the glacier, bringing large amounts of heat into contact with the ice and ____________ the glacier's melting.

① separating
② delaying
③ preventing
④ accelerating

16 밑줄 친 부분에 들어갈 말로 가장 적절한 것은?

2022. 지방직 9급

One of the most frequently used propaganda techniques is to convince the public that the propagandist's views reflect those of the common person and that he or she is working in their best interests. A politician speaking to a blue-collar audience may roll up his sleeves, undo his tie, and attempt to use the specific idioms of the crowd. He may even use language incorrectly on purpose to give the impression that he is "just one of the folks." This technique usually also employs the use of glittering generalities to give the impression that the politician's views are the same as those of the crowd being addressed. Labor leaders, businesspeople, ministers, educators, and advertisers have used this technique to win our confidence by appearing to be ________________________.

① beyond glittering generalities
② just plain folks like ourselves
③ something different from others
④ better educated than the crowd

17 밑줄 친 부분에 들어갈 말로 가장 적절한 것은?

2022. 지방직 9급

As a roller coaster climbs the first lift hill of its track, it is building potential energy — the higher it gets above the earth, the stronger the pull of gravity will be. When the coaster crests the lift hill and begins its descent, its potential energy becomes kinetic energy, or the energy of movement. A common misperception is that a coaster loses energy along the track. An important law of physics, however, called the law of conservation of energy, is that energy can never be created nor destroyed. It simply changes from one form to another. Whenever a track rises back uphill, the cars' momentum — their kinetic energy — will carry them upward, which builds potential energy, and roller coasters repeatedly convert potential energy to kinetic energy and back again. At the end of a ride, coaster cars are slowed down by brake mechanisms that create ____________ between two surfaces. This motion makes them hot, meaning kinetic energy is changed to heat energy during braking. Riders may mistakenly think coasters lose energy at the end of the track, but the energy just changes to and from different forms.

① gravity
② friction
③ vacuum
④ acceleration

18 다음 빈칸에 들어갈 말로 가장 적절한 것은?

2022. 법원직 9급

There are a few jobs where people have had to ________________________________. We see referees and umpires using their arms and hands to signal directions to the players — as in cricket, where a single finger upwards means that the batsman is out and has to leave the wicket. Orchestra conductors control the musicians through their movements. People working at a distance from each other have to invent special signals if they want to communicate. So do people working in a noisy environment, such as in a factory where the machines are very loud, or lifeguards around a swimming pool full of school children.

* wicket (크리켓에서) 삼주문

① support their parents and children
② adapt to an entirely new work style
③ fight in court for basic human rights
④ develop their signing a bit more fully

19 다음 빈칸에 들어갈 말로 가장 적절한 것은?

2022. 법원직 9급

Water and civilization go hand-in-hand. The idea of a "*hydraulic civilization" argues that water is the unifying context and justification for many large-scale civilizations throughout history. For example, the various multi-century Chinese empires survived as long as they did in part by controlling floods along the Yellow River. One interpretation of the hydraulic theory is that the justification for gathering populations into large cities is to manage water. Another interpretation suggests that large water projects enable the rise of big cities. The Romans understood the connections between water and power, as the Roman Empire built a vast network of **aqueducts throughout land they controlled, many of which remain intact. For example, Pont du Gard in southern France stands today as a testament to humanity's investment in its water infrastructure. Roman governors built roads, bridges, and water systems as a way of ______________________.

* hydraulic : 수력학의

** aqueduct : 송수로

① focusing on educating young people
② prohibiting free trade in local markets
③ concentrating and strengthening their authority
④ giving up their properties to other countries

20 밑줄 친 부분에 들어갈 말로 가장 적절한 것은?

2021. 국가직 9급

Social media, magazines and shop windows bombard people daily with things to buy, and British consumers are buying more clothes and shoes than ever before. Online shopping means it is easy for customers to buy without thinking, while major brands offer such cheap clothes that they can be treated like disposable items — worn two or three times and then thrown away. In Britain, the average person spends more than £ 1,000 on new clothes a year, which is around four percent of their income. That might not sound like much, but that figure hides two far more worrying trends for society and for the environment. First, a lot of that consumer spending is via credit cards. British people currently owe approximately £ 670 per adult to credit card companies. That's 66 percent of the average wardrobe budget. Also, not only are people spending money they don't have, they're using it to buy things ______________. Britain throws away 300,000 tons of clothing a year, most of which goes into landfill sites.

① they don't need
② that are daily necessities
③ that will be soon recycled
④ they can hand down to others

21 밑줄 친 부분에 들어갈 말로 가장 적절한 것은?

2021. 국가직 9급

Excellence is the absolute prerequisite in fine dining because the prices charged are necessarily high. An operator may do everything possible to make the restaurant efficient, but the guests still expect careful, personal service: food prepared to order by highly skilled chefs and delivered by expert servers. Because this service is, quite literally, manual labor, only marginal improvements in productivity are possible. For example, a cook, server, or bartender can move only so much faster before she or he reaches the limits of human performance. Thus, only moderate savings are possible through improved efficiency, which makes an escalation of prices ____________. (It is an axiom of economics that as prices rise, consumers become more discriminating.) Thus, the clientele of the fine-dining restaurant expects, demands, and is willing to pay for excellence.

① ludicrous
② inevitable
③ preposterous
④ inconceivable

22 밑줄 친 부분에 들어갈 말로 가장 적절한 것은?

2021. 지방직 9급

As more and more leaders work remotely or with teams scattered around the nation or the globe, as well as with consultants and freelancers, you'll have to give them more ____________. The more trust you bestow, the more others trust you. I am convinced that there is a direct correlation between job satisfaction and how empowered people are to fully execute their job without someone shadowing them every step of the way. Giving away responsibility to those you trust can not only make your organization run more smoothly but also free up more of your time so you can focus on larger issues.

① work
② rewards
③ restrictions
④ autonomy

23 다음 빈칸에 들어갈 말로 가장 적절한 것은?

2021. 법원직 9급

Beeches, oaks, spruce and pines produce new growth all the time, and have to get rid of the old. The most obvious change happens every autumn. The leaves have served their purpose: they are now worn out and riddled with insect damage. Before the trees bid them adieu, they pump waste products into them. You could say they are taking this opportunity to relieve themselves. Then they grow a layer of weak tissue to separate each leaf from the twig it's growing on, and the leaves tumble to the ground in the next breeze. The rustling leaves that now blanket the ground — and make such a satisfying scrunching sound when you scuffle through them — are basically ____________.

① tree toilet paper
② the plant kitchen
③ lungs of the tree
④ parents of insect

24 다음 빈칸에 들어갈 말로 가장 적절한 것은?

2021. 법원직 9급

The seeds of willows and poplars are so minuscule that you can just make out two tiny dark dots in the fluffy flight hairs. One of these seeds weighs a mere 0.0001 grams. With such a meagre energy reserve, a seedling can grow only 1–2 millimetres before it runs out of steam and has to rely on food it makes for itself using its young leaves. But that only works in places where there's no competition to threaten the tiny sprouts. Other plants casting shade on it would extinguish the new life immediately. And so, if a fluffy little seed package like this falls in a spruce or beech forest, the seed's life is over before it's even begun. That's why willows and poplars ____________________.

* minuscule 아주 작은

① prefer settling in unoccupied territory
② have been chosen as food for herbivores
③ have evolved to avoid human intervention
④ wear their dead leaves far into the winter

Chapter 06

25 밑줄 친 (A), (B)에 들어갈 말로 가장 적절한 것은?

2020. 국가직 9급

When an organism is alive, it takes in carbon dioxide from the air around it. Most of that carbon dioxide is made of carbon-12, but a tiny portion consists of carbon-14. So the living organism always contains a very small amount of radioactive carbon, carbon-14. A detector next to the living organism would record radiation given off by the carbon-14 in the organism. When the organism dies, it no longer takes in carbon dioxide. No new carbon-14 is added, and the old carbon-14 slowly decays into nitrogen. The amount of carbon-14 slowly ___(A)___ as time goes on. Over time, less and less radiation from carbon-14 is produced. The amount of carbon-14 radiation detected for an organism is a measure, therefore, of how long the organism has been ___(B)___. This method of determining the age of an organism is called carbon-14 dating. The decay of carbon-14 allows archaeologists to find the age of once-living materials. Measuring the amount of radiation remaining indicates the approximate age.

	(A)		(B)
①	decreases	……	dead
②	increases	……	alive
③	decreases	……	productive
④	increases	……	inactive

26 밑줄 친 부분에 들어갈 말로 가장 적절한 것은?

2020. 국가직 9급

All creatures, past and present, either have gone or will go extinct. Yet, as each species vanished over the past 3.8-billion-year history of life on Earth, new ones inevitably appeared to replace them or to exploit newly emerging resources. From only a few very simple organisms, a great number of complex, multicellular forms evolved over this immense period. The origin of new species, which the nineteenth-century English naturalist Charles Darwin once referred to as "the mystery of mysteries," is the natural process of speciation responsible for generating this remarkable ________________ with whom humans share the planet. Although taxonomists presently recognize some 1.5 million living species, the actual number is possibly closer to 10 million. Recognizing the biological status of this multitude requires a clear understanding of what constitutes a species, which is no easy task given that evolutionary biologists have yet to agree on a universally acceptable definition.

① technique of biologists
② diversity of living creatures
③ inventory of extinct organisms
④ collection of endangered species

27 밑줄 친 부분에 들어갈 말로 가장 적절한 것은?

2020. 지방직 9급

All of us inherit something: in some cases, it may be money, property or some object — a family heirloom such as a grandmother's wedding dress or a father's set of tools. But beyond that, all of us inherit something else, something ________________________, something we may not even be fully aware of. It may be a way of doing a daily task, or the way we solve a particular problem or decide a moral issue for ourselves. It may be a special way of keeping a holiday or a tradition to have a picnic on a certain date. It may be something important or central to our thinking, or something minor that we have long accepted quite casually.

① quite unrelated to our everyday life
② against our moral standards
③ much less concrete and tangible
④ of great monetary value

28 다음 빈칸에 들어갈 말로 가장 적절한 것은?

2020. 법원직 9급

Impressionable youth are not the only ones subject to ____________. Most of us have probably had an experience of being pressured by a salesman. Have you ever had a sales rep try to sell you some "office solution" by telling you that 70 percent of your competitors are using their service, so why aren't you? But what if 70 percent of your competitors are idiots? Or what if that 70 percent were given so much value added or offered such a low price that they couldn't resist the opportunity? The practice is designed to do one thing and one thing only—to pressure you to buy. To make you feel you might be missing out on something or that everyone else knows but you.

① peer pressure
② impulse buying
③ bullying tactics
④ keen competition

29 다음 빈칸에 들어갈 말로 가장 적절한 것은?

2020. 법원직 9급

Much is now known about natural hazards and the negative impacts they have on people and their property. It would seem obvious that any logical person would avoid such potential impacts or at least modify their behavior or their property to minimize such impacts. However, humans are not always rational. Until someone has a personal experience or knows someone who has such an experience, most people subconsciously believe "It won't happen here" or "It won't happen to me." Even knowledgeable scientists who are aware of the hazards, the odds of their occurrence, and the costs of an event ____________________.

① refuse to remain silent
② do not always act appropriately
③ put the genetic factor at the top end
④ have difficulty in defining natural hazards

30 밑줄 친 부분에 들어갈 말로 가장 적절한 것은?

2019. 국가직 9급

Why bother with the history of everything? ____________________. In literature classes you don't learn about genes; in physics classes you don't learn about human evolution. So you get a partial view of the world. That makes it hard to find meaning in education. The French sociologist Emile Durkheim called this sense of disorientation and meaninglessness anomie, and he argued that it could lead to despair and even suicide. The German sociologist Max Weber talked of the "disenchantment" of the world. In the past, people had a unified vision of their world, a vision usually provided by the origin stories of their own religious traditions. That unified vision gave a sense of purpose, of meaning, even of enchantment to the world and to life. Today, though, many writers have argued that a sense of meaninglessness is inevitable in a world of science and rationality. Modernity, it seems, means meaninglessness.

① In the past, the study of history required disenchantment from science
② Recently, science has given us lots of clever tricks and meanings
③ Today, we teach and learn about our world in fragments
④ Lately, history has been divided into several categories

31 밑줄 친 (A), (B)에 들어갈 말로 가장 적절한 것은?

2019. 지방직 9급

In the 1840s, the island of Ireland suffered famine. Because Ireland could not produce enough food to feed its population, about a million people died of ___(A)___; they simply didn't have enough to eat to stay alive. The famine caused another 1.25 million people to ___(B)___; many left their island home for the United States; the rest went to Canada, Australia, Chile, and other countries. Before the famine, the population of Ireland was approximately 6 million. After the great food shortage, it was about 4 million.

	(A)		(B)
①	dehydration	······	be deported
②	trauma	······	immigrate
③	starvation	······	emigrate
④	fatigue	······	be detained

32 밑줄 친 부분에 들어갈 말로 가장 적절한 것은?

2019. 지방직 9급

Language proper is itself double-layered. Single noises are only occasionally meaningful: mostly, the various speech sounds convey coherent messages only when combined into an overlapping chain, like different colors of ice-cream melting into one another. In birdsong also, ______________________: the sequence is what matters. In both humans and birds, control of this specialized sound-system is exercised by one half of the brain, normally the left half, and the system is learned relatively early in life. And just as many human languages have dialects, so do some bird species: in California, the white-crowned sparrow has songs so different from area to area that Californians can supposedly tell where they are in the state by listening to these sparrows.

① individual notes are often of little value
② rhythmic sounds are important
③ dialects play a critical role
④ no sound-system exists

33 밑줄 친 부분에 들어갈 말로 가장 적절한 것은?

2019. 지방직 9급

Nobel Prize-winning psychologist Daniel Kahneman changed the way the world thinks about economics, upending the notion that human beings are rational decision-makers. Along the way, his discipline-crossing influence has altered the way physicians make medical decisions and investors evaluate risk on Wall Street. In a paper, Kahneman and his colleagues outline a process for making big strategic decisions. Their suggested approach, labeled as "Mediating Assessments Protocol," or MAP, has a simple goal: To put off gut-based decision-making until a choice can be informed by a number of separate factors. "One of the essential purposes of MAP is basically to ____________ intuition," Kahneman said in a recent interview with The Post. The structured process calls for analyzing a decision based on six to seven previously chosen attributes, discussing each of them separately and assigning them a relative percentile score, and finally, using those scores to make a holistic judgment.

① improve
② delay
③ possess
④ facilitate

34 글의 흐름상 빈칸에 들어갈 말로 가장 적절한 것은?

2019. 서울시 9급

"Highly conscientious employees do a series of things better than the rest of us," says University of Illinois psychologist Brent Roberts, who studies conscientiousness. Roberts owes their success to "hygiene" factors. Conscientious people have a tendency to organize their lives well. A disorganized, unconscientious person might lose 20 or 30 minutes rooting through their files to find the right document, an inefficient experience conscientious folks tend to avoid. Basically, by being conscientious, people ________________ they'd otherwise create for themselves.

① deal with setbacks
② do thorough work
③ follow norms
④ sidestep stress

35 글의 흐름상 빈칸에 들어갈 말로 가장 적절한 것은?

2019. 서울시 9급

Climate change, deforestation, widespread pollution and the sixth mass extinction of biodiversity all define living in our world today — an era that has come to be known as "the Anthropocene". These crises are underpinned by production and consumption which greatly exceeds global ecological limits, but blame is far from evenly shared. The world's 42 wealthiest people own as much as the poorest 3.7 billion, and they generate far greater environmental impacts. Some have therefore proposed using the term "Capitalocene" to describe this era of ecological devastation and growing inequality, reflecting capitalism's logic of endless growth and ________________.

① the better world that is still within our reach
② the accumulation of wealth in fewer pockets
③ an effective response to climate change
④ a burning desire for a more viable future

36 다음 빈칸에 들어갈 말로 가장 적절한 것은?

2019. 법원직 9급

With the present plummeting demand market for office buildings, resulting in many vacant properties, we need to develop plans that will enable some future exchange between residential and commercial or office functions. This vacancy has reached a historic level; at present the major towns in the Netherlands have some five million square metres of unoccupied office space, while there is a shortage of 160,000 homes. At least a million of those square metres can be expected to stay vacant, according to the association of Dutch property developers. There is a real threat of 'ghost towns' of empty office buildings springing up around the major cities. In spite of this forecast, office building activities are continuing at full tilt, as these were planned during a period of high returns. Therefore, it is now essential that ________________.

① a new design be adopted to reduce costs for the maintenance of buildings
② a number of plans for office buildings be redeveloped for housing
③ residential buildings be converted into commercial buildings
④ we design and deliver as many shops as possible

37 다음 빈칸에 들어갈 말로 가장 적절한 것은?

2019. 법원직 9급

Although we all possess the same physical organs for sensing the world — eyes for seeing, ears for hearing, noses for smelling, skin for feeling, and mouths for tasting — our perception of the world depends to a great extent on the language we speak, according to a famous hypothesis proposed by linguists Edward Sapir and Benjamin Lee Whorf. They hypothesized that language is like a pair of eyeglasses through which we "see" the world in a particular way. A classic example of the relationship between language and perception is the word snow. Eskimo languages have as many as 32 different words for snow. For instance, the Eskimos have different words for falling snow, snow on the ground, snow packed as hard as ice, slushy snow, wind-driven snow, and what we might call "cornmeal" snow. The ancient Aztec languages of Mexico, in contrast, used only one word to mean snow, cold, and ice. Thus, if the Sapir-Whorf hypothesis is correct and we can perceive only things that we have words for, the Aztecs perceived snow, cold, and ice as ________________________.

① one and the same phenomenon
② being distinct from one another
③ separate things with unique features
④ something sensed by a specific physical organ

38 밑줄 친 부분에 들어갈 말로 가장 적절한 것은?

2018. 국가직 9급

Kisha Padbhan, founder of Everonn Education, in Mumbai, looks at his business as nation-building. India's student-age population of 230 million (kindergarten to college) is one of the largest in the world. The government spends \$83 billion on instruction, but there are serious gaps. "There aren't enough teachers and enough teacher-training institutes," says Kisha. "What children in remote parts of India lack is access to good teachers and exposure to good-quality content." Everonn's solution? The company uses a satellite network, with two-way video and audio ________________________. It reaches 1,800 colleges and 7,800 schools across 24 of India's 28 states. It offers everything from digitized school lessons to entrance exam prep for aspiring engineers and has training for job-seekers, too.

① to improve the quality of teacher training facilities
② to bridge the gap through virtual classrooms
③ to get students familiarized with digital technology
④ to locate qualified instructors across the nation

39 밑줄 친 부분에 들어갈 말로 가장 적절한 것은?

2018. 지방직 9급

> In our time it is not only the law of the market which has its own life and rules over man, but also the development of science and technique. For a number of reasons, the problems and organization of science today are such that a scientist does not choose his problems; the problems force themselves upon the scientist. He solves one problem, and the result is not that he is more secure or certain, but that ten other new problems open up in place of the single solved one. They force him to solve them; he has to go ahead at an ever-quickening pace. The same holds true for industrial techniques. The pace of science forces the pace of technique. Theoretical physics forces atomic energy on us; the successful production of the fission bomb forces upon us the manufacture of the hydrogen bomb. We do not choose our problems, we do not choose our products; we are pushed, we are forced — by what? By a system which has no purpose and goal transcending it, and which ____________________.

① makes man its appendix
② creates a false sense of security
③ inspires man with creative challenges
④ empowers scientists to control the market laws

40 밑줄 친 부분에 들어갈 말로 가장 적절한 것은?

2018. 지방직 9급

> The secret of successful people is usually that they are able to concentrate totally on one thing. Even if they have a lot in their head, they have found a method that the many commitments don't impede each other, but instead they are brought into a good inner order. And this order is quite simple: ____________________. In theory, it seems to be quite clear, but in everyday life it seems rather different. You might have tried to decide on priorities, but you have failed because of everyday trivial matters and all the unforeseen distractions. Separate off disturbances, for example, by escaping into another office, and not allowing any distractions to get in the way. When you concentrate on the one task of your priorities, you will find you have energy that you didn't even know you had.

① the sooner, the better
② better late than never
③ out of sight, out of mind
④ the most important thing first

41 다음 글의 빈칸에 들어갈 말로 가장 적절한 것은?

2018. 법원직 9급

A great ad is a wonderful thing; it's why you love advertising. But what you're looking at is only half of what's there, and the part you can't see has more to do with that ad's success than the part you can. Before those surface features (the terrific headline or visual or storyline or characters or voiceover or whatever) can work their wonders, the ad has to have something to say, something that matters. Either it addresses real consumer motives and real consumer problems, or it speaks to no one. To make great ads, then, you have to start where they start: with ______________________.

① the effective tool
② the invisible part
③ the corporate needs
④ the surface features

42 빈칸 (A), (B)에 들어갈 말로 가장 적절한 것은?

2017. 국가직 9급

The amount of information gathered by the eyes as contrasted with the ears has not been precisely calculated. Such a calculation not only involves a translation process, but scientists have been handicapped by lack of knowledge of what to count. A general notion, however, of the relative complexities of the two systems can be obtained by ___(A)___ the size of the nerves connecting the eyes and the ears to the centers of the brain. Since the optic nerve contains roughly eighteen times as many neurons as the cochlear nerve, we assume it transmits at least that much more information. Actually, in normally alert subjects, it is probable that the eyes may be as much as a thousand times as effective as the ears in ___(B)___ information.

* cochlear: 달팽이관의

	(A)		(B)
①	comparing	……	sweeping up
②	comparing	……	reducing
③	adding	……	disseminating
④	adding	……	clearing up

43 밑줄 친 부분에 들어갈 말로 가장 적절한 것은?

2017. 국가직 9급

Why might people hovering near the poverty line be more likely to help their fellow humans? Part of it, Keltner thinks, is that poor people must often band together to make it through tough times — a process that probably makes them more socially astute. He says, "When you face uncertainty, it makes you orient to other people. You build up these strong social networks." When a poor young mother has a new baby, for instance, she may need help securing food, supplies, and childcare, and if she has healthy social times, members of her community will pitch in. But limited income is hardly a prerequisite for developing this kind of empathy and social responsiveness. Regardless of the size of our bank accounts, suffering becomes a conduit to altruism or heroism when our own pain compels us to be ________________ other people's needs and to intervene when we see someone in the clutches of the kind of suffering we know so well.

① more indifferent to
② more attentive to
③ less preoccupied with
④ less involved in

44 밑줄 친 부분에 들어갈 말로 가장 적절한 것은?

2017. 국가직 9급

The Soleil department store outlet in Shanghai would seem to have all the amenities necessary to succeed in modern Chinese retail: luxury brands and an exclusive location. Despite these advantages, however, the store's management thought it was still missing something to attract customers. So next week they're unveiling a gigantic, twisting, dragon-shaped slide that shoppers can use to drop from fifth-floor luxury boutiques to first-floor luxury boutiques in death-defying seconds. Social media users are wondering, half-jokingly, whether the slide will kill anyone. But Soleil has a different concern that Chinese shopping malls will go away completely. Chinese shoppers, once seemingly in endless supply, are no longer turning up at brick-and-mortar outlets because of the growing online shopping, and they still go abroad to buy luxury goods. So, repurposing these massive spaces for consumers who have other ways to spend their time and money is likely to require a lot of creativity. ________________________________.

① Luxury brands are thriving at Soleil
② Soleil has decided against making bold moves
③ Increasing the online customer base may be the last hope
④ A five-story dragon slide may not be a bad place to start

45 밑줄 친 부분에 들어갈 말로 가장 적절한 것은?

2017. 국가직 9급

It is easy to devise numerous possible scenarios of future developments, each one, on the face of it, equally likely. The difficult task is to know which will actually take place. In hindsight, it usually seems obvious. When we look back in time, each event seems clearly and logically to follow from previous events. Before the event occurs, however, the number of possibilities seems endless. There are no methods for successful prediction, especially in areas involving complex social and technological changes, where many of the determining factors are not known and, in any event, are certainly not under any single group's control. Nonetheless, it is essential to __________________________________. We do know that new technologies will bring both dividends and problems, especially human, social problems. The more we try to anticipate these problems, the better we can control them.

① work out reasonable scenarios for the future
② legitimize possible dividends from future changes
③ leave out various aspects of technological problems
④ consider what it would be like to focus on the present

46 밑줄 친 부분에 들어갈 말로 가장 적절한 것은?

2017. 지방직 9급

One of the tricks our mind plays is to highlight evidence which confirms what we already believe. If we hear gossip about a rival, we tend to think "I knew he was a nasty piece of work"; if we hear the same about our best friend, we're more likely to say "that's just a rumour." Once you learn about this mental habit—called confirmation bias—you start seeing it everywhere. This matters when we want to make better decisions. Confirmation bias is OK as long as we're right, but all too often we're wrong, and we only pay attention to the deciding evidence when it's too late. How __________________________________ depends on our awareness of why, psychologically, confirmation bias happens. There are two possible reasons. One is that we have a blind spot in our imagination and the other is we fail to ask questions about new information.

① we make our rivals believe us
② our blind spot helps us make better decisions
③ we can protect our decisions from confirmation bias
④ we develop exactly the same bias

47 밑줄 친 부분에 들어갈 말로 가장 적절한 것은?

2017. 지방직 9급

For many big names in consumer product brands, exporting and producing overseas with local labor and for local tastes have been the right thing to do. In doing so, the companies found a way to improve their cost structure, to grow in the rapidly expanding consumer markets in emerging countries. But, Sweets Co. remains stuck in the domestic market. Even though its products are loaded with preservatives, which means they can endure long travel to distant markets, Sweets Co. ____________________, let alone produce overseas. The unwillingness or inability to update its business strategy and products for a changing world is clearly damaging to the company.

① is intent on importing
② does very little exporting
③ has decided to streamline operations
④ is expanding into emerging markets

48 밑줄 친 부분에 들어갈 말로 가장 적절한 것은?

2017. 지방직 9급

London taxi drivers have to undertake years of intense training known as "the knowledge" to gain their operating license, including learning the layout of over twenty-five thousand of the city's streets. A researcher and her team investigated the taxi drivers and the ordinary people. The two groups were asked to watch videos of routes unfamiliar to them through a town in Ireland. They were then asked to take a test about the video that included sketching out routes, identifying landmarks, and estimating distances between places. Both groups did well on much of the test, but the taxi drivers did significantly better on identifying new routes. This result suggests that the taxi drivers' mastery can be ____________ to new and unknown areas. Their years of training and learning through deliberate practice prepare them to take on similar challenges even in places they do not know well or at all.

① confined
② devoted
③ generalized
④ contributed

06 빈칸 추론 유형 기출 독해 어휘 복습 TEST

1	unemployment		21	standardization	
2	income		22	roll out	
3	substitute		23	uniform	
4	predominant		24	disparate	
5	inevitably		25	empirical	
6	disastrous		26	distraction	
7	project		27	persist	
8	population		28	immerse	
9	aging		29	buffer	
10	demographic		30	break off	
11	elderly		31	massive	
12	inattention		32	propaganda	
13	comprehend		33	plain	
14	appeal		34	misperception	
15	persuasion		35	interpretation	
16	devote		36	authority	
17	settle down		37	throw away	
18	mortgage		38	budget	
19	existing		39	hand down	
20	paradoxical		40	prerequisite	

06 빈칸 추론 유형 기출 독해 어휘 복습 TEST

41	discriminate		61	outline	
42	scattered		62	intuition	
43	autonomy		63	conscientious	
44	unoccupied		64	setback	
45	determine		65	underpin	
46	decay		66	plummet	
47	measure		67	hypothesis	
48	approximate		68	entrance	
49	extinct		69	manufacture	
50	constitute		70	transcend	
51	concrete		71	impede	
52	subject to		72	trivial	
53	keen		73	matter	
54	modify		74	calculate	
55	subconscious		75	alert	
56	odds		76	astute	
57	bother		77	altruism	
58	famine		78	legitimize	
59	coherent		79	nasty	
60	sequence		80	streamline	

MEMO

진가영

주요 약력

現) 박문각 공무원 영어 온라인, 오프라인 대표교수
서강대학교 우수 졸업
서강대학교 영미어문 심화 전공
중등학교 정교사 2급 자격증
단기 공무원 영어 전문 강의(개인 운영)

주요 저서

New Trend 진가영 영어 단기합격 문법 All In One(박문각)
New Trend 진가영 영어 단기합격 독해 All In One(박문각)
New Trend 진가영 영어 단기합격 VOCA(박문각)
New Trend 진가영 영어 단판승 문법 적중 포인트 100(박문각)
New Trend 진가영 영어 반한다 기출 문법·어휘 & 생활영어(박문각)
New Trend 진가영 영어 반한다 기출 독해(박문각)
진가영 영어 신독기 구문독해(박문각)
진가영 영어 신경향 어휘 마스터(박문각)
진가영 영어 신경향 독해 마스터 시즌1(박문각)
진가영 영어 신경향 독해 마스터 시즌2(박문각)
진가영 영어 독해끝판왕[독판왕](박문각)
진가영 영어 문법끝판왕[문판왕](박문각)
진가영 영어 진독기 구문독해 시즌1(박문각)
진가영 영어 단판승 생활영어 적중 70(박문각)
진가영 영어 하프 모의고사(박문각)
2024 박문각 공무원 봉투모의고사(박문각)

진가영 영어 ✧✦ 반한다 기출 독해

초판 발행 2024. 9. 20. | **2쇄 발행** 2024. 12. 10. | **편저자** 진가영
발행인 박 용 | **발행처** (주)박문각출판 | **등록** 2015년 4월 29일 제2019-000137호
주소 06654 서울시 서초구 효령로 283 서경 B/D 4층 | **팩스** (02)584-2927
전화 교재 문의 (02)6466-7202

저자와의 협의하에 인지생략

정가 23,000원
ISBN 979-11-7262-208-4

꿈은 이루어진다

Dreams come true!

★★★★★ 철도경찰직 합격, 영어 95점 이**

저는 공부 마무리를 교수님의 단판승 문법 킬포인트 100이라는 강의로 했습니다. **잠깐 까먹었던 개념들이나 아직 살짝 헷갈렸던 개념들을 빠르게 정리하는 강의**였습니다. 마무리로 양을 늘리는 것이 아니라 아는 내용, **시험에 꼭 나오는 내용을 다시 한 번 꼼꼼히 짚고 넘어갈 수 있어 좋았습니다.** 또 마지막엔 안 그래도 짧은 단판승을 3시간으로 요약한 강의를 제공해 주셔서 시험 직전 마무리 공부에 정말 큰 도움을 받았습니다.

★★★★★ 충남 교행 수석 합격, 영어 100점 김**

매번 가영쌤이 고유명사처럼 Mr.판승을 애타게 부르짖으며 홍보하는 **존재감 넘치는 강의**입니다.
문법의 핵심 킬포인트를 **반복하며 확실하게 내 것으로 만들 수 있도록** 많은 노력을 기울여 주십니다. 기존에 확실히 배우고 넘어갔다 생각한 문법 포인트들도 어느 순간 기억 속에서 잘 안 꺼내지는 경우가 많은데 그런 상황을 해결하는 데 많은 도움을 줍니다. 더 확실하게 기억할 수 있게 매번 특강들을 통해서도 요점들을 반복하여 계속 언급해 주시기 때문에 수험생 입장에서는 **반복 회독하는 부분까지 그냥 떠먹여주는 대로 받아먹으면 되는** 든든한 강의입니다.

★★★★★ 일반행정직 합격, 영어 95점 김**

가영쌤의 수업이 정말 좋았던 이유는 문법, 독해를 체계적으로 잘 가르쳐 주시고 매일매일 단어인증을 숙제로 내주셔서 의무감으로라도 단어를 꾸준히 외울 수 있도록 도와 주셨다는 점입니다!! 또, 엄청나게 지엽적인 문제들 위주로 가르쳐 주시기보다는 정말 시험에 나오는 것들, **출제 포인트를 딱 집어서 가르쳐 주셔서 시험장 가서도 '내가 어떤 출제 포인트에 집중하면 되겠다!'라는 부분을 알 수 있도록 도와 주셨습니다.** 가영쌤 400제, 동형, 단판승 **정말 최고입니다!!! 이 세 개의 커리만 제대로 따라가도 충분히 고득점 가능하다고 생각합니다.**

★★★★★ 사회복지직 합격, 영어 95점 강**

선생님은 자칫 지루할 수 있는 **문법 수업을 정말 쉽고 재미있고 어려운 부분까지 정확하게 다루어 주셨습니다!** 선생님의 단판승 요약서를 보고 선생님의 문법 특강 강좌에 참여하면서 선생님과 호흡하는 재미있는 수업을 하였고, 수업이 끝난 후에는 **어느 순간 리틀 가영(?)이 되어 선생님이 알려준 재밌는 암기법과 챈트들로 재미있게 문법을 푸는 제 자신을 발견하게 되었습니다.** 단판승 요약서를 활용한 문법 강의를 진행하여 수험생들에게 문법에 대한 두려움을 없애고 중요한 내용을 토가 나올 정도로 반복하여 시험이 가까워질 때는 완벽에 가깝게 암기하여 적용을 원활하게 잘할 수 있도록 좋은 강의를 진행해 주셨습니다.

9급 공무원 시험대비 **개정판**

박문각 공무원

기출문제

브랜드만족 **1위** 박문각

2025

수석합격 **2연속** 배출
산출근거 후면표기

진가영 영어

진가영 편저

New Trend
단기합격 길라잡이

- 2025 출제 기조 전환 1차, 2차 예시 문제 반영
- 국가직과 지방직 및 기타 9급 핵심 기출 반영
- 기출 독해 유형별 문제 풀이 전략 수록
- 9급 기출 핵심 어휘 총정리 자료 수록

반한다 기출 독해

정답 및 해설

동영상 강의 www.pmg.co.kr

박문각

반한다 기출 정답 및 해설
독해

브랜드만족
1위
박문각

2025

수석합격
2연속
배출

9급 공무원 시험대비 **개정판**

박문각 공무원

기출문제

진가영 영어

진가영 편저

New Trend
단기합격 길라잡이

- 2025 출제 기조 전환 1차, 2차 예시 문제 반영
- 국가직과 지방직 및 기타 9급 핵심 기출 반영
- 기출 독해 유형별 문제 풀이 전략 수록
- 9급 기출 핵심 어휘 총정리 자료 수록

반한다 기출 독해

정답 및 해설

동영상 강의 www.pmg.co.kr

박문각

chapter 01 신경향 유형 정답 및 해설

ANSWER

01 ①	02 ①	03 ④	04 ①	05 ③
06 ③	07 ④	08 ③	09 ②	10 ②
11 ③	12 ④	13 ②	14 ③	

01 다음 글의 목적으로 가장 적절한 것은?

2025. 출제 기조 전환 2차

Send Preview Save

To: cbsclients@calbank.com

From: calbanks@calmail.com

Date: May 7, 2024

Subject: Important notice

My PC Browse

Times New 10pt

Dear Valued Clients,

In today's world, cybercrime poses a serious threat to your security. As your trusted partner, we want to help you protect your personal and business information. Here are five easy ways to safeguard yourself from cyber threats:

1. Use strong passwords and change them frequently.
2. Keep your software and devices up to date.
3. Be wary of suspicious emails, links, or telephone calls that pressure you to act quickly or give out sensitive information.
4. Enable Two Factor authentication and use it whenever possible. When contacting California Bank & Savings, you will be asked to use a One Time Passcode (OTP) to verify your identity.
5. Back up your data regularly.

Visit our Security Center to learn more about how you can stay safe online. Remember, cybersecurity is a team effort. By working together, we can build a safer online environment for ourselves and the world.

Sincerely,

California Bank & Savings

① to inform clients of how to keep themselves safe from cyber threats
② to inform clients of how to update their software and devices
③ to inform clients of how to make their passwords stronger
④ to inform clients of how to safeguard their OTPs

해설

이 전자우편의 주요 목적은 고객들에게 사이버 범죄로부터 자신을 보호하는 방법에 대한 정보를 제공하는 것이다. 전자 우편의 내용은 다양한 안전 수칙을 제시하고 있으며, 전체적으로 사이버 위협에 대한 경각심을 일깨우고 있다. 따라서 글의 목적으로 가장 적절한 것은 ① '고객에게 사이버 위협으로부터 자신을 안전하게 지키는 방법을 알리기 위해서'이다.
② 고객에게 소프트웨어와 장비를 업데이트하는 방법을 알리기 위해서
③ 고객에게 비밀번호를 더 강하게 만드는 방법을 알리기 위해서
④ 고객에게 OTP를 보호하는 방법을 알리기 위해서

해석

수신인: cbsclients@calbank.com
발신인: calbanks@calmail.com
날짜: 2024년 5월 7일
제목: 중요 공지

소중한 고객님들께,

오늘날 사이버 범죄는 여러분의 보안에 심각한 위협을 가하고 있습니다. 신뢰받는 파트너로서, 우리는 여러분의 개인 및 비즈니스 정보를 보호하는 데 도움을 드리고자 합니다. 사이버 위협으로부터 자신을 보호하는 다섯 가지 간단한 방법은 다음과 같습니다:

1. 강력한 비밀번호를 사용하고 자주 변경하세요.
2. 소프트웨어와 장비를 최신 상태로 유지하세요.
3. 빠르게 행동하거나 민감한 정보를 제공하라는 압박을 가하는 의심스러운 전자 우편, 링크, 전화에 주의하세요.
4. 이중 인증을 활성화하고 가능한 경우 항상 사용하세요. 캘리포니아 저축은행에 연락할 때, 신원을 확인하기 위해 일회용 비밀번호(OTP)를 사용해야 합니다.
5. 데이터를 정기적으로 백업하세요.

온라인에서 안전을 유지하는 방법에 대해 더 알아보려면 보안 센터를 방문하세요. 사이버 보안은 팀의 노력입니다. 함께 협력하여 우리와 전 세계를 위한 더 안전한 온라인 환경을 만들어 나가도록 합시다.

진심으로
캘리포니아 저축은행

어휘

- □ valued 소중한, 존중되는, 평가된
- □ cybercrime 사이버 범죄
- □ frequently 자주, 흔히
- □ up to date 최신의, 최근의, 현대식의
- □ suspicious 의심스러운, 수상쩍은
- □ sensitive 민감한, 예민한, 세심한
- □ authentication 인증, 입증, 증명
- □ verify 확인하다, 입증하다
- □ regularly 정기[규칙]적으로, 자주

정답 ①

[02-03] 다음 글을 읽고 물음에 답하시오.

2025. 출제 기조 전환 2차

dagov ×

http://dagov.com/our-agency

HOME ABOUT US CONTACT US SEARCH

Agricultural Marketing Office

Mission

We administer programs that create domestic and international marketing opportunities for national producers of food, fiber, and specialty crops. We also provide the agriculture industry with valuable services to ensure the quality and availability of wholesome food for consumers across the country and around the world.

Vision

We facilitate the strategic marketing of national agricultural products in domestic and international markets while ensuring <u>fair</u> trading practices and promoting a competitive and efficient marketplace to the benefit of producers, traders, and consumers of national food, fiber, and specialty crops.

Core Values

- Honesty & Integrity: We expect and require complete honesty and integrity in all we do.
- Independence & Objectivity: We act independently and objectively to create trust in our programs and services.

02 윗글에서 Agricultural Marketing Office에 관한 내용과 일치하는 것은?

① It creates marketing opportunities for domestic producers.
② It limits wholesome food consumption around the world.
③ It is committed to benefiting consumers over producers.
④ It receives mandates from other agencies before making decisions.

03 밑줄 친 fair의 의미와 가장 가까운 것은?

① free ② mutual
③ profitable ④ impartial

해설

02. 농업 마케팅 사무소의 임무에서 'domestic and international marketing opportunities(국내외 마케팅 기회)'를 창출한다는 내용이 명시되어 있다. 따라서 다음 글에 관한 내용과 일치하는 것은 ① '국내 생산자들에게 마케팅 기회를 제공한다.'이다.
② 전 세계적으로 건강한 음식 소비를 제한한다.
③ 생산자보다 소비자에게 혜택을 주는 데 전념한다.
④ 결정을 내리기 전에 다른 기관으로부터 지시를 받는다.

[오답 해설]
② Agricultural Marketing Office의 목적과 반대되는 내용이다. 사무소는 소비자에게 건강한 식품의 품질과 가용성을 보장하는 데 초점을 맞추고 있으므로, 식품 소비를 제한하지 않는다.
③ 이 기관은 생산자, 거래자 및 소비자 모두의 혜택을 위해 노력하며, 특정 그룹에 대한 편향에 대한 언급은 없다.
④ Agricultural Marketing Office는 프로그램과 서비스에 대한 신뢰를 형성하기 위해 독립적이고 객관적으로 행동하므로, 다른 기관으로부터의 지시를 받지 않는다.

03. 'fair'는 '박람회, 전시회, 공정한'이라는 의미로, 선정의 기준이나 처리 방식에서 편견이 없음을 나타낸다. 따라서 'fair'의 의미와 가장 가까운 것은 ④ 'impartial(공평한, 공정한)'이다.

[오답 해설]
① 'free'는 '자유로운, 무료의, ~이 없는'이라는 의미로, 문맥상 'fair'와는 다른 의미이다.
② 'mutual'은 '상호간의, 서로의'라는 의미로, 문맥상 'fair'와는 다른 의미이다.
③ 'profitable'은 '수익성이 있는, 이득이 되는'이라는 의미로, 문맥상 'fair'와는 다른 의미이다.

해석

농업 마케팅 사무소

사명
우리는 식품, 섬유 및 특수 작물의 국내 생산자를 위한 국내외 마케팅 기회를 창출하는 프로그램을 운영합니다. 또한, 우리는 농업 산업에 가치 있는 서비스를 제공하여 국내외 소비자에게 건강에 좋은 식품의 품질과 가용성을 보장합니다.

비전
우리는 국내외 시장에서 국가 농산물의 전략적 마케팅을 촉진하며, 공정한 거래 관행을 보장하고 생산자, 거래자 및 소비자에게 이익이 되는 경쟁력 있고 효율적인 시장을 촉진합니다.

핵심 가치
- 정직과 진실성: 우리는 우리가 하는 모든 일에서 완벽한 정직과 진실성을 기대하고 요구합니다.
- 독립성과 객관성: 우리는 프로그램과 서비스에 대한 신뢰를 형성하기 위해 독립적이고 객관적으로 행동합니다.

어휘

- □ agricultural 농업의, 농사의
- □ administer 운영하다, 관리하다
- □ domestic 국내의, 가정의
- □ international 국제적인
- □ fiber 섬유(질)
- □ wholesome 건강에 좋은, 건전한, 유익한
- □ facilitate 촉진하다, 가능[용이]하게 하다
- □ competitive 경쟁력 있는, 뒤지지 않는
- □ integrity 진실성, 완전한 상태, 온전함
- □ independence 독립(성), 자립(성)
- □ objectivity 객관성

정답 ①

정답 ④

[04-05] 다음 글을 읽고 물음에 답하시오.

2025. 출제 기조 전환 2차

(A)

As a close neighbor, you will want to learn how to save your lake.

While it isn't dead yet, Lake Dimmesdale is heading toward this end. So pay your respects to this beautiful body of water while it is still alive.

Some dedicated people are working to save it now. They are having a special meeting to tell you about it. Come learn what is being done and how you can help. This affects your property value as well.

Who wants to live near a dead lake?

Sponsored by Central State Regional Planning Council

- Location: Green City Park Opposite Southern State College
  (in case of rain: College Library Room 203)
- Date: Saturday, July 6, 2024
- Time: 2:00 p.m.

For any questions about the meeting, please visit our website at www.planningcouncilsavelake.org or contact our office at (432) 345-6789.

04 (A)에 들어갈 윗글의 제목으로 가장 적절한 것은?

① Lake Dimmesdale Is Dying
② Praise to the Lake's Beauty
③ Cultural Value of Lake Dimmesdale
④ Significance of the Lake to the College

05 위 안내문의 내용과 일치하지 않는 것은?

① 호수를 살리기 위해 노력하는 사람들이 있다.
② 호수를 위한 활동이 주민들의 재산에 영향을 미친다.
③ 우천 시에는 대학의 구내식당에서 회의가 열린다.
④ 웹사이트 방문이나 전화로 회의에 관해 질문할 수 있다.

해설

04. 본문에서는 Lake Dimmesdale가 죽어가고 있다는 경고와 함께 이를 구하기 위한 노력을 강조하고 있으므로, 글의 제목으로 가장 적절한 것은 ① '딤즈데일 호수가 죽어가고 있다'이다.
② 호수의 아름다움에 대한 찬사
③ 딤즈데일 호수의 문화적 가치
④ 대학에 대한 호수의 중요성

[오답 해설]
② 본문에서는 호수의 아름다움에 대한 찬사를 담고 있지만, 글의 주된 내용이 아니다. 이 글은 호수의 위기에 대한 경각심을 일깨우는 데 중점을 두고 있다.
③ 본문에서는 호수의 문화적 가치를 언급하고 있지만, 글에서는 그런 측면이 강조되지 않는다. 대신 호수를 구하기 위한 현재의 위기와 노력이 중점적으로 다뤄진다.
④ 대학에 대한 호수의 중요성은 글의 목적과 관련이 없다.

05. 안내문에 따르면, 우천 시 회의는 'College Library Room 203'에서 열린다고 명시되어 있으므로, 위 안내문의 내용과 일치하지 않는 것은 ③이다.

[오답 해설]
①은 안내문에서 분명히 언급된 내용이며, 글의 핵심 메시지와 일치한다.
②은 안내문에서 호수의 상태가 주민들의 재산 가치에 영향을 미친다고 언급하고 있으므로, 이 내용도 사실이다.
④은 안내문에서 웹사이트와 전화 연락처를 제공하고 있으므로, 이 내용 역시 일치한다.

해석

딤즈데일 호수가 죽어가고 있다

가까운 이웃으로서, 여러분은 호수를 구하는 방법을 알아야 할 것입니다.

아직 호수가 죽지는 않았지만, 딤즈데일 호수는 그 방향으로 나아가고 있습니다. 그러니 이 아름다운 수역이 아직 살아 있는 동안에 경의를 표해주세요.

지금 몇몇 헌신적인 사람들이 호수를 구하기 위해 노력하고 있습니다. 그들은 이에 대해 여러분에게 알리기 위해 특별 회의를 개최할 예정입니다. 무엇이 이루어지고 있으며, 어떻게 도움을 줄 수 있는지 배워보세요. 이것은 여러분의 재산 가치에도 영향을 미칩니다.

누가 죽어가는 호수 근처에 살고 싶겠어요?

중앙 주 지역 계획 위원회 주최

- 장소: 그린 시티 공원, 서던 주립 대학 맞은편
  (비가 올 경우: 대학 도서관 203호)
- 날짜: 2024년 7월 6일 토요일
- 시간: 오후 2시

회의에 관한 질문은 저희 웹사이트 www.planningcouncilsavelake.org을 방문하시거나 사무실(432) 345-6789로 연락해 주시기 바랍니다.

어휘

□ pay respect to ~에 경의를 표하다, ~를 존중하다
□ dedicated 헌신적인, 전념하는
□ affect 영향을 미치다, 발생하다
□ property 재산, 소유물, 부동산, 건물
□ sponsor 주최[주관]하다, 후원하다, 후원자
□ council 의회, 자문 위원회
□ opposite 맞은편의, 다른 쪽의, 반대, 반의어
□ in case of ~의 경우, ~에 대비해서

정답 ①

정답 ③

06 다음 글의 내용과 일치하지 않는 것은?

2025. 출제 기조 전환 2차

The David Williams Library and Museum is open 7 days a week, from 9:00 a.m. to 5:00 p.m. (NOV－MAR) and 9:00 a.m. to 6:00 p.m. (APR－OCT). Online tickets may be purchased at the link below. You will receive an email confirmation after making a purchase (be sure to check your SPAM folder). Bring this confirmation — printed or on smart device — as proof of purchase.

- **Online tickets**: buy.davidwilliams.com/events

The David Williams Library and Museum and the Home of David Williams (operated by the National Heritage Service) offer separate $10.00 adult admission tickets. Tickets for tours of the Home may be purchased on-site during normal business hours.

- **CLOSED**: Thanksgiving, Christmas and New Year's Day

There is no charge for conducting research in the David Williams Library research room.

For additional information, call 1 (800) 333-7777.

① The Library and Museum closes at 5:00 p.m. in December.
② Visitors can buy tour tickets for the Home on-site.
③ The Home of David Williams is open all year round.
④ One can do research in the Library research room for free.

해설

David Williams 도서관 및 박물관 운영 안내에 대한 글로, David Williams 도서관 및 박물관은 매일 운영되며, 온라인 티켓 구매가 가능하고, 연구는 무료로 진행할 수 있으며, 휴무일은 추수감사절, 크리스마스, 새해 첫날임을 설명하고 있다. 따라서 글의 내용과 일치하지 않는 것은 ③ 'The Home of David Williams는 연중무휴로 열려 있습니다.'이다.
① 도서관과 박물관은 12월에 오후 5시에 문을 닫습니다.
② 방문객들은 현장에서 집 투어 티켓을 구매할 수 있습니다.
④ 도서관 연구실에서 연구를 무료로 진행할 수 있습니다.

[오답 해설]
① 본문에서 12월의 운영 시간을 명시하고 있다.
② 본문에서 현장에서 티켓 구매 가능성을 언급하고 있다.
④ 본문에서 연구실 이용이 무료라고 명시되어 있다.

해석

David Williams 도서관 및 박물관은 매주 7일 운영되며, 11월부터 3월까지는 오전 9시부터 오후 5시까지, 4월부터 10월까지는 오전 9시부터 오후 6시까지 열려 있습니다. 온라인 티켓은 아래 링크에서 구매할 수 있습니다. 구매 후 이메일로 확인서를 받게 됩니다(스팸 메일 폴더를 반드시 확인하시기 바랍니다). 이 확인서를 인쇄하여 지참하거나 스마트 기기에서 제시하여 구매 증빙으로 사용하세요.

• 온라인 티켓: buy.davidwilliams.com/events

데이비드 윌리엄스 도서관 및 박물관과 David Williams의 집(국가문화유산 서비스 운영)은 성인 입장권을 각각 $10.00에 판매합니다. 집 투어 티켓은 정상 업무 시간 중 현장에서 구매할 수 있습니다.

• 휴무: 추수감사절, 크리스마스, 새해 첫날

David Williams 도서관 연구실에서 연구를 진행하는 데는 비용이 들지 않습니다.

추가 정보는 1 (800) 333-7777로 문의해 주세요.

어휘

□ purchase 구매[구입]하다, 구매, 구입
□ below 아래에, 밑에
□ confirmation 확인, 확증, 증거
□ be sure to 반드시 ~하다
□ separate 각각의, 별개의, 분리된, 분리되다, 나누다
□ admission 입장, 입학, 시인, 인정
□ on-site 현장의, 현지의
□ charge 비용, 요금, 고발, 비난, 청구하다, 고소하다, 비난하다

정답 ③

07 Enter-K 앱에 관한 다음 글의 내용과 일치하지 않는 것은?

2025. 출제 기조 전환 1차

Enter-K ×
https://enter-k.org
MENU

Use the new Enter-K app for your customs declaration.

Use the new Enter-K app upon your arrival at the airport. One notable feature offered by Enter-K is the Advance Declaration, which allows travellers the option to submit their customs declaration in advance, enabling them to save time at all our international airports. As part of the ongoing Traveller Modernization initiative, Enter-K will continue to introduce additional border-related features in the future, further improving the overall border experience. Simply download the latest version of the app from the online store before your arrival. There is also a web version of the app for those who are not comfortable using mobile devices.

① It allows travellers to declare customs in advance.
② More features will be added later.
③ Travellers can download it from the online store.
④ It only works on personal mobile devices.

해설

윗글에 따르면, 마지막 문장에 'There is also a web version of the app…'이라고 명시되어 있으므로, 윗글의 내용과 일치하지 않는 것은 ④ '그것은 개인 모바일 장치에서만 작동한다.'이다.
① 그것은 여행자들이 미리 세관 신고를 할 수 있게 해준다.
② 더 많은 기능이 나중에 추가될 것이다.
③ 여행자들은 온라인 상점에서 이것을 다운로드할 수 있다.
[오답 해설]
① 글의 두 번째 문장에 명시되어 있다.
② 글의 세 번째 문장에 명시되어 있다.
③ 글의 네 번째 문장에 명시되어 있다.

해석

당신의 세관 신고를 위해 새로운 Enter-K 앱을 사용하세요.

공항에 당신이 도착하자마자 새로운 Enter-K 앱을 사용하세요. Enter-K에 의해 제공되는 한 가지 주목할 만한 특징은 Advance Declaration(사전 신고)인데, 이것은 여행자들에게 미리 그들의 세관

신고서를 제출할 수 있는 옵션을 허용하고 그들이 우리의 모든 국제 공항에서 시간을 절약할 수 있게 합니다. Enter-K는 계속 진행 중인 Traveller Modernization(여행자 현대화) 계획의 일환으로 미래에 국경 관련 추가 기능을 계속 도입하여 전체적인 국경 경험을 더욱 향상시킬 것입니다. 당신이 도착하기 전에 온라인 스토어에서 최신 버전의 앱을 간단히 다운로드 하세요. 모바일 기기 사용이 불편한 사람들을 위한 웹 버전의 앱 또한 있습니다.

어휘

- ☐ customs 세관, 관세
- ☐ declaration 신고, 선언, 발표, 공표
- ☐ arrival 도착, 도래, 도입
- ☐ in advance 미리, 전부터
- ☐ enable ~을 할 수 있게 하다, 가능하게 하다
- ☐ international 국제적인
- ☐ ongoing 계속 진행 중인
- ☐ introduce 도입하다, 소개하다, 시작하다
- ☐ comfortable 편안한, 쾌적한

정답 ④

[08-09] 다음 글을 읽고 물음에 답하시오.

2025. 출제 기조 전환 1차

Send Preview Save

To	Clifton District Office
From	Rachael Beasly
Date	June 7
Subject	Excessive Noise in the Neighborhood

My PC Browse

Times New 10pt

To whom it may concern,

I hope this email finds you well. I am writing to express my concern and frustration regarding the excessive noise levels in our neighborhood, specifically coming from the new sports field.

As a resident of Clifton district, I have always appreciated the peace of our community. However, the ongoing noise disturbances have significantly impacted my family's well-being and our overall quality of life. The sources of the noise include crowds cheering, players shouting, whistles, and ball impacts.

I kindly request that you look into this matter and take appropriate <u>steps</u> to address the noise disturbances. Thank you for your attention to this matter, and I appreciate your prompt response to help restore the tranquility in our neighborhood.

Sincerely,
Rachael Beasley

08 윗글의 목적으로 가장 적절한 것은?

① 체육대회 소음에 대해 주민들의 양해를 구하려고
② 새로 이사 온 이웃 주민의 소음에 대해 항의하려고
③ 인근 스포츠 시설의 소음에 대한 조치를 요청하려고
④ 늦은 시간 악기 연주와 같은 소음의 차단을 부탁하려고

09 밑줄 친 "steps"의 의미와 가장 가까운 것은?

① movements ② actions
③ levels ④ stairs

해설

08. 새로운 스포츠 경기장 소음으로 인한 불편함에 대한 우려를 나타내기 위해 Clifton 구청에 보낸 이메일이다. 따라서 글의 목적으로 적절한 것은 ③이다.

[오답 해설]
① 소음의 소재는 맞지만, 체육대회 소음이 아니다.
② 소음의 소재는 맞지만, 이웃 주민의 소음이 아니다.
④ 소음의 소재는 맞지만, 악기 연주와 같은 소음이 아니다.

09. '이 문제에 대해서 적합한 조치'를 취하기를 원한다는 문맥에서 steps와 가장 의미가 가까운 것은 ② 'actions(조치들)'이다.

[오답 해설]
① 'movement'는 '움직임, 이동'이라는 의미로, 문맥상 'step'과는 다른 의미이다.
③ 'level'은 '정도, 단계, 관점'이라는 의미로, 문맥상 'step'과는 다른 의미이다.
④ 'stair'는 '계단, 층계'라는 의미로, 문맥상 'step'과는 다른 의미이다.

해석

수신인: 클리프턴 구청
발신인: Rachael Beasly
날짜: 6월 7일
제목: 인근의 과도한 소음

담당자분께,
이 이메일이 당신에게 잘 도착하기를 바랍니다. 저는 특히 새로운 스포츠 경기장에서 오는 우리 동네의 과도한 소음 수준에 대하여 우려와 좌절감을 표현하기 위해 글을 씁니다.

클리프턴 지역 주민으로서, 저는 항상 우리 지역 사회의 평화를 높이 평가해왔습니다. 그러나, 계속되는 소음으로 인한 방해는 우리 가족의 안녕과 우리 삶의 전반적인 질에 상당히 영향을 미치고 있습니다. 소음의 원인은 군중 응원, 선수들의 함성, 휘파람, 공의 충돌을 포함합니다.

저는 당신이 이 문제를 조사하여 소음으로 인한 방해를 해결하기 위한 적절한 조치를 취해 주시기를 부탁드립니다. 이 문제에 관한 당신의 관심에 감사드리며, 우리 인근의 평온을 회복하는 데 도움이 될 수 있는 신속한 대응에 감사드립니다.

진심을 담아,
Rachael Beasly

어휘

□ concern
관계하다, 관련되다, 걱정시키다, 염려[우려]하게 만들다, 일, 관계, 관심, 걱정, 우려
□ regarding ~에 대하여, ~에 관하여
□ excessive 과도한, 지나친
□ district 지역, 지방
□ look into ~을 조사하다, ~을 들여다 보다, 주의 깊게 살피다
□ matter 문제, 물질, 재료, 중요하다, 문제가 되다
□ take steps 조치를 취하다
□ address 해결하다, 다루다, 처리하다, 주소를 쓰다, 연설하다
□ prompt 신속한, 즉각적인, 자극하다, 촉구하다
□ tranquility 평온, 고요, 차분함

정답 ③

정답 ②

[10–11] 다음 글을 읽고 물음에 답하시오.

2025. 출제 기조 전환 1차

(A) ____________________

We're pleased to announce the upcoming City Harbour Festival, an annual event that brings our diverse community together to celebrate our shared heritage, culture, and local talent. Mark your calendars and join us for an exciting weekend!

Details
- **Dates**: Friday, June 16 – Sunday, June 18
- **Times**: 10 : 00 a.m. – 8 : 00 p.m. (Friday & Saturday)
  10 : 00 a.m. – 6 : 00 p.m. (Sunday)
- **Location**: City Harbour Park, Main Street, and surrounding areas

Highlights
- **Live Performances**
  Enjoy a variety of live music, dance, and theatrical performances on multiple stages throughout the festival grounds.
- **Food Trucks**
  Have a feast with a wide selection of food trucks offering diverse and delicious cuisines, as well as free sample tastings.

For the full schedule of events and activities, please visit our website at www.cityharbourfestival. org or contact the Festival Office at (552) 234-5678.

10 (A)에 들어갈 윗글의 제목으로 가장 적절한 것은?

① Make Safety Regulations for Your Community
② Celebrate Our Vibrant Community Events
③ Plan Your Exciting Maritime Experience
④ Recreate Our City's Heritage

11 **City Harbour Festival에 관한 윗글의 내용과 일치하지 않는 것은?**

① 일 년에 한 번 개최된다.
② 일요일에는 오후 6시까지 열린다.
③ 주요 행사로 무료 요리 강습이 진행된다.
④ 웹사이트나 전화 문의를 통해 행사 일정을 알 수 있다.

해설

10. 연간 행사인 도시 항만 축제의 일정과 세부 프로그램에 대한 공지의 글이다. 따라서 글의 제목으로 가장 적절한 것은 ② '활기찬 커뮤니티 이벤트를 기념하세요'이다.
① 커뮤니티를 위한 안전 규정을 만들어 보세요
③ 신나는 해양 체험을 계획하세요
④ 우리 도시의 유산을 재현하세요

[오답 해설]
① 본문에서는 커뮤니티에 대한 언급은 있지만, 안전 규정과 관련된 내용은 아니다.
③ 지역 행사 이름이 '도시 항구 축제'이긴 하지만 해양 체험과는 거리가 멀다.
④ 유산, 문화 등을 기념하기 위한 행사는 맞지만 그것을 재현하고자 하는 목적은 아니다.

11. 윗글에 따르면, 주요 행사로 무료 시식을 제공한다고 명시되어 있으므로, 윗글의 내용과 일치하지 않는 것은 ③이다.

[오답 해설]
① 글의 첫 부분에 명시되어 있다.
② 세부 사항의 날짜와 시간에 명시되어 있다.
④ 글의 마지막 부분에 명시되어 있다.

해석

우리의 활기찬 지역사회 행사를 기념하세요

우리는 우리의 공유된 유산, 문화, 그리고 지역 재능을 기념하기 위해 우리의 다양한 지역 사회를 화합하게 하는 연례행사인 곧 있을 City Harbour Festival을 발표하게 되어 기쁩니다. 여러분의 달력에 표시하고 신나는 주말에 우리와 함께 하세요!

세부 사항
- **날짜**: 6월 16일, 금요일 – 6월 18일, 일요일
- **시간**: 오전 10 : 00 – 오후 8 : 00 (금, 토)
  오전 10 : 00 – 오후 6 : 00 (일)
- **장소**: City Harbour 공원, 시내 중심가, 주변 지역

하이라이트
- **라이브 공연**
  축제장 곳곳에 다수의 무대에서 다양한 라이브 음악, 춤, 그리고 연극 공연을 즐기세요.
- **푸드 트럭**
  무료 시식뿐만 아니라 다양하고 맛있는 요리를 제공하는 다양한 푸드 트럭과 함께 잔치를 즐기세요.

행사 및 활동의 전체 일정은 당사 웹사이트 www.cityharbourfestival.org를 방문하거나 축제사무소인 (552) 234-5678로 연락주세요.

어휘

- ☐ vibrant 활기찬, 생기가 넘치는, 강렬한, 선명한
- ☐ upcoming 곧 있을, 다가오는
- ☐ bring together 화합하게 하다, 모으다, 화해시키다
- ☐ heritage 유산, 전승, 전통
- ☐ a variety of 다양한, 여러 가지의
- ☐ throughout 곳곳에, 도처에, ~동안, ~내내
- ☐ feast 잔치, 연회, 축제일, 포식하다
- ☐ cuisine 요리, 요리법

정답 ②

정답 ③

12 **Office of the Labor Commissioner에 관한 다음 글의 내용과 일치하는 것은?** 2025. 출제 기조 전환 1차

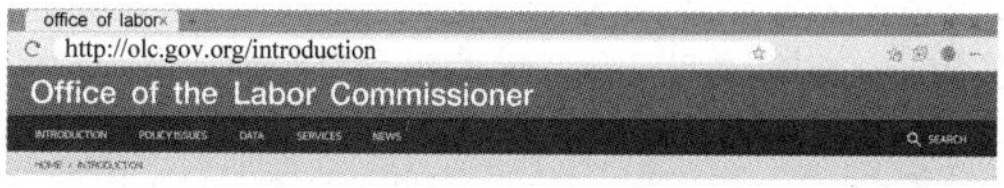

Office of the Labor Commissioner(OLC) Responsibilities

The OLC is the principal labor regulatory agency for the state. The OLC is responsible for ensuring that minimum wage, prevailing wage, and overtime are paid to employees, and that employee break and lunch periods are provided. In addition, the OLC has authority over the employment of minors. It is the vision and mission of this office to resolve labor-related problems in an efficient, professional, and effective manner. This includes educating employers and employees regarding their rights and responsibilities under the law. The OLC takes enforcement action when necessary to ensure that workers are treated fairly and compensated for all time worked.

① It ensures that employees pay taxes properly.
② It has authority over employment of adult workers only.
③ It promotes employers' business opportunities.
④ It takes action when employees are unfairly treated.

해설

윗글에 따르면, 마지막 문장에 '…to ensure that workers are treated fairly…'라고 명시되어 있으므로, 윗글의 내용과 일치하는 것은 ④ '그것은 직원들이 불공정하게 대우 받을 때 조치를 취한다.'이다.
① 그것은 직원들이 세금을 제대로 납부하도록 보장한다.
② 그것은 성인 근로자의 고용에만 권한을 가지고 있다.
③ 그것은 고용주의 사업 기회들을 촉진한다.

[오답 해설]
① 글에서 해당 내용을 언급한 부분이 없으므로 일치하지 않는다.
② 글의 세 번째 문장에서 '미성년자 고용에 관한 권한을 가지고 있다'라고 명시되어 있으므로 일치하지 않는다.
③ 글에서 해당 내용을 언급한 부분이 없으므로 일치하지 않는다.

해석

노동위원회(OLC) 사무소의 책임

OLC는 국가의 주요 노동 규제 기관입니다. OLC는 최저 임금, 적정 임금, 그리고 초과 근무 수당 등이 종업원에게 지급되고 종업원의 휴식 및 점심시간이 제공되도록 보장하는 것에 책임이 있습니다. 게다가, OLC는 미성년자 고용에 관한 권한을 가지고 있습니다. 노동과 관련된 문제들을 효율적이고 전문적이며 효과적인 방법으로 해결하는 것이 본 사무소의 비전이자 임무입니다. 이것은 고용주와 종업원에게 법에 따른 그들의 권리와 책임에 대해 교육하는 것을 포함합니다. OLC는 근로자가 공정하게 대우받고 모든 근무 시간에 대해 보상을 받는 것을 보장할 수 있도록 필요할 때 집행 조치를 취합니다.

어휘

□ principal 주된, 주요한, 학장, 총장
□ regulatory 규제의, 통제의, 단속의
□ minimum 최저의, 최소한의
□ wage 임금, 급료
□ employee 종업원
□ minor 미성년자, 부전공, 작은, 가벼운
□ employer 고용주
□ enforcement 집행, 시행, 실시
□ compensate 보상하다, 보상금을 주다

정답 ④

13 Northeastern Wildlife Exposition에 관한 다음 글의 내용과 일치하는 것은? 2024. 국가직 9급

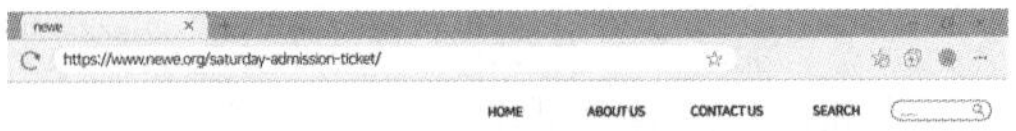

NORTHEASTERN WILDLIFE EXPOSITION (NEWE)

Admission ticket for Saturday, March 30th, 2024
- **Price**: $40.00
- **Opening hours**: 10:00 a.m. – 6:00 p.m.

Kids 10 and under are free. Entry to shows and lectures are first-come, first-served. All venues open rain or shine.

March 20th is the last day to buy tickets online for the 2024 Northeastern Wildlife Exposition.

Please note: Purchasing NEWE tickets in advance is the best way to guarantee entry into all exhibits. NEWE organizers may discontinue in-person ticket sales should any venue reach capacity.

① 10세 어린이는 입장료 40불을 지불해야 한다.
② 공연과 강연의 입장은 선착순이다.
③ 비가 올 경우에는 행사장을 닫는다.
④ 입장권은 온라인으로만 구매할 수 있다.

해설

윗글에 따르면, 첫 번째 단락 부분에 'Entry to shows and lectures are first-come, first-served.'라고 명시되어 있으므로, 윗글의 내용과 일치하는 것은 ②이다.

[오답 해설]
① 글의 첫 번째 단락 부분에 10세 이하는 무료라고 명시되어 있으므로 일치하지 않는다.
③ 글의 첫 번째 단락 부분에 날씨와 관계없이 열린다고 명시되어 있으므로 일치하지 않는다.
④ 글의 마지막 단락 참고 부분에 현장 입장권 판매를 중단할 수 있다고 명시되어 있으므로 일치하지 않는다.

해석

북동부 야생 동물 전시회(NEWE)

2024년 3월 30일 토요일 입장권
• 가격: 40달러
• 개장 시간: 오전 10:00 – 오후 6:00

10세 이하의 아이들은 무료입니다. 공연과 강연의 입장은 선착순입니다. 모든 장소는 날씨에 관계없이 열립니다.

3월 20일은 2024 북동부 야생 동물 전시회의 온라인 입장권 구매 마지막 날입니다.

참고: NEWE의 입장권을 미리 구매하는 것이 모든 전시회 입장을 보장하는 최고의 방법입니다. NEWE의 주최자는 장소가 수용 범위에 도달한다면 현장 입장권 판매를 중단할 수 있습니다.

어휘

- ☐ exposition 전시회
- ☐ admission 입장료
- ☐ first-come, first-served 선착순
- ☐ venue 개최지, 장소
- ☐ rain or shine 비가 오든 말든, 무조건
- ☐ in advance 미리, 사전에
- ☐ guarantee 보장하다, 보증하다
- ☐ exhibit 전시품, 전시하다
- ☐ organizer 주최자
- ☐ capacity 수용 능력, 용적량

정답 ②

14 **다음 이메일의 내용과 일치하지 않는 것은?**

2024. 지방직 9급

Send Preview Save

To reserve@metropolitan.com
From BruceTaylor@westcity.com
Date June 22, 2024
Subject Venue facilities

My PC Browse

Times New 10pt

Dear Sir,

I am writing to ask for information about Metropolitan Conference Center.

We are looking for a venue for a three-day conference in September this year. We need to have enough room for over 200 delegates in your main conference room, and we would also like three small conference rooms for meetings. Each conference room needs wi-fi as well. We need to have coffee available mid-morning and mid-afternoon, and we would also like to book your restaurant for lunch on all three days.

In addition, could you please let me know if there are any local hotels with discount rates for Metropolitan clients or large groups? We will need accommodations for over 100 delegates each night.

I look forward to hearing from you.

Best regards,
Bruce Taylor, Event Manager

① 주 회의실은 200명 이상의 대표자를 수용할 수 있어야 한다.
② wi-fi가 있는 작은 회의실 3개가 필요하다.
③ 3일간의 저녁 식사를 위한 식당 예약이 필요하다.
④ 매일 밤 100명 이상의 대표자를 위한 숙박시설이 필요하다.

해설

윗글에 따르면, 두 번째 단락 마지막 부분에 '3일 간의 점심식사를 위해 예약하고 싶다.'라고 명시되어 있으므로, 윗글의 내용과 일치하지 않는 것은 ③이다.

[오답 해설]
① 글의 두 번째 단락 2번째 문장에 명시되어 있다.
② 글의 두 번째 단락 2~3번째 문장에 명시되어 있다.
④ 글의 세 번째 단락 2번째 문장에 명시되어 있다.

해석

수신인: reserve@metropolitan.com
발신인: BruceTaylor@westcity.com
날짜: 2024년 6월 22일
제목: 행사 시설

친애하는 분께,

Metropolitan 컨퍼런스 센터에 대한 정보를 요청 드립니다.

우리는 올해 9월에 3일간의 컨퍼런스를 위한 장소를 찾고 있습니다. 주 회의실에 200명 이상의 대표자를 수용할 수 있어야 하며, 회의를 위한 3개의 작은 회의실도 필요합니다. 각 회의실에는 wi-fi가 필요합니다. 또한 오전과 오후에 커피를 제공해 주시기 바라며, 3일 간의 점심 식사를 위해 귀사의 레스토랑을 예약하고 싶습니다.

추가로, Metropolitan 고객 또는 대규모 단체를 위해 요금을 할인해 주는 지역 호텔이 있는지 알려주시기 바랍니다. 매일 밤 100명 이상의 대표자를 위한 숙박시설이 필요합니다.

답변을 기다리고 있겠습니다.

감사합니다.
Bruce Taylor, 행사 담당자

어휘

☐ venue 장소, 개최지
☐ delegate 대표(자), 위임하다
☐ discount 할인하다, 할인
☐ accommodation 숙박 시설, 협상

정답 ③

01 신 경향 유형 기출 독해 어휘 복습 TEST 정답

정답

1	valued	소중한, 존중되는, 평가된	21	regarding	~에 대하여, ~에 관하여
2	frequently	자주, 흔히	22	excessive	과도한, 지나친
3	up to date	최신의, 최근의, 현대식의	23	district	지역, 지방
4	suspicious	의심스러운, 수상쩍은	24	look into	~을 조사하다, ~을 들여다 보다, 주의 깊게 살피다
5	sensitive	민감한, 예민한, 세심한	25	matter	문제, 물질, 재료, 중요하다, 문제가 되다
6	authentication	인증, 입증, 증명	26	take steps	조치를 취하다
7	verify	확인하다, 입증하다	27	address	해결하다, 다루다, 처리하다, 주소를 쓰다, 연설하다
8	regularly	정기[규칙]적으로, 자주	28	prompt	신속한, 즉각적인, 자극하다, 촉구하다
9	agricultural	농업의, 농사의	29	tranquility	평온, 고요, 차분함
10	administer	운영하다, 관리하다	30	vibrant	활기찬, 생기가 넘치는, 강렬한, 선명한
11	domestic	국내의, 가정의	31	upcoming	곧 있을, 다가오는
12	international	국제적인	32	heritage	유산, 전승, 전통
13	fiber	섬유(질)	33	a variety of	다양한, 여러 가지의
14	wholesome	건강에 좋은, 건전한, 유익한	34	throughout	곳곳에, 도처에, ~동안, ~내내
15	facilitate	촉진하다, 가능[용이]하게 하다	35	feast	잔치, 연회, 축제일, 포식하다
16	competitive	경쟁력 있는, 뒤지지 않는	36	cuisine	요리, 요리법
17	integrity	진실성, 완전한 상태, 온전함	37	pay respect to	~에 경의를 표하다, ~를 존중하다
18	independence	독립(성), 자립(성)	38	dedicated	헌신적인, 전념하는
19	objectivity	객관성	39	affect	영향을 미치다, 발생하다
20	concern	관계하다, 관련되다, 걱정시키다, 염려[우려]하게 만들다, 일, 관계, 관심, 걱정, 우려	40	property	재산, 소유물, 부동산, 건물

01 신경향 유형 기출 독해 어휘 복습 TEST 정답

정답

41	sponsor	주최[주관]하다, 후원하다, 후원자	61	compensate	보상하다, 보상금을 주다
42	council	의회, 자문 위원회	62	purchase	구매[구입]하다, 구매, 구입
43	opposite	맞은편의, 다른 쪽의, 반대, 반의어	63	below	아래에, 밑에
44	in case of	~의 경우, ~에 대비해서	64	confirmation	확인, 확증, 증거
45	customs	세관, 관세	65	be sure to	반드시 ~하다
46	declaration	신고, 선언, 발표, 공표	66	separate	각각의, 별개의, 분리된, 분리되다, 나누다
47	arrival	도착, 도래, 도입	67	admission	입장, 입학, 시인, 인정
48	in advance	미리, 전부터	68	on-site	현장의, 현지의
49	enable	~을 할 수 있게 하다, 가능하게 하다	69	charge	비용, 요금, 고발, 비난, 청구하다, 고소하다, 비난하다
50	ongoing	계속 진행 중인	70	exposition	전시회
51	introduce	도입하다, 소개하다, 시작하다	71	admission	입장료
52	comfortable	편안한, 쾌적한	72	first-come, first-served	선착순
53	principal	주된, 주요한, 학장, 총장	73	venue	개최지, 장소
54	regulatory	규제의, 통제의, 단속의	74	in advance	미리, 사전에
55	minimum	최저의, 최소한의	75	guarantee	보장하다, 보증하다
56	wage	임금, 급료	76	organizer	주최자
57	employee	종업원	77	capacity	수용 능력, 용적량
58	minor	미성년자, 부전공, 작은, 가벼운	78	delegate	대표(자), 위임하다
59	employer	고용주	79	discount	할인하다, 할인
60	enforcement	집행, 시행, 실시	80	accommodation	숙박 시설, 협상

chapter 02

중심 내용 파악 유형 정답 및 해설

ANSWER

01 ④	02 ②	03 ④	04 ①	05 ④
06 ①	07 ③	08 ③	09 ③	10 ①
11 ②	12 ②	13 ②	14 ④	15 ②
16 ③	17 ①	18 ③	19 ①	20 ④
21 ①	22 ②	23 ③	24 ④	25 ④
26 ①	27 ③	28 ②	29 ①	30 ③
31 ③	32 ④	33 ①	34 ④	35 ③
36 ③	37 ②			

01 다음 글의 주제로 가장 적절한 것은?

2025. 출제 기조 전환 2차

The International Space Station, orbiting some 240 miles above the planet, is about to join the effort to monitor the world's wildlife — and to revolutionize the science of animal tracking. A large antenna and other equipment aboard the orbiting outpost, installed by spacewalking Russian astronauts in 2018, are being tested and will become fully operational this summer. The system will relay a much wider range of data than previous tracking technologies, logging not just an animal's location but also its physiology and environment. This will assist scientists, conservationists and others whose work requires close monitoring of wildlife on the move and provide much more detailed information on the health of the world's ecosystems.

① evaluation of sustainability of global ecosystems
② successful training projects of Russian astronauts
③ animal experiments conducted in the orbiting outpost
④ innovative wildlife monitoring from the space station

해설

우주 정거장에서의 혁신적인 야생 동물 모니터링에 대한 글로, 국제 우주 정거장이 새로운 장비를 통해 야생 동물 모니터링을 혁신하고, 동물의 위치와 생리학적 데이터, 환경 정보를 수집하여 생태계 건강을 분석함을 설명하고 있다. 따라서 글의 주제로 가장 적절한 것은 ④이다.

해석

국제 우주 정거장이 지구에서 약 240마일 상공을 돌며 세계의 야생 동물을 모니터링하고 동물 추적 과학에 혁신을 일으킬 준비를 하고 있다. 2018년 우주 유영을 한 러시아 우주인들이 설치한 대형 안테나와 기타 장비가 테스트 중이며, 올 여름에는 완전히 운영될 예정이다. 이 시스템은 이전 추적 기술보다 훨씬 넓은 범위의 데이터를 전달하며, 동물의 위치뿐만 아니라 생리학과 환경까지 기록할 수 있다. 이는 야생 동물의 이동을 밀접하게 모니터링을 해야 하는 과학자, 환경 보호 활동가 및 기타 연구자들에게 도움을 주며, 세계 생태계의 건강에 대한 보다 자세한 정보를 제공할 것이다.

① 지구 생태계의 지속 가능성 평가
② 러시아 우주비행사들의 성공적인 훈련 프로젝트
③ 궤도 전초기지에서 행해진 동물 실험
④ 우주 정거장에서 혁신적인 야생 동물 모니터링

어휘

□ space station 우주 정거장
□ orbit 궤도를 돌다, 궤도, 영향권
□ revolutionize 혁신을 일으키다
□ install 설치하다, 설비하다
□ spacewalk 우주 유영
□ relay 전달하다, 중계하다
□ previous 이전의, 바로 앞의
□ physiology 생리학
□ conservationist 환경 보호 활동가

정답 ④

02 다음 글의 요지로 가장 적절한 것은?

2025. 출제 기조 전환 2차

Animal Health Emergencies

Preparedness for animal disease outbreaks has been a top priority for the Board of Animal Health (BOAH) for decades. A highly contagious animal disease event may have economically devastating effects as well as public health or food safety and security consequences.

Foreign Animal Diseases

A foreign animal disease (FAD) is a disease that is not currently found in the country, and could cause significant illness or death in animals or cause extensive economic harm by eliminating trading opportunities with other countries and states.

Several BOAH veterinarians who are trained in diagnosing FADs are available 24 hours a day to investigate suspected cases of a FAD. An investigation is triggered when report of animals with clinical signs indicative of a FAD is received or when diagnostic laboratory identifies a suspicious test result.

① BOAH focuses on training veterinarians for FADs.
② BOAH's main goal is to repsond to animal disease epidemic.
③ BOAH actively promotes international trade opportunities.
④ BOAH aims to lead laboratory research on the causes of FADs.

해설

글의 주된 내용은 동물 질병 발생에 대한 준비와 대응의 중요성을 강조하고 있다. BOAH는 동물 질병 발생에 대비하는 것을 최우선 과제로 삼고 있으며, 이는 동물 질병 전염이 경제적 피해와 공공 건강에 미치는 영향을 고려한 것이다. 따라서 글의 요지로 가장 적절한 것은 ②이다.

해석

동물 건강 비상 사태

동물 질병 발생에 대한 준비는 수십 년 동안 동물 건강 위원회(BOAH)의 최우선 과제가 되어 왔습니다. 전염성이 매우 높은 동물 질병 사건은 공중 보건이나 식품 안전 및 보안 결과뿐만 아니라 경제적으로 파괴적인 영향을 미칠 수 있습니다.

외국 동물 질병

외국 동물 질병(FAD)은 현재 해당 국가에서 발견되지 않는 질병으로, 동물에게 심각한 질병이나 사망을 초래할 수 있으며, 다른 국가 및 주와의 무역 기회를 없애 경제적으로 큰 피해를 줄 수 있습니다.

FAD 진단 교육을 받은 여러 BOAH 수의사들이 24시간 대기 중이며, FAD 의심 사례를 조사합니다. 조사는 FAD를 나타내는 임상 징후가 있는 동물에 대한 보고가 접수되거나 진단 실험실에서 의심스러운 검사 결과를 확인할 때 시작됩니다.

① BOAH는 FAD를 위한 수의사 교육에 중점을 둔다.
② BOAH의 주요 목표는 동물 질병 전염에 대응하는 것이다.
③ BOAH는 국제 무역 기회를 적극적으로 추진한다.
④ BOAH는 FAD의 원인에 대한 연구를 주도하는 것을 목표로 한다.

어휘

□ preparedness 준비, 각오
□ outbreak 발생, 발발
□ top priority 최우선(과제)
□ contagious 전염되는, 전염성의
□ devastating 파괴적인, 충격적인
□ consequence 결과, 중요함
□ currently 현재, 지금
□ extensive 아주 넓은, 대규모의, 광범위한
□ eliminate 없애다, 제거하다
□ veterinarian 수의사
□ diagnose 진단하다
□ investigate 조사하다, 수사하다
□ clinical 임상의
□ indicative ~을 나타내는[보여주는], 직설법의

정답 ②

03 다음 글의 주제로 가장 적절한 것은?

2025. 출제 기조 전환 1차

The Ministry of Food and Drug Safety warned that cases of food poisoning have occurred as a result of cross-contamination, where people touch eggs and neglect to wash their hands before preparing food or using utensils. To mitigate such risks, the ministry advised refrigerating eggs and ensuring they are thoroughly cooked until both the yolk and white are firm. Over the past five years, a staggering 7,400 people experienced food poisoning caused by Salmonella bacteria. Salmonella thrives in warm temperatures, with approximately 37 degrees Celsius being the optimal growth condition. Consuming raw or undercooked eggs and failing to separate raw and cooked foods were identified as the most common causes of Salmonella infection. It is crucial to prioritize food safety measures and adhere to proper cooking practices to minimize the risk of Salmonella-related illnesses.

① Benefits of consuming eggs to the immune system
② Different types of treatments for Salmonella infection
③ Life span of Salmonella bacteria in warm temperatures
④ Safe handling of eggs for the prevention of Salmonella infection

해설

살모넬라에 의한 식중독의 예방을 위한 글로, 식약처는 식중독 증가 사례를 경고하며, 계란을 만질 때 손을 씻지 않아 음식이나 도구를 준비할 때 식품 중독이 발생할 수 있다고 경고했다. 특히, 살모넬라 박테리아에 의한 식중독이 증가하고 있으며, 식품 안전을 위해 계란을 냉장하고 완전히 익혀야 함을 강조하고 있다. 따라서 글의 주제로 적절한 것은 ④이다.

해석

식품의약품안전처는 음식을 준비하거나 도구를 사용하기 전에 사람들이 달걀을 만지고 손을 씻는 것에 소홀하는 교차 오염의 결과로 식중독 사례가 발생했다고 경고했다. 이러한 위험을 완화시키기 위해 식약처는 달걀을 냉장 보관하고 노른자와 흰자가 모두 단단해질 때까지 그것들을 완전히 익힐 것을 권고했다. 지난 5년간, 놀랍게도 7,400명의 사람들이 살모넬라균에 의해 야기된 식중독을 경험했다. 살모넬라균은 따뜻한 온도에서 번성하며, 대략 섭씨 37도가 최적의 성장 조건이다. 날달걀 또는 설익은 달걀을 먹고 날음식과 익힌 음식을 분리하지 못하는 것이 살모넬라균 감염의 가장 흔한 원인으로 확인되었다. 살모넬라균과 관련된 질병의 위험을 최소화하기 위해 식품 안전 조치를 우선시하고 적절한 조리 관행을 지키는 것이 중요하다.

① 면역 체계에 계란 섭취가 미치는 이점들
② 살모넬라 감염에 대한 다양한 치료법들
③ 따뜻한 온도에서 살모넬라 박테리아의 수명
④ 살모넬라 감염 예방을 위한 계란의 안전한 취급 방법

어휘

- □ ministry (정부의 각) 부처, 목사, 성직자
- □ food poisoning 식중독
- □ utensil 도구, 기구, 가정용품
- □ advise 권고하다, 충고하다, 조언하다
- □ yolk (달걀 등의) 노른자(위)
- □ firm 단단한, 확고한, 회사
- □ staggering 놀랍게도, 충격적인, 믿기 어려운, 비틀거리는
- □ thrive 번성하다, 번영하다, 성장하다, 잘 자라다
- □ temperature 온도, 기온, 체온
- □ degree (온도 단위인) 도, 정도, 학위, 등급
- □ optimal 최적의, 최선의
- □ raw 날것의, 익히지 않은, 가공되지 않은
- □ undercooked (음식이) 설익은
- □ common 흔한, 공동의, 공통의
- □ infection 감염, 전염병
- □ prioritize 우선시하다, 우선순위를 매기다, 우선적으로 처리하다
- □ adhere to 지키다, ~을 고수하다
- □ minimize 최소화하다, 축소하다
- □ illness 질병, 질환, 아픔

정답 ④

04 다음 글의 요지로 가장 적절한 것은?

2025. 출제 기조 전환 1차

Despite ongoing efforts to address educational disparities, the persistent achievement gap among students continues to highlight significant inequities in the education system. Recent data reveal that marginalized students, including those from low-income back grounds and vulnerable groups, continue to lag behind their peers in academic performance. The gap poses a challenge to achieving educational equity and social mobility. Experts emphasize the need for targeted interventions, equitable resource allocation, and inclusive policies to bridge this gap and ensure equal opportunities for all students, irrespective of their socioeconomic status or background. The issue of continued educational divide should be addressed at all levels of education system in an effort to find a solution.

① We should deal with persistent educational inequities.
② Educational experts need to focus on new school policies.
③ New teaching methods are necessary to bridge the achievement gap.
④ Family income should not be considered in the discussion of education.

해설

교육격차 해소를 위한 노력과 과제에 대한 글로, 전문가들이 격차를 줄이기 위해 효과적인 개입, 공정한 자원 할당, 포용적인 정책이 필요하고 강조하고 있다. 따라서 글의 요지로 적절한 것은 ①이다.

해석

교육 격차를 해결하기 위한 지속적인 노력에도 불구하고, 학생들 간의 끊임없이 지속되는 성취 격차는 교육 체제의 상당한 불평등을 계속해서 강조하고 있다. 최근 자료들은 저소득층 배경과 취약 계층을 포함한 소외된 학생들이 학업 성적에서 동료들보다 계속 뒤처지고 있음을 보여준다. 격차는 교육 형평성과 사회 이동성을 달성하는 데 어려움을 제기한다. 전문가들은 이러한 격차를 해소하고 사회경제적 지위나 배경에 관계없이 모든 학생들에게 균등한 기회를 보장하기 위해 표적적 개입, 공평한 자원 배분, 포용적 정책의 필요성을 강조한다. 지속적인 교육 격차의 문제는 교육 체제의 모든 수준에서 해결책을 찾기 위한 노력으로 해결되어야 한다.

① 우리는 지속적인 교육 불평등을 해결해야 한다.
② 교육 전문가들은 새로운 학교 정책에 초점을 맞출 필요가 있다.
③ 성취 격차를 해소하기 위해 새로운 교수 방법이 필요하다.
④ 교육 논의에서 가정 소득은 고려되지 않아야 한다.

어휘

□ despite ~에도 불구하고
□ ongoing 지속적인, 계속 진행 중인
□ disparity 격차, 차이
□ persistent 끊임없이 지속되는, 끈질긴, 집요한
□ highlight 강조하다, 돋보이게 하다
□ inequity 불공평, 불공정
□ reveal 드러내다, 나타내다, 밝히다
□ marginalize ~을 소외되게 하다, 사회적으로 무시하다
□ low-income 저소득의
□ background 배경, 배후 사정
□ vulnerable 취약한, 연약한
□ lag behind ~보다 뒤(처)지다, 뒤떨어지다
□ pose 제기하다, 두다, 놓다, 자세[태도]를 취하다, ~인 체하다
□ challenge 어려움, 도전, 이의를 제기하다
□ mobility 이동성, 기동성, 유동성
□ emphasize 강조하다
□ intervention 개입, 간섭
□ equitable 공평한, 공정한
□ allocation 배분, 할당
□ inclusive 포용적인, 포괄적인, 포함된
□ bridge the gap 격차를 해소하다
□ status 지위, 신분, 자격
□ address 해결하다, 다루다, 연설하다, 주소, 연설

정답 ①

05 다음 글의 주제로 적절한 것은? 2024. 국가직 9급

It seems incredible that one man could be responsible for opening our eyes to an entire culture, but until British archaeologist Arthur Evans successfully excavated the ruins of the palace of Knossos on the island of Crete, the great Minoan culture of the Mediterranean was more legend than fact. Indeed its most famed resident was a creature of mythology: the half-man, half-bull Minotaur, said to have lived under the palace of mythical King Minos. But as Evans proved, this realm was no myth. In a series of excavations in the early years of the 20th century, Evans found a trove of artifacts from the Minoan age, which reached its height from 1900 to 1450 B.C.: jewelry, carvings, pottery, altars shaped like bull's horns, and wall paintings showing Minoan life.

① King Minos' successful excavations
② Appreciating artifacts from the Minoan age
③ Magnificence of the palace on the island of Crete
④ Bringing the Minoan culture to the realm of reality

해설

Arthur Evans는 크레타 섬의 크노소스 궁전 발굴을 통해 미노아 문화를 실제로 확인했다는 것을 설명하는 글로, 이 글이 강조하는 것은 이것은 신화적 이야기가 아닌 실제 유물과 벽화를 통해 기원전 1900년부터 1450년까지의 미노아 문명이였다는 것이다. 따라서 글의 주제로 가장 적절한 것은 ④이다.

해석

한 사람이 하나의 전체 문화에 우리의 눈을 뜨게 하는 데 책임을 질 수 있다는 것은 믿기 힘든 것 같지만, 영국의 고고학자 Arthur Evans가 크레타섬에 있는 크노소스 궁전의 유적을 성공적으로 발굴하기 전까지 지중해의 위대한 미노스 문화는 사실보다 더 전설에 가까웠다. 실제로 그곳의 가장 유명한 거주자는 신화의 한 생명체였는데, 반인반우 미노타우로스였고, 신화 속에 나오는 미노스 왕의 궁전 아래에서 살았다고 전해진다. 그러나 Evans가 증명했듯이 이 왕국은 신화가 아니었다. 20세기 초의 일련의 발굴에서 Evans는

> 보석류, 조각품, 도자기, 황소의 뿔 모양을 한 제단, 그리고 미노아의 삶을 보여주는 벽화 등 기원전 1900년부터 1450년까지 절정에 달했던 미노스 시대의 귀중한 인공물을 발견했다.

① 미노스 왕의 성공적인 발굴
② 미노아 시대의 유물을 감상하기
③ 크레타섬에 있는 궁전의 웅장함
④ 미노아 문화를 현실의 영역으로 가져오기

어휘

- ☐incredible 믿기 어려운, 놀라운
- ☐excavate 발굴하다
- ☐famed 유명한, 명성이 있는
- ☐resident 거주자
- ☐mythology 신화학, 신화
- ☐excavation 발굴 작업, 발굴 지역
- ☐jewelry 보석류
- ☐carving 조각품, 새긴 무늬
- ☐pottery 도기, 도자기
- ☐altar 제단

정답 ④

06 다음 글의 제목으로 적절한 것은? 2024. 국가직 9급

> Currency debasement of a good money by a bad money version occurred via coins of a high percentage of precious metal, reissued at lower percentages of gold or silver diluted with a lower value metal. This adulteration drove out the good coin for the bad coin. No one spent the good coin, they kept it, hence the good coin was driven out of circulation and into a hoard. Meanwhile the issuer, normally a king who had lost his treasure on interminable warfare and other such dissolute living, was behind the move. They collected all the good old coins they could, melted them down and reissued them at lower purity and pocketed the balance. It was often illegal to keep the old stuff back but people did, while the king replenished his treasury, at least for a time.

① How Bad Money Replaces Good
② Elements of Good Coins
③ Why Not Melt Coins?
④ What Is Bad Money?

해설

나쁜 화폐의 높은 비율의 귀금속 동전으로 인해 좋은 화폐의 품위가 저하되었다. 좋은 동전은 퇴출되고 나쁜 동전이 유통되며, 왕들은 재발행으로 자금을 보충했음을 설명하는 글이다. 따라서 글의 제목으로 가장 적절한 것은 ①이다.

해석

> 나쁜 화폐 형태에 의한 좋은 화폐의 통화 가치 저하는 더 낮은 가치의 금속으로 희석된 더 낮은 비율의 금이나 은으로 재발행된 귀금속의 비율이 높은 동전을 통해 발생했다. 이러한 품질의 조악화는 나쁜 동전으로 좋은 동전을 몰아냈다. 아무도 그들이 보유하고 있던 좋은 동전을 쓰지 않았고 이런 이유로 좋은 동전이 유통에서 사라지게 되었고 비축되었다. 한편, 보통 끊이지 않는 전쟁과 그 밖의 방탕한 생활로 보물을 잃은 왕이었던 발행인이 이러한 조치의 배후였다. 그들은 할 수 있는 모든 좋은 옛 동전을 모아 녹여서 낮은 순도로 재발행하고, 차액을 착복했다. 옛 물건을 다시 보관하는 것은 종종 불법이었지만, 왕이 국고를 보충하는 동안, 적어도 한동안은 사람들은 그렇게 했다.

① 나쁜 화폐가 좋은 화폐를 대체하는 방법
② 좋은 동전의 요소들
③ 왜 동전을 녹이지 말아야 하는가?
④ 나쁜 화폐란 무엇인가?

어휘

- ☐currency debasement 통화 훼손, 화폐 가치 하락
- ☐occur 발생하다, 일어나다
- ☐precious 귀중한, 소중한
- ☐dilute 희석하다, 약화시키다
- ☐adulteration 불순물 첨가, 오염
- ☐out of circulation 순환에서 제외된, 유통에서 제외된
- ☐hoard 비축하다, 저장하다
- ☐treasure 보물, 귀중품
- ☐dissolute 방탕한, 타락한
- ☐melt 녹다, 용해되다
- ☐illegal 불법적인, 불법의
- ☐replenish 보충하다, 채우다
- ☐treasury 국고, 재무부
- ☐at least 최소한, 적어도

정답 ①

07 다음 글의 주제로 적절한 것은? 2024. 지방직 9급

In recent years Latin America has made huge strides in exploiting its incredible wind, solar, geothermal and biofuel energy resources. Latin America's electricity sector has already begun to gradually decrease its dependence on oil. Latin America is expected to almost double its electricity output between 2015 and 2040. Practically none of Latin America's new large-scale power plants will be oil-fueled, which opens up the field for different technologies. Countries in Central America and the Caribbean, which traditionally imported oil, were the first to move away from oil-based power plants, after suffering a decade of high and volatile prices at the start of the century.

① booming oil industry in Latin America
② declining electricity business in Latin America
③ advancement of renewable energy in Latin America
④ aggressive exploitation of oil-based resources in Latin America

해설

라틴 아메리카의 재생 에너지 확대와 그에 따른 석유 의존도 감소에 대한 글이다. 첫 번째 문장에서의 라틴아메리카의 재생 가능한 에너지의 큰 발전에 대한 진술을 바탕으로 석유 의존도가 감소함의 구체적인 사례를 들고 있다. 따라서 글의 주제로 적절한 것은 ③이다.

해석

최근 몇 년 동안 라틴 아메리카는 풍력, 태양력, 지열 및 바이오연료 등 놀라운 재생 에너지 자원을 적극적으로 활용하는 데 큰 진전을 이루었다. 라틴 아메리카의 전력 부문은 이미 석유에 대한 의존도를 점차적으로 줄이기 시작했다. 2015년에서 2040년 사이에 라틴 아메리카의 전력 생산량은 거의 두 배로 늘어날 것으로 예상된다. 라틴 아메리카의 새로운 대규모 발전소 중 사실상 석유를 연료로 사용하는 곳은 없어질 것이며, 이는 다양한 기술의 발전을 가져올 것이다. 전통적으로 석유를 수입해 왔던 중앙아메리카와 카리브해 국가들이 이 세기 초반 10년 동안 높고 불안정한 가격에 시달리다가 가장 먼저 석유 기반 발전소에서 벗어나기 시작했다.

① 라틴 아메리카의 호황을 누리는 석유 산업
② 라틴 아메리카의 쇠퇴하는 전력 사업
③ 라틴 아메리카의 재생 가능 에너지 발전
④ 라틴 아메리카의 석유 기반 자원의 공격적인 개발

어휘

- □ stride 큰 발전, 큰 걸음, 성큼성큼 걷다
- □ exploit 이용하다, 착취하다
- □ geothermal 지열의
- □ biofuel 바이오 연료
- □ large-scale 대규모의, 광범한
- □ import 수입하다, 수입(품)
- □ volatile 변동성이 큰, 불안한, 휘발성의

정답 ③

08 다음 글의 제목으로 적절한 것은? 2024. 지방직 9급

Every organization has resources that it can use to perform its mission. How well your organization does its job is partly a function of how many of those resources you have, but mostly it is a function of how well you use the resources you have, such as people and money. You as the organization's leader can always make the use of those resources more efficient and effective, provided that you have control of the organization's personnel and agenda, a condition that does not occur automatically. By managing your people and your money carefully, by treating the most important things as the most important, by making good decisions, and by solving the problems that you encounter, you can get the most out of what you have available to you.

① Exchanging Resources in an Organization
② Leaders' Ability to Set up External Control
③ Making the Most of the Resources: A Leader's Way
④ Technical Capacity of an Organization: A Barrier to Its Success

해설

조직 리더로서 자원 관리의 중요성을 강조하는 글로, 두 번째 그리고 세 번째 문장에서 '조직의 리더로서 그러한 자원의 사용을 더 효율적 그리고 효과적으로 만들어야 한다'고 진술하고 있다. 따라서 글의 제목으로 적절한 것은 ③이다.

해석

모든 조직은 자신의 목표를 달성하기 위해 사용할 수 있는 자원을 가지고 있다. 당신의 조직이 얼마나 잘 수행하는지는 부분적으로 보유한 자원의 양에 달려있지만, 대부분은 사람과 돈과 같은 자원을

얼마나 잘 활용하는지에 달려있다. 당신이 조직의 리더로서 조직의 인력과 의제를 통제할 수 있다면, 언제든 그 자원의 활용을 더 효율적이고 효과적으로 만들 수 있다. 이는 자동적으로 일어나는 것은 아니다. 사람과 자금을 신중하게 관리하고, 가장 중요한 것을 가장 중요한 것으로 여기며, 좋은 결정을 내리고, 마주하는 문제를 해결함으로써, 당신이 가진 것을 최대한 활용할 수 있다.

① 조직 내 자원 교환하기
② 외부 통제를 설정하는 리더의 능력
③ 자원을 최대한 활용하기: 리더의 방식
④ 조직의 기술적 역량: 성공의 장애물

어휘

☐ organization 조직, 단체, 준비, 구성
☐ function 기능, 행사, 기능하다
☐ efficient 효율적인, 능률적인, 유능한
☐ effective 효과적인, 실질적인
☐ control 통제, 지배, 지배하다, 제한하다
☐ personnel 인원, 직원들, 인사과
☐ agenda 의제, 안건
☐ encounter 만나다, 직면하다
☐ available 이용할[구할] 수 있는

정답 ③

09 다음 글의 제목으로 알맞은 것은? 2023. 국가직 9급

The feeling of being loved and the biological response it stimulates is triggered by nonverbal cues: the tone in a voice, the expression on a face, or the touch that feels just right. Nonverbal cues — rather than spoken words — make us feel that the person we are with is interested in, understands, and values us. When we're with them, we feel safe. We even see the power of nonverbal cues in the wild. After evading the chase of predators, animals often nuzzle each other as a means of stress relief. This bodily contact provides reassurance of safety and relieves stress.

① How Do Wild Animals Think and Feel?
② Communicating Effectively Is the Secret to Success
③ Nonverbal Communication Speaks Louder than Words
④ Verbal Cues: The Primary Tools for Expressing Feelings

해설

사랑과 안전감을 만드는 비언어적인 신호의 힘을 주제로 하는 글로, 비언어적인 신호는 우리에게 사랑받는 느낌을 줄 뿐 아니라 안전하고 스트레스를 완화하는 효과가 있다는 것을 강조하는 글이다. 첫 번째 문장이 이 글의 주제문으로 '사랑받는 느낌과 그것이 유발하는 생물학적 반응은 언어적인 요소가 아닌 비언어적인 신호에 의해 유발된다'고 진술한 다음 동물에서의 구체적인 예를 들어 설명하고 있다. 따라서 글의 제목으로 가장 알맞은 것은 ③이다.

해석

사랑받는 느낌과 그것이 자극하는 생물학적 반응은 목소리의 톤, 얼굴 표정, 적절한 감촉 같은 비언어적인 신호에 의해 유발된다. 비언어적인 신호는 발화되는 말보다 우리가 함께 있는 사람이 우리에게 관심이 있고, 우리를 이해하며 소중하게 여기고 있다고 느끼게 해준다. 우리가 그들과 함께 있을 때, 우리는 안전하다고 느낀다. 우리는 심지어 야생에서 비언어적인 신호의 힘을 본다. 포식자들의 추적을 피한 후에, 동물들은 종종 스트레스 해소의 수단으로 서로 코를 비빈다. 이러한 신체 접촉은 안전에 대한 확신을 제공하고 스트레스를 완화한다.

① 야생 동물은 어떻게 생각하고 느끼는가?
② 효과적인 의사소통이 성공의 비결이다
③ 비언어적인 의사소통은 말보다 더 크게 말한다
④ 언어적인 신호: 감정을 표현하는 주요 수단

어휘

☐ biological 생물학의
☐ trigger 촉발시키다, 일으키다, 방아쇠
☐ nonverbal 비언어적인
☐ evade 피하다, 회피하다
☐ chase 뒤쫓다, 추적하다
☐ predator 포식자
☐ nuzzle 코를 비벼대다, 코로 구멍을 파다
☐ means 수단, 방법, 수입
☐ reassurance 안심, 안도, 확신
☐ relieve 완화하다, 줄이다

정답 ③

10 다음 글의 주제로 알맞은 것은? 2023. 국가직 9급

There are times, like holidays and birthdays, when toys and gifts accumulate in a child's life. You can use these times to teach a healthy nondependency on things. Don't surround your child with toys. Instead, arrange them in baskets, have one basket out at a time, and rotate baskets occasionally. If a cherished object is put away for a time, bringing it out creates a delightful remembering and freshness of outlook. Suppose your child asks for a toy that has been put away for a while. You can direct attention toward an object or experience that is already in the environment. If you lose or break a possession, try to model a good attitude ("I appreciated it while I had it!") so that your child can begin to develop an attitude of nonattachment. If a toy of hers is broken or lost, help her to say, "I had fun with that."

① building a healthy attitude toward possessions
② learning the value of sharing toys with others
③ teaching how to arrange toys in an orderly manner
④ accepting responsibility for behaving in undesirable ways

해설

장난감을 통해 아이에게 건강한 비의존성을 가르치는 방법을 주제로 하는 글로, 장난감과 선물이 많이 모일 때, 건강한 비의존성을 가르치기 위해 아이를 장난감으로 둘러싸지 않고, 바구니에 정리하고, 회전시키며, 애착 없는 태도를 모델로 삼도록 하라는 제안을 하는 글이다. 특히 2번째 문장의 '당신은 이 시간들을 사물에 대한 건강한 비의존성을 가르치기 위해 사용할 수 있다'의 내용을 바탕으로 글의 주제로 가장 알맞은 것은 ①이다.

해석

명절이나 생일처럼 아이의 삶에서 장난감과 선물이 모이는 시기가 있다. 당신은 이러한 시기들을 물건에 대한 건강한 비의존성을 가르치는 데 사용할 수 있다. 당신의 아이를 장난감들로 둘러싸지 마라. 대신에, 그것들을 바구니에 정리하고, 한 번에 한 바구니씩 꺼내 놓고, 가끔 바구니를 교체해라. 소중히 간직한 물건을 잠시 치워두면, 그것을 꺼내는 것이 즐거운 기억과 관점의 새로움을 만든다. 당신의 아이가 잠시 치워둔 장난감을 요구한다고 가정해 보자. 당신은 이미 주변 환경에 있는 물건 혹은 경험으로 주의를 돌릴 수 있다. 만약 당신이 소유물을 잃어버리거나 깨뜨린다면, 당신의 아이가 애착이 없는 태도를 발달시키기 시작할 수 있도록 좋은 태도("나는 그것을 가지고 있는 동안 감사했어!")를 만들도록 노력해라. 만약 그녀의 장난감이 망가지거나 잃어버린다면, "나는 그것으로 즐거운 시간을 보냈어."라고 말할 수 있도록 도와줘라.

① 소유물에 대한 건강한 태도를 형성하는 것
② 다른 사람들과 장난감을 공유하는 것의 가치를 배우는 것
③ 장난감을 질서정연하게 정리하는 방법을 가르치는 것
④ 좋지 않은 방식으로 행동한 책임을 받아들이는 것

어휘

□ accumulate 모으다, 축적하다
□ nondependency 비의존성
□ surround 둘러싸다, 에워싸다
□ rotate 회전시키다
□ cherish 소중히 여기다, 아끼다, 간직하다
□ put away 넣다, 치우다
□ delightful 즐거운, 매우 기쁜
□ freshness 새로움, 신선함
□ outlook 관점, 전망, 시야
□ possession 소유물, 소지품
□ nonattachment 비애착
□ direct ~로 돌리다, 향하다, 겨냥하다
□ broken 깨진, 부서진, 고장난

정답 ①

11 다음 글의 요지로 알맞은 것은? 2023. 국가직 9급

Many parents have been misguided by the "self-esteem movement," which has told them that the way to build their children's self-esteem is to tell them how good they are at things. Unfortunately, trying to convince your children of their competence will likely fail because life has a way of telling them unequivocally how capable or incapable they really are through success and failure. Research has shown that how you praise your children has a powerful influence on their development. Some researchers found that children who were praised for their intelligence, as compared to their effort, became overly focused on results. Following a failure, these same children persisted less, showed less enjoyment, attributed their failure to a lack of ability, and performed poorly in future achievement efforts. Praising children for intelligence made them fear difficulty because they began to equate failure with stupidity.

① Frequent praises increase self-esteem of children.
② Compliments on intelligence bring about negative effect.
③ A child should overcome fear of failure through success.
④ Parents should focus on the outcome rather than the process.

해설

자녀 칭찬 방법이 자녀들의 발달에 영향을 미치는 중요성을 주제로 하는 글로, 부모들이 자녀의 자존감을 높이기 위해 자녀의 지능을 칭찬하는 것은 자녀들이 실패했을 때 능력 부족의 탓으로 보고 미래의 성취노력에서 성과가 좋지 않음을 지적하고 있다. 따라서 글의 요지로 가장 알맞은 것은 '자녀의 칭찬하는 방법'의 핵심어가 있고, '지능에 대한 칭찬의 부정적인 진술'이 있는 ②이다.

해석

많은 부모들은 "자존감 운동"에 의해 잘못 인도되었는데, 이 운동은 그들의 아이들의 자존감을 높이는 방법이 자녀들에게 그들이 일을 얼마나 잘 하는지 알려주는 것이라고 말해왔다. 불행하게도, 자녀에게 그들의 능력에 대해 확신시키려는 시도는 실패할 가능성이 높은데, 왜냐하면 인생은 성공과 실패를 통해 그들이 실제로 얼마나 능력이 있고 능력이 없는지를 분명하게 말해주기 때문이다. 연구는 자녀를 어떻게 칭찬하는지가 자녀의 발달에 강력한 영향을 미친다는 것을 보여준다. 몇몇 연구원들은 그들의 노력에 비해 그들의 지능으로 칭찬받은 아이들이 결과에 지나치게 집중하게 되었다는 것을 발견했다. 실패 후에 이러한 아이들은 덜 지속했고, 적은 즐거움을 보여주며, 실패를 능력 부족의 탓으로 여기고, 미래의 성취 노력에서도 저조한 성과를 보였다. 아이들의 지능을 칭찬하는 것은 그들이 실패를 어리석음과 동일시하기 시작했기 때문에 어려움을 두려워하게 만들었다.

① 빈번한 칭찬이 아이들의 자존감을 높인다.
② 지능에 대한 칭찬은 부정적인 효과를 초래한다.
③ 아이는 성공을 통해 실패에 대한 두려움을 극복해야 한다.
④ 부모는 과정보다 결과에 집중해야 한다.

어휘

□ misguide 잘못 이끌다, 그릇되게 지도하다, 잘못 인식시키다
□ self-esteem 자부심, 자존감
□ movement 움직임, 행동
□ competence 능력, 능숙함
□ fail 실패하다
□ unequivocally 명백하게, 분명하게
□ influence 영향
□ development 발달
□ praise 칭찬, 칭찬하다
□ intelligence 지능
□ focused 집중한, 집중적인
□ persist 지속하다, 집요하게[끈질기게] 계속하다
□ attribute ~의 탓으로 보다, 속성, 특성, 특질
□ equate 동일시하다
□ stupidity 어리석음, 우둔함

정답 ②

12 다음 글의 제목으로 가장 적절한 것은? 2023. 지방직 9급

Well-known author Daniel Goleman has dedicated his life to the science of human relationships. In his book *Social Intelligence* he discusses results from neuro-sociology to explain how sociable our brains are. According to Goleman, we are drawn to other people's brains whenever we engage with another person. The human need for meaningful connectivity with others, in order to deepen out relationships, is what we all crave, and yet there are countless articles and studies suggesting that we are lonelier than we ever have been and loneliness is now a world health epidemic. Specifically, in Australia, according to a national Lifeline survey, more than 80% of those surveyed believe our society is becoming a lonelier place. Yet, our brains crave human interaction.

① Lonely People
② Sociable Brains
③ Need for Mental Health Survey
④ Dangers of Human Connectivity

해설

인간의 뇌의 사교적인 기능을 주제로 하는 글로, Daniel Goleman의 연구결과를 인용하면서 자신의 주장을 펼치고 있다. 우리의 뇌는 상대방과의 관계에 끌리며, 의미 있는 연결성이 필요하지만 우리는 점점 외로움을 느끼고 외로워지고 있다고 믿는다고 말한다. 그럼에도 불구하고 우리의 뇌는 인간과의 상호작용을 갈망한다고 진술하고 있다. 따라서 글의 제목으로 가장 적절한 것은 ②이다.

해석

유명한 작가인 Daniel Goleman은 인간관계의 과학에 평생을 바쳐왔다. 그의 책 '사회적 지능'에서는 우리의 뇌가 얼마나 사교적인지 설명하기 위해 신경 사회학의 결과들을 논한다. Goleman에 따르면, 우리는 다른 사람과 관계를 맺을 때마다 다른 사람의 뇌에 끌린다. 우리의 관계를 깊게 하기 위해 다른 사람들과 의미 있는 연결성을 가지고자 하는 인간의 욕구는 우리가 갈망하는 것이지만 우리가 어느 때보다 더 외롭고, 외로움은 전 세계적인 건강 유행병이라

는 것을 시사하는 수많은 기사와 연구들이 있다. 특히 호주에서 실시된 국립 Lifeline 조사에 따르면 조사대상자들의 80% 이상이 우리 사회가 더 외로운 곳이 되어가고 있다고 믿고 있다. 하지만 우리의 뇌는 인간과의 상호 작용을 갈망한다.

① 외로운 사람들
② 사교적인 두뇌
③ 정신 건강 조사의 필요성
④ 인간과의 연결성의 위험성

어휘

□well-known 유명한, 잘 알려진
□author 작가
□dedicate 바치다, 전념하다
□discuss 논의하다, 상의하다
□neuro-sociology 신경 사회학
□sociable 사교적인, 붙임성 있는
□engage 관여하다
□connectivity 연결성
□ be drawn (마음이) 끌리다
□crave 갈망하다, 열망하다
□countless 무수한
□lonely 외로운
□article 글, 기사
□epidemic 유행성의, 전염성의, 유행병

정답 ②

13 다음 글의 주제로 가장 적절한 것은? 2023. 지방직 9급

Certainly some people are born with advantages (e.g., physical size for jockeys, height for basketball players, an "ear" for music for musicians). Yet only dedication to mindful, deliberate practice over many years can turn those advantages into talents and those talents into successes. Through the same kind of dedicated practice, people who are not born with such advantages can develop talents that nature put a little farther from their reach. For example, even though you may feel that you weren't born with a talent for math, you can significantly increase your mathematical abilities through mindful, deliberate practice. Or, if you consider yourself "naturally" shy, putting in the time and effort to develop your social skills can enable you to interact with people at social occasions with energy, grace, and ease.

① advantages some people have over others
② importance of constant efforts to cultivate talents
③ difficulties shy people have in social interactions
④ need to understand own strengths and weaknesses

해설

잠재된 재능을 성공으로 이끌기 위한 방법을 주제로 하는 글로, 장점을 타고난 사람들도 수년간의 신중한 연습으로 그 장점을 재능으로 발전시킬 수 있고, 장점이 없는 사람들 또한 의도적인 연습을 통해 멀리 놓은 재능을 개발할 수 있음을 강조하고 있다. 따라서 글의 주제로 가장 적절한 것은 ②이다.

해석

확실히 일부 사람들은 장점을 가지고 태어난다 (예를 들어, 기수에 적합한 신체 크기, 농구 선수에 적합한 키, 음악가에 적합한 "귀"). 그러나 수년간의 의식하고 의도적인 연습에 대한 전념만이 그러한 장점들을 재능으로 그리고 그 재능을 성공으로 바꿀 수 있다. 동일한 종류의 헌신적인 연습을 통해, 그러한 장점을 타고나지 않은 사람들도 천성이 그들이 닿기 어려운 곳에 조금 더 멀리 놓은 재능을 개발할 수 있다. 예를 들어, 당신은 수학에 재능이 없다고 느낄지라도, 의식하고 의도적인 연습을 통해 수학적 능력을 상당히 향상시킬 수 있다. 또는 자기 자신이 "본래" 수줍음이 많다고 생각한다면, 시간과 노력을 들여 사교적 기술을 개발함으로써 사회적인 행사에서 활기 있게, 우아하게, 그리고 쉽게 사람들과 상호작용할 수 있다.

① 어떤 사람들이 다른 사람들에 비해 가지고 있는 장점들
② 재능을 기르기 위한 끊임없는 노력의 중요성
③ 수줍은 사람들이 사회적 상호작용에서 겪는 어려움들
④ 자신의 강점과 약점을 이해할 필요성

어휘

□jockey (경마에서 특히 직업적으로 말을 타는) 기수
□height 키, 신장
□dedication 헌신, 전념
□deliberate 고의의, 의도적인, 신중한, 사려 깊은
□shy 수줍음을 타는
□put in 쏟다, 들이다
□grace 우아함
□ease 쉬움, 용이함

정답 ②

14 다음 글의 요지로 가장 적절한 것은? 2023. 지방직 9급

Dr. Roossinck and her colleagues found by chance that a virus increased resistance to drought on a plant that is widely used in botanical experiments. Their further experiments with a related virus showed that was true of 15 other plant species, too. Dr. Roossinck is now doing experiments to study another type of virus that increases heat tolerance in a range of plants. She hopes to extend her research to have a deeper understanding of the advantages that different sorts of viruses give to their hosts. That would help to support a view which is held by an increasing number of biologists, that many creatures rely on symbiosis, rather than being self-sufficient.

① Viruses demonstrate self-sufficiency of biological beings.
② Biologists should do everything to keep plants virus-free.
③ The principle of symbiosis cannot be applied to infected plants.
④ Viruses sometimes do their hosts good, rather than harming them.

해설

바이러스와 식물의 상호작용을 주제로 하는 글로, Roossinck 박사와 동료들은 우연히 바이러스가 가뭄에 대한 내성을 증가시키는 것을 발견하고, 추가 실험을 통해 이것이 여러 식물에도 적용된다는 것을 확인했음을 보여주는 글이다. 따라서 글의 요지로 가장 적절한 것은 ④이다.

해석

Roossinck 박사와 그녀의 동료들은 우연히 한 바이러스가 식물 실험에서 널리 사용되는 식물에서 가뭄에 대한 저항성을 증가시키는 것을 발견했다. **관련된 바이러스로 진행된 추가 실험은 그것이 15개의 다른 식물 종에도 사실이라는 것을 보여줬다. Roossinck 박사는 지금 다양한 식물의 내열성을 증가시키는 다른 유형의 바이러스를 연구하기 위한 실험을 진행하고 있다.** 그녀는 다양한 종류의 바이러스가 숙주에게 제공하는 이점들에 대한 더 깊은 이해를 하기 위해 자신의 연구를 확장하기를 희망한다. 이는 점점 더 많은 생물학자들이 가지고 있는 견해인 많은 생물들이 자립이 아닌 공생에 의존한다는 것을 뒷받침하는 데 도움이 될 것이다.

① 바이러스는 생물학적 존재의 자급자족을 보여준다.
② 생물학자들은 식물들을 바이러스가 없는 상태로 유지하기 위해 모든 것을 해야 한다.
③ 공생의 원리는 감염된 식물에 적용될 수 없다.
④ 바이러스는 때때로 숙주에게 해를 끼치기보다는 이롭다.

어휘

- □ colleague 동료
- □ resistance 저항력, 내성
- □ drought 가뭄
- □ botanical 식물(학)의
- □ further 더 이상의, 추가의
- □ related 관련된
- □ heat tolerance 내열성
- □ a range of 다양한
- □ extend 확장하다, 연장하다
- □ host 숙주
- □ biologist 생물학자
- □ rely on 의지하다
- □ symbiosis 공생
- □ do good (~에게) 이롭다, 도움이 되다

정답 ④

15 다음 글의 주제로 가장 적절한 것은? 2023. 법원직 9급

Do you want to be a successful anchor? If so, keep this in mind. As an anchor, the individual will be called upon to communicate news and information to viewer during newscasts, special reports and other types of news programs. This will include interpreting news events, adlibbing, and communicating breaking news effectively when scripts are not available. Anchoring duties also involve gathering and writing stories. The anchor must be able to deliver scripts clearly and effectively. Strong writing skills, solid news judgement and a strong sense of visual storytelling are essential skills. This individual must be a self-starter who cultivates sources and finds new information as a regular part of job. Live reporting skills are important, as well as the ability to adlib and describe breaking news as it takes place.

① difficulties of producing live news
② qualifications to become a news anchor
③ the importance of the social role of journalists
④ the importance of forming the right public opinion

해설

성공적인 앵커가 되기 위한 자격들을 설명하는 글로, 앵커로서의 역할과 필요한 능력에 대한 가이드라인을 제시하고 있다. 2번째 문장부터 앵커로서 가져야 할 능력들을 나열하고 있다. 따라서 글의 주제로 가장 적절한 것은 ②이다.

해석

당신은 성공적인 앵커가 되고 싶은가? 그렇다면 이 점을 명심해라. 앵커로서, 개인은 뉴스 방송, 특별 보도 및 기타 유형의 뉴스 프로그램 동안 시청자에게 뉴스와 정보를 전달하도록 요청받을 것이다. 이것은 뉴스 사건을 해석하는 것, 즉흥적으로 이야기하는 것, 그리고 대본을 사용할 수 없을 때 효과적으로 뉴스 속보를 전달하는 것을 포함할 것이다. 앵커 업무는 또한 이야기를 모으고 쓰는 것을 포함한다. 앵커는 대본을 명확하고 효과적으로 전달할 수 있어야 한다. 강력한 글쓰기 능력, 믿을 수 있는 뉴스 판단력, 그리고 시각적 스토리텔링의 강한 감각은 필수적인 기술이다. 이 사람은 정보원을 양성하고 새로운 정보를 직업의 정기적인 부분으로 찾는 자발적으로 행동하는 사람이어야 한다. 발생하는 대로 뉴스 속보를 즉흥적으로 하고 설명할 수 있는 능력뿐만 아니라 생방송 보도 기술도 중요하다.

① 생방송 뉴스 제작의 어려움들
② 뉴스 앵커가 되기 위한 자격들
③ 저널리스트의 사회적 역할의 중요성
④ 올바른 여론 형성의 중요성

어휘

□anchor 앵커
□call upon 요청하다
□communicate 전달하다, 의사소통을 하다
□script 원고, 대본
□interpret 해석하다, 이해하다
□adlib 각본에 없는 대사를 말하다, 즉흥적으로 하다
□breaking news 뉴스 속보
□gathering 수집, 모임
□solid 믿을 수 있는, 견고한, 고체의, 단단한
□self-starter 자발적으로 행동하는 사람
□cultivate 양성하다, 경작하다, 재배하다
□journalist 저널리스트, 기자, 언론인

정답 ②

16 다음 글의 주제로 가장 적절한 것은? 2023. 법원직 9급

Cosmetics became so closely associated with portraiture that some photography handbooks included recipes for them. American photographers also, at times, used cosmetics to retouch negatives and prints, enlivening women's faces with traces of rouge. Some customers with dark skin requested photographs that would make them look lighter. A skin lightener advertisement that appeared in an African American newspaper in 1935 referenced this practice by promising that its product could achieve the same look produced by photographers: a lighter skin Cop free of blemishes. By drawing attention to the face and encouraging cosmetics use, portrait photography heightened the aesthetic valuation of smooth and often light-colored skin.

* blemish (피부 등의) 티

① side effects of excessive use of cosmetics
② overuse of cosmetics promoted by photographers
③ active use of cosmetics to make the face look better
④ decreased use of cosmetics due to advances in photography

해설

화장품과 초상화 사진의 상호작용에 대한 글로, 화장품이 초상화와 어떻게 상호작용하며 미적 가치를 높였는지에 대해 설명하고 있다. 특히, 자신의 초상화 사진의 피부를 더 밝게 보이게 원하는 사람들의 요청으로, 초상화 사진에 화장품을 사용한다는 진술과 이러한 사진들을 바탕으로 화장품 광고를 한다는 진술이 '3번째, 4번째' 문장을 통해서 설명하고 있다. 따라서 글의 주제로 가장 적절한 것은 ③이다.

해석

화장품은 인물 사진 기법과 매우 밀접하게 연관되어 있어서 일부 사진술 입문서들은 그것들을 위한 비법이 포함되어 있었다. 미국의 사진작가들도, 때때로, 원판과 인화사진을 수정하기 위해 화장품을 사용했고, 약간의 루즈로 여성들의 얼굴에 활기를 띠게 했다. 어두운 피부를 가진 몇몇 고객들은 그들을 더 밝아 보일 수 있는 사진을 요청했다. 1935년 아프리카계 미국인 신문에 등장한 피부 미백 광고는 잡티가 없는 더 밝은 피부를 만들 수 있는 그것의 제품이 사진작가들이 만들어낸 것과 같은 모습을 이룰 수 있다고 약속함으로써 이 관행을 언급했다. 얼굴에 관심을 끌고 화장품 사용을 장려함으로써, 인물 사진은 매끄럽고 종종 밝은 색의 피부에 대한 미적 가치를 높였다.

① 화장품의 과도한 사용의 부작용
② 사진작가들에 의해 조장된 화장품의 남용
③ 얼굴을 더 좋게 만들기 위한 화장품의 적극적인 사용
④ 사진술의 발달로 인한 줄어든 화장품의 사용

어휘

□ cosmetic 화장품
□ photography 사진술, 사진 찍기
□ portraiture 인물 사진 기법, 초상화, 초상화법
□ handbook 입문서, 안내서
□ recipe 비결, 비법, 요리법
□ retouch 수정하다, 손질하다
□ negative 원판, 음화, 부정적인
□ trace 약간, 조금, 자취, 흔적, 추적하다
□ enliven 생기를 주다, 활기를 띠게 하다
□ skin lightener 피부 미백제
□ aesthetic 미적인
□ excessive 과도한, 지나친
□ overuse 남용, 남용하다
□ decreased 줄어든

정답 ③

17 다음 글의 제목으로 가장 적절한 것은? 2022. 국가직 9급

Lasers are possible because of the way light interacts with electrons. Electrons exist at specific energy levels or states characteristic of that particular atom or molecule. The energy levels can be imagined as rings or orbits around a nucleus. Electrons in outer rings are at higher energy levels than those in inner rings. Electrons can be bumped up to higher energy levels by the injection of energy — for example, by a flash of light. When an electron drops from an outer to an inner level, "excess" energy is given off as light. The wavelength or color of the emitted light is precisely related to the amount of energy released. Depending on the particular lasing material being used, specific wavelengths of light are absorbed (to energize or excite the electrons) and specific wavelengths are emitted (when the electrons fall back to their initial level).

① How Is Laser Produced?
② When Was Laser Invented?
③ What Electrons Does Laser Emit?
④ Why Do Electrons Reflect Light?

해설

전자와 빛의 상호작용하는 방식으로 레이저 발생 원리를 설명하는 글이다. 따라서 글의 제목으로 가장 적절한 것은 ①이다.

해석

레이저는 빛이 전자와 상호작용하는 방식 때문에 가능하다. 전자는 그 특정한 원자나 분자의 특정한 에너지 준위 또는 상태에서 존재한다. 에너지 준위는 고리 또는 핵 주위의 궤도로 생각될 수 있다. 외부 고리의 전자는 내부 고리에 있는 전자들보다 더 높은 에너지 준위에 있다. 전자는 예를 들어, 빛의 섬광과 같은 에너지 주입에 의해 더 높은 에너지 준위로 상승할 수 있다. 전자가 외부에서 내부로 떨어질 때, "과잉" 에너지는 빛으로 방출된다. 방출된 빛의 파장 또는 색상은 방출되는 에너지의 양과 정확하게 관련이 있다. 사용되는 특정 레이저 물질에 따라, 특정 파장의 빛이 흡수되고 (전자를 활성화하거나 촉발시키기 위해) 특정 파장이 방출된다 (전자가 초기의 준위로 떨어질 때).

① 레이저는 어떻게 만들어지는가?
② 레이저는 언제 발명되었는가?
③ 레이저는 어떤 전자를 방출하는가?
④ 전자는 왜 빛을 반사하나?

어휘

□ electron 전자
□ atom 원자
□ molecule 분자
□ particular 특정한, 특별한, 개별적인
□ orbit 궤도, 궤도를 돌다
□ nucleus (원자)핵, 중심
□ injection 주입
□ bump up ~을 올리다
□ give off (냄새·열·빛 등을) 내다[발하다]
□ emit 방출하다, 내뿜다
□ wavelength 파장 길이
□ energize 활성화시키다, 활기를 돋우다
□ excite 흥분시키다, 자극하다, 불러일으키다, 촉발시키다

정답 ①

18 다음 글의 제목으로 가장 적절한 것은? 2022. 국가직 9급

Do people from different cultures view the world differently? A psychologist presented realistic animated scenes of fish and other underwater objects to Japanese and American students and asked them to report what they had seen. Americans and Japanese made about an equal number of references to the focal fish, but the Japanese made more than 60 percent more references to background elements, including the water, rocks, bubbles, and inert plants and animals. In addition, whereas Japanese and American participants made about equal numbers of references to movement involving active animals, the Japanese participants made almost twice as many references to relationships involving inert, background objects. Perhaps most tellingly, the very first sentence from the Japanese participants was likely to be one referring to the environment, whereas the first sentence from Americans was three times as likely to be one referring to the focal fish.

① Language Barrier Between Japanese and Americans
② Associations of Objects and Backgrounds in the Brain
③ Cultural Differences in Perception
④ Superiority of Detail-oriented People

해설

일본과 미국 학생들을 예로 들면서, 문화마다 다른 시각을 가지고 있음을 설명하는 글이다. 실험의 결과로 중심의 물고기에 대해서는 동일한 수를 언급했지만, 일본 학생들은 미국 학생들에 비해 비활성화된 것들에 대해서는 60% 이상 혹은 두 배 이상 언급을 했음을 밝히고 있다. 따라서 글의 제목으로 가장 적절한 것은 ③이다.

해석

다른 문화권의 사람들은 세상을 다르게 보는가? 한 심리학자가 일본과 미국 학생들에게 물고기와 다른 수중 물체의 사실적인 동영상으로 된 장면을 보여주고 그들이 본 것을 보고하도록 요청했다. 미국인들과 일본인들은 중심의 물고기에 대해서는 거의 같은 수로 언급했지만, 일본인들은 물, 바위, 거품, 그리고 비활성 동식물을 포함한 배경 요소에 대해 60% 이상 더 많은 언급을 했다. 게다가, 일본인과 미국인 참가자들이 활동적인 동물들과 관련된 움직임에 대해 거의 같은 수의 언급을 한 반면, 일본인 참가자들은 비활성적이고 배경적인 물체들과 관련된 관계에 대해 거의 두 배나 더 많은 언급을 했다. 아마도 가장 강력하게, 일본 참가자들의 맨 처음 문장은 환경을 언급하는 반면, 미국인들의 첫 번째 문장은 초점 물고기를 언급하는 것일 가능성이 세 배 더 높았다.

① 일본인과 미국인 사이의 언어 장벽
② 뇌에서 물체와 배경의 연관성
③ 인식에 있어서의 문화적 차이
④ 세부적인 것에 더 집중하는 사람들의 우월성

어휘

- □ view 보다, 여기다
- □ psychologist 심리학자
- □ animated 동영상으로 된, 만화 영화로 된, 활기찬
- □ scene 장면
- □ make (a) reference 언급하다
- □ focal 중심의, 초점의
- □ element 요소
- □ including ~을 포함하여
- □ inert 움직이지 않는, 비활성의
- □ participant 참가자
- □ tellingly 강력하게
- □ sentence 문장, 판결, 선고
- □ refer to ~을 언급[지칭]하다
- □ the very first 맨 처음
- □ perception 인지, 자각

정답 ③

19 다음 글의 요지로 가장 적절한 것은? 2022. 국가직 9급

If someone makes you an offer and you're legitimately concerned about parts of it, you're usually better off proposing all your changes at once. Don't say, "The salary is a bit low. Could you do something about it?" and then, once she's worked on it, come back with "Thanks. Now here are two other things I'd like..." If you ask for only one thing initially, she may assume that getting it will make you ready to accept the offer (or at least to make a decision). If you keep saying "and one more thing...," she is unlikely to remain in a generous or understanding mood. Furthermore, if you have more than one request, don't simply mention all the things you want — A, B, C, and D; also signal the relative importance of each to you. Otherwise, she may pick the two things you value least, because they're pretty easy to give you, and feel she's met you halfway.

① Negotiate multiple issues simultaneously, not serially.
② Avoid sensitive topics for a successful negotiation.
③ Choose the right time for your negotiation.
④ Don't be too direct when negotiating salary.

해설

누군가 제안을 했을 때 그 제안과 관련된 변경사항들을 어떻게 제안해야 하는지 설명하는 글이다. 여러 가지의 사항들이 있더라도 한 번에 제안해야 하는 이유와 그 예시들을 상세히 설명하고 있다. 따라서 글의 요지로 가장 적절한 것은 ①이다.

해석

만약 누군가가 당신에게 제안을 하고 당신이 정당하게 그것의 일부를 걱정한다면, 당신은 보통 당신의 모든 변경사항을 한 번에 제안하는 것이 더 낫다. "월급이 좀 적습니다. 그것에 대해 어떻게 해주실 수 있나요?"라고 말하지 말고, 그러고 나서 그녀가 그것에 노력을 들이자마자, "감사합니다. 이제 제가 원하는 것이 두 가지가 더 있습니다..."라고 되돌아가지도 마라. 처음에 한 가지만 요구한다면, 그녀는 그것을 얻는 것이 당신이 그 제안을 받아들일 (또는 최소한의 결정을 내릴) 준비가 될 것으로 생각할지도 모른다. 만약 당신이 계속해서 "그리고 한 가지 더..."라고 말한다면, 그녀는 관대하거나 이해심 있는 기분을 유지할 것 같지 않다. 게다가, 만약 당신이 한 가지 이상의 요청이 있다면, 당신이 원하는 — A, B, C, 그리고 D — 모든 것을 단순하게 언급하지 말아라; 또한 당신에게 있어 각각의 상대적인 중요성을 신호로 보내라. 그렇지 않으면, 그녀는 가장 중요하게 생각하지 않는 두 가지를 선택할 수도 있는데, 왜냐하면 그것들은 당신에게 주기 매우 쉽기 때문이고, 그녀는 당신과 타협했다고 느낄지도 모른다.

① 여러 문제를 연속적으로 하지 말고, 동시에 협상하라.
② 성공적인 협상을 위해 민감한 주제를 피하라.
③ 당신의 협상에 적절한 시간을 선택하라.
④ 급여를 협상할 때 너무 직접적이지 않도록 해라.

어휘

□legitimately 정당하게, 합법적으로
□concerned 걱정하는, 관심이 있는
□work on ~에 노력을 들이다, 착수하다
□once ~하자마자, ~할 때
□assume 추정하다, 알다, 띠다
□generous 관대한
□understanding 이해심 있는
□request 요청
□mention 언급하다
□relative 상대적인
□meet halfway 타협하다, 절충하다
□multiple 다수의, 다양한, 복잡한

정답 ①

20 **다음 글의 제목으로 가장 적절한 것은?** 2022. 지방직 9급

One of the areas where efficiency can be optimized is the work force, through increasing individual productivity — defined as the amount of work (products produced, customers served) an employee handles in a given time. In addition to making sure you have invested in the right equipment, environment, and training to ensure optimal performance, you can increase productivity by encouraging staffers to put an end to a modern-day energy drain: multitasking. Studies show it takes 25 to 40 percent longer to get a job done when you're simultaneously trying to work on other projects. To be more productive, says Andrew Deutscher, vice president of business development at consulting firm The Energy Project, "do one thing, uninterrupted, for a sustained period of time."

① How to Create More Options in Life
② How to Enhance Daily Physical Performance
③ Multitasking is the Answer for Better Efficiency
④ Do One Thing at a Time for Greater Efficiency

해설

인력 생산성 향상을 위한 다중 작업 방지를 주장하는 글이다. 이 글 곳곳에서 생산성을 향상시키기 위해 에너지 낭비인 다중 작업을 끝내도록 장려해야 한다고 주장하며 글 마지막에 전문가의 견해를 인용하여 하나의 일에 집중하라고 이야기하고 있다. 따라서 글의 제목으로 가장 적절한 것은 ④이다.

해석

직원이 주어진 시간 내에 처리하는 작업(생산된 제품들, 응대받은 고객들)의 양으로 정의되는 — 개인 생산성 향상을 통한 효율성을 최적화할 수 있는 영역 중 하나는 인력이다. 최적의 성과를 보장하기 위해 당신이 올바른 장비, 환경 및 교육에 투자했는지 확인하는 것뿐만 아니라, 현재의 에너지 낭비인 다중 작업을 끝내도록 장려하여 생산성을 높일 수 있다. 연구들은 당신이 동시에 다른 프로젝트들을 수행하려고 할 때 작업을 완료하는 데 25%에서 40% 더 오래 걸린다는 것을 보여준다. 컨설팅 회사인 The Energy Project의 사업 개발 부사장인 Andrew Deutsher는 생산성을 높이기 위해 "지속적인 기간 동안 중단 없이 한 가지 일을 수행하라."라고 말한다.

① 인생에서 더 많은 선택지를 만드는 방법
② 일상의 신체적 기능을 향상시키는 방법
③ 다중 작업은 더 나은 효율성을 위한 답이다
④ 더 큰 효율성을 위해 하나의 일에 집중하라

어휘

- □efficiency 효율성
- □optimize 최적화하다
- □customer 손님, 고객
- □employee 직원, 고용인, 종업원
- □equipment 장비
- □encourage 장려하다, 격려하다
- □multitasking 다중 작업, 멀티태스킹
- □energy drain 에너지 낭비
- □simultaneously 동시에
- □vice president 부사장
- □uninterrupted 중단 없는, 방해받지 않는
- □sustain 유지하다, 지속시키다

정답 ④

21 다음 글의 요지로 가장 적절한 것은? 2022. 지방직 9급

In one study, done in the early 1970s when young people tended to dress in either "hippie" or "straight" fashion, experimenters donned hippie or straight attire and asked college students on campus for a dime to make a phone call. When the experimenter was dressed in the same way as the student, the request was granted in more than two-thirds of the instances; when the student and requester were dissimilarly dressed, the dime was provided less than half the time. Another experiment showed how automatic our positive response to similar others can be. Marchers in an antiwar demonstration were found to be more likely to sign the petition of a similarly dressed requester and to do so without bothering to read it first.

① People are more likely to help those who dress like themselves.
② Dressing up formally increases the chance of signing the petition.
③ Making a phone call is an efficient way to socialize with other students.
④ Some college students in the early 1970s were admired for their unique fashion.

해설

사람들이 자신과 비슷하게 옷을 입은 사람들에게 더 많은 도움을 주는 이유에 대한 글이다. 다른 옷을 입은 경우보다 비슷한 옷을 입은 사람들끼리는 상호작용에서 더 긍정적으로 대한다는 것을 보여주는 실험 결과를 설명하고 있다. 따라서 글의 요지로 가장 적절한 것은 ①이다.

해석

젊은이들이 '히피' 또는 '스트레이트' 패션으로 옷을 입는 경향이 있었던 때인 1970년대 초에 행해진 한 연구에서, 실험자들은 히피나 스트레이트 복장을 하고 대학생들에게 전화를 걸어 10센트를 달라고 요청했다. 실험자가 학생과 같은 방식으로 옷을 입었을 때, 그 요청은 사례 중 3분의 2 이상이 받아들여졌고, 학생과 요청자가 다르게 옷을 입었을 때, 10센트짜리 동전은 절반 미만으로 제공되었다. 또 다른 실험은 비슷한 다른 사람에 대한 우리의 긍정적인 반응이 얼마나 자동적일 수 있는지를 보여줬다. 반전 시위에 참가한 시위자들은 비슷한 복장을 한 요청자의 탄원서에 서명할 가능성이 더 높았으며, 그것을 우선 읽어보려고 애를 쓰지 않고도 그렇게 할 가능성이 더 높은 것으로 밝혀졌다.

① 사람들은 자신과 비슷하게 옷을 입은 사람들을 도와줄 가능성이 더 높다.
② 옷을 갖춰 입는 것은 청원서에 서명할 확률을 높인다.
③ 전화를 거는 것은 다른 학생들과 어울리는 효율적인 방법이다.
④ 1970년대 초반에는 일부 대학생들이 독특한 패션으로 인해 동경받았다.

어휘

- □experimenter 실험자
- □attire 복장, 의복
- □dime 10센트
- □requester 요청자
- □dissimilarly 닮지 않게, 다르게
- □automatic 자동의, 무의식적인, 반사적인
- □marcher 시위자, 가두 행진 참가자
- □antiwar 반전의, 전쟁 반대의
- □petition 청원(서), 탄원(서), 신청서, 청원하다, 탄원하다
- □dress up 옷을 갖춰[격식을 차려] 입다
- □socialize 어울리다, 교제하다, 사귀다
- □admire 동경하다, 존경하다, 칭찬하다

정답 ①

22 다음 글의 주제로 가장 적절한 것은? 2022. 법원직 9급

Daily training creates special nutritional needs for an athlete, particularly the elite athlete whose training commitment is almost a fulltime job. But even recreational sport will create nutritional challenges. And whatever your level of involvement in sport, you must meet these challenges if you're to achieve the maximum return from training. Without sound eating, much of the purpose of your training might be lost. In the worst-case scenario, dietary problems and deficiencies may directly impair training performance. In other situations, you might improve, but at a rate that is below your potential or slower than your competitors. However, on the positive side, with the right everyday eating plan your commitment to training will be fully rewarded.

① how to improve body flexibility
② importance of eating well in exercise
③ health problems caused by excessive diet
④ improving skills through continuous training

해설

영양과 스포츠 훈련의 관계에 대한 글로, 스포츠 훈련을 위해서는 올바른 영양 섭취와 규칙적인 식사 계획이 필요하며, 이를 소홀히 하면 훈련 성과가 손상될 수 있음을 설명하고 있다. 따라서 글의 주제로 가장 적절한 것은 ②이다.

해석

매일의 훈련은 운동선수, 특히 훈련에 전념하는 것이 거의 전업인 엘리트 운동선수에게 특별한 영양적 필요를 만들어 낸다. 하지만 레크리에이션 스포츠조차도 영양상의 문제를 만들어낼 것이다. 그리고 스포츠에 당신의 관여 수준이 어떻든 간에, 만약 당신이 훈련으로부터 최대의 이득을 달성하려면 이러한 문제들에 대응해야 한다. 건강한 식사 없이는, 당신의 훈련 목적의 많은 부분이 손실될 수 있다. 최악의 경우, 식사 문제와 결핍은 직접적으로 훈련 성과를 손상시킬 수 있다. 다른 상황에서는, 당신은 향상될 수 있지만, 당신의 잠재력에 미치지 못하거나 당신의 경쟁자들보다 느린 속도로 향상될 수 있다. 그러나 긍정적인 측면에서는, 매일 올바른 식사 계획으로, 훈련에 대한 당신의 헌신은 완전히 보상받을 것이다.

① 신체의 유연성을 향상시키는 방법
② 운동에서 잘 먹는 것의 중요성
③ 과도한 다이어트로 인한 건강 문제점들
④ 지속적인 훈련을 통해 기술들을 향상시키기

어휘

- □ nutritional 영양적인, 영양상의
- □ athlete 운동선수
- □ commitment 전념, 헌신, 약속
- □ recreational 레크리에이션, 오락의
- □ involvement 관련, 관여, 몰두
- □ return 이득, 수익, 돌아옴, 반납
- □ sound 건강한, 철저한, 타당한
- □ dietary 식사의, 식이요법의
- □ deficiency 결핍, 부족
- □ flexibility 유연성, 신축성
- □ continuous 지속적인, 계속되는

정답 ②

23 다음 글의 제목으로 가장 적절한 것은? 2021. 국가직 9급

Warming temperatures and loss of oxygen in the sea will shrink hundreds of fish species — from tunas and groupers to salmon, thresher sharks, haddock and cod — even more than previously thought, a new study concludes. Because warmer seas speed up their metabolisms, fish, squid and other water-breathing creatures will need to draw more oxygen from the ocean. At the same time, warming seas are already reducing the availability of oxygen in many parts of the sea. A pair of University of British Columbia scientists argue that since the bodies of fish grow faster than their gills, these animals eventually will reach a point where they can't get enough oxygen to sustain normal growth. "What we found was that the body size of fish decreases by 20 to 30 percent for every 1 degree Celsius increase in water temperature," says author William Cheung.

① Fish Now Grow Faster than Ever
② Oxygen's Impact on Ocean Temperatures
③ Climate Change May Shrink the World's Fish
④ How Sea Creatures Survive with Low Metabolism

해설

따뜻해지는 기온과 바다의 산소 감소로 인하여 다양한 어종들과 해양 생물들이 줄어들고 있음을 설명하는 글이다. 이에 대해 과학자와 작가 William Cheung의 주장을 추가적으로 부연 설명하고 있다. 따라서 글의 제목으로 가장 적절한 것은 ③이다.

해석

따뜻해지는 기온과 바다의 산소 감소가 — 참다랑어와 농어부터 연어, 진환도 상어, 해덕 그리고 대구까지 — 수백 어종을 이전에 생각했던 것보다 훨씬 더 줄어들게 할 것이라고 새로운 연구는 결론을 내린다. 더 따뜻해진 바다가 그것들의 신진대사를 촉진하기 때문에, 물고기, 오징어 그리고 다른 수중에서 호흡하는 생물들이 바다에서 더 많은 산소를 들이마셔야 할 것이다. 동시에, 따뜻해지고 있는 바다는 이미 바다의 많은 부분에서 산소의 이용 가능성을 줄이고 있다. British Columbia 대학교의 한 쌍의 과학자들은 물고기의 몸이 그것들의 아가미보다 더 빠르게 자라고 있기 때문에, 이러한 동물들은 결국 정상적인 성장을 지속하는 데 충분한 산소를 얻지 못하는 지점에 이를 것이라고 주장한다. "우리가 발견한 것은 물의 온도가 섭씨 1도 높아질 때 물고기의 크기가 20~30퍼센트씩 줄어든다는 것이었다,"라고 저자 William Cheung은 말한다.

① 지금은 물고기가 예전보다 더 빠르게 자란다
② 바다의 온도에 대한 산소의 영향
③ 기후 변화가 세계 어종을 줄어들게 할 수 있다
④ 바다 생물들이 낮은 신진대사로 어떻게 생존하는가

어휘

□ oxygen 산소
□ shrink 줄어들게 하다, 감소하다
□ tuna 참치, 참다랑어
□ grouper 농어
□ salmon 연어
□ thresher shark 진환도 상어
□ haddock 해덕
□ cod 대구
□ metabolism 신진대사
□ squid 오징어
□ availability 이용 가능성
□ gill 아가미
□ eventually 결국
□ sustain 유지하다, 지속시키다
□ Celsius 섭씨의

정답 ③

24 다음 글의 주제로 가장 적절한 것은? 2021. 국가직 9급

During the late twentieth century socialism was on the retreat both in the West and in large areas of the developing world. During this new phase in the evolution of market capitalism, global trading patterns became increasingly interlinked, and advances in information technology meant that deregulated financial markets could shift massive flows of capital across national boundaries within seconds. 'Globalization' boosted trade, encouraged productivity gains and lowered prices, but critics alleged that it exploited the low-paid, was indifferent to environmental concerns and subjected the Third World to a monopolistic form of capitalism. Many radicals within Western societies who wished to protest against this process joined voluntary bodies, charities and other non-governmental organizations, rather than the marginalized political parties of the left. The environmental movement itself grew out of the recognition that the world was interconnected, and an angry, if diffuse, international coalition of interests emerged.

① The affirmative phenomena of globalization in the developing world in the past
② The decline of socialism and the emergence of capitalism in the twentieth century
③ The conflict between the global capital market and the political organizations of the left
④ The exploitative characteristics of global capitalism and diverse social reactions against it

해설

세계화 시대의 비판과 급진주의자들의 새로운 움직임을 주제로 하는 글이다. 사회주의가 후퇴하고 시장 자본주의가 도입되면서 자본주의가 발달하게 되었지만 자본주의의 발달에 따른 문제점들로 인하여 서구 사회에서 자발적인 기구와 자선단체, 비정부기구들에 참여하고 환경운동에 관한 연합이 생겨났다는 내용이다. 따라서 글의 주제로 가장 적절한 것은 ④이다.

해석

> 20세기 후반 동안 사회주의는 서구와 개발도상국의 많은 지역에서 후퇴하는 중이었다. 시장 자본주의의 진화의 이 새로운 단계 동안, 세계 무역 양식은 점점 더 상호 연결되게 되었고, 정보 기술의 발전은 규제가 완화된 금융 시장이 국경을 넘어 거대한 자본의 흐름을 몇 초 안에 이동할 수 있다는 것을 의미했다. '세계화'는 무역을 증가시키고, 생산성 향상을 장려하며, 가격을 낮추었지만, 비평가들은 그것이 저임금층을 착취하고, 환경 문제에 무관심하며, 제3세계가 독점적인 형태의 자본주의의 지배를 받게 했다고 주장했다. 이 과정에 항의하기를 원했던 서구 사회 내의 많은 급진주의자들은 좌파의 소외된 정당보다는 자발적인 단체, 자선 단체 그리고 다른 비정부 조직에 가입했다. 환경운동 자체는 세계가 서로 상호 연결되어 있다는 인식에서 시작되었고, 흩어져 있지만, 분노한 국제적인 이해관계의 연합이 등장했다.

① 과거 개발도상국에서의 세계화의 긍정적인 현상
② 20세기 사회주의의 쇠퇴와 자본주의의 출현
③ 세계 자본시장과 좌파 정치 조직 사이의 갈등
④ 세계 자본주의의 착취적 특성과 다양한 사회적 반응들

어휘

- □ socialism 사회주의
- □ retreat 퇴각, 후퇴, 후퇴하다, 쇠퇴하다
- □ capitalism 자본주의
- □ interlink 연결하다
- □ deregulate 규제를 철폐하다
- □ developing world 개발도상국
- □ national boundary 국경
- □ boost 촉진시키다
- □ allege 혐의를 제기하다
- □ exploit 착취하다, 이용하다
- □ low-paid 저임금의
- □ subject 지배하에 두다, 종속시키다
- □ monopolistic 독점적인
- □ capitalism 자본주의
- □ radical 급진주의자
- □ marginalized 소외된
- □ voluntary 자발적인, 임의적인
- □ charity 자선, 자선 단체
- □ non-governmental organization 비정부 단체
- □ political party 정당
- □ diffuse 분산되다, 확산되다
- □ international coalition 국제 연합
- □ interest 이해관계, 이익, 관심, 흥미
- □ affirmative 긍정적인, 확언적인

정답 ④

25 다음 글의 제목으로 가장 적절한 것은? 2021. 지방직 9급

> The definition of 'turn' casts the digital turn as an analytical strategy which enables us to focus on the role of digitalization within social reality. As an analytical perspective, the digital turn makes it possible to analyze and discuss the societal meaning of digitalization. The term 'digital turn' thus signifies an analytical approach which centers on the role of digitalization within a society. If the linguistic turn is defined by the epistemological assumption that reality is constructed through language, the digital turn is based on the assumption that social reality is increasingly defined by digitalization. Social media symbolize the digitalization of social relations. Individuals increasingly engage in identity management on social networking sites(SNS). SNS are polydirectional, meaning that users can connect to each other and share information.
>
> ※ epistemological 인식론의

① Remaking Identities on SNS
② Linguistic Turn Versus Digital Turn
③ How to Share Information in the Digital Age
④ Digitalization Within the Context of Social Reality

해설

디지털 전환(디지털화에 초점을 맞춘 분석적 전략)이 사회적으로 어떠한 의미를 가지는지에 대해 이야기 하는 글이다. 디지털화에 대한 개념의 설명이 5번째 줄의 '소셜미디어'를 예를 들면서 구체적으로 이해가 되는 글이다. 따라서 글의 제목으로 가장 적절한 것은 ④이다.

해석

> '전환'의 정의는 우리가 사회적 현실 내에서 디지털화의 역할에 집중할 수 있도록 하는 분석적 전략으로서 디지털 전환을 제시한다. 분석적인 관점으로서 디지털 전환은 디지털화의 사회적 의미를 분석하고 논의할 수 있게 한다. 따라서 '디지털 전환'이라는 용어는 한 사회 내에서 디지털화의 역할에 초점을 맞춘 분석적 접근 방식을 의미한다. 만약 언어적 전환이 언어를 통해 현실이 구성된다는 인식론적 가정에 의해 정의된다면, 디지털 전환은 사회적 현실이 디지털화에 의해 점점 더 정의된다는 가정에 기초한다. 소셜미디어는 사회적 관계의 디지털화를 상징한다. 개인들은 소셜 네트워킹 사이트(SNS)에서 정체성 관리에 점점 더 참여하고 있다. SNS는 다방향성인데, 이것은 사용자들이 서로 연결하여 정보를 공유할 수 있다는 것을 의미한다.

① SNS에서 정체성 재창조하기
② 언어학적 전환 대 디지털 전환
③ 디지털 시대에서 정보 공유하는 방법
④ 사회적 현실 안에서의 디지털화

어휘

□ definition 정의
□ cast A as B A를 B로 제시하다, 묘사하다, 간주하다
□ digitalization 디지털화
□ perspective 관점, 시각
□ societal 사회의, 사회적인
□ term 용어
□ signify 의미하다
□ linguistic 언어적
□ assumption 가정, 추정
□ construct 구성하다, 건설하다
□ symbolize 상징하다
□ engage in ~에 참여하다, 종사하다
□ identity 정체성, 신원
□ polydirectional 다방향적인

정답 ④

26 다음 글의 요지로 가장 적절한 것은? 2021. 지방직 9급

"In Judaism, we're largely defined by our actions," says Lisa Grushcow, the senior rabbi at Temple Emanu-El-Beth Sholom in Montreal. "You can't really be an armchair do-gooder." This concept relates to the Jewish notion of tikkun olam, which translates as "to repair the world." Our job as human beings, she says, "is to mend what's been broken. It's incumbent on us to not only take care of ourselves and each other but also to build a better world around us." This philosophy conceptualizes goodness as something based in service. Instead of asking "Am I a good person?" you may want to ask "What good do I do in the world?" Grushcow's temple puts these beliefs into action inside and outside their community. For instance, they sponsored two refugee families from Vietnam to come to Canada in the 1970s.

① We should work to heal the world.
② Community should function as a shelter.
③ We should conceptualize goodness as beliefs.
④ Temples should contribute to the community.

해설

이 글은 유대교의 철학인 "tikkun olam"에 대해 이야기 하면서, 이것은 '세상을 고치기'라는 뜻임을 밝히고 있다. 그리고, 인간으로서 우리의 일은 망가진 것을 고치는 것이 이 철학의 핵심임을 강조하면서, 우리가 세상을 개선하는 데 노력해야 한다고 주장한다. 그리고 '치료' 등의 표현이 반복적으로 나타나고 있다. 따라서 글의 요지로 가장 적절한 것은 ①이다.

해석

"유대교에서, 우리는 주로 우리의 행동에 의해 정의된다,"라고 몬트리올에 있는 Emanu-El-Beth Sholom 사원 선임 랍비 Lisa Grushcow는 말한다. "당신은 절대 관념적인 개혁가가 되어서는 안 된다." 이 개념은 유대인의 틱쿤 올람의 개념과 관련이 있는데, 이것은 "세상을 고치기"라고 번역이 된다. 인간으로서 우리의 일은 "망가진 것을 고치는 것이다. 우리 자신과 서로를 돌볼 뿐만 아니라 우리 주위에 더 나은 세상을 만드는 것이 우리의 의무이다."라고 그녀는 말했다. 이 철학은 선함을 서비스에 기반을 둔 것으로 개념화한다. "나는 좋은 사람인가?"라고 묻는 대신에, "내가 세상에서 무슨 도움이 되는가?"라고 묻고 싶을지도 모른다. Grushcow의 사원은 이러한 믿음들을 그들의 공동체 안팎에서 실천한다. 예를 들어, 그들은 1970년대에 두 명의 난민 가족을 베트남에서 캐나다로 오도록 지원했다.

① 우리는 세상을 치유하기 위해 노력해야 한다.
② 공동체는 피난처로서 기능해야 한다.
③ 우리는 선량함을 믿음으로 개념화해야 한다.
④ 사원은 지역사회에 기여해야 한다.

어휘

□ Judaism 유대교
□ rabbi (유대교의 지도자교사인) 라비, 선생님
□ armchair 안락의자
□ do-gooder 공상적 박애주의자[개혁가]
□ translate 번역하다, 해석하다
□ repair 수리하다, 바로잡다
□ mend 고치다, 수리하다
□ incumbent 의무적인, 재임 중인
□ take care of ~을 돌보다
□ conceptualize 개념화하다, 개념적으로 설명하다
□ goodness 선량함, 착함
□ put A into action A를 행동으로 옮기다
□ sponsor 후원하다
□ refugee 난민

정답 ①

27 다음 글의 요지로 가장 알맞은 것은? 2021. 법원직 9급

> If your kids fight every time they play video games, make sure you're close enough to be able to hear them when they sit down to play. Listen for the particular words or tones of voice they are using that are aggressive, and try to intervene before it develops. Once tempers have settled, try to sit your kids down and discuss the problem without blaming or accusing. Give each kid a chance to talk, uninterrupted, and have them try to come up with solutions to the problem themselves. By the time kids are elementary-school age, they can evaluate which of those solutions are win-win solutions and which ones are most likely to work and satisfy each other over time. They should also learn to revisit problems when solutions are no longer working.

① Ask your kids to evaluate their test.
② Make your kids compete each other.
③ Help your kids learn to resolve conflict.
④ Teach your kids how to win an argument.

해설

아이들 간의 비디오 게임 중 분쟁을 해결하는 방법에 대한 글로, 아이들이 비디오 게임 중에 싸울 때, 부모는 가까이 있어서 상황을 모니터하고, 대화와 문제 해결 능력을 통해 해결책을 찾도록 도와야 함을 3번째 문장 "아이들을 비난하거나 비난하지 않고 앉아서 그 문제에 대해 토론하도록 노력하세요"의 진술을 통해서 강조하고 있다. 따라서 글의 요지로 가장 알맞은 것은 ③이다.

해석

> 만약 당신의 아이들이 비디오 게임을 할 때마다 싸운다면, 그들이 게임을 하기 위해 앉을 때 그들의 말을 들을 수 있을 만큼 충분히 가까이에 있는지 확인해라. 그들이 사용하고 있는 공격적인 단어나 목소리의 톤을 듣고, 그것이 발전하기 전에 개입하려고 노력해라. 일단 화가 풀리면, 아이들을 탓하거나 비난하지 않고 앉아서 그 문제에 대해 토론하도록 노력해라. 각각의 아이들에게 말할 기회를 주고, 중단하지 않고, 그들 스스로 문제에 대한 해결책을 생각해 내도록 해라. 아이들이 초등학생이 될 때까지, 그들은 어떤 해결책들이 윈윈의 솔루션이고 어떤 것들이 시간이 지남에 따라 서로 작용하고 만족시킬 수 있는지를 평가할 수 있다. 그들은 또한 해결책이 더 이상 효과가 없을 때 문제를 다시 논의하는 법을 배워야 한다.

① 당신의 아이들에게 그들의 시험을 평가하도록 요청하라.
② 당신의 아이들이 서로 경쟁하도록 하라.
③ 아이들이 갈등을 해결하는 법을 배울 수 있도록 도와줘라.
④ 아이들에게 논쟁에서 이기는 법을 가르쳐줘라.

어휘

- □ close 가까이, 가까운
- □ aggressive 공격적인
- □ intervene 개입하다, 간섭하다
- □ temper 화, 기질, 분노
- □ discuss 토론하다, 상의하다
- □ uninterrupted 중단되지 않는, 연속된
- □ come up with ~을 제시하다, 생각해내다
- □ resolve 해결하다, 결심하다
- □ revisit 다시 논의하다, 다시 방문하다

정답 ③

28 다음 글의 요지로 가장 적절한 것은? 2020. 국가직 9급

> Listening to somebody else's ideas is the one way to know whether the story you believe about the world — as well as about yourself and your place in it — remains intact. We all need to examine our beliefs, air them out and let them breathe. Hearing what other people have to say, especially about concepts we regard as foundational, is like opening a window in our minds and in our hearts. Speaking up is important. Yet to speak up without listening is like banging pots and pans together: even if it gets you attention, it's not going to get you respect. There are three prerequisites for conversation to be meaningful: 1. You have to know what you're talking about, meaning that you have an original point and are not echoing a worn-out, hand- me-down or pre-fab argument; 2. You respect the people with whom you're speaking and are authentically willing to treat them courteously even if you disagree with their positions; 3. You have to be both smart and informed enough to listen to what the opposition says while handling your own perspective on the topic with uninterrupted good humor and discernment.

① We should be more determined to persuade others.
② We need to listen and speak up in order to communicate well.
③ We are reluctant to change our beliefs about the world we see.
④ We hear only what we choose and attempt to ignore different opinions.

해설

다른 이들의 아이디어를 듣는 것의 중요성을 대화의 의미 있는 전제조건으로 설명하는 글이다. 글의 초반부에 다른 사람의 아이디어를 듣는 것은 당신이 믿는 세상과 당신 자신과 그 안에서 당신의 위치에 대한 이야기가 그대로 남아 있는지 알 수 있는 한 가지 방법이라고 하였고 중간 부분에서 그러나 듣지 않고 목소리를 높이는 것은 냄비와 냄비를 함께 두드리는 것과 같다고 진술하고 있다. 따라서 글의 요지로 가장 적절한 것은 ②이다.

해석

> 다른 사람의 생각들을 듣는 것은 당신 자신과 그 안에서 당신의 위치에 대한 이야기뿐만 아니라 세상에 대해 당신이 믿는 이야기가 여전히 그대로 남아 있는지 아는 한 가지 방법이다. 우리 모두는 우리의 신념을 조사하고, 그것들을 환기시키고, 그것들이 숨을 쉬게 할 필요가 있다. 다른 사람들이, 특히 우리가 기본적이라고 여기는 개념에 대해 말해야 하는 것을 듣는 것은 우리 머리와 마음의 창문을 여는 것과 같다. 목소리를 높이는 것은 중요하다. 그러나 듣지 않고 목소리를 높이는 것은 냄비와 팬을 함께 세게 치는 것과 같다: 비록 그것이 당신이 주목받게 할지라도 존중받도록 하지는 않을 것이다. 대화를 의미 있게 하기 위한 세 가지 전제 조건이 있다: 1. 당신은 당신이 무슨 말을 하고 있는지 알아야 하고, 이는 당신이 독창적인 의견을 가지고 있고 진부하거나, 독창성이 없거나, 이미 만들어진 주장을 되풀이하지 않는다는 것을 의미한다; 2. 당신은 상대방을 존중하고 비록 당신이 그들의 입장에 동의하지 않더라도 진정으로 그들을 예의 바르게 대한다; 3. 당신은 연속된 좋은 유머와 통찰력으로 주제에 대한 자신의 관점을 다루면서 상대방의 말을 경청할 수 있을 만큼 똑똑하고 충분한 정보를 가지고 있어야 한다.

① 우리는 다른 사람들을 설득하기 위해 더 단호해야 한다.
② 우리는 원활하게 의사소통하기 위해 듣고 목소리를 높일 필요가 있다.
③ 우리는 우리가 보는 세상에 대한 믿음을 바꾸는 것을 꺼린다.
④ 우리는 선택한 것만 듣고 다른 의견들을 애써 무시한다.

어휘

□ intact 그대로의, 온전한, 손상되지 않은
□ foundational 기본적인, 근본적인
□ speak up 큰소리로 말하다, 거리낌 없이 말하다
□ pot 냄비, 항아리
□ pan (손잡이가 달린 얕은) 팬, 냄비
□ bang 세게 치다, 쾅 하고 치다
□ attention 주목, 주의
□ worn-out 진부한, 써서 낡은, 지친
□ hand-me-down 독창성이 없는, 만들어 놓은, 헌 옷의
□ pre-fab 미리 만들어진
□ authentically 확실히, 진정하게
□ willing 기꺼이 하는, 꺼리지 않는
□ courteously 정중히, 공손하게
□ informed 알고 있는
□ opposition 상대방, 반대
□ uninterrupted 중단되지 않은, 연속된
□ discernment 통찰력, 식별, 인식

정답 ②

29 다음 글의 제목으로 가장 적절한 것은? 2020. 국가직 9급

> The future may be uncertain, but some things are undeniable: climate change, shifting demographics, geopolitics. The only guarantee is that there will be changes, both wonderful and terrible. It's worth considering how artists will respond to these changes, as well as what purpose art serves, now and in the future. Reports suggest that by 2040 the impacts of human-caused climate change will be inescapable, making it the big issue at the centre of art and life in 20 years' time. Artists in the future will wrestle with the possibilities of the post-human and post-Anthropocene — artificial intelligence, human colonies in outer space and potential doom. The identity politics seen in art around the #MeToo and Black Lives Matter movements will grow as environmentalism, border politics and migration come even more sharply into focus. Art will become increasingly diverse and might not 'look like art' as we expect. In the future, once we've become weary of our lives being visible online for all to see and our privacy has been all but lost, anonymity may be more desirable than fame. Instead of thousands, or millions, of likes and followers, we will be starved for authenticity and connection. Art could, in turn, become more collective and experiential, rather than individual.

① What will art look like in the future?
② How will global warming affect our lives?
③ How will artificial intelligence influence the environment?
④ What changes will be made because of political movements?

해설

예술이 미래에서 가질 목적과 역할을 예술가들이 직면할 미래 인간의 문제들, 즉 예술에서 보이는 정체성 정치학과 환경 운동 등을 설명하는 글이다. 3번째 문장에서 미래에 예술이 어떤 역할을 하고 어떤 모습을 띠게 될 것인가에 대해 생각해 볼만하다고 제시하고 있고 이후의 내용에서 변화하는 미래에 예술이 어떤 모습을 띠게 될지 반복적으로 진술하고 있다. 따라서 글의 제목으로 가장 적절한 것은 ①이다.

해석

미래는 불확실할 수 있지만, 기후 변화, 변화하는 인구 통계, 지정학과 같은 어떤 것들은 확실하다. 유일한 보장은 변화가 있을 것이라는 거고, 그 중에는 멋진 것과 끔찍한 것이 모두 있을 것이다. 예술이 현재와 미래에 어떤 도움이 될지 뿐만 아니라, 예술가들이 이러한 변화에 어떻게 반응할 것인지는 고려할 가치가 있다. 보고서는 2040년까지 인간이 초래한 기후 변화의 영향을 피할 수 없게 될 것이며, 20년 후에는 예술과 삶의 중심에서 그것은 큰 이슈가 될 것을 시사한다. 미래의 예술가들은 미래 인간과 인공지능, 우주 공간의 인류 식민지 그리고 잠재적인 파멸과 같은 포스트 휴먼과 포스트 인류세의 가능성과 씨름할 것이다. 미투 운동과 흑인 민권 운동(흑인의 생명은 소중하다)과 관련된 예술에서 보이는 정체성 정치는 환경 보호주의, 경계 정치학 그리고 이주가 훨씬 더 뚜렷하게 집중을 받으면서 더 성장할 것이다. 예술은 점점 다양해지고 우리가 기대하는 것처럼 '예술처럼' 보이지 않을 수도 있다. 미래에는, 모두가 볼 수 있는 온라인에 우리의 삶이 보이는 것에 싫증나게 되고 우리의 사생활이 거의 없어지면, 익명성이 명성보다 더 바람직할 수도 있다. 수천, 혹은 수백만 개의 좋아요와 팔로워들 대신, 우리는 진실성과 관계에 굶주릴 것이다. 예술은, 결국, 개인적이기 보다는, 더 집단적이고 경험적이 된다.

① 미래의 예술은 어떤 모습일까?
② 지구 온난화가 우리의 삶에 어떤 영향을 미칠까?
③ 인공지능이 환경에 어떤 영향을 미칠까?
④ 정치적 운동 때문에 어떤 변화가 일어날까?

어휘

□ demographics 인구 통계학
□ geopolitics 지정학
□ wrestle with ~과 씨름하다
□ post-human 포스트휴먼
(인간과 로봇 및 기술의 경계가 사라져 현존하는 인간을 넘어선 신인류)
□ Anthropocene 인류세(人類世)
(인류가 지질학과 생태계에 상당한 영향력을 미치기 시작한 이후의 시대)
□ doom 파멸, 죽음
□ identity politics 정체성 정치
(인종·성·종교·계급 등 여러 기준으로 분화된 집단이 각 집단의 권리를 주장하는 데 주력하는 정치)
□ environmentalism 환경 보호주의, 환경 결정론
□ migration 이주, 이동
□ diverse 다양한
□ anonymity 익명성
□ fame 명성
□ authenticity 진실성
□ collective 집단적인

정답 ①

30 다음 글의 주제로 가장 적절한 것은? 2020. 국가직 9급

For many people, work has become an obsession. It has caused burnout, unhappiness and gender inequity, as people struggle to find time for children or passions or pets or any sort of life besides what they do for a paycheck. But increasingly, younger workers are pushing back. More of them expect and demand flexibility — paid leave for a new baby, say, and generous vacation time, along with daily things, like the ability to work remotely, come in late or leave early, or make time for exercise or meditation. The rest of their lives happens on their phones, not tied to a certain place or time — why should work be any different?

① ways to increase your paycheck
② obsession for reducing inequity
③ increasing call for flexibility at work
④ advantages of a life with long vacations

해설

일을 강박적으로 느끼는 젊은 근로자들의 업무 환경 변화를 요구한다는 내용의 글이다. 글의 첫 부분에 많은 사람들이 일에 강박을 느낀다고 하며 일을 하면서 개인 시간을 보내기 위해 많은 노력을 하며 생기는 여러 부작용을 제시하고 있다. 그러나 점점 더 많은 젊은 근로자들이 이에 대해 반발하며 유연성을 요구하고 있다고 진술하고 있다. 따라서 글의 주제로 가장 적절한 것은 ③이다.

해석

많은 사람들에게 일은 강박이 되었다. 그것은 사람들이 급여를 위해 하는 일 이외에 아이, 열정, 애완동물, 또는 어떤 종류의 삶을 위한 시간을 찾기 위해 애쓰면서 극도의 피로, 불행, 그리고 성 불평등을 야기했다. 그러나 점점 더 젊은 근로자들이 반발하고 있다. 그들 중 더 많은 이들이 원격 근무를 할 수 있고 늦게 출근하거나 일찍 퇴근할 수 있는 혹은 운동 혹은 명상을 위한 시간을 낼 수 있는 능력과 같은 일상적인 것들과 함께, 이를테면, 새로 태어난 아기를 위한 유급휴가와 넉넉한 휴가 시간과 같은 유연성을 기대하고 요구한다. 그들 삶의 나머지는 특정 장소와 시간에 묶여 있지 않고 그들의 전화에서 일어나는데, ― 일은 왜 달라야 하는가?

① 급여를 늘리는 방법들
② 불평등 해소에 대한 강박관념
③ 일에서 유연성 증대에 대한 요구 증가
④ 긴 휴가가 주는 이점들

어휘

□obsession 강박, 집착, 사로잡힘
□burnout 업무 스트레스로 인한 심리적, 육체적 지침
□inequity 불공평
□paycheck 급여
□flexibility 유연성
□paid leave 유급 휴가
□generous 넉넉한, 관대한, 너그러운
□work remotely 원격 근무
□meditation 명상

정답 ③

31 다음 글의 주제로 가장 적절한 것은? 2020. 지방직 9급

> The e-book applications available on tablet computers employ touchscreen technology. Some touchscreens feature a glass panel covering two electronically-charged metallic surfaces lying face- to-face. When the screen is touched, the two metallic surfaces feel the pressure and make contact. This pressure sends an electrical signal to the computer, which translates the touch into a command. This version of the touchscreen is known as a resistive screen because the screen reacts to pressure from the finger. Other tablet computers feature a single electrified metallic layer under the glass panel. When the user touches the screen, some of the current passes through the glass into the user's finger. When the charge is transferred, the computer interprets the loss in power as a command and carries out the function the user desires. This type of screen is known as a capacitive screen.

① how users learn new technology
② how e-books work on tablet computers
③ how touchscreen technology works
④ how touchscreens have evolved

해설

태블릿 컴퓨터에서 사용되는 터치스크린 기술에 관해 설명하는 글이다. 터치스크린 기술의 작동 원리를 열거하고 터치스크린의 유형에 대해서 소개하고 있다. 따라서 글의 주제로 가장 적절한 것은 ③이다.

해석

> 태블릿 컴퓨터에서 사용할 수 있는 전자책 애플리케이션은 터치스크린 기술을 사용한다. 몇몇 터치스크린들은 마주 보도록 놓인 두 개의 금속 표면들을 덮고 있는 유리판을 특징으로 한다. 스크린이 만져지면, 두 개의 금속 표면들은 압력을 느끼고 접촉한다. 이 압력은 전기 신호를 컴퓨터로 보내고, 이것은 그 접촉을 명령어로 전환한다. 이 버전의 터치스크린은 손가락의 압력에 반응하기 때문에 저항식 스크린으로 알려져 있다. 다른 태블릿 컴퓨터들은 유리판 아래에 하나의 전기가 흐르는 금속 막을 특징으로 한다. 사용자가 스크린을 터치하면 전류 중 일부가 유리를 통해 사용자의 손가락으로 지나간다. 전하가 이동되면 컴퓨터는 전력 손실을 명령으로 해석해 사용자가 원하는 기능을 수행한다. 이러한 유형의 화면을 정전식 화면으로 알려져 있다.

① 사용자가 새로운 기술을 배우는 방법
② 태블릿 컴퓨터에서 전자책이 작동하는 방법
③ 터치스크린 기술이 작동하는 방법
④ 터치스크린의 발전 과정

어휘

□e-book 전자책
□glass panel 유리판
□electronically-charged 전자적으로 충전된
□metallic 금속의, 금속으로 만든
□translate 전환하다, 바꾸다, 번역하다
□command (컴퓨터에 대한) 명령어, 명령, 명령하다
□version 버전, 형태
□pressure 압력, 압박
□resistive screen 저항식 스크린
□pass through 지나가다, 거쳐가다
□charge 전하, 충전, 책임 , 요금
□transfer 이동하다, 옮기다
□capacitive screen 정전식 스크린

정답 ③

32 다음 글의 제목으로 가장 적절한 것은? 2020. 지방직 9급

Louis XIV needed a palace worthy of his greatness, so he decided to build a huge new house at Versailles, where a tiny hunting lodge stood. After almost fifty years of labor, this tiny hunting lodge had been transformed into an enormous palace, a quarter of a mile long. Canals were dug to bring water from the river and to drain the marshland. Versailles was full of elaborate rooms like the famous Hall of Mirrors, where seventeen huge mirrors stood across from seventeen large windows, and the Salon of Apollo, where a solid silver throne stood. Hundreds of statues of Greek gods such as Apollo, Jupiter, and Neptune stood in the gardens; each god had Louis's face!

① True Face of Greek Gods
② The Hall of Mirrors vs. the Salon of Apollo
③ Did the Canal Bring More Than Just Water to Versailles?
④ Versailles: From a Humble Lodge to a Great Palace

해설

루이 14세가 '베르사유 궁전'을 건설하는 과정(기원)에 대한 이야기이다. 베르사유의 보잘것없는 오두막에서 엄청난 궁전으로 변하는 과정을 설명하고 있다. 따라서 글의 제목으로 가장 적절한 것은 ④이다.

해석

루이 14세는 그의 위대함에 걸맞은 궁전이 필요해서, 그는 베르사유에 거대한 새 집을 짓기로 결정했는데, 그곳에는 작은 사냥꾼 오두막집이 있었다. 거의 50년의 노동 끝에, 이 작은 사냥꾼 오두막은 4분의 1마일 길이의 거대한 궁전으로 바뀌었다. 강에서 물을 끌어오고 습지대의 물을 빼내기 위해 운하를 팠다. 베르사유는 유명한 거울의 방 같은 정교한 방들로 가득 차 있었는데, 그곳에는 17개의 거울들이 17개의 커다란 창문 맞은편에 있었고, 아폴론 방에는 순은빛 왕좌가 있었다. Apollo와 Jupiter, Neptune과 같은 그리스 신들 수백 개의 동상들이 정원들에 서 있었다; 각각의 신은 루이의 얼굴을 하고 있었다!

① 그리스 신들의 진면목
② 거울의 방 vs. 아폴로의 살롱
③ 운하가 베르사유에 물 이상의 것을 가져다 주었나?
④ 베르사유: 초라한 오두막에서 엄청난 궁전으로

어휘

□ palace 궁전, 왕궁
□ lodge 오두막
□ canal 운하
□ statue 조각상
□ drain 물을 빼내다, 배수하다, 고갈시키다
□ marshland 습지대
□ throne 왕좌
□ humble 변변치 않은, 초라한, 겸손한

정답 ④

33 다음 글의 요지로 가장 적절한 것은? 2020. 지방직 9급

Evolutionarily, any species that hopes to stay alive has to manage its resources carefully. That means that first call on food and other goodies goes to the breeders and warriors and hunters and planters and builders and, certainly, the children, with not much left over for the seniors, who may be seen as consuming more than they're contributing. But even before modern medicine extended life expectancies, ordinary families were including grandparents and even great-grandparents. That's because what old folk consume materially, they give back behaviorally — providing a leveling, reasoning center to the tumult that often swirls around them.

① Seniors have been making contributions to the family.
② Modern medicine has brought focus to the role of old folk.
③ Allocating resources well in a family determines its prosperity.
④ The extended family comes at a cost of limited resources.

해설

노인들의 중요성과 현대 사회에서의 역할을 강조하는 글이다. 글의 초반부에서는 노인들이 공동체에서 배제되는 것이 합리적이라는 내용으로 제시하였으나 3번째 문장에서 역접 표현인 But 이하의 내용으로 노인들이 공동체 내에서 흔들리지 않는 중심점을 제공함으로써 가족들에게 물질적인 것에 대한 보상을 제공한다고 설명하고 있다. 따라서 글의 요지로 가장 적절한 것은 ①이다.

해석

진화론적으로, 살아남기를 원하는 모든 종들은 그것의 자원을 신중하게 관리해야 한다. 이것은 음식과 다른 맛있는 것들이 우선적으로 사육가들, 전사들, 사냥꾼들, 농부들, 건설가들 그리고 분명히, 아이들에게 우선적으로 가야하고, 그들이 기여하는 것보다 소비하는 것으로 여겨질 수 있는 노인들을 위해 남겨지는 것은 많이 없다는 것을 의미한다. 그러나, 심지어 현대의학이 기대수명들을 늘리기 전에도, 보통 가정들은 조부모들과 심지어 증조부모들을 포함하고 있었다. 그것은 가족들 주변에 종종 몰아치는 혼란에 침착하고 논리적인 사유를 하는 중심을 제공하면서, 나이든 사람들이 소비하는 것을 행동적으로 되돌려 주기 때문이다ㅡ즉, 노인들은 종종 그들 주변에서 소용돌이치는 소동에 평준화, 합리적인 중심을 제공한다.

① 노인들은 가족에게 기여해왔다.
② 현대 의학은 노인들의 역할에 초점을 두었다.
③ 한 가정에 자원을 잘 배분하는 것이 그것의 번영을 결정한다.
④ 대가족은 한정된 자원의 희생으로 이루어진다.

어휘

□ evolutionarily 진화론적으로
□ species 종
□ breeder 사육사, 양성자
□ contribute 기여하다
□ extend 확장하다, 연장하다
□ life expectancy 기대 수명, 평균 수명
□ old folk 노인들
□ great-grandparent 증조부모
□ materially 물질적으로
□ leveling 평준화, 평등화, 단순화
□ tumult 소란, 소동
□ swirl 소용돌이치다, 빙빙 돌다, 소용돌이
□ prosperity 번영, 번성, 번창
□ extended family 대가족

정답 ①

34 다음 글의 제목으로 가장 적절한 것은? 2019. 국가직 9급

Mapping technologies are being used in many new applications. Biological researchers are exploring the molecular structure of DNA ("mapping the genome"), geophysicists are mapping the structure of the Earth's core, and oceanographers are mapping the ocean floor. Computer games have various imaginary "lands" or levels where rules, hazards, and rewards change. Computerization now challenges reality with "virtual reality," artificial environments that stimulate special situations, which may be useful in training and entertainment. Mapping techniques are being used also in the realm of ideas. For example, relationships between ideas can be shown using what are called concept maps. Starting from a general or "central" idea, related ideas can be connected, building a web around the main concept. This is not a map by any traditional definition, but the tools and techniques of cartography are employed to produce it, and in some ways it resembles a map.

① Computerized Maps vs. Traditional Maps
② Where Does Cartography Begin?
③ Finding Ways to DNA Secrets
④ Mapping New Frontiers

해설

다양한 분야에서 활용되는 현대 지도 기술의 다양한 응용에 대한 글로, 생물학, 지구 물리학, 컴퓨터 게임, 가상 현실, 개념도 등 다양한 분야에서 활용되는 현대 지도 기술의 응용 형태와 그 중요성에 대한 설명하고 있다. 따라서 글의 제목으로 가장 적절한 것은 ④이다.

해석

지도 제작 기술은 많은 새로운 응용 프로그램들에서 사용되고 있다. 생물학 연구원들은 DNA의 분자 구조("게놈의 지도화")를 탐색하고 있고, 지구 물리학자들은 지구의 중심핵의 구조를 지도화하고 있고, 해양학자들은 해저를 지도화하고 있다. 컴퓨터 게임들은 규칙들, 위험들, 보상들이 변화하는 다양한 가상의 "땅" 혹은 단계들을 가지고 있다. 컴퓨터화는 이제 훈련과 오락에 유용할 수 있는 특별한 상황을 가장하는 인공적인 환경인 "가상 현실"로 현실에 도전한다. 지도 제작 기술은 관념 영역에서도 사용되고 있다. 예를 들어, 생각들 사이의 관계는 개념도라고 불리는 것을 사용하여 보일 수 있다. 일반적인 또는 "중심적인" 생각에서 시작하여, 관련된 생각들이 연결되고, 주요 개념 주위에 망을 구축할 수 있다. 이것은 전통적인 정의에 의한 지도는 아니지만 지도 제작의 도구와 기술이 사용되었고, 어떤 면에서는 지도와 유사하다.

① 컴퓨터화된 지도 vs. 전통적인 지도
② 지도 제작법은 어디에서 시작되었는가?
③ DNA의 비밀에 대한 방법들을 찾기
④ 새로운 영역을 지도로 표현하기

어휘

□ mapping technology 지도제작 기술
□ map 지도, 지도를 만들다
□ application 응용 프로그램, 응용, 적용, 지원, 신청
□ genome 게놈(유전자 총체)
□ molecular 분자
□ geophysicist 지구 물리학자
□ Earth's core 지구의 중심핵
□ oceanographer 해양학자
□ ocean floor 해저
□ reward 보상, 보상하다
□ virtual reality 가상 현실
□ artificial 인공의, 인위적인
□ realm 영역, 범위
□ concept map 개념도
□ central 중심적인
□ cartography 지도 제작(법)

정답 ④

35 다음 글의 요지로 가장 적절한 것은? 2019. 국가직 9급

When giving performance feedback, you should consider the recipient's past performance and your estimate of his or her future potential in designing its frequency, amount, and content. For high performers with potential for growth, feedback should be frequent enough to prod them into taking corrective action, but not so frequent that it is experienced as controlling and saps their initiative. For adequate performers who have settled into their jobs and have limited potential for advancement, very little feedback is needed because they have displayed reliable and steady behavior in the past, knowing their tasks and realizing what needs to be done. For poor performers — that is, people who will need to be removed from their jobs if their performance doesn't improve — feedback should be frequent and very specific, and the connection between acting on the feedback and negative sanctions such as being laid off or fired should be made explicit.

① Time your feedback well.
② Customize negative feedback.
③ Tailor feedback to the person.
④ Avoid goal-oriented feedback.

해설

성과 피드백의 적절한 설계와 전략에 대한 글로, 성과 피드백을 제공할 때 고려해야 할 요소와 다양한 성과 수준에 따른 효과적인 피드백 전략에 대한 설명하고 있다. 첫 문장에서 주제를 제시하고 2번째에서 4번째 문장의 예시를 통해서 개별적인 피드백의 방법을 제시하고 있으므로 글의 요지로 가장 적절한 것은 ③이다.

해석

성과에 대한 피드백을 줄 때, 당신은 받는 사람의 과거의 성과와 그것의 빈도, 양 그리고 내용을 설계하는 데 있어서 그 또는 그녀의 미래 잠재력에 대한 당신의 추정치를 고려해야 한다. 성장 가능성이 있는 고성과자들에게는, 피드백은 그들이 교정적인 행동을 하게끔 촉구하기에 충분할 정도로 자주 있어야 하지만, 너무 자주 이루어져 그것이 통제하는 것으로서 여겨지고 그들의 주도권을 약화시킬 정도로 자주 있어서는 안 된다. 그들의 일에 정착하고 발전에 제한된 가능성을 가진 적합한 성과를 내는 수행자들에게는 거의 피드백이 필요하지 않은데, 왜냐하면 그들이 믿을 수 있고 꾸준한 행동을 과거에 보여주었고 과거에 그들의 업무를 알고, 무엇이 완료될 필요가 있는지 알아차리고 있기 때문이다. 그들의 직장에서 내보내질 필요가 있을 좋지 못한 성과를 내는 사람들에게는 그들의 성과가 향상되지 않으면 피드백은 자주 있어야 하고 매우 구체적이어야 하며, 피드백에 근거하여 행동하는 것과 일시적으로 해고되거나 해고되는 것과 같은 부정적인 제재 사이의 연관성이 분명하게 만들어져야 한다.

① 당신의 피드백의 시기를 잘 맞춰라.
② 부정적인 피드백을 사용자의 사정에 맞춰서 하라.
③ 피드백을 그 사람에 맞춰라.
④ 목표 지향적인 피드백을 피하라.

어휘

□ performance 성과, 수행
□ recipient 받는 사람, 수령인, 수취인
□ potential 잠재력, 잠재적인
□ frequency 빈도
□ amount 양
□ prod 촉구하다, 자극하다
□ corrective 바로잡는, 교정의
□ sap 수액, 원기, 약화시키다
□ initiative 진취성, 결단력, 주도권
□ adequate 적합한, 충분한
□ sanction 제재, 허가, 제재를 가하다, 허가하다
□ lay off 해고하다
□ fire 해고하다
□ explicit 분명한, 명백한, 노골적인

□customize 사용자의 사정[희망]에 맞추다. 주문에 응하여 만들다
□tailor (특정한 목적·사람 등에) 맞추다[조정하다], 재단사
□goal-oriented 목표 지향적인

정답 ③

36 다음 글의 주제로 가장 적절한 것은? 2019. 국가직 9급

Imagine that two people are starting work at a law firm on the same day. One person has a very simple name. The other person has a very complex name. We've got pretty good evidence that over the course of their next 16 plus years of their career, the person with the simpler name will rise up the legal hierarchy more quickly. They will attain partnership more quickly in the middle parts of their career. And by about the eighth or ninth year after graduating from law school the people with simpler names are about seven to ten percent more likely to be partners—which is a striking effect. We try to eliminate all sorts of other alternative explanations. For example, we try to show that it's not about foreignness because foreign names tend to be harder to pronounce. But even if you look at just white males with Anglo-American names. so really the true in-group, you find that among those white males with Anglo names they are more likely to rise up if their names happen to be simpler. So simplicity is one key feature in names that determines various outcomes.

① the development of legal names
② the concept of attractive names
③ the benefit of simple names
④ the roots of foreign names

해설

단순한 이름이 커리어에 미치는 영향에 대한 글로, 이름의 단순성이 커리어 성과에 영향을 미치는 것을 조사한 결과, 더 단순한 이름을 가진 사람들이 더 빨리 진급하고 파트너십을 획득하는 경향이 있다는 연구결과를 근거로 설명하고 있다. 따라서 글의 주제로 가장 적절한 것은 ③이다.

해석

두 사람이 같은 날에 법률 사무소에서 일하기 시작한다고 상상해보자. 한 사람은 매우 단순한 이름을 가지고 있다. 다른 사람은 매우 복잡한 이름을 가지고 있다. 우리는 이후 16년간의 그들의 경력에 있어 더 간단한 이름을 가지고 있는 사람이 더 빨리 법조계 서열이 올라갈 것이라는 꽤나 타당한 증거를 가지고 있다. 그들은 그들의 경력의 중반부에 파트너십을 더 빨리 획득할 것이다. 그리고 로스쿨에서 졸업하고 8년 또는 9년차 정도가 되었을 때 더 단순한 이름을 가진 사람들은 파트너(이사)가 될 가능성이 대략 7에서 10퍼센트 더 높은데, 이것은 인상적인 결과이다. 우리는 여기에서 모든 종류의 다른 대안적인 설명들을 제거하고자 한다. 예를 들어, 외국 이름이 발음하기 더 어려운 경향이 있기 때문에, 우리는 그것이 외래성에 관한 것이 아님을 보여주려 한다. 그러나 당신이 그렇게 정말 진정한 내집단에 속한 영국계 미국인 이름들을 가지고 있는 백인 남성들을 본다고 하더라도, 당신은 영국계 미국 이름들을 가진 그러한 백인 남성들 중에서 그들의 이름들이 더 단순하다면 그들은 위로 올라갈 가능성이 더 높다는 것을 알게 된다. 그러므로 간단함은 다양한 결과들을 결정하는 이름에 있어서의 하나의 핵심적인 특징이다.

① 법적 이름의 발달
② 매력적인 이름의 개념
③ 간단한 이름의 이점
④ 외국 이름의 뿌리

어휘

□hierarchy 계층, 계급
□attain 이루다, 달성하다
□striking 인상적인, 현저한, 두드러진
□eliminate 제거하다
□alternative 대안적인
□foreignness 외래성, 이질성
□pronounce 발음하다
□in-group 내집단
□outcome 결과

정답 ③

37 다음 글의 주제로 가장 적절한 것은? 2019. 지방직 9급

As the digital revolution upends newsrooms across the country, here's my advice for all the reporters. I've been a reporter for more than 25 years, so I have lived through a half dozen technological life cycles. The most dramatic transformations have come in the last half dozen years. That means I am, with increasing frequency, making stuff up as I go along. Much of the time in the news business, we have no idea what we are doing. We show up in the morning and someone says, "Can you write a story about (pick one) tax policy/immigration/climate change?" When newspapers had once-a-day deadlines, we said a reporter would learn in the morning and teach at night — write a story that could inform tomorrow's readers on a topic the reporter knew nothing about 24 hours earlier. Now it is more like learning at the top of the hour and teaching at the bottom of the same hour. I'm also running a political podcast, for example, and during the presidential conventions, we should be able to use it to do real-time interviews anywhere. I am just increasingly working without a script.

① a reporter as a teacher
② a reporter and improvisation
③ technology in politics
④ fields of journalism and technology

해설

디지털 혁명과 뉴스룸의 변화에 따르는 기자들에게 주는 조언을 주제로 하는 글로, 디지털 혁명으로 인해 뉴스룸에서의 변화와 기자들에게 필요한 새로운 접근 방식을 설명하고 있다. 따라서 글의 주제로 가장 적절한 것은 ②이다.

해석

디지털 혁명이 전국의 뉴스룸에 근본적인 변화를 일으키게 됨에 따라 여기에 모든 기자들을 위한 내 조언이 있다. 나는 25년 동안 기자였기 때문에 여섯 번의 기술적 라이프 사이클을 겪었다. 가장 극적인 변화들은 마지막의 6년간에 왔다. 이는 내가 더욱 잦은 빈도로 진행하면서 뭔가를 만들어가고 있음을 의미한다. 뉴스 업계에 있어 많은 시간 동안 우리는 우리가 하고 있는 것에 관해 모른다. 우리는 아침에 출근을 하고, 누군가는 '세금 정책, 이민, 기후 변화에 관해 글을 써주실래요?'라고 말한다. 기자들이 하루에 한 번씩 마감이 있었을 때, 우리는 기자들은 아침에는 배우고 밤에는 가르쳐야 한다고 말을 했다 — 그 기자가 24시간 전에는 알지 못했던 주제에 관해 내일의 독자들에게 알려주는 기사를 쓰는 것 말이다. 이제 이것은 마치 정시에는 배우고 30분에는 가르치는 것과 같다. 예를 들면 나는 또한 정치 팟캐스트를 운영 중인데 우리는 실시간 인터뷰를 하기 위해 어디에서든 그것을 이용할 수 있어야만 한다. 나는 점점 더 대본 없이 일하고 있다.

① 선생님으로서의 기자
② 기자와 즉석에서 하기
③ 정치학에서의 기술
④ 저널리즘과 기술의 영역들

어휘

- □ upend 철저한[근본적인] 영향을 주다, 거꾸로 세우다, 엎어놓다
- □ dramatic 극적인
- □ transformation 변화, 변신
- □ make up 만들어 내다, 꾸미다, 구성하다, 화장하다
- □ once-a-day 하루에 한 번의
- □ deadline 마감 기한
- □ inform 알리다, 통지하다
- □ real-time 실시간
- □ script 대본, 원고
- □ improvisation 즉석에서 하기

정답 ②

02 중심 내용 파악 유형 기출 독해 어휘 복습 TEST 정답

정답

1	contagious	전염되는, 전염성의	21	crave	갈망하다, 열망하다
2	eliminate	없애다, 제거하다	22	countless	무수한
3	ministry	(정부의 각) 부처, 목사, 성직자	23	deliberate	고의의, 의도적인, 신중한, 사려 깊은
4	infection	감염, 전염병	24	resistance	저항력, 내성
5	install	설치하다, 설비하다	25	further	더 이상의, 추가의
6	disparity	격차, 차이	26	extend	확장하다, 연장하다
7	emphasize	강조하다, 두드러지게 하다	27	interpret	해석하다, 이해하다
8	excavate	발굴하다	28	solid	믿을 수 있는, 견고한, 고체의, 단단한
9	exploit	이용하다, 착취하다	29	cultivate	양성하다, 경작하다, 재배하다
10	dilute	희석하다, 약화시키다	30	negative	원판, 음화, 부정적인
11	replenish	보충하다, 채우다	31	excessive	과도한, 지나친
12	organization	조직, 단체, 준비, 구성	32	overuse	남용, 남용하다
13	means	수단, 방법, 수입	33	give off	(냄새·열·빛 등을) 내다[발하다]
14	relieve	완화하다, 줄이다	34	emit	방출하다, 내뿜다
15	cherish	소중히 여기다, 아끼다, 간직하다	35	excite	흥분시키다, 자극하다, 불러일으키다, 촉발시키다
16	competence	능력, 능숙함	36	focal	중심의, 초점의
17	attribute	~의 탓으로 보다, 속성, 특성, 자질	37	inert	움직이지 않는, 비활성의
18	equate	동일시하다	38	perception	인지, 자각
19	dedicate	바치다, 전념하다	39	concerned	걱정하는, 관심이 있는
20	discuss	논의하다, 상의하다	40	assume	추정하다, 알다, 띠다

02 중심 내용 파악 유형 기출 독해 어휘 복습 TEST 정답

정답

41	meet halfway	타협하다, 절충하다	61	uninterrupted	중단되지 않는, 연속된
42	optimize	최적화하다	62	intact	그대로의, 온전한, 손상되지 않은
43	simultaneously	동시에	63	courteously	정중히, 공손하게
44	sustain	유지하다, 지속시키다	64	discernment	통찰력, 식별, 인식
45	attire	복장, 의복	65	migration	이주, 이동
46	petition	청원(서), 탄원(서), 신청서, 청원하다, 탄원하다	66	anonymity	익명성
47	flexibility	유연성, 신축성	67	obsession	강박, 집착, 사로잡힘
48	shrink	줄어들게 하다, 감소하다	68	generous	넉넉한, 관대한, 너그러운
49	allege	혐의를 제기하다	69	meditation	명상
50	subject	지배하에 두다, 종속시키다	70	pressure	압력, 압박
51	diffuse	분산되다, 확산되다	71	palace	궁전, 왕궁
52	merit	받을 만하다[자격/가치가 있다], 가치, 장점	72	statue	조각상
53	perspective	관점, 시각	73	leveling	평준화, 평등화, 단순화
54	assumption	가정, 추정	74	tumult	소란, 소동
55	construct	구성하다, 건설하다	75	prosperity	번영, 번성, 번창
56	signify	의미하다	76	artificial	인공의, 인위적인
57	identity	정체성, 신원	77	sanction	제재, 허가, 제재를 가하다, 허가하다
58	mend	고치다, 수리하다	78	striking	인상적인, 현저한, 두드러진
59	incumbent	의무적인, 재임 중인	79	transformation	변화, 변신
60	intervene	개입하다, 간섭하다	80	inform	알리다, 통지하다

chapter 03 문장 제거 유형 정답 및 해설

ANSWER

01 ②	02 ③	03 ④	04 ③	05 ③
06 ④	07 ②	08 ①	09 ③	10 ④
11 ②	12 ②	13 ②	14 ④	15 ③
16 ②	17 ④	18 ③	19 ③	20 ④
21 ④	22 ④	23 ③	24 ③	25 ④
26 ③	27 ④	28 ②	29 ③	

01 다음 글의 흐름상 어색한 문장은? 2025. 출제 기조 전환 2차

A very common type of writing task — one that appears in every academic discipline — is a reaction or response. ① In a reaction essay, the writer is usually given a "prompt" — a visual or written stimulus — to think about and then respond to. ② It is very important to gather reliable facts so that you can defend your argument effectively. ③ Common prompts or stimuli for this type of writing include quotes, pieces of literature, photos, paintings, multimedia presentations, and news events. ④ A reaction focuses on the writer's feelings, opinions, and personal observations about the particular prompt. Your task in writing a reaction essay is twofold: to briefly summarize the prompt and to give your personal reaction to it.

해설

반응 에세이의 개념과 작성 방법에 대한 글로, 반응 에세이는 주어진 자극에 대한 개인의 감정과 의견을 표현하는 글쓰기 과제로, 글쓴이는 자극을 요약하고 자신의 반응을 제시해야 함을 설명하고 있다. 반응 에세이에서 중요한 것은 주어진 자극에 대한 개인의 감정이나 의견을 표현하는 것이며, 사실을 수집하여 주장을 방어하는 것이 아니다. 따라서 글의 흐름상 어색한 문장은 사실수집의 중요성을 말하는 ②이다.

해석

매우 일반적인 종류의 글쓰기 과제는 모든 학문 분야에서 나타나는 반응 또는 응답이다. ① 반응 에세이에서는 보통 "프롬프터" — 시각적이거나 서면 자극 — 가 제공되어 이에 대해 생각하고 응답하는 방식이다. (② 당신의 주장을 효과적으로 방어하기 위해 신뢰할 수 있는 사실을 모으는 것이 매우 중요하다.) ③ 이 유형의 글쓰기를 위한 일반적인 프롬프트나 자극에는 인용문, 문학 작품, 사진, 그림, 멀티미디어 프레젠테이션, 뉴스 사건 등이 포함된다. ④ 반응은 특정 프롬프트에 대한 작가의 감정, 의견 및 개인적인 관찰에 중점을 둔다. 반응 에세이를 작성할 때의 작업은 두 가지이다: 프롬프트를 간결하게 요약하고 이에 대한 개인적인 반응을 제시하는 것이다.

어휘

- □ discipline 분야, 훈육, 규율, 훈육하다, 징계하다
- □ prompt 프롬프터의, 즉각적인, 신속한, 촉발하다, 유도하다
- □ reliable 신뢰할[믿을] 수 있는
- □ argument 주장, 논쟁, 언쟁
- □ quote 인용문, 인용하다
- □ literature 문학, 문헌
- □ focus on 중점을 두다, 초점을 맞추다
- □ opinion 의견, 견해
- □ briefly 간결하게, 간단히, 잠시
- □ summarize 요약하다

정답 ②

02 다음 글의 흐름상 어색한 문장은? 2025. 출제 기조 전환 1차

Every parent or guardian of small children will have experienced the desperate urge to get out of the house and the magical restorative effect of even a short trip to the local park. ① There is probably more going on here than just letting off steam. ② The benefits for kids of getting into nature are huge, ranging from better academic performance to improved mood and focus. ③ Outdoor activities make it difficult for them to spend quality time with their family. ④ Childhood experiences of nature can also boost environmentalism in adulthood. Having access to urban green spaces can play a role in children's social networks and friendships.

해설

어린이들의 성장에서 중요한 '자연'을 강조하는 글이다. 어린이와 함께 도시 공원을 방문하는 것은 단순히 스트레스 해소뿐만 아니라 학업 성과 향상, 기분 및 집중력 향상과 같은 거대한 이점을 가져올 수 있음을 설명하고 있다. 그러나 ③번의 진술은 '자연에서의 활동의 단점'을 언급하고 있으므로 글의 일관성에서 위배가 된다. 따라서 글의 흐름상 어색한 문장은 ③이다.

해석

어린 아이들의 모든 부모나 보호자는 집에서 나가고 싶은 필사적인 충동과 심지어 지역 공원으로의 짧은 여행의 마법 같은 회복 효과를 경험했을 것이다. ① 여기서 아마도 단지 기분을 푸는 것 이상의 일이 일어나고 있을 것이다. ② 더 나은 학업 성취로부터 향상된 기분과 집중에 이르기까지, 아이들에게 자연에 들어가는 것의 이점들은 엄청나다. (③ 야외 활동들은 그들이 가족과 양질의 시간을 보내는 것을 어렵게 만든다.) ④ 자연에 대한 어린 시절의 경험들은 성인기에 환경 보호주의를 신장시킬 수도 있다. 도시의 녹지 공간에 접근하는 것은 아이들의 사회적 관계망과 우정에 역할을 할 수 있다.

어휘

□guardian 보호자, 후견인
□desperate 필사적인, 절망적인
□urge 충동, 욕구, 충고하다, 권고하다
□get out of ~에서 나오다, 도망치다
□restorative 회복하는, 복원하는
□probably 아마
□going on (일이) 일어나고 있는
□let off steam 기분을 풀다, 울분[열기 등]을 발산하다
□get into ~에 들어가다, ~에 도착하다

정답 ③

03 다음 글의 흐름상 어색한 문장은? 2024. 국가직 9급

In spite of all evidence to the contrary, there are people who seriously believe that NASA's Apollo space program never really landed men on the moon. These people claim that the moon landings were nothing more than a huge conspiracy, perpetuated by a government desperately in competition with the Russians and fearful of losing face. ① These conspiracy theorists claim that the United States knew it couldn't compete with the Russians in the space race and was therefore forced to fake a series of successful moon landings. ② Advocates of a conspiracy cite several pieces of what they consider evidence. ③ Crucial to their case is the claim that astronauts never could have safely passed through the Van Allen belt, a region of radiation trapped in Earth's magnetic field. ④ They also point to the fact that the metal coverings of the spaceship were designed to block radiation. If the astronauts had truly gone through the belt, say conspiracy theorists, they would have died.

해설

일부 사람들은 NASA의 아폴로 프로그램이 달 착륙을 가짜로 만들었다고 주장하며, 미국의 우주 경쟁에서의 패배와 방사선에 대한 우려를 근거로 한다. ④번의 진술이 사실이라면, 달 착륙에 대한 근거가 되므로, 다음 글에서 제거가 되어야 한다. 따라서 글의 흐름상 어색한 문장은 ④이다.

해석

반대되는 모든 증거들에도 불구하고, NASA의 아폴로 우주 프로그램이 실제로 달에 사람을 착륙시킨 적이 없다고 진지하게 믿는 사람들이 있다. 이 사람들은 달 착륙이 러시아와 필사적으로 경쟁하며 체면을 잃을까봐 두려워하는 정부에 의해 영구화된 거대한 음모에 불과하다고 주장한다. ① 이 음모론자들은 미국이 우주 개발 경쟁에서 러시아와 경쟁할 수 없다는 것을 알았고 따라서 하는 수 없이 일련의 성공적인 달 착륙을 조작했다고 주장한다. ② 음모론 옹호자들은 그들이 증거라고 간주하는 것 중에 몇 가지를 인용한다. ③ 그들의 논거에 결정적인 것은 우주 비행사들이 지구의 자기장에 갇힌 방사선의 지역인 밴 앨런 벨트를 결코 안전하게 통과할 수 없었을 것이라는 주장이다. (④ 그들은 또한 우주선의 금속 덮개가 방사선을 차단하도록 설계되었다는 사실을 지적한다.) 만약 우주 비행사들이 진정으로 벨트를 통과했다면, 그들은 죽었을 것이라고 음모론자들은 말한다.

어휘

□land 상륙시키다, 상륙하다
□landing 착륙
□conspiracy 음모
□perpetuate 계속되게 하다, 영속시키다
□competition 경쟁
□therefore 그러므로, 따라서
□advocate 옹호하다, 지지하다
□radiation 방사선
□trapped 갇힌, 가두어진

정답 ④

04 다음 글의 흐름상 어색한 문장은? 2024. 지방직 9급

Critical thinking sounds like an unemotional process but it can engage emotions and even passionate responses. In particular, we may not like evidence that contradicts our own opinions or beliefs. ① If the evidence points in a direction that is challenging, that can rouse unexpected feelings of anger, frustration or anxiety. ② The academic world traditionally likes to consider itself as logical and free of emotions, so if feelings do emerge, this can be especially difficult. ③ For example, looking at the same information from several points of view is not important. ④ Being able to manage your emotions under such circumstances is a useful skill. If you can remain calm, and present your reasons logically, you will be better able to argue your point of view in a convincing way.

해설

비판적 사고와 감정과 관계가 있고, 감정 관리의 중요성을 강조하는 글이다. 글의 전개가 '감정이 관련됨의 여부'의 비교의 논리로 이어지고 있는데, '동일한 정보를 여러 관점에서 보는 것이 중요하지 않다'는 ③번이 '감정과 관련됨의 여부'와는 관련이 없는 진술로, 일관성에서 위반된다. 따라서 글의 흐름상 어색한 문장은 ③이다.

해석

비판적 사고는 감정 없는 과정처럼 들릴 수 있지만, 감정과 열정적인 반응을 불러일으킬 수 있다. 특히 우리는 자신의 의견이나 신념에 반하는 증거를 좋아하지 않을 수 있다. ① 만약 증거가 도전적인 방향을 가리킨다면, 그것은 예상치 못한 분노, 좌절, 불안의 감정을 불러일으킬 수 있다. ② 학계는 전통적으로 자신을 논리적이고 감정 없는 것으로 간주하려 하지만, 만약 감정이 드러나면 이는 특히 어려운 일이 될 수 있다. (③ 예를 들어, 같은 정보를 여러 관점에서 바라보는 것은 중요하지 않다.) ④ 이러한 상황에서 자신의 감정을 관리할 수 있는 능력은 유용한 기술이다. 당신이 침착하게 행동하고 논리적으로 자신의 이유를 제시할 수 있다면, 설득력 있게 자신의 관점을 주장할 수 있을 것이다.

어휘

- □critical thinking 비판적 사고
- □unemotional 감정 없는, 감정을 드러내지 않는
- □process 과정, 절차, 처리하다
- □passionate 열정적인, 열렬한
- □contradict 모순되다, 부정하다
- □challenging 도전적인, 저항하는
- □rouse 불러일으키다, 깨우다
- □frustration 좌절감, 불만
- □anxiety 불안, 염려, 걱정거리, 열망
- □convincing 설득력 있는, 확실한

정답 ③

05 다음 글의 흐름상 어색한 문장은? 2023. 국가직 9급

In our monthly surveys of 5,000 American workers and 500 U. S. employers, a huge shift to hybrid work is abundantly clear for office and knowledge workers. ① An emerging norm is three days a week in the office and two at home, cutting days on site by 30 % or more. You might think this cutback would bring a huge drop in the demand for office space. ② But our survey data suggests cuts in office space of 1 % to 2 % on average, implying big reductions in density not space. We can understand why. High density at the office is uncomfortable and many workers dislike crowds around their desks. ③ Most employees want to work from home on Mondays and Fridays. Discomfort with density extends to lobbies, kitchens, and especially elevators. ④ The only sure-fire way to reduce density is to cut days on site without cutting square footage as much. Discomfort with density is here to stay according to our survey evidence.

해설

하이브리드 근무로의 전환과 사무실 밀도에 미치는 영향을 주제로, 미국인 근로자와 고용주를 대상으로 한 조사 결과, 하이브리드 업무로의 변화가 명확하게 드러나고 있으며, 이로 인한 사무실에서 일하는 시간이 줄어들었지만, 사무실 공간 수요는 크게 감소하지 않았고, 밀도 문제는 여전히 존재한다는 것을 설명하는 글이다. ③ 문장의 '대부분의 직원들은 월요일과 금요일에 집에서 일하기를 원한다'는 진술은 글의 주제인 '하이브리드 업무'의 주제와 벗어나는 진술이다. 따라서 글의 흐름상 어색한 문장은 ③이다.

해석

5,000명의 미국 근로자와 500개의 미국 기업을 대상으로 실시한 우리의 월간조사에서, 사무직 및 지식노동자들 사이에서 하이브리드 근무로의 큰 변화가 명확하게 드러나고 있다. ① 최근에 생긴 표준은 사무실에서 주 3일, 집에서 주 2일로 현장 근무 일수를 30% 이상 단축하는 것이다. 당신은 이러한 삭감이 사무실 공간에 대한

수요를 크게 감소시킬 것이라고 생각할지도 모른다. ② 그러나 우리의 설문조사 데이터는 사무실 공간이 평균 1%에서 2% 감소하는 것을 시사하고, 이는 공간이 아닌 밀도에서의 큰 감소를 의미한다.. 우리는 그 이유를 이해할 수 있다. 사무실의 고밀도는 불편하고 많은 직원들은 그들 책상 주위에 사람들이 붐비는 것을 싫어한다. (③ 대부분의 직원들은 월요일과 금요일에 집에서 일하기를 원한다.) 밀도에 대한 불편함은 로비, 주방, 특히 엘리베이터까지 확대된다. ④ 밀도를 줄일 수 있는 유일한 확실한 방법은 평방 피트를 크게 줄이지 않고 현장에서의 근무일을 줄이는 것이다. 우리의 조사 증거에 따르면 밀도에 대한 불편함은 계속 남아 있다.

어휘

- □ shift 전환, 전환하다
- □ hybrid work 하이브리드 업무
  (온라인과 오프라인의 작업 방식을 조합한 새로운 업무 방식)
- □ emerging 최근 생겨난
- □ norm 기준
- □ density 밀도, 농도
- □ uncomfortable 불편한
- □ sure-fire 확실한, 틀림없는, 실패하지 않는
- □ reduce 줄이다, 축소하다, 감소시키다
- □ square footage 평방 피트
- □ here to stay 계속 유지될

정답 ③

06 다음 글의 흐름상 어색한 문장은? 2023. 지방직 9급

I once took a course in short-story writing and during that course a renowned editor of a leading magazine talked to our class. ① He said he could pick up any one of the dozens of stories that came to his desk every day and after reading a few paragraphs he could feel whether or not the author liked people. ② "If the author doesn't like people," he said, "people won't like his or her stories." ③ The editor kept stressing the importance of being interested in people during his talk on fiction writing. ④ Thurston, a great magician, said that every time he went on stage he said to himself, "I am grateful because I'm successful." At the end of the talk, he concluded, "Let me tell you again. You have to be interested in people if you want to be successful writer of stories."

해설

단편 소설 작가의 성공 비결로서의 인간에 대한 관심을 주제로 하는 글로, 작가로서 사람들을 좋아하는 태도는 작품을 좋아하게 만들며, 사람들에게 관심을 가져야 작가로서 성공할 수 있다는 편집장의 말을 강조하는 글이다. ④는 '자기 자신에게 긍정적인 말을 하는 마술사의 예'이므로 글의 맥락과 맞지 않다. 따라서 글의 흐름상 어색한 문장은 ④이다.

해석

나는 한때 단편 소설 쓰기 수업을 들었고, 그 과정 중에 일류의 잡지의 저명한 편집장이 우리 수업에서 강연했다. ① 그는 매일 자신의 책상에 온 수십 편의 이야기 중 아무거나 골라서 몇 단락을 읽은 후에 저자가 사람들을 좋아하는지 아닌지를 느낄 수 있다고 말했다. ② "만약 저자가 사람들을 좋아하지 않는다면, 사람들도 그의 이야기를 좋아하지 않을 것입니다."라고 그는 말했다. ③ 그 편집장은 소설 작성에 관한 강연 중에 계속해서 사람들에 관심을 가져야 하는 중요성을 강조했다. (④ 위대한 마술사인 Thurston은 무대에 올라갈 때마다 자신에게 "나는 성공해서 감사하다"라고 말했다고 한다.) 강연의 끝에서 그는 "다시 말하지만, 성공한 소설 작가가 되길 원한다면 사람들에게 관심을 가져야 합니다."라고 끝마쳤다.

어휘

- □ short-story 단편 소설
- □ renowned 유명한, 명성 있는
- □ editor 편집장, 편집자
- □ leading 주요한
- □ pick up 고르다
- □ paragraph 문단, 단락, 절
- □ stress 강조하다
- □ conclude 결론을 내리다, 끝내다

정답 ④

07 다음 글에서 전체 흐름과 가장 관계없는 문장은?

2023. 법원직 9급

One of the most interesting discoveries in the field of new sources of sustainable energy is bio-solar energy from jellyfish. Scientists have discovered that the fluorescent protein in this animal can be used to generate solar energy in a more sustainable way than current photovoltaic energy. How is this energy generated? ① The process involves converting the jellyfish's fluorescent protein into a solar cell that is capable of generating energy and transferring it to small devices. ② There has been constant criticism that the natural environment is being damaged by reckless solar power generation. ③ The main advantage of using these living beings as a natural energy source is that they are a clean alternative that does not use fossil fuels or require the use of limited resources. ④ Although this project is still currently in the trial phase, the expectation is that this source of energy will be able to be expanded and become a green alternative for powering the type of small electronic devices that are becoming more and more common.

* photovoltaic 광전기성의

해설

해파리의 형광 단백질을 활용하여 태양 에너지를 생성하는 새로운 방법을 소개하는 글이며, 이것이 지속 가능한 에너지의 중요한 대안임을 강조하고 있다. ②는 '태양광 발전의 폐해'에 대한 진술로, 해파리의 형광 단백질을 이용한, 미래 깨끗한 에너지의 대안이라는 글의 주제와는 관계가 없다. 따라서 전체 흐름과 가장 관계없는 문장은 ②이다.

해석

지속 가능한 에너지의 새로운 원천 분야에서 가장 흥미로운 발견 중 하나는 해파리의 바이오 태양 에너지이다. 과학자들은 이 동물의 형광 단백질이 현재의 광전 에너지보다 더 지속 가능한 방법으로 태양 에너지를 생성하는 데 사용될 수 있다는 것을 발견했다. 이 에너지는 어떻게 생성될까? ① 그 과정은 해파리의 형광 단백질을 에너지를 생성하고 작은 장치로 전달할 수 있는 태양 전지로 변환하는 것을 포함한다. (② 무분별한 태양광 발전으로 인해 자연환경이 훼손되고 있다는 지적이 끊이지 않고 있다.) ③ 이 생명체들을 자연적인 에너지원으로 사용하는 것의 주요 이점은 화석 연료를 사용하지 않거나 제한된 자원의 사용을 요구하는 깨끗한 대안이라는 것이다. ④ 비록 이 프로젝트가 아직 시험 단계에 있지만, 이 에너지원은 점점 더 보편화되고 있는 소형 전자 장치 유형에 전력을 공급하기 위한 친환경 대안이 될 수 있을 것으로 기대된다.

어휘

- □ jellyfish 해파리
- □ fluorescent 형광성의, 선명한
- □ reckless 무분별한, 무모한, 신중하지 못한
- □ fossil fuel 화석 연료
- □ limited 제한된, 한정된
- □ trial phase 시험 단계
- □ expand 확대시키다, 팽창하다
- □ green 환경보호의, 친환경적인
- □ device 장치, 기구

정답 ②

08 다음 글에서 전체 흐름과 가장 관계없는 문장은?

2023. 법원직 9급

Fast fashion is a method of producing inexpensive clothing at a rapid pace to respond to the latest fashion trends. With shopping evolving into a form of entertainment in the age of fast fashion, customers are contributing to what sustainability experts refer to as a throwaway culture. This means customers simply discard products once they are deemed useless rather than recycling or donating them. ① The consumers are generally satisfied with the quality of fast fashion brand clothing. ② As a result, these discarded items add a huge burden to the environment. ③ To resolve the throwaway culture and fast fashion crisis, the concept of sustainability in fashion is brought to the spotlight. ④ Sustainable fashion involves apparel, footwear, and accessories that are produced, distributed, and utilized as sustainably as possible while taking into account socio-economic and environmental concerns.

해설

패스트 패션과 그로 인한 일회용 문화에 대한 문제를 제기하고, 이를 해결하기 위한 지속 가능한 패션의 중요성을 강조하고 있다. 작가가 강조하는 문장은 마지막 문장인 '일회용 문화와 빠른 패션 위기를 해결하기 위해 패션의 지속 가능성이라는 개념이 주목받고 있다'를 통해 '지속 가능한 패션'을 강조하고 있다. 그러나 ① 문장은 '소비자들이 패스트 패션의 품질에 만족한다'는 패스트 패션에 대한 긍정적인 진술로 글의 흐름과 관계가 없다. 따라서 전체 흐름과 가장 관계없는 문장은 ①이다.

해석

패스트 패션은 최신 패션 트렌드에 대응하기 위해 빠른 속도로 저렴한 의류를 생산하는 방법이다. 패스트 패션 시대에 쇼핑이 오락 형태로 진화하면서 고객들은 지속 가능성 전문가들이 말하는 일회용 문화에 기여하고 있다. 이것은 고객들이 제품을 재활용하거나 기부하는 것이 아니라 쓸모없는 것으로 간주되면 그냥 폐기한다는 것을 의미한다. (① 소비자들은 일반적으로 패스트 패션 브랜드 의류의 품질에 만족한다.) ② 결과적으로, 이러한 버려진 물건들은 환경에 큰 부담을 더한다. ③ 일회용 문화와 패스트 패션 위기를 해결하기 위해 패션의 지속 가능성이라는 개념이 주목받고 있다. ④ 지속 가능한 패션은 사회경제적, 환경적 관심사를 고려하여 가능한 지속 가능하게 생산, 유통 및 활용되는 의류, 신발 및 액세서리를 포함한다.

어휘

- □ sustainability 지속 가능성
- □ throwaway 일회용
- □ socio-economic 사회 경제적인
- □ environmental 환경적인
- □ concern 관심사, 중요한 것, 걱정, 염려, 영향을 미치다

정답 ①

09 글의 흐름상 가장 어색한 문장은? 2022. 지방직 9급

The skill to have a good argument is critical in life. But it's one that few parents teach to their children. ① We want to give kids a stable home, so we stop siblings from quarreling and we have our own arguments behind closed doors. ② Yet if kids never get exposed to disagreement, we may eventually limit their creativity. ③ Children are most creative when they are free to brainstorm with lots of praise and encouragement in a peaceful environment. ④ It turns out that highly creative people often grow up in families full of tension. They are not surrounded by fistfights or personal insults, but real disagreements. When adults in their early 30s were asked to write imaginative stories, the most creative ones came from those whose parents had the most conflict a quarter-century earlier.

해설

어떻게 아이들이 논쟁 능력을 배울 수 있는지와 논쟁의 중요성을 강조하는 글로, 논쟁과 긴장된 환경이 창의력에 기여할 수 있다는 것을 강조하고 있다. ③은 '평화로운 환경이 창의력에 기여한다'고 진술하고 있으므로 글의 일관성에서 벗어난다. 따라서 글의 흐름상 가장 어색한 문장은 ③이다.

해석

좋은 논쟁을 하는 기술은 인생에서 매우 중요하다. 하지만 그것은 소수의 부모들이 그들의 아이들에게 가르치는 것이다. ① 우리는 아이들에게 안정적인 가정을 제공해 주고 싶어서 우리는 형제자매들이 싸우는 것을 막고 우리만의 논쟁을 비공개로 한다. ② 하지만 아이들이 의견 차이에 절대 노출되지 않는다면, 우리는 결국 그들의 창의력을 제한할 수도 있다. (③ 아이들은 평화로운 환경에서 많은 칭찬과 격려를 받으며 자유롭게 브레인스토밍을 할 때 가장 창의적이다.) ④ 대단히 창의력이 뛰어난 사람들은 종종 긴장감이 가득한 가정에서 성장하는 것으로 나타났다. 그들은 주먹다짐이나 개인적인 모욕에 둘러싸여 있는 것이 아니라, 진정한 의견 차이로 둘러싸여 있다. 30대 초반의 성인들에게 상상력이 풍부한 이야기를 쓰라고 했을 때, 가장 창의적인 이야기들은 25년 전에 가장 갈등이 많았던 부모님들에게서 나왔다.

어휘

- □ argument 논쟁, 주장
- □ stable 안정적인
- □ quarrel 말다툼, 언쟁
- □ disagreement 불일치, 의견 차이
- □ creativity 창의성
- □ brainstorm 아이디어 회의
- □ encouragement 격려
- □ peaceful 평화로운
- □ tension 긴장, 긴장감
- □ fistfight 주먹싸움
- □ insult 모욕, 모욕하다
- □ imaginative 상상력이 풍부한
- □ conflict 갈등, 충돌
- □ quarter-century 25년, 1/4세기
- □ exposure 노출, 폭로
- □ limit 제한하다

정답 ③

10 다음 글의 흐름상 가장 어색한 문장은? 2021. 국가직 9급

The term burnout refers to a "wearing out" from the pressures of work. Burnout is a chronic condition that results as daily work stressors take their toll on employees. ① The most widely adopted conceptualization of burnout has been developed by Maslach and her colleagues in their studies of human service workers. Maslach sees burnout as consisting of three interrelated dimensions. The first dimension — emotional exhaustion — is really the core of the burnout phenomenon. ② Workers suffer from emotional exhaustion when they feel fatigued, frustrated, used up, or unable to face another day on the job. The second dimension of burnout is a lack of personal accomplishment. ③ This aspect of the burnout phenomenon refers to workers who see themselves as failures, incapable of effectively accomplishing job requirements. ④ Emotional labor workers enter their occupation highly motivated although they are physically exhausted. The third dimension of burnout is depersonalization. This dimension is relevant only to workers who must communicate interpersonally with others (e.g. clients, patients, students) as part of the job.

해설

일상 업무 스트레스로 인한 지침의 만성적인 질환인 번아웃을 주제로 하는 글이다. 본문의 내용은 번아웃이라는 개념과 유형에 대해서 나열하고 있는데 ④는 감정노동자들은 그들의 직업에 매우 의욕적으로 들어간다고 진술하고 있으므로 글의 일관성에서 벗어난다. 따라서 글의 흐름상 가장 어색한 문장은 ④이다.

해석

번아웃이라는 용어는 업무 압박으로 인한 "지치는 것"을 의미한다. 번아웃은 일상의 업무 스트레스 요인이 직원들에게 피해를 입히면서 발생하는 만성적인 질환이다. ① 번아웃에 대한 가장 널리 채택된 개념화는 Maslach와 그녀의 동료들이 인간 서비스 노동자에 대한 연구에서 발전되어 왔다. Maslach는 번아웃이 서로 연관된 3개의 차원으로 이루어져 있다고 본다. 첫 번째 요소인 감정적인 소모는 실제로 번아웃 현상의 핵심이다. ② 근로자들은 피곤하거나, 좌절하거나, 지치거나, 직장에서 다른 날을 맞이할 수 없을 때 감정적인 피로로 고통 받는다. 번아웃 현상의 두 번째 요소는 개인적인 성취의 결여이다. ③ 이러한 번아웃 현상의 차원은 자신을 실패자로 간주하고, 업무 요건을 효과적으로 이행할 수 없는 근로자를 나타낸다. (④ 감정노동자들은 육체적으로 지쳤음에도 불구하고 매우 의욕적으로 그들의 직업에 들어간다.) 번아웃의 세 번째 요소는 비인격화이다. 이 요소는 직무의 일부로 다른 사람들(예를 들어, 고객들, 환자들, 학생들)과 대인 관계에서 의사소통해야 하는 노동자들과만 관련된다.

어휘

- □ burnout 번아웃, 극도의 피로
- □ chronic 만성적인, 장기적인
- □ stressor 스트레스를 유발하는 요인
- □ toll 대가, 비용, 통행료
- □ conceptualization 개념화, 개념적인 해석
- □ interrelated 상호 관련된, 연결된
- □ dimension 요소, 차원
- □ exhaustion 탈진, 피로
- □ core 핵심
- □ phenomenon 현상
- □ fatigued 피로한, 지친
- □ frustrated 좌절한, 좌절감을 느끼는
- □ used up 다 쓴, 지친
- □ incapable 무능한, ~을 할 수 없는
- □ effectively 효과적으로
- □ requirement 요구사항
- □ depersonalization 비인격화, 몰개성화, 객관화
- □ interpersonally 대인 관계에서

정답 ④

11 다음 글의 흐름상 적절하지 않은 문장은? 2021. 지방직 9급

There was no divide between science, philosophy, and magic in the 15th century. All three came under the general heading of 'natural philosophy'. ① Central to the development of natural philosophy was the recovery of classical authors, most importantly the work of Aristotle. ② Humanists quickly realized the power of the printing press for spreading their knowledge. ③ At the beginning of the 15th century Aristotle remained the basis for all scholastic speculation on philosophy and science. ④ Kept alive in the Arabic translations and commentaries of Averroes and Avicenna, Aristotle provided a systematic perspective on mankind's relationship with the natural world. Surviving texts like his *Physics*, *Metaphysics*, and *Meteorology* provided scholars with the logical tools to understand the forces that created the natural world.

해설

아리스토텔레스의 작품과 자연 철학의 발전에 대한 글로, 체계적인 자연 세계와의 인류의 관계적인 측면에서 아리스토텔레스의 역할을 강조하고 있다. 본문의 내용은 아리스토텔레스 철학이 현재 학문들에 영향을 미쳤다는 내용의 글인데, '그들의 지식을 전파하는 인쇄기의 힘'을 강조하는 ②는 아리스토텔레스의 철학에 벗어나는 내용이다. 따라서 글의 흐름상 적절하지 않은 문장은 ②이다.

해석

15세기에는 과학, 철학, 마술 사이에 어떤 구분도 없었다. 이 세 가지 모두 '자연 철학'이라는 일반적인 주제에 포함되었다. ① 고전 작가들의 재발견이 자연 철학의 발전에 중요했는데, 가장 중요하게는 아리스토텔레스의 작품들이었다. (② 인문주의자들은 그들의 지식을 전파하는 인쇄기의 힘을 빠르게 깨달았다.) ③ 15세기 초에 아리스토텔레스는 스콜라 학파 철학과 과학의 논쟁에 기초가 되었다. ④ 아랍어 번역 작품들과 Averroes와 Avicenna의 논평 안에서 살아 있는, 아리스토텔레스는 자연세계와의 인류의 관계에 대한 체계적인 관점을 제공했다. 그의 물리학, 형이상학, 그리고 기상학과 같은 살아남은 문헌들은 학자들에게 자연계를 창조한 힘을 이해할 수 있는 논리적 도구를 제공했다.

어휘

- ☐natural philosophy 자연 철학
- ☐recovery 회복
- ☐humanist 인문주의자
- ☐printing press 인쇄기
- ☐scholastic 스콜라 철학의, 학문적인
- ☐speculation 추측, 사색
- ☐systematic 체계적인
- ☐perspective 시각, 관점
- ☐physics 물리학
- ☐metaphysics 형이상학
- ☐meteorology 기상학
- ☐logical 논리적인
- ☐force 힘, 역력

정답 ②

12 글의 흐름상 가장 어색한 문장은? 2021. 법원직 9급

Fiction has many uses and one of them is to build empathy. When you watch TV or see a film, you are looking at things happening to other people. Prose fiction is something you build up from 26 letters and a handful of punctuation marks, and you, and you alone, using your imagination, create a world and live there and look out through other eyes. ① <u>You get to feel things, and visit places and worlds you would never otherwise know.</u> ② <u>Fortunately, in the last decade, many of the world's most beautiful and unknown places have been put in the spotlight.</u> ③ <u>You learn that everyone else out there is a me, as well.</u> ④ <u>You're being someone else, and when you return to your own world, you're going to be slightly changed.</u>

해설

산문 소설을 통해 상상력을 발휘하고 다른 세계를 탐험하며 공감을 형성하는 경험을 강조하는 글이다. 그러나 ②의 내용은 '실제 세계에서의 장소'를 언급하고 있으므로, '소설과 상상력을 통한 세계'라는 주제와 거리가 있다. 따라서 글의 흐름상 가장 어색한 문장은 ②이다.

해석

소설은 많은 용도를 가지고 있고 그것들 중 하나는 공감을 형성하는 것이다. 당신이 TV 를 보거나 영화를 볼 때, 당신은 다른 사람들에게 일어나는 일들을 보고 있다. 산문 소설은 26개의 글자[알파벳]와 몇 개의 구두점을 통해 쌓아올린 것이다. 그리고 당신과 당신만이 상상력을 발휘하여 세상을 창조하고 그곳에서 살고 다른 눈을 통해 관찰한다. ① 당신은 무언가를 느끼고, 그렇지 않았다면 당신이 결코 알지 못할 장소와 세상들을 방문한다. (② 다행히도, 지난 10년 동안, 세계에서 가장 아름답고 알려지지 않은 많은 장소들이 주목을 받았다.) ③ 저 밖에 있는 다른 사람들도 모두 나라는 것을 알게 된다. ④ 당신은 다른 사람이 되고 있고, 당신이 당신의 세상으로 돌아가면, 당신은 약간 달라질 것이다.

어휘

- ☐empathy 감정 이입, 공감
- ☐prose 산문(체)
- ☐punctuation mark 구두점
- ☐imagination 상상력
- ☐spotlight 주목을 받다
- ☐slightly 약간, 조금

정답 ②

13 다음 글에서 전체 흐름과 관계없는 문장은? 2021. 법원직 9급

Medical anthropologists with extensive training in human biology and physiology study disease transmission patterns and how particular groups adapt to the presence of diseases like malaria and sleeping sickness. ① Because the transmission of viruses and bacteria is strongly influenced by people's diets, sanitation, and other behaviors, many medical anthropologists work as a team with epidemiologists to identify cultural practices that affect the spread of disease. ② Though it may be a commonly held belief that most students enter medicine for humanitarian reasons rather than for the financial rewards of a successful medical career, in developed nations the prospect of status and rewards is probably one incentive. ③ Different cultures have different ideas about the causes and symptoms of disease, how best to treat illnesses, the abilities of traditional healers and doctors, and the importance of community involvement in the healing process. ④ By studying how a human community perceives such things, medical anthropologists help hospitals and other agencies deliver health care services more effectively.

* epidemiologist 유행[전염]병학자

해설

의학 인류학자들이 질병 전염 패턴과 인간의 적응에 대한 연구를 통해 어떻게 의료 서비스를 개선하는 데 기여하는지를 다루고 있는 글이다. ②는 '인도주의적인 동기에서의 전망과 지위와 보상의 고려'에 대한 진술로, '인류 인류학자들의 의료에 대한 기여'와는 관계가 없는 문장이다. 따라서 전체 흐름과 관계없는 문장은 ②이다.

해석

인간 생물학 및 생리학에 대한 폭넓은 교육을 받은 의학 인류학자들은 질병 전염 패턴과 말라리아나 수면병과 같은 질병의 존재에 어떻게 적응하는지를 연구한다. ① 바이러스와 박테리아의 전염은 사람들의 식생활, 위생, 다른 행동의 영향을 많이 받기 때문에 많은 의학 인류학자들은 전염병학자와 팀을 이루어 질병의 확산에 영향을 미치는 문화적 관행을 파악한다. (② 비록 대부분의 학생들이 성공적인 의학 경력의 금전적 보상보다는 인도주의적 이유로 의학을 입학한다는 것이 일반적인 믿음일 수 있지만, 선진국에서는 지위와 보상에 대한 전망이 아마도 하나의 동기일 것이다.) ③ 질병의 원인과 증상, 어떻게 질병을 가장 잘 치료하는지, 전통 치료사와 의사의 능력, 치유 과정에 지역사회가 참여하는 중요성에 대해 서로 다른 문화들은 다른 생각을 갖고 있다. ④ 의료 인류학자는 인간 공동체가 이러한 것들을 어떻게 인식하는지 연구함으로써 병원 및 다른 기관이 보다 효과적으로 의료 서비스를 제공할 수 있도록 지원한다.

어휘

- □ transmission 전염, 전파, 전달
- □ practice 관행, 관례, 실행, 실천
- □ cause 원인, 이유
- □ symptom 증상, 징후
- □ traditional healer 전통 치료사
- □ involvement 참여, 개입, 몰두, 열중
- □ perception 인식, 지각

정답 ②

14 다음 글의 흐름상 가장 어색한 문장은? 2020. 국가직 9급

When the brain perceives a threat in the immediate surroundings, it initiates a complex string of events in the body. It sends electrical messages to various glands, organs that release chemical hormones into the bloodstream. Blood quickly carries these hormones to other organs that are then prompted to do various things. ① The adrenal glands above the kidneys, for example, pump out adrenaline, the body's stress hormone. ② Adrenaline travels all over the body doing things such as widening the eyes to be on the lookout for signs of danger, pumping the heart faster to keep blood and extra hormones flowing, and tensing the skeletal muscles so they are ready to lash out at or run from the threat. ③ The whole process is called the fight-or-flight response, because it prepares the body to either battle or run for its life. ④ Humans consciously control their glands to regulate the release of various hormones. Once the response is initiated, ignoring it is impossible, because hormones cannot be reasoned with.

해설

위협 감지 시 신체 반응을 할 때의 호르몬의 역할에 대한 설명을 하는 글이다. ④ 문장은 인간이 의식적으로 호르몬을 분비한다는 내용으로 글의 일관성에서 벗어난다. 따라서 글의 흐름상 가장 어색한 문장은 ④이다.

해석

두뇌가 인접한 환경에서 위협을 감지할 때, 그것은 신체에서 복잡한 일련의 사건들을 일으킨다. 그것은 화학 호르몬을 혈류로 방출하는 기관인 다양한 분비샘에 전기적 신호를 보낸다. 혈액은 이 호르몬들을 그 다음에 다양한 일을 하도록 유도되는 다른 기관으로 빠르게 운반한다. ① 예를 들어, 신장 위의 부신은 신체의 스트레스 호르몬인 아드레날린을 배출한다. ② 아드레날린은 위험의 징후를 경계하기 위해 눈을 크게 뜨고, 혈액과 여분의 호르몬이 계속 흐르게 하기 위해 심장을 더 빠르게 펌프질하고, 골격 근육을 긴장시켜서 그들이 위협에 맞서거나 도망칠 준비를 하는 것과 같은 일들을 하면서 몸 전체를 돌아다닌다. ③ 그 전체 과정은 몸을 자신의 생명을 위해 싸우거나 뛸 수 있도록 준비시키기 때문에 투쟁－도피 반응이라고 불린다. (④ 인간은 의식적으로 다양한 호르몬의 분비를 통제하기 위해 그들의 분비샘을 조절한다.) 일단 그 반응이 시작되면, 호르몬은 논리적으로 설득할 수 없기 때문에 그것을 무시하는 것은 불가능하다.

어휘

☐ threat 위협
☐ initiate 시작하다, 착수시키다
☐ complex 복잡한
☐ a string of 일련의, 연속적인
☐ electrical 전기적인
☐ gland (내분비)샘
☐ chemical 화학적인
☐ hormone 호르몬
☐ bloodstream 혈류
☐ pump out 내보내다
☐ widen 넓히다, 커지다
☐ be on the lookout 주의를 기울이다, 세심히 살피다
☐ skeletal muscle 골격근
☐ lash out 공격하다, 싸우다, 혹평하다, 비난하다
☐ fight-or-flight response 투쟁 혹은 도피 반응
☐ consciously 의식적으로

정답 ④

15 글의 흐름상 가장 어색한 문장은? 2020. 지방직 9급

Philosophers have not been as concerned with anthropology as anthropologists have with philosophy. ① Few influential contemporary philosophers take anthropological studies into account in their work. ② Those who specialize in philosophy of social science may consider or analyze examples from anthropological research, but do this mostly to illustrate conceptual points or epistemological distinctions or to criticize epistemological or ethical implications. ③ In fact, the great philosophers of our time often drew inspiration from other fields such as anthropology and psychology. ④ Philosophy students seldom study or show serious interest in anthropology. They may learn about experimental methods in science, but rarely about anthropological fieldwork.

해설

이 글의 주제는 '철학자들은 인류학자의 연구에 관심이 없다'이다. ③은 '훌륭한 철학자들이 인류학과 같은 분야에서 영감을 얻는다'는 내용이므로 주제와 반대가 되는 진술이다. 따라서 글의 흐름상 가장 어색한 문장은 ③이다.

해석

철학자들은 인류학자들이 철학에 관심을 갖는 것만큼 인류학에 관심을 갖지 않았다. ① 영향력 있는 현대의 철학자들 중 그들의 연구에 인류학적 연구를 고려한 사람은 거의 없었다. ② 사회과학 철학을 전공하는 사람들은 인류학 연구의 사례를 고려하거나 분석할 수 있지만, 대부분 개념적 요점이나 인식론적 차이를 설명하거나 인식론적 또는 윤리적 영향을 비판하기 위해서였다. (③ 사실, 우리 시대의 위대한 철학자들은 종종 인류학과 심리학 같은 다른 분야로부터 영감을 얻는다.) ④ 철학과 학생들은 인류학에 대해 공부하거나 진지한 관심을 보이지 않는다. 그들은 과학에서 실험적인 방법에 대해 배울 수는 있지만, 인류학적 현장 연구에 대해서는 거의 배우지 않는다.

어휘

☐ anthropology 인류학
☐ influential 영향력 있는
☐ contemporary 현대의, 동시대의
☐ specialize in 전공하다
☐ analyze 분석하다
☐ research 연구
☐ illustrate 설명하다, 실증하다

□ conceptual 개념적인
□ epistemological 인식론의
□ distinction 구분
□ ethical 윤리적인
□ implication 함축, 암시, 영향, 결과
□ inspiration 영감
□ fieldwork 현장 연구

정답 ③

16 밑줄 친 부분 중 글의 흐름상 가장 어색한 것은?

2019. 국가직 9급

In 2007, our biggest concern was "too big to fail." Wall Street banks had grown to such staggering sizes, and had become so central to the health of the financial system, that no rational government could ever let them fail. ① Aware of their protected status, banks made excessively risky bets on housing markets and invented ever more complicated derivatives. ② New virtual currencies such as bitcoin and ethereum have radically changed our understanding of how money can and should work. ③ The result was the worst financial crisis since the breakdown of our economy in 1929. ④ In the years since 2007, we have made great progress in addressing the too-big-to-fail dilemma. Our banks are better capitalized than ever. Our regulators conduct regular stress tests of large institutions.

해설

금융 위기와 금융 체계 안정화의 발전에 대한 글로, 2007년의 금융 위기를 겪은 후, 금융 체계 안정화를 위해 은행들의 자본화와 규제 강화 등의 발전이 이루어지고 있음을 보여주고 있다. 이 글은 문제점으로 '너무 커진 월스트리트의 은행들'을 언급하고, 글의 전개방향은 이의 해결책이 진술되어야 하는데, ②에서 언급한 '가상화폐'는 이 글의 주제와 상관없다. 따라서 글의 흐름상 가장 어색한 것은 ②이다.

해석

2007년, 우리의 가장 큰 걱정은 "파산하기에는 너무 크다"는 것이었다. Wall Street의 은행들은 그렇게 어마어마한 크기로 성장했고, 금융 체계의 안정에 있어 너무도 중심이 되어 합리적인 정부라면 그들을 파산하도록 내버려둘 수가 없었다. ① 그들이 보호 받는 상태임을 알고 있기 때문에, 은행들은 과도하게 위험한 투자를 주택 시장에 하고 훨씬 복잡한 금융파생상품들을 고안해 냈다. (② 비트코인과 이더리움과 같은 새로운 가상 화폐들은 어떻게 돈이 작용 할 수 있고 작용해야 하는지에 대한 우리의 이해를 급진적으로 변화시켰다.) ③ 그 결과는 1929년 우리 경제의 붕괴 이후 최악의 금융 위기였다. ④ 2007년 이래로 파산하기에는 너무 큰 것에 대한 딜레마를 해결하는 데 있어서 큰 발전을 해오고 있다. 우리의 은행들 은 그 어느 때보다 더 잘 투자를 받는다. 우리의 단속 기관들은 대형 기관들의 규칙적인 스트레스 테스트를 시행한다.

어휘

□ concern 걱정, 염려
□ staggering 충격적인, 믿기 어려운
□ financial 금융의
□ rational 합리적인
□ excessively 과도하게, 지나치게
□ complicated 복잡한
□ derivative 파생상품
□ virtual currency 가상 화폐
□ financial crisis 금융 위기
□ breakdown 붕괴
□ progress 진전, 진척, 진행하다, 나아가다
□ address 다루다, 연설하다
□ capitalize 투자하다, 자본화하다
□ institution 기관

정답 ②

17 글의 흐름상 가장 어색한 문장은?

2019. 지방직 9급

Children's playgrounds throughout history were the wilderness, fields, streams, and hills of the country and the roads, streets, and vacant places of villages, towns, and cities. ① The term playground refers to all those places where children gather to play their free, spontaneous games. ② Only during the past few decades have children vacated these natural playgrounds for their growing love affair with video games, texting, and social networking. ③ Even in rural America few children are still roaming in a free-ranging manner, unaccompanied by adults. ④ When out of school, they are commonly found in neighborhoods digging in sand, building forts, playing traditional games, climbing, or playing ball games. They are rapidly disappearing from the natural terrain of creeks, hills, and fields, and like their urban counterparts, are turning to their indoor, sedentary cyber toys for entertainment.

해설

아이들의 놀이터와 변화된 환경에 대한 글로, 역사 속 아이들의 놀이터가 자연적인 장소에서 현대의 디지털 환경으로 변화하면서 아이들의 놀이 습관과 활동이 변화되어 전통적인 놀이터에서 아이들이 보이지 않음을 강조하는 글이다. 아이들의 자연의 놀이터가 점점 역할을 못하고 있다는 진술의 글인데, ④는 아이들이 '자연에서의 놀이터'에서 놀고 있다는 진술이므로 글의 일관성에서 벗어난다. 따라서 글의 흐름상 가장 어색한 문장은 ④이다.

해석

역사를 통틀어 아이들의 놀이터는 황야, 들판, 개울, 그리고 도시의 언덕과 도로, 거리, 마을, 시내, 도시의 공터였다. ① 놀이터라는 용어는 아이들이 자유롭고 자발적인 게임을 하기 위해 모인 모든 장소들을 나타낸다. ② 불과 지난 몇십 년 사이에 아이들은 비디오 게임, 문자, 그리고 사회 연결망과의 사랑이 커짐에 따라 이런 자연적 놀이터를 떠나 왔다. ③ 심지어 미국의 시골에서도 조금밖에 없는 아이들이 어른들과 동반되지 않은 채 여전히 자유롭게 돌아다니는 방식으로 한다. (④ 학교 밖에 있을 때, 그들은 모래를 파거나, 요새를 짓거나, 전통 게임을 하거나, 등산하거나, 혹은 공놀이를 하면서 흔히 동네에서 발견된다.) 그들은 계곡, 언덕 그리고 들판의 자연적 지역으로부터 빠르게 사라지고 있고 도시 거주자처럼 오락을 위해 실내에서 앉아 하는 사이버 장난감으로 눈을 돌리고 있다.

어휘

- □ playground 놀이터
- □ wilderness 황야, 황무지
- □ spontaneous 자발적인, 즉흥적인
- □ free-ranging 자유롭게 돌아다니는
- □ unaccompanied 동반되지 않은
- □ terrain 지역, 지형
- □ sedentary 정적인, 주로 앉아서 하는

정답 ④

18 글의 흐름상 가장 적절하지 않은 문장은? 2019. 서울시 9급

It seems to me possible to name four kinds of reading, each with a characteristic manner and purpose. The first is reading for information — reading to learn about a trade, or politics, or how to accomplish something. ① We read a newspaper this way, or most textbooks, or directions on how to assemble a bicycle. ② With most of this material, the reader can learn to scan the page quickly, coming up with what he needs and ignoring what is irrelevant to him, like the rhythm of the sentence, or the play of metaphor. ③ We also register a track of feeling through the metaphors and associations of words. ④ Courses in speed reading can help us read for this purpose, training the eye to jump quickly across the page.

해설

다양한 독서 형식의 분류와 목적에 대한 글로, 다양한 독서 형식 중 정보 획득을 위한 독서, 실용서나 설명서의 읽기, 그리고 속독 수업을 통한 빠른 훑어보기의 필요성에 대해 설명하고 있다. 즉, '정보를 목적으로 한 독서'가 주제인데, ③의 '일련의 감정과 은유와 단어들의 결합'은 정보를 목적으로 한 독서가 아니기 때문에 글의 일관성에서 벗어난다. 따라서 글의 흐름상 가장 적절하지 않은 문장은 ③이다.

해석

내가 보기에는 각각 독특한 방식과 목적을 가진 네 종류의 독서를 이름 짓는 것은 가능할 것 같다. 첫 번째는 정보를 얻기 위한 독서 ─ 무역, 정치, 또는 무언가를 성취하는 방법에 관해 배우기 위해 읽는 것이다. ① 우리는 이런 식으로 신문을 읽거나, 대부분의 교과서 또는 자전거를 조립하는 방법에 대한 설명서를 읽는다. ② 이러한 자료의 대부분을 가지고 독자는 페이지를 빨리 훑어보는 법을 배울 수 있고, 필요한 것을 찾아내고, 문장의 운율이나 은유 구사와 같은 자신과 무관한 것을 무시한다. (③ 우리는 또한 은유와 단어들의 연관성을 통해 감정의 궤적을 나타낸다.) ④ 속독 수업은 페이지 전체에 걸쳐 빠르게 움직이도록 눈을 훈련시키면서 우리가 이러한 목적을 위해 책을 읽는 데 도움을 줄 수 있다.

어휘

- □ accomplish 성취하다, 달성하다
- □ direction 안내, 지시사항, 방향
- □ assemble 조립하다, 모으다
- □ scan 빠르게 훑어보다
- □ irrelevant 무관한, 관련 없는
- □ metaphor 은유, 비유

□ register 나타내다, 기록하다. 등록하다
□ association 연관, 연상

정답 ③

19 다음 글에서 전체의 흐름과 가장 관계없는 문장은?

2019. 법원직 9급

The immortal operatically styled single Bohemian Rhapsody by Queen was released in 1975 and proceeded to the top of the UK charts for 9 weeks. ① A song that was nearly never released due to its length and unusual style but which Freddie insisted would be played became the instantly recognizable hit. ② By this time Freddie's unique talents were becoming clear, a voice with a remarkable range and a stage presence that gave Queen its colorful, unpredictable and flamboyant personality. ③ The son of Bomi and Jer Bulsara, Freddie spent the bulk of his childhood in India where he attended St. Peter's boarding school. ④ Very soon Queen's popularity extended beyond the shores of the UK as they charted and triumphed around Europe, Japan and the USA where in 1979 they topped the charts with Freddie's song Crazy Little thing Called Love.

해설

프레디 머큐리와 그가 이끈 밴드 Queen의 음악과 스타일에 대한 이야기를 다루고 있는 글이며, ②에서 'Queen의 음악과 스타일'이 뚜렷해 졌음을 강조하고 있다. 그러나 ③은 'Freddie의 유년시절'에 대한 진술로, 글의 주제인 'Freddie의 음악스타일'과는 거리가 있다. 따라서 글의 흐름과 가장 관계없는 문장은 ③이다.

해석

Queen에 의한 불멸의 오페라 풍으로 스타일된 싱글 보헤미안 랩소디는 1975년에 발표되어 9주 동안 영국 차트의 정상에 올랐다. ① 길이와 독특한 스타일 때문에 거의 발매되지 않을 뻔했지만, Freddie가 들려지게 될 것이라고 강력히 주장했던 노래는 즉시 눈에 띄는 히트를 쳤다. ② 이때쯤에 Freddie의 독특한 재능들은 분명해지고 있었는데, 그것들은 놀랄 만한 음역대의 목소리, 그리고 Queen에게 그것의 다채롭고 예측할 수 없으며 이색적인 개성을 주었던 무대에서의 존재감이었다. (③ Bomi와 Jer Bulsara의 아들인 Freddie는 어린 시절의 대부분을 인도에서 보냈고 그곳에서 St. Peter의 기숙학교에 다녔다.) ④ 곧 그들이 유럽, 일본과 Freddie의 노래 Crazy Little thing Called Love로 1979년 차트에서 1위를 차지했던 미국에서까지 성공하면서, Queen의 인기는 영국의 해안을 넘어 뻗어나갔다.

어휘

□ nearly 거의
□ release 발매하다, 풀어주다
□ remarkable 놀라운, 주목할 만한
□ range 음역대
□ presence 있음, 존재, 참석
□ flamboyant 이색적인, 화려한
□ boarding school 기숙학교
□ extend 뻗다, 연장하다, 확장하다
□ triumph 성공하다, 승리를 거두다

정답 ③

20 다음 글에서 전체 흐름과 관계없는 문장은?

2019. 소방직 9급

Gum disease is frequently to blame for bad breath. In fact, bad breath is a warning sign for gum disease. ① This issue occurs initially as a result of plaque buildup on the teeth. ② Bacteria in the plaque irritate the gums and cause them to become tender, swollen and prone to bleeding. ③ Foul-smelling gases emitted by the bacteria can also cause bad breath. ④ Smoking damages your gum tissue by affecting the attachment of bone and soft tissue to your teeth. If you pay attention when you notice that bacteria-induced bad breath, though, you could catch gum disease before it gets to its more advanced stages.

해설

입냄새와 잇몸 질환 사이의 관계에 대해 다루며 조기 발견의 중요성을 강조하고 있는 글이다. 특히 강조하고 있는 것은 '박테리아로 말미암은 문제'인데, ④는 '흡연으로 말미암은 잇몸 조직의 손상'에 대한 내용으로 글의 일관성에서 벗어난다, 따라서 글의 흐름과 관계없는 문장은 ④이다.

해석

잇몸 질환은 종종 입 냄새의 원인으로 지목된다. 사실, 입냄새는 잇몸 질환의 경고 신호다. ① 이 문제는 치아에 플라크가 축적된 결과로 처음 발생한다. ② 치석 속의 박테리아는 잇몸을 자극하여 잇몸이 연해지고 부어오르고 출혈이 일어나기 쉽다. ③ 박테리아가 내뿜는 냄새가 역겨운 가스도 입냄새를 유발할 수 있다. (④ 흡연은 당신의 치아에 뼈와 부드러운 조직의 부착에 영향을 미침으로써 당신의 잇몸 조직을 손상시킨다.) 하지만 박테리아가 유발하는 입냄새를 알아차릴 때 주의를 기울인다면, 더 발전된 단계에 이르기 전에 잇몸 질환을 발견할 수 있을 것이다.

어휘

□gum disease 잇몸 질환
□plaque 치석
□irritate 자극하다, 짜증나게 하다
□tender 부드러운, 연한
□swollen 부어오른, 불어난
□prone to ~하기 쉬운
□advanced 진행된
□attachment 부착

정답 ④

21 다음 글의 흐름상 가장 어색한 문장은? 2018. 국가직 9급

Biologists have identified a gene that will allow rice plants to survive being submerged in water for up to two weeks — over a week longer than at present. Plants under water for longer than a week are deprived of oxygen and wither and perish. ① The scientists hope their discovery will prolong the harvests of crops in regions that are susceptible to flooding. ② Rice growers in these flood-prone areas of Asia lose an estimated one billion dollars annually to excessively waterlogged rice paddies. ③ They hope the new gene will lead to a hardier rice strain that will reduce the financial damage incurred in typhoon and monsoon seasons and lead to bumper harvests. ④ This is dreadful news for people in these vulnerable regions, who are victims of urbanization and have a shortage of crops. Rice yields must increase by 30 percent over the next 20 years to ensure a billion people can receive their staple diet.

해설

벼의 유전자 발견으로 홍수에 강한 농작물 생산 가능성 증대에 대한 글로, 생물학자들은 벼의 유전자를 통해 1주일 이상의 물에 잠기는 환경에서 생존할 수 있는 능력을 이끌었고, 이러한 발견은 홍수 위험 지역에서의 농작물 수확 증가를 희망하며, 풍년을 이끌어내고 경제적 손실을 감소시키기 위한 가능성을 열어 놓았음을 설명하고 있다. '벼를 생존하게 하는 유전자를 발견한 것'은 좋은 소식인데, 이것을 '무서운 소식'이라고 진술한 ④ 문장의 내용이 글의 일관성에 벗어난다. 따라서 글의 흐름상 가장 어색한 문장은 ④이다.

해석

생물학자들은 벼가 현재보다 일주일 이상 더 긴 2주까지 물속에 잠긴 채로 생존하게 할 수 있는 유전자를 찾아냈다. 일주일 이상 물속에 있는 식물들은 산소를 빼앗기고 시들어 죽는다. ① 과학자들은 그들의 발견이 홍수에 취약한 지역에서의 작물 수확을 연장시킬 것을 희망한다. ② 이러한 범람하기 쉬운 아시아 지역의 벼 재배자들은 과도하게 물에 잠긴 논 때문에 매년 10억 달러로 추정되는 돈을 잃는다. ③ 그들은 새로운 유전자가 태풍과 장마철에 발생하는 재정적 피해를 줄이고 풍작을 가져오고 더 강인한 벼 품종을 가져오기를 희망한다. (④ 이것은 이러한 취약한 지역의 사람들에게 끔찍한 소식이고, 그들은 도시화의 피해자이며 작물 부족을 겪는다.) 쌀 생산량은 다음 20년에 걸쳐 10억 명의 사람들이 그들의 주식을 얻을 수 있는 것을 확실하게 하기 위해 30퍼센트만큼 증가해야 한다.

어휘

□submerge 물속에 잠기다, 잠수하다
□deprive of 빼앗다, 박탈하다
□perish 죽다, 사라지다, 소멸되다
□prolong 연장시키다, 늘이다
□susceptible 취약한, 민감한, 영향을 받기 쉬운
□water logged 물에 잠긴
□rice paddy 쌀, 벼
□lead to 가져오다, 이끌다
□incur 발생시키다, 초래하다
□bumper 풍작의, 대단히 큰
□vulnerable 취약한
□urbanization 도시화

정답 ④

22 밑줄 친 부분 중 글의 흐름상 가장 어색한 것은?

2018. 국가직 9급

Most people like to talk, but few people like to listen, yet listening well is a ① rare talent that everyone should treasure. Because they hear more, good listeners tend to know more and to be more sensitive to what is going on around them than most people. In addition, good listeners are inclined to accept or tolerate rather than to judge and criticize. Therefore, they have ② fewer enemies than most people. In fact, they are probably the most beloved of people. However, there are ③ exceptions to that generality. For example, John Steinbeck is said to have been an excellent listener, yet he was hated by some of the people he wrote about. No doubt his ability to listen contributed to his capacity to write. Nevertheless, the result of his listening didn't make him ④ unpopular.

해설

듣는 능력과 사랑받음의 관계에 대한 글로, 대부분의 사람들은 말하기를 좋아하며, 듣는 능력은 귀하게 여겨지는 흔하지 않은 재능임을 강조하는 글이다. 문제에서 요구하는 것은 문맥에서 바르지 않은 단어를 고르는 것으로, 듣는 것이 더 적은 적들을 만든다는 일반론의 예외적인 사항을 예시를 통해 이야기를 하는 ④는 부정적인 진술이 되어야 한다. 따라서 '그럼에도 불구하고, 그의 듣기의 결과는 그를 인기 있게 만들지 않았다'의 의미가 되어야 한다. 따라서 '인기 없는(unpopular)' 대신에 인기 있는(popular)'이 들어가야 한다.

해석

대부분의 사람들은 말하는 것을 좋아하나 듣는 것을 좋아하는 사람들은 거의 없다, 하지만 잘 듣는 것은 모든 사람들이 귀하게 여겨야 하는 ① 흔하지 않은 재능이다. 그들은 더 많이 듣기 때문에, 주변사람들에게 일어나는 일에 대하여 대부분의 사람들보다 더 많이 알고 더 민감한 경향이 있다. 게다가 좋은 청자들은 받아들이거나 견뎌내는 것을, 판단하거나 비판하는 것보다 더 잘하게 된다. 그러므로 그들은 대부분의 사람들보다 ② 더 적은 적을 가지고 있다. 사실, 그들이 아마도 가장 사랑받는 사람일 것이다. 그러나 그러한 일반론에도 ③ 예외는 있다. 예를 들어 John Steinback은 훌륭한 청자였다고 알려졌지만 그는 그가 글을 썼던 일부 사람들에게 미움을 받았다. 경청하는 그의 능력이 그의 쓰기 능력에 기여한 것은 틀림없다. 그럼에도 불구하고, 그의 경청의 결과는 그를 ④ 인기 없게(→ 인기 있게) 만들지 않았다.

어휘

- □ treasure 보물, 귀하게 여기다
- □ go on 시작하다
- □ inclined ~을 하고 싶은, ~할 것 같은
- □ tolerate 용인하다, 참다, 견디다
- □ beloved 인기 많은, 사랑받는
- □ generality 일반론
- □ no doubt 틀림없는, 아마
- □ contribute 기여하다, 헌신하다, ~의 원인이 되다
- □ capacity 능력, 수용력

정답 ④

23 다음 글의 흐름상 가장 어색한 문장은?

2018. 지방직 9급

The Renaissance kitchen had a definite hierarchy of help who worked together to produce the elaborate banquets. ① At the top, as we have seen, was the scalco, or steward, who was in charge of not only the kitchen, but also the dining room. ② The dining room was supervised by the butler, who was in charge of the silverware and linen and also served the dishes that began and ended the banquet — the cold dishes, salads, cheeses, and fruit at the beginning and the sweets and confections at the end of the meal. ③ This elaborate decoration and serving was what in restaurants is called "the front of the house." ④ The kitchen was supervised by the head cook, who directed the undercooks, pastry cooks, and kitchen help.

해설

르네상스 시대 주방과 식당의 계층과 역할에 대한 글로, 르네상스 시대 주방과 식당 내에서 각 역할의 분명한 계층과 있음과, 주방에서 만찬을 준비하기 위해 협력하는 다양한 사람들의 역할과 책임을 설명하고 하고 있다. 르네상스 시대의 주방에서 일하는 사람들의 위계질서를 주제로 한 글로, ③ '이러한 공들인 장식들과 음식을 전달하는 것은 "the front of the house"라고 식당에서 불리는 것이다'의 진술은 사람들의 위계와는 상관없는 내용이다. 따라서 글의 흐름상 가장 어색한 문장은 ③이다.

해석

르네상스 시대 주방에는 정성을 들인 만찬을 만들기 위해 함께 일하는 도움을 주는 사람들의 분명한 계급이 있었다. ① 최고의 위치에는, 우리가 보았던 것처럼, 집사라는 scalco가 있었는데, 그 사람은 주방을 책임졌을 뿐만 아니라 식당도 책임을 지고 있었다. ② 식당은 집사에 의해 감독이 되었는데, 이 사람은 은식기와 식탁용 리넨

제품들을 책임을 졌고 만찬을 시작하고 끝내는 요리들을 제공했다 —식사를 시작할 때의 차가운 요리, 샐러드, 치즈 그리고 과일과 식사의 끝에는 디저트들과 과자들이 있었다. (③ 이러한 공들인 장식들과 음식을 전달하는 것은 "the front of the house"라고 식당에서 불리는 것이다.) ④ 주방은 주방장들에 의해 감독되었고, 그는 요리사의 조수들, 페이스트리 요리사들과 주방 보조들을 지휘했다.

어휘

- □ hierarchy 계급, 계층
- □ elaborate 정성을 들인, 정교한
- □ banquet 연회, 만찬
- □ scalco (식당의) 집사
- □ steward 지배인, 집사
- □ supervise 감독하다, 지휘하다
- □ butler 집사, 하인 우두머리
- □ silverware 은제품, 은식기류
- □ serve 섬기다, 제공하다, 주다
- □ head cook 주방장

정답 ③

24 글의 흐름상 가장 어색한 문장은?

2017. 국가직 9급

Children's book awards have proliferated in recent years; today, there are well over 100 different awards and prizes by a variety of organizations. ① The awards may be given for books of a specific genre or simply for the best of all children's books published within a given time period. An award may honor a particular book or an author for a lifetime contribution to the world of children's literature. ② Most children's book awards are chosen by adults, but now a growing number of children's choice book awards exist. The larger national awards given in most countries are the most influential and have helped considerably to raise public awareness about the fine books being published for young readers. ③ An award ceremony for outstanding services to the publishing industry is put on hold. ④ Of course, readers are wise not to put too much faith in award-winning books. An award doesn't necessarily mean a good reading experience, but it does provide a starting place when choosing books.

해설

아동문학상의 증가와 그것의 의미를 주제로 하는 글로, 최근 아동문학상의 급증과 다양성에 대해 설명하며, 이러한 상들이 어린이들과 어른들의 선택을 통해 아동문학의 영향력을 인정받고, 좋은 독서 경험을 위한 출발점을 제공한다는 내용을 다루고 있다. 아동 문학상에 대한 전반적으로 설명하고 있는데 ③은 출판 산업에 대한 기여에 대한 시상식에 대해 진술하고 있다. 따라서 글의 흐름상 가장 어색한 문장은 ③이다.

해석

최근에 아동문학상이 급증하고 있다; 오늘날 다양한 기관에서 수여하는 100여개가 넘는 다양한 상이 있다. ① 이 상들은 특정한 장르의 책이나 단순히 일정 기간 안에 출간된 모든 아동문학 중 최고의 도서에 주어질 수 있다. 상은 특정한 책이나 아동 문학 세계에 공헌한 작가의 일생에 줄 수도 있다. ② 대부분의 아동문학상은 어른들에 의해 선택되나 현재는 더욱 많은 어린이들이 선정한 도서상이 존재한다. 대부분의 국가에서 주어지는 더 큰 국가적인 상은 가장 영향력이 있으며, 어린 독자를 위해 출간되는 훌륭한 책들이라는 대중적인 인식을 높이는 데 상당히 기여한다. (③ 출판 산업에 대한 뛰어난 기여에 대한 한 시상식이 보류되었다.) ④ 물론 독자들은 수상한 책에 대해 너무 많은 신뢰를 주지 않을 정도로 현명하다. 상이 필연적으로 좋은 독서 경험을 의미하지는 않으나, 책을 선정할 때 좋은 출발점을 제공한다.

어휘

- □ proliferate 급증하다, 확산되다
- □ a variety of 다양한
- □ publish 출간하다, 발표하다
- □ lifetime 일생, 생애
- □ contribution 기여, 공헌
- □ influential 영향력 있는
- □ awareness 인식, 의식
- □ outstanding 뛰어난, 두드러진
- □ put on hold 보류하다, 연기하다
- □ faith 믿음, 신뢰, 신앙

정답 ③

25 다음 글의 흐름상 가장 어색한 문장은?

2017. 국가직 9급 하반기

Researchers have developed a new model that they said will provide better estimates about the North Atlantic right whale population, and the news isn't good. ① The model could be critically important to efforts to save the endangered species, which is in the midst of a year of high mortality, said Peter Corkeron, who leads the large whale team for the National Oceanic and Atmospheric Administration's Northeast Fisheries Science Center. ② The agency said the analysis shows the probability the population has declined since 2010 is nearly 100 percent. ③ "One problem was, are they really going down or are we not seeing them? They really have gone down, and that's the bottom line," Corkeron said. ④ The new research model has successfully demonstrated that the number of right whales has remained intact despite the worrisome, widening population gap between whale males and females.

해설

북대서양 참고래 개체 수 감소의 심각성과 구조적 문제에 대한 새로운 모델 분석에 대한 글로, 첫 문장에서 참고래의 개체 수 조사내용이 좋지 않다고 설명했다. 2번째 문장부터는 참고래의 개체 수의 부정적인 결과를 나열하고 있는데, ④는 고래가 온전한 상태로 남아있다는 긍정적인 내용으로 글의 주제문에 맞지 않고 새로운 내용이 추가될 수 있는 연결사도 없다. 그리고 고래의 수컷과 암컷의 개체 수의 비교도 이 글하고는 상관없는 내용이다. 따라서 글의 흐름상 가장 어색한 문장은 ④이다.

해석

연구원들은 북방긴수염고래 개체 수에 대해 더 나은 추정치를 제공할 수 있을 것이라고 말한 새로운 모델을 개발했지만 그 소식은 좋지 않다. ① 그 모델은 멸종 위기에 처한 종들을 살리기 위한 노력의 일환으로 멸종 위기에 처한 동물을 구하는 데 결정적으로 중요할 수 있다고 Peter Corken 국립해양 과학 연구소장은 말했다. ② 그 기관은 이 분석이 2010년 이래로 개체 수가 거의 100퍼센트 감소했다고 말하고 있다. ③ "한 가지 문제는 개체 수가 정말로 줄어들고 있는가? 아니면 단지 우리가 그걸 보지 못하고 있는 것인가? 이것이 문제였다. 개체 수는 정말로 줄어들고 있으며, 그게 요점이다."라고 Corkeron이 말했다. (④ 그 새로운 조사 모델은 수많은 긴수염고래들이 온전한 상태로 남아 있다는 것이 성공적으로 입증되었으며 그런 걱정에도 불구하고, 고래 수컷과 암컷 사이의 개체 수 격차가 커지고 있다.)

어휘

- □ North Atlantic right whale 북방긴수염고래
- □ critically 결정적으로, 중대하게
- □ endangered 멸종 위기에 처한
- □ species 종, 종류
- □ mortality 사망률, 사망
- □ agency 기관, 단체
- □ decline 감소하다, 줄어들다
- □ bottom line 핵심, 요점
- □ intact 온전한, 전혀 다치지 않은
- □ worrisome 걱정스러운, 귀찮은
- □ widen 커지다, 확대되다
- □ gap 격차, 간격, 차이

정답 ④

26 다음 글의 흐름상 가장 어색한 문장은?

2017. 지방직 9급

Whether you've been traveling, focusing on your family, or going through a busy season at work, 14 days out of the gym takes its toll — not just on your muscles, but your performance, brain, and sleep, too. ① Most experts agree that after two weeks, you're in trouble if you don't get back in the gym. "At the two week point without exercising, there are a multitude of physiological markers that naturally reveal a reduction of fitness level," says Scott Weiss, a New York-based exercise physiologist and trainer who works with elite athletes. ② After all, despite all of its abilities, the human body (even the fit human body) is a very sensitive system and physiological changes (muscle strength or a greater aerobic base) that come about through training will simply disappear if your training load dwindles, he notes. Since the demand of training isn't present, your body simply slinks back toward baseline. ③ More protein is required to build more muscles at a rapid pace in your body. ④ Of course, how much and how quickly you'll decondition depends on a slew of factors like how fit you are, your age, and how long sweating has been a habit. "Two to eight months of not exercising at all will reduce your fitness level to as if you never exercised before," Weiss notes.

해설

체육관을 벗어난(운동하지 않은) 14일간의 영향과 회복에 대한 글이다. 당신이 14일 동안 운동을 하지 않으면(체육관으로 돌아오지 않으면) 당신의 근육뿐만 아니라 당신의 수행능력, 뇌, 잠 등에도 영향을 미친다는 주제를 바탕으로 글이 이어진다. 하지만 ③은 단백질(먹는 것)에 대한 내용으로 운동과 관련된 글의 일관성에서 벗어난다. 따라서 글의 흐름상 가장 어색한 문장은 ③이다.

해석

> 당신이 여행을 하는 중이거나, 당신의 가족에 집중을 하거나, 혹은 직장에서의 바쁜 시즌을 경험하는 것과는 상관없이, 체육관을 벗어난 14일은 이것의 대가를 치를 것이다 — 이것은 단지 당신의 근육뿐만 아니라, 당신의 수행능력, 뇌, 그리고 수면에 대해서 역시 대가를 치를 것이다. ① 대부분의 전문가들은 2주후에 당신이 체육관으로 돌아오지 않는다면, 당신은 어려움에 처할 것이라는 것에 동의한다. "운동을 하지 않은 2주의 시점에, 건강한 상태의 감소를 자연적으로 나타내는 수많은 생리학적인 표식들이 있다"고 엘리트 운동선수들과 일을 하는 뉴욕에 있는 운동 생리학자이자 트레이너인 Scott Weiss가 말한다. ② 결국, 모든 사람의 인체의 능력에도 불구하고, 인체(심지어 건강한 인체)는 매우 민감한 시스템이며, 훈련을 통해 발생하는 생리적 변화(근육의 힘 또는 더 큰 호기성 기저)는 훈련 부담이 줄어들면 간단히 사라질 것이라고 그는 언급한다. 훈련의 요구가 현재에 있지 않기 때문에 당신의 몸은 단순히 기준선을 향하여 갈 것이다. (③ 더 많은 단백질이 더 많은 근육들을 당신의 몸에서 빠른 속도로 만드는 데 요구되어진다.) ④ 물론, 얼마나 많이 그리고 얼마나 빨리 건강을 손상시킬 것인지는 당신이 얼마나 건강한지, 나이가 몇 살인지, 그리고 얼마나 오랜 기간 동안 땀을 흘리는 습관을 가지고 있었는지와 같은 많은 요소들에 따라 달라진다. Weiss는 "2~8개월 동안 운동을 전혀 하지 않으면 마치 전에 운동을 하지 않은 것처럼 체력 수준이 떨어질 것"이라고 언급한다.

어휘

- □toll 대가, 영향
- □physiological 생리적인
- □marker 지표, 표시
- □fitness 신체 단련, 건강
- □physiologist 생리학자
- □aerobic 호기성의, 유산소의
- □load 부담, 짐
- □dwindle 줄어들다, 감소하다
- □note 언급하다, 주목하다
- □baseline 기준선
- □protein 단백질
- □decondition 건강을 손상시키다
- □a slew of 많은

정답 ③

27 글의 흐름상 가장 어색한 것은? 2017. 지방직 9급 하반기

> A story that is on the cutting edge of modern science began in an isolated part of northern Sweden in the 19th century. ① <u>This area of the country had unpredictable harvests through the first half of the century</u>. In years that the harvest failed, the population went hungry. However, the good years were very good. ② <u>The same people who went hungry during bad harvests overate significantly during the good years</u>. A Swedish scientist wondered about the long-term effects of these eating patterns. He studied the harvest and health records of the area. He was astonished by what he found. ③ <u>Boys who overate during the good years produced children and grandchildren who died about six years earlier than the children and grandchildren of those who had very little to eat</u>. Other scientists found the same result for girls. ④ <u>Both boys and girls benefited greatly from the harvests of the good years</u>. The scientists were forced to conclude that just one reason of overeating could have a negative impact that continued for generations.

해설

과식의 장기적 영향 연구와 세대 간 건강에 대한 글로, 19세기 스웨덴에서 시작된 연구에서 수확 변동에 따른 과식과 영양 부족이 세대 간 건강에 미치는 영향이 밝혀져, 과식의 부정적인 영향이 지속됨을 발견하게 되었음을 설명하고 있다. 그런데 ④는 '자손들(소년과 소녀 모두)이 좋은 수확으로 이익을 보았다'는 긍정적인 진술의 내용으로 글의 일관성에서 벗어난다. 따라서 글의 흐름상 가장 어색한 것은 ④이다.

해석

> 최첨단 현대 과학의 한 이야기는 19세기 북부 스웨덴의 고립된 지역에서 시작되었다. ① 그 국가의 이 지역은 그 세기 전반에 걸쳐 예측할 수 없는 수확을 하였다. 수확이 실패했던 수년 동안, 주민들은 굶주렸다. 그러나, 수확이 좋았던 해에는 상황이 매우 좋았다. ② 수확이 안 좋았던 시기 동안에 굶주렸던 사람들이, 수확이 좋았던 시기에는 상당히 과식을 하게 되었다. 한 스웨덴 과학자가 이러한 식습관의 장기적인 영향에 대해 의문을 가졌다. 그는 그 지역의 건강기록과 수확과의 관계를 연구하였다. 그는 그가 발견한 것에 놀랐다. ③ 수확이 좋았던 시기에 과식을 했던 소년들은 거의 먹지 못했던 소년들의 자녀들과 손주들보다 약 6년 정도 더 일찍 죽는 후손들을 낳았다. 다른 과학자들도 소녀들에게 똑같은 결과를 발견하였다. (④ 소년들과 소녀들 모두 풍년이었던 수확기로부터 상당히 혜택을

받았다.) 과학자들은 과식의 단 한 가지 이유가 수 세대에 걸쳐 계속되는 부정적인 영향을 가질 수 있다는 결론을 내릴 수밖에 없었다.

어휘

☐ cutting edge 최첨단
☐ isolated 고립된, 외딴
☐ unpredictable 예측할 수 없는, 불확실한
☐ harvest 수확, 수확하다, 거둬들이다
☐ overeat 과식하다, 지나치게 먹다
☐ astonish 깜짝 놀라게 하다
☐ effect 영향, 결과, 효과
☐ conclude 끝내다, 결론을 내리다

정답 ④

28 글의 흐름상 가장 어색한 문장은? 2016. 국가직 9급

One of the largest celebrations of the passage of young girls into womanhood occurs in Latin American and Hispanic cultures. This event is called La Quinceañera, or the fifteenth year. ① It acknowledges that a young woman is now of marriageable age. The day usually begins with a Mass of Thanksgiving. ② By comparing the rites of passage of one culture with those of another, we can assess differences in class status. The young woman wears a full-length white or pastel-colored dress and is attended by fourteen friends and relatives who serve as maids of honor and male escorts. ③ Her parents and godparents surround her at the foot of the altar. When the Mass ends, other young relatives give small gifts to those who attended, while the Quinceañera herself places a bouquet of flowers on the altar of the Virgin. ④ Following the Mass is an elaborate party, with dancing, cake, and toasts. Finally, to end the evening, the young woman dances a waltz with her favorite escort.

해설

라틴 아메리카와 히스패닉 문화에서의 어린 소녀의 성인의식인 La Quinceanera를 설명하고 있는 글이다. 하지만 ②는 이 문화와 다른 문화 사이의 성인의식을 비교하여 계급적 차이를 알아낼 수 있다는 내용으로 글의 일관성에서 벗어난다. 따라서 글의 흐름상 가장 어색한 문장은 ②이다.

해석

어린 소녀들이 여성으로 인정받는 통과의례의 가장 큰 축하행사 중 하나가 라틴 아메리카와 히스패닉 문화에 있다. 이 행사는 La Quinceanera 또는 15번째 생일이라고 불린다. ① 이것은 어린 여성이 이제 결혼할 나이가 되었음을 알려주는 것이다. 이날은 보통 감사의 미사로 시작한다. (② 한 문화에서의 통과 의식을 다른 문화의 그것과 비교함으로써, 우리는 계급의 지위에서의 차이를 가늠할 수 있다.) 어린 여성은 완전한 길이의 흰색 또는 파스텔 색의 드레스를 입고 들러리와 남성 호위자로 봉사하는 14명의 친구들과 친척들에 의해 수행된다. ③ 그녀의 부모와 대부모는 제단의 발치에서 그녀를 둘러싼다. 미사가 끝날 때, 주인공인 어린 여성 자신은 처녀의 제단에 꽃다발을 바치는 동안 다른 어린 친척들은 참석한 사람들에게 작은 선물을 준다. ④ 미사에 이어 춤과 케익과 토스트 등이 있는 화려한 파티가 있게 된다. 마지막으로 저녁을 마치기 위해 이 어린 여성은 자신이 가장 좋아하는 호위자와 왈츠를 춘다.

어휘

☐ passage 통행, 통과
☐ Mass (특히 로마 가톨릭교에서) 미사
☐ rite 의식, 의례
☐ assess 가늠하다, 재다, 평가하다
☐ status 신분, 지위
☐ surround 둘러싸다, 포위하다
☐ relative 친척, 동족, 상대적인, 비교상의
☐ altar 제단

정답 ②

29 글의 흐름상 가장 어색한 문장은? 2016. 지방직 9급

Progress is gradually being made in the fight against cancer. ① In the early 1900s, few cancer patients had any hope of long-term survival. ② But because of advances in medical technology, progress has been made so that currently four in ten cancer patients survive. ③ It has been proven that smoking is a direct cause of lung cancer. ④ However, the battle has not yet been won. Although cures for some forms of cancer have been discovered, other forms of cancer are still increasing.

해설

암과의 싸움(암 치료법)에서 점점 진전되는 과정에 대해 설명하는 글이다. 그런데 ③의 흡연이 폐암의 직접적인 원인이라고 밝혀졌다는 내용은 글의 일관성에서 벗어난다. 따라서 글의 흐름상 가장 어색한 문장은 ③이다.

해석

암과의 싸움에서의 진전은 점차적으로 이루어지고 있다. ① 1900년대 초반에 암 환자들은 장기간 생존에 대한 희망은 거의 가질 수 없었다. ② 그러나 의료 기술의 발전으로 인해 10명 중 4명의 암 환자들이 생존할 수 있게 진전되어 왔다. (③ 흡연이 폐암의 직접적 원인이라는 것이 밝혀졌다.) ④ 그러나, 그 전투가 아직 승리한 것은 아니다. 암의 몇몇 형태에 대한 치료법이 발견되었지만, 다른 형태의 암 종류는 여전히 증가하고 있다.

어휘

- ☐ progress 진전, 진척, 진보, 발달
- ☐ gradually 점차적으로, 서서히
- ☐ survival 생존
- ☐ advance 진전, 발전
- ☐ proven 입증된, 증명된
- ☐ lung cancer 폐암
- ☐ discover 발견하다, 찾다

정답 ③

03 문장 제거 유형 기출 독해 어휘 복습 TEST 정답

정답

1	discipline	분야, 훈육, 규율, 훈육하다, 징계하다	21	reckless	무분별한, 무모한, 신중하지 못한
2	quote	인용문, 인용하다	22	limited	제한된, 한정된
3	summarize	요약하다	23	argument	논쟁, 주장
4	briefly	간결하게, 간단히, 잠시	24	quarrel	말다툼, 언쟁
5	desperate	필사적인, 절망적인	25	insult	모욕, 모욕하다
6	urge	충동, 욕구, 충고하다, 권고하다	26	exposure	노출, 폭로
7	get out of	~에서 나오다, 도망치다	27	toll	대가, 비용, 통행료
8	let off steam	기분을 풀다, 울분[열기 등]을 발산하다	28	fatigued	피로한, 지친
9	conspiracy	음모	29	incapable	무능한, ~을 할 수 없는
10	advocate	옹호하다, 지지하다	30	depersonalization	비인격화, 몰개성화, 객관화
11	trapped	갇힌, 가두어진	31	speculation	추측, 사색
12	contradict	모순되다, 부정하다	32	metaphysics	형이상학
13	rouse	불러일으키다, 깨우다	33	meteorology	기상학
14	anxiety	불안, 염려, 걱정거리, 열망	34	empathy	감정 이입, 공감
15	norm	기준	35	slightly	약간, 조금
16	density	밀도, 농도	36	transmission	전염, 전파, 전달
17	reduce	줄이다, 축소하다, 감소시키다	37	practice	관행, 관례, 실행, 실천
18	renowned	유명한, 명성 있는	38	involvement	참여, 개입, 몰두, 열중
19	paragraph	문단, 단락, 절	39	initiate	시작하다, 착수시키다
20	conclude	끝내다, 결론을 내리다	40	a string of	일련의, 연속적인

03 문장 제거 유형 기출 독해 어휘 복습 TEST 정답

정답

41	chemical	화학적인	61	irritate	자극하다, 짜증나게 하다
42	widen	넓히다, 커지다	62	tender	부드러운, 연한
43	lash out	공격하다, 싸우다, 혹평하다, 비난하다	63	submerge	물속에 잠기다, 잠수하다
44	anthropology	인류학	64	deprive of	빼앗다, 박탈하다
45	contemporary	현대의, 동시대의	65	prolong	연장시키다, 늘이다
46	illustrate	설명하다, 실증하다	66	incur	발생시키다, 초래하다
47	implication	함축, 암시, 영향, 결과	67	urbanization	도시화
48	progress	진전, 진척, 진행하다, 나아가다	68	inclined	~을 하고 싶은, ~할 것 같은
49	spontaneous	자발적인, 즉흥적인	69	tolerate	용인하다, 참다, 견디다
50	sedentary	정적인, 주로 앉아서 하는	70	no doubt	틀림없는, 아마
51	direction	안내, 지시사항, 방향	71	hierarchy	계급, 계층
52	assemble	조립하다, 모으다	72	supervise	감독하다, 지휘하다
53	irrelevant	무관한, 관련 없는	73	proliferate	급증하다, 확산되다
54	metaphor	은유, 비유	74	outstanding	뛰어난, 두드러진
55	register	나타내다, 기록하다, 등록하다	75	put on hold	보류하다, 연기하다
56	association	연관, 연상	76	intact	온전한, 전혀 다치지 않은
57	remarkable	놀라운, 주목할 만한	77	dwindle	줄어들다, 감소하다
58	presence	있음, 존재, 참석	78	isolated	고립된, 외딴
59	flamboyant	이색적인, 화려한	79	astonish	깜짝 놀라게 하다
60	triumph	성공하다, 승리를 거두다	80	status	신분, 지위

chapter

04 문장 삽입 유형 정답 및 해설

ANSWER

01 ②	02 ③	03 ③	04 ④	05 ③
06 ②	07 ③	08 ②	09 ③	10 ④
11 ③	12 ②	13 ③	14 ④	15 ②
16 ④	17 ④	18 ④	19 ④	20 ④
21 ③	22 ③	23 ④	24 ④	25 ④
26 ③	27 ③	28 ②	29 ④	

01 주어진 문장이 들어갈 위치로 가장 적절한 것은?

2025. 출제 기조 전환 2차

For others, activism is controversial and disruptive; after all, it often manifests as confrontational activity that directly challenges the order of things.

Activism is frequently defined as intentional, vigorous or energetic action that individuals and groups practice to bring about a desired goal. (①) For some, activism is a theoretically or ideologically focused project intended to effect a perceived need for political or social change. (②) Activism is uncomfortable, sometimes messy, and almost always strenuous. (③) In addition, it does not occur without the presence and commitment of activists, that is, folks who develop workable strategies, focus a collective spotlight onto particular issues, and ultimately move people into action. (④) As a noted scholar suggests, effective activists also make noise, sometimes loudly.

해설

행동주의의 정의와 특성에 대한 글로, 행동주의는 목표 달성을 위한 의도적이고 에너지가 넘치는 행동으로 정의되며, 때로는 대립적이고 논란이 많은 활동으로 나타남을 설명하고 있다. 주어진 문장은 활동주의의 특성을 설명하는 내용으로, 활동주의가 대립적이고 혼란스러운 성격을 가지고 있음을 강조한다. 따라서 주어진 문장이 들어갈 위치로 가장 적절한 것은 ②이다.

해석

행동주의는 종종 개인과 집단이 원하는 목표를 달성하기 위해 연습하는 의도적이고, 격렬하거나 에너지가 넘치는 행동으로 정의된다. (①) 어떤 사람들에게 행동주의는 정치적 또는 사회적 변화에 대한 인식된 필요에 영향을 미치기 위한 이론적 또는 이념적으로 집중된 프로젝트이다. (② <u>다른 사람들에게 행동주의는 논란이 많고 파괴적이다; 결국에는, 그것은 종종 사물의 질서에 직접적으로 도전하는 대립적인 활동으로 나타난다.</u>) 행동주의는 불편하고, 때로는 지저분하며, 거의 항상 격렬하다. (③) 게다가, 행동주의자들, 즉 실행 가능한 전략을 개발하고, 특정 문제에 집단적인 스포트라이트를 집중하고, 궁극적으로 사람들을 행동으로 옮기는 사람들의 존재와 헌신 없이는 발생하지 않는다. (④) 저명한 학자가 시사하듯이, 효과적인 활동가들은 또한 때때로 큰 소리로 소음을 낸다.

어휘

- □ activism 행동주의, 능동주의
- □ controversial 논란이 많은
- □ disruptive 파괴적인, 분열시키는, 지장을 주는
- □ after all 결국에는, 어쨌든
- □ confrontational 대립의, 모순되는
- □ define 정의하다, 규정하다
- □ vigorous 격렬한, 활발한, 건강한
- □ theoretically 이론적으로
- □ ideologically 이념적으로, 사상적으로
- □ messy 지저분한, 엉망인, 골치 아픈
- □ strenuous 격렬한, 몹시 힘든, 완강한, 불굴의
- □ presence 존재, 참석, 있음
- □ commitment 헌신, 약속, 전념
- □ scholar 학자, 장학생

정답 ②

02 주어진 문장이 들어갈 위치로 가장 적절한 것은?

2025. 출제 기조 전환 1차

In particular, in many urban counties, air pollution, as measured by the amount of total suspended particles, had reached dangerous levels.

Economists Chay and Greenstone evaluated the value of cleaning up of air pollution after the Clean Air Act of 1970. (①) Before 1970, there was little federal regulation of air pollution, and the issue was not high on the agenda of state legislators. (②) As a result, many counties allowed factories to operate without any regulation on their pollution, and in several heavily industrialized counties, pollution had reached very high levels. (③) The Clean Air Act established guidelines for what constituted excessively high levels of five particularly dangerous pollutants. (④) Following the Act in 1970 and the 1977 amendment, there were improvements in air quality.

해설

Clean Air Act(1970년) 후, Chay와 Greenstone의 경제학적 평가에 따르면, 미 연방 정부의 공기 오염 규제는 공장 및 도시에서의 대기 질을 개선하고, 경제적 가치를 창출했음을 과거의 상황과 대비시킨 글이다. 주어진 제시문은 과거의 문제점을 강조하고 있으므로 ②번의 '그 결과 오염에 대한 규제 없이 가동을 허용했고, 오염이 매우 높은 수준에 도달함'의 진술 다음에 위치해야 한다. 따라서 주어진 문장이 들어갈 위치로 가장 적절한 것은 ③이다.

해석

경제학자 Chay와 Greenstone은 1970년 청정대기법 이후 대기오염 정화의 가치를 평가했다. (①) 1970년 이전에는 대기오염에 대한 연방 정부의 규제가 거의 없었고, 주 의원들의 의제에서 그 문제가 중요하지 않았다. (②) 결과적으로, 많은 주들이 오염에 대한 규제 없이 공장들이 가동하는 것을 허용했고, 몇몇 고도로 산업화된 주들에서는 오염이 매우 높은 수준에 도달했다. (③ <u>특히 많은 도시의 주들에서는 총 부유입자의 양으로 측정되는 대기오염이 위험 수준에 도달했다.</u>) (④) 청정대기법은 무엇이 5가지 특히 위험한 오염물질의 과도하게 높은 수준을 구성하는 지에 대한 지침을 제정했다. 1970년 이 법령과 1977년 개정에 이후에, 대기의 질에 개선이 있었다.

어휘

- □ act 법령, 행동, 행동하다
- □ federal 연방 정부의, 연방제의
- □ agenda 의제, 안건
- □ legislator 입법자, 법률 제정자, 의회[국회]의원
- □ county (자치)주, 군
- □ operate 가동[작동]하다, 작용하다, 수술하다
- □ suspend 부유시키다, 매달다, 중지하다, 연기하다
- □ particle 입자, 조각, 미립자
- □ constitute ~을 구성하다, 이루다, 설립하다
- □ excessively 과도하게, 지나치게
- □ pollutant 오염 물질, 오염원
- □ amendment 개정, 수정

정답 ③

03 주어진 문장이 들어갈 위치로 적절한 것은?

2024. 국가직 9급

Tribal oral history and archaeological evidence suggest that sometime between 1500 and 1700 a mudslide destroyed part of the village, covering several longhouses and sealing in their contents.

From the village of Ozette on the westernmost point of Washington's Olympic Peninsula, members of the Makah tribe hunted whales. (①) They smoked their catch on racks and in smokehouses and traded with neighboring groups from around the Puget Sound and nearby Vancouver Island. (②) Ozette was one of five main villages inhabited by the Makah, an Indigenous people who have been based in the region for millennia. (③) Thousands of artifacts that would not otherwise have survived, including baskets, clothing, sleeping mats, and whaling tools, were preserved under the mud. (④) In 1970, a storm caused coastal erosion that revealed the remains of these longhouses and artifacts.

해설

고래 사냥과 무역을 중심으로 한 마카 부족의 중요한 거점인 워싱턴 올림픽 반도의 Ozette 마을이 진흙 사태로 인해 그들의 생활과 유물이 보존되었고, 최근의 폭풍으로 인한 침식으로 인해 그들의 생활과 유물이 밝혀졌음을 설명하는 글이다. 주어진 제시문은 진흙이 집들을 덮쳐, 그들의 생활상을 알 수 있게 봉인했다는 것이고 이와 관련된 부가 설명을 ③번이 하고 있으므로, 주어진 문장이 들어갈 위치로 가장 적절한 것은 ③이다.

해석

워싱턴주 올림픽 반도의 최서단에 있는 Ozette 마을에서 Makah 부족 구성원들은 고래를 사냥했다. (①) 그들은 선반과 훈제장 안에서 그들의 어획물을 훈제했으며, 퓨젓 사운드와 인근 밴쿠버섬 주변의 이웃 그룹들과 거래했다. (②) Ozette는 그 지역에 수천 년 동안 기반을 두고 살아온 원주민인 Makah 부족에 의해 거주된 다섯 개의 주요 마을 중 하나였다. (③ 부족의 구전 역사와 고고학적 증거는 1500년에서 1700년 사이 어느 때에 이류가 마을의 일부를 파괴하였고 여러 개의 전통가옥들을 덮어 내용물을 봉인했다는 것을 시사한다.) 그렇지 않았다면 살아남지 못했을 바구니, 옷, 수면요, 포경 도구를 포함한 수천 개의 인공물들이 진흙 속에 보존되었다. (④) 1970년, 한 폭풍은 이러한 전통가옥들의 잔해와 인공물들을 드러내는 해안의 침식을 야기했다.

어휘

- □westernmost 서쪽 최고의
- □peninsula 반도
- □rack 선반, 벽걸이
- □smokehouses 훈연 공장
- □inhabit 거주하다, 살다
- □archaeological 고고학적인
- □mudslide 산사태
- □longhouse 길게 붙은 공동 주택, 일잣(一字)집
- □artifact 유물, 유적
- □preserve 보존하다, 지키다, 전유물
- □reveal 드러내다, 밝히다

정답 ③

04 주어진 문장이 들어갈 위치로 적절한 것은? 2024. 지방직 9급

But she quickly popped her head out again.

The little mermaid swam right up to the small window of the cabin, and every time a wave lifted her up, she could see a crowd of well-dressed people through the clear glass. Among them was a young prince, the handsomest person there, with large dark eyes. (①) It was his birthday, and that's why there was so much excitement. (②) When the young prince came out on the deck, where the sailors were dancing, more than a hundred rockets went up into the sky and broke into a glitter, making the sky as bright as day. (③) The little mermaid was so startled that she dove down under the water. (④) And look! It was just as if all the stars up in heaven were falling down on her. Never had she seen such fireworks.

해설

인어공주의 왕자의 생일 파티를 몰래 구경한 경험에 대한 글로, '인어가 빠르게 그녀의 머리를 밖으로 다시 드러냈다'는 부분 전에는 '물에 들어갔다'는 진술이 나와야 하며, 이 진술 다음에는 머리를 드러내고 보았다는 진술이 나와야 한다. 따라서 주어진 문장이 들어갈 위치로 적절한 것은 ④이다.

해석

작은 인어공주는 선실 작은 창문까지 곧장 헤엄쳐 갔고, 파도가 그녀를 들어 올릴 때마다 투명한 유리를 통해 잘 차려입은 사람들의 무리를 볼 수 있었다. 그들 중에는 젊은 왕자가 있었는데, 그는 그 자리에서 가장 잘생긴 사람이었고 큰 검은 눈을 가지고 있었다. (①) 그날은 그의 생일이었기 때문에 그렇게 많은 흥분이 있었다. (②) 젊은 왕자가 선원들이 춤추고 있는 갑판으로 나왔을 때, 100개가 넘는 로켓이 하늘로 쏘아 올라가 반짝이며 터졌고, 하늘을 낮처럼 밝게 만들었다. (③) 작은 인어공주는 너무 놀라서 물속으로 잠수했다. (④ 그러나 그녀는 곧 다시 머리를 내밀었다.) 그리고 보라! 마치 하늘에 있는 모든 별들이 그녀 쪽으로 떨어지는 것 같았다. 그녀는 이런 불꽃놀이를 본 적이 없었다.

어휘

- □cabin 선실, 오두막
- □prince 왕자
- □mermaid 인어
- □startle 깜짝 놀라게 하다

정답 ④

05 주어진 문장이 들어갈 위치로 알맞은 것은? 2023. 국가직 9급

They installed video cameras at places known for illegal crossings, and put live video feeds from the cameras on a Web site.

Immigration reform is a political minefield. (①) About the only aspect of immigration policy that commands broad political support is the resolve to secure the U. S. border with Mexico to limit the flow of illegal immigrants. (②) Texas sheriffs recently developed a novel use of the Internet to help them keep watch on the border. (③) Citizens who want to help monitor the border can go online and serve as "virtual Texas deputies." (④) If they see anyone trying to cross the border, they send a report to the sheriff's office, which follows up, sometimes with the help of the U. S. Border Patrol.

해설

텍사스 보안관들의 인터넷을 활용한 국경 감시를 주제로 하는 글로, 텍사스 보안관들이 인터넷을 이용해 불법 횡단을 감시하는 '가상 텍사스 의원' 시스템을 도입했다는 것을 소개하는 글이다. 주어진 문장에서 '그들(They)'은 ② 다음 문장에서 언급되고 있는 '텍사스 보안관들 (Texas sheriffs)'을 의미한다. 따라서 주어진 문장이 들어갈 위치로 알맞은 것은 ③이다.

해석

이민 개혁은 정치적 지뢰밭이다. (①) 광범위한 정치적 지지를 받는 이민 정책의 유일한 측면은 불법 이민자들의 유입을 제한하기 위해 멕시코와의 미국 국경을 확보하겠다는 결의이다. (②) 텍사스 보안관들은 최근 국경을 감시하는 것을 돕기 위해 인터넷의 새로운 사용법을 개발했다. (③ 그들은 불법 횡단으로 알려진 장소에 비디오 카메라를 설치했고, 카메라의 라이브 비디오 자료를 웹 사이트에 게시했다.) (④) 국경 감시를 돕고자 하는 시민들은 온라인에 접속해 "가상 텍사스 보안관" 역할을 할 수 있다. 국경을 넘으려는 사람을 보면 보안관 사무실로 보고서를 보내고, 때때로 미국 국경 순찰대의 도움을 받아 더 알아보기도 한다.

어휘

□ install 설치하다
□ known for ~로 알려진
□ feed 먹이다, 먹이, 자료, 원료
□ immigration 이주, 이민, 출입국 관리소
□ reform 개혁, 개선, 개혁하다, 개선하다
□ minefield 지뢰밭
□ policy 정책
□ command 명령하다, 지시하다, 지휘하다
□ resolve 결의, 결심, 결심하다, 해결하다
□ sheriff 대리인, 의원, 보안관
□ novel 소설, 새로운, 기발한
□ monitor 감시하다
□ virtual 가상의
□ deputy 대리인, 의원, 보안관
□ border 국경, 경계, 가장자리
□ follow up 더 알아보다, ~을 덧붙이다
□ Border Patrol 국경 순찰대

정답 ③

06 주어진 문장이 들어갈 위치로 가장 적절한 것은?

2023. 지방직 9급

Yet, requests for such self-assessments are pervasive throughout one's Career.

The fiscal quarter just ended. Your boss comes by to ask you how well you performed in terms of sales this quarter. How do you describe your performance? As excellent? Good? Terrible? (①) Unlike when someone asks you about an objective performance metric (e.g., how many dollars in sales you brought in this quarter), how to subjectively describe your performance is often unclear. There is no right answer. (②) you are asked to subjectively describe your own performance in school applications, in job applications, in interviews, in performance reviews, in meetings — the list goes on. (③) How you describe your performance is what we call your level of self-promotion. (④) Since self-promotion is a pervasive part of work, people who do more self-promotion may have better chances of being hired, being promoted, and getting a raise or a bonus.

해설

자기 평가의 중요성을 강조하는 글로, 자기 평가 요청은 자신의 성과를 주관적으로 설명하는 것으로, 자기 홍보는 채용과 승진 등에 유리한 기회를 제공할 수 있으므로 더 많은 자기 홍보를 하는 사람들이 더 좋은 결과를 얻을 수 있음을 강조하고 있다. 주어진 문장은 글의 주제문에 해당하며,

그 다음에 구체적인 예시가 이어져야 한다. 그 구체적인 예시의 시작이 ② 다음의 '학교 지원서, 취업 지원서, 면접, 성과 평가, 회의' 등이 구체적인 예시가 된다. 따라서 주어진 문장이 들어갈 위치로 알맞은 것은 ② 이다.

해석

회계 분기가 막 끝났다. 상사가 당신에게 이번 분기의 판매 성과에 대해 얼마나 잘 수행했는지 묻기 위해서 왔다. 당신은 어떻게 자신의 성과를 설명할까? 훌륭하다고? 좋다고? 형편없다고? (①) 객관적인 성과 지표(예를 들어 이번 분기에 얼마나 매출을 올렸는지)에 관해 묻는 경우와 달리, 주관적으로 성과를 설명하는 것은 종종 명확하지 않다. 정답이 없다. (② 그러나 이러한 자기 평가 요청은 경력 전반에 걸쳐 만연하다). 당신은 학교 지원서, 취업 지원서, 면접, 업무 평가, 회의 그리고 계속되는 목록에서 자신의 성과를 주관적으로 설명하라는 요청을 받는다. (③) 당신이 성과를 어떻게 설명하는지가 우리가 자기 홍보의 수준이라고 부르는 것이다. (④) 자기 홍보는 업무의 만연한 부분이기 때문에, 자기 홍보를 더 많이 하는 사람들은 채용되는 기회, 승진, 급여 인상 또는 보너스를 받을 가능성이 더 높을 수 있다.

어휘

- □ pervasive 만연하는, 스며드는
- □ fiscal quarter 회계 분기, 재무 분기
- □ come by 잠깐 들르다, 얻다
- □ describe 말로 설명하다, 묘사하다
- □ objective 목적, 목표, 객관적인
- □ bring in 벌다, 이익을 가져오다
- □ subjectively 주관적으로
- □ self-promotion 자기 홍보
- □ pervasive 만연하는, 스며드는

정답 ②

07 글의 흐름으로 보아, 주어진 문장이 들어가기에 가장 적절한 곳은?

2023. 법원직 9급

> Healthcare chatbots have been purposed to solve this problem and ensure proper diagnosis and advice for people from the comfort of their homes.

People have grown hesitant to approach hospitals or health centers due to the fear of contracting a disease or the heavy sum of consultation fees. (①) This leads them to self-diagnose themselves based upon unverified information sources on the Internet. (②) This often proves harmful effects on the person's mental and physical health if misdiagnosed and improper medicines are consumed. (③) Based upon the severity of the diagnosis, the chatbot prescribes over the counter treatment or escalates the diagnosis to a verified healthcare professional. (④) Interactive chatbots that have been trained on a large and wide variety of symptoms, risk factors, and treatment can handle user health queries with ease, especially in the case of COVID-19.

해설

헬스케어 챗봇의 역할과 중요성에 대한 글로, 헬스케어 챗봇이 진단과 조언을 제공하여 사람들이 질병에 대한 정보를 얻고 집에서 편안하게 사용할 수 있도록 도와주는 중요성을 강조하고 있다. 주어진 문장에서 '이 문제 (this problem)'를 해결한다고 한 것으로 보아 앞에 문제점의 내용이 나와야 한다. 따라서 주어진 문장이 들어가기에 가장 적절한 곳은 ③이다.

해석

질병에 걸리는 것에 대한 두려움 혹은 막대한 진료비 때문에 병원이나 보건소에 가는 것을 망설이는 사람들이 많아졌다. (①) 이것은 그들로 하여금 인터넷상에서 검증되지 않은 정보원에 근거하여 스스로 자가 진단하게 한다. (②) 이것은 종종 오진되고 부적절한 약을 먹을 경우 사람의 정신적, 신체적 건강에 해로운 영향을 미친다는 것을 증명한다. (③ 건강 관리 챗봇은 이 문제를 해결하고 집에서 편안하게 사용할 수 있는 사람들을 위한 적절한 진단과 조언을 보장하는 것을 목적으로 한다.) 챗봇은 진단의 심각도에 따라 처방전 없이 살 수 있는 약을 처방하거나 검증된 의료 전문가에게의 진단을 확대한다. (④) 광범위하고 다양한 증상, 위험 요인 및 치료에 대해 교육을 받은 대화형 챗봇은 특히 COVID-19의 경우 사용자 건강 문의를 쉽게 처리할 수 있다.

어휘

☐ensure 보장하다, 반드시 ~하게 하다
☐comfort 위로하다, 위안하다, 편하게 하다
☐contract (병에) 걸리다
☐consultation fee 진료비, 진찰료
☐unverified 검증되지 않은
☐misdiagnosed 오진을 받은
☐over the counter 처방전 없이 살 수 있는
☐escalate 확대하다, 증가되다
☐symptom 증상, 징후
☐risk factor 위험 인자, 위험 요인

정답 ③

08 글의 흐름으로 보아, 주어진 문장이 들어가기에 가장 적절한 곳은?

2023. 법원직 9급

> But here it's worth noting that more than half the workforce has little or no opportunity for remote work.

COVID-19's spread flattened the cultural and technological barriers standing in the way of remote work. One analysis of the potential for remote work to persist showed that 20 to 25 percent of workforces in advanced economies could work from home in the range of three to five days a week. (①) This is four to five times more remote work than pre-COVID-19. (②) Moreover, not all work that can be done remotely should be; for example, negotiations, brainstorming, and providing sensitive feedback are activities that may be less effective when done remotely. (③) The outlook for remote work, then, depends on the work environment, job, and the tasks at hand, so *hybrid work setups, where some work happens on-site and some remotely, are likely to persist. (④) To unlock sustainable performance and well-being in a hybrid world, the leading driver of performance and productivity should be the sense of purpose work provides to employees, not compensation.

* hybrid 혼합체

해설

이 글은 COVID-19로 인한 원격 근무의 증가와 함께 미래의 일자리와 작업 환경이 어떻게 형성될 수 있는지를 탐구하며, 하이브리드 작업 모델의 중요성을 강조하고 있다. 주어진 문장은 역접(But)으로 시작하고 '원격 근무의 기회가 없다'는 부정적 진술로, 앞에 원격 근무의 긍정적인 진술이 나와야 한다. 따라서 주어진 문장이 들어가기에 가장 적절한 곳은 ②이다.

해석

> COVID-19의 확산은 원격 근무에 방해가 되는 문화적 및 기술적 장벽을 깨부수었다. 원격 근무가 지속될 가능성에 대한 분석에서 선진국의 노동력의 20~25%가 일주일에 3~5일 범위에서 재택 근무를 할 수 있는 것으로 나타났다. (①) 이는 COVID-19 이전보다 원격 근무가 4~5배 더 많은 것이다. (② 그러나 여기서 주목할 점은 노동자의 절반 이상이 원격 근무의 기회가 거의 없거나 아예 없다는 것이다.) 게다가 원격으로 할 수 있는 모든 일이 되어서는 안 된다; 예를 들어 협상, 브레인스토밍 및 민감한 피드백 제공은 원격으로 했을 때 덜 효과적일 수 있는 활동이다. (③) 원격 근무의 전망은 작업 환경, 직무 및 당면한 작업에 따라 달라지므로 일부 작업은 현장에서 발생하고 일부는 원격에서 발생하는 혼합체 근무 상황은 지속될 가능성이 높다. (④) 혼합체 세계에서 지속 가능한 성과와 행복을 실현하려면 성과와 생산성의 주요 동력은 보상이 아니라 직원에게 제공되는 목적 의식이어야 한다.

어휘

☐workforce 노동자, 노동력
☐flatten 깨부수다, 납작하게 만들다
☐negotiation 협상, 절충
☐effective 효과적인
☐outlook 전망, 관점
☐persist 지속되다, 끝까지 하다
☐sustainable 지속 가능한
☐productivity 생산성
☐compensation 보상

정답 ②

09 글의 흐름으로 보아, 주어진 문장이 들어가기에 가장 적절한 곳은?

2023. 법원직 9급

These may appear as challenges which may be impossible to address because of the uncertainty in our ability to predict future climate.

Global warming is a reality man has to live with. (①) This is a very important issue to recognize, because, of all the parameters that affect human existence, on planet earth, it is the food security that is of paramount importance to life on earth and which is most threatened by global warming. (②) Future food security will be dependent on a combination of the stresses, both biotic and *abiotic, imposed by climate change, variability of weather within the growing season, development of **cultivars more suited to different ***ambient conditions, and, the ability to develop effective adaptation strategies which allow these cultivars to express their genetic potential under the changing climate conditions. (③) However, these challenges also provide us the opportunities to enhance our understanding of soil-plant-atmosphere interaction and how one could utilize this knowledge to enable us achieve the ultimate goal of enhanced food security across all areas of the globe. (④)

* abiotic 비생물적인
** cultivar 품종
*** ambient 주변의

해설

이 글은 기후 변화와 식량 안보 문제를 다루며, 이 도전적인 과제들이 동시에 기회를 제공한다는 관점을 강조하고 있다. 주어진 문장의 '이것들(These)'은 앞 문장에서 언급한 '생물적 및 비생물적 스트레스, 적응 전략 개발, 품종 개발, 유전적 잠재력 발현'을 지칭하는 지시대명사이다. 따라서 ② 문장의 다음에 위치해야 한다. 따라서 주어진 문장이 들어가기에 가장 적절한 곳은 ③이다.

해석

지구 온난화는 인간이 함께 살아가야 하는 현실이다. (①) 이것은 지구에 있는 인간의 존재에 영향을 미치는 모든 매개 변수들 중에서 지구상의 생명체에게 가장 중요하고 지구 온난화로 인해 가장 위협을 받는 것은 식량 안전 보장이기 때문에 인지해야 할 매우 중요한 문제이다. (②) 미래의 식량 안전보장은 기후 변화로 인해 야기되는 생물적 및 비생물적인 스트레스의 결합, 성장기의 날씨 변동성, 다양한 주변 조건에 더 적합한 품종의 개발, 그리고 이러한 품종들이 변화하는 기후 조건하에서 유전적 잠재력을 발현할 수 있도록 하는 효과적인 적응 전략을 개발하는 능력에 의존한다. (③ <u>이것들은 미래의 기후를 예측하는 우리의 능력의 불확실성 때문에 해결하기 불가능한 난제로 보일 수 있다.</u>) 하지만, 이러한 난제들은 또한 우리에게 토양과 식물, 대기의 상호 작용에 대한 이해를 높일 수 있는 기회를 제공하며, 이러한 지식을 어떻게 활용하여 전 세계 모든 지역에 걸쳐 식량 안전보장을 향상시키는 궁극적인 목표를 달성할 수 있도록 할 수 있는지를 보여준다. (④)

어휘

- □ predict 예측하다, 예견하다
- □ global warming 지구 온난화
- □ food security 식량 안전보장
- □ be dependent on ~에 의존하다
- □ variability 변동성, 가변성
- □ adaptation 적응, 각색
- □ interaction 상호 작용
- □ enhanced 향상된, 높아진
- □ ultimate 궁극적인, 최후의

정답 ③

10 주어진 문장이 들어갈 위치로 가장 적절한 곳은?

2022. 국가직 9급

> Thus, blood, and life-giving oxygen, are easier for the heart to circulate to the brain.

> People can be exposed to gravitational force, or g-force, in different ways. It can be localized, affecting only a portion of the body, as in getting slapped on the back. It can also be momentary, such as hard forces endured in a car crash. A third type of g-force is sustained, or lasting for at least several seconds. (①) Sustained, body-wide g-forces are the most dangerous to people. (②) The body usually withstands localized or momentary g-force better than sustained g-force, which can be deadly because blood is forced into the legs, depriving the rest of the body of oxygen. (③) Sustained g-force applied while the body is horizontal, or lying down, instead of sitting or standing tends to be more tolerable to people, because blood pools in the back and not the legs. (④) Some people, such as astronauts and fighter jet pilots, undergo special training exercises to increase their bodies' resistance to g-force.

해설

중력에 대한 신체적 영향(반응)과 대처법에 대한 글이다. 혈액이 다리에 강제로 들어가 신체의 나머지 산소를 빼앗을 때 치명적일 수 있다는 진술을 ② 다음 문장에서 진술하고 있고, 그 ③ 다음 문장에서 그 해결책으로 몸을 수평으로 유지하는 것을 제시하고 있다. 그리고 그 결과로 주어진 문장에서 이야기하는 '혈액과 생명을 유지하는 산소는 심장이 뇌로 순환하기가 더 쉽다'고 진술하고 있다. 따라서 주어진 문장의 들어갈 위치로 가장 적절한 곳은 ④이다.

해석

> 사람들은 다양한 방식으로 중력, 또는 g-force에 노출될 수 있다. 등을 때리는 것과 같이 신체의 일부에만 영향을 미치는 국부적일 수 있다. 그것은 또한 자동차 충돌에서 겪게 되는 강력한 힘과 같이 순간적일 수 있다. 세 번째 유형의 중력은 지속되거나 적어도 몇 초 동안 지속된다. (①) 지속적이고 신체적인 중력은 사람들에게 가장 위험하다. (②) 신체는 일반적으로 지속적인 중력보다 국부적이거나 순간적인 중력을 더 잘 견디는데, 이는 혈액이 다리에 강제로 들어가 신체의 나머지 산소를 빼앗기 때문에 치명적일 수 있다. (③) 앉거나 서 있는 대신에 몸이 수평이거나 눕는 동안 지속적인 중력을 가하는 것은 다리가 아닌 등에 피가 고이기 때문에 사람들이 더 견딜 수 있는 경향이 있다. (④ <u>따라서 혈액과, 생명을 유지하는 산소는 심장이 뇌로 순환하기가 더 쉽다.</u>) 우주비행사와 전투기 조종사와 같은 어떤 사람들은 그들의 신체의 중력에 대한 저항력을 높이기 위해 특별한 훈련을 받는다.

어휘

- □ circulate 순환하다, 유포하다
- □ be exposed to ~에 노출되다
- □ gravitational force 중력
- □ localized 국부적인, 국지적인
- □ affect 영향을 미치다
- □ slap 때리다
- □ momentary 순간적인, 잠깐의
- □ endure 견디다
- □ sustained 지속된, 한결같은, 일관된
- □ lasting 영속적인, 지속적인
- □ deadly 치명적인
- □ deprive 빼앗다
- □ horizontal 수평의, 가로의
- □ lie down 눕다
- □ tolerable 견딜 수 있는
- □ astronaut 우주 비행사
- □ resistance 저항, 저항력

정답 ④

11 주어진 문장이 들어갈 위치로 가장 적절한 곳은?

2022. 지방직 9급

> The comparison of the heart to a pump, however, is a genuine analogy.

> An analogy is a figure of speech in which two things are asserted to be alike in many respects that are quite fundamental. Their structure, the relationships of their parts, or the essential purposes they serve are similar, although the two things are also greatly dissimilar. Roses and carnations are not analogous. (①) They both have stems and leaves and may both be red in color. (②) But they exhibit these qualities in the same way; they are of the same genus. (③) These are disparate things, but they share important qualities: mechanical apparatus, possession of valves, ability to increase and decrease pressures, and capacity to move fluids. (④) And the heart and the pump exhibit these qualities in different ways and in different contexts.

해설

비유와 유사성의 본질적인 특징들을 주제로 하는 글이다. 주어진 문장은 심장을 펌프에 비교하는 것이 진정한 비유라고 진술하고 있으며, 심장과 펌프에 대한 설명이 ③ 다음 문장부터 이어지고 있다. 따라서 주어진 문장이 들어갈 위치로 가장 적절한 곳은 ③이다.

해석

> 비유는 두 가지가 상당히 근본적인 많은 점에서 유사하다고 가정되는 비유적 표현이다. 그 두개는 크게 다르지만, 그것들의 구조, 그것들 일부의 관계들 혹은 그것들이 제공하는 핵심적인 목적들은 유사하다. 장미와 카네이션은 유사하지 않다. (①) 그들은 둘 다 줄기와 잎을 가지고 있고 둘 다 빨간색일 수 있다. (②) 하지만 그들은 같은 방식으로 이러한 특성들을 보여준다; 그들은 같은 속에 속한다. (③ 그러나, 심장을 펌프에 비유하는 것은 진정한 비유이다.) 이것들은 서로 전혀 다른 것들이지만, 그것들은 중요한 특성들을 공유한다: 기계 장치, 밸브의 보유, 압력을 증가시키고 감소시키는 능력, 그리고 유체를 이동시키는 능력. (④) 그리고 심장과 펌프는 이러한 특성들을 다른 방식과 다른 맥락에서 보여준다.

어휘

□ comparison 비유, 비교
□ analogy 비유, 유추
□ alike 비슷한, 유사한
□ fundamental 근본적인, 기본적인
□ structure 구조, 체계
□ relationship 관계, 연결
□ essential 필수적인, 본질적인
□ dissimilar 같지 않은, 다른
□ genus (생물 분류상의) 속
□ disparate 서로 전혀 다른, 이질적인
□ apparatus 기구, 장치
□ possession 소유, 소지, 보유
□ capacity 능력
□ fluid 유체, 유동체

정답 ③

12 글의 흐름으로 보아, 주어진 문장이 들어가기에 가장 적절한 곳은?

2022. 법원직 9급

> The effect, however, was just the reverse.

> How we dress for work has taken on a new element of choice, and with it, new anxieties. (①) The practice of having a "dress-down day" or "casual day," which began to emerge a decade or so ago, was intended to make life easier for employees, to enable them to save money and feel more relaxed at the office. (②) In addition to the normal workplace wardrobe, employees had to create a "workplace casual" wardrobe. (③) It couldn't really be the sweats and T-shirts you wore around the house on the weekend. (④) It had to be a selection of clothing that sustained a certain image — relaxed, but also serious.
>
> * wardrobe 옷, 의류

해설

직장에서의 복장이 어떻게 변화하고 그에 따른 걱정거리가 생겨났는지에 대해 다룬 글이며, 직장 캐주얼의 의미와 영향에 대해 설명하고 있다. 주어진 문장에 '그러나 (however)'로 문장의 앞뒤에 대조적인 내용이 진술되어야 한다. ② 이전에는 "dress-down day"와 "casual day" 관행의 의도를 진술하고 있고, ② 다음에 원래의 긍정적인 의도와 다른 부작용에 대한 내용을 진술하고 있다. 따라서 주어진 문장이 들어가기에 가장 적절한 곳은 ②이다.

해석

우리가 직장에서 어떻게 옷을 입는 지는 새로운 선택 요소가 되었으며, 그것과 함께 새로운 걱정거리가 되었다. (①) "약식 복장으로 근무하는 날" 또는 "평상복 출근일"이 가지는 관행은, 10년 전 쯤에 나타나기 시작했는데, 직원들에게 생활이 더 편안해지도록, 그들이 돈을 절약하고 사무실에서 더 편안함을 느낄 수 있게 하도록 의도되었다. (② 그러나, 그 효과는 정반대였다.) 평범한 직장 옷 외에도, 직원들은 "직장 캐주얼" 옷을 만들어내야 했다. (③) 그것은 정말, 당신이 주말에 집에서 입는 운동복과 티셔츠일 수는 없었다. (④) 그것은 특정한 이미지를 — 느긋하지만 또한 진지한 이미지를 — 유지하는 엄선된 옷이어야 했다.

어휘

- □ reverse (정)반대, 뒤바꾸다
- □ dress-down day 약식 복장으로 근무하는 날
- □ casual day 평상복 출근일
- □ workplace 직장
- □ relaxed 편안한, 여유 있는

정답 ②

13 글의 흐름으로 보아, 주어진 문장이 들어가기에 가장 적절한 곳은? 2022. 법원직 9급

But the demand for food isn't *elastic; people don't eat more just because food is cheap.

The free market has never worked in agriculture and it never will. (①) The economics of a family farm are very different than a firm's: When prices fall, the firm can lay off people and idle factories. (②) Eventually the market finds a new balance between supply and demand. (③) And laying off farmers doesn't help to reduce supply. (④) You can fire me, but you can't fire my land, because some other farmer who needs more cash flow or thinks he's more efficient than I am will come in and farm it.

* elastic 탄력성 있는

해설

농업 분야에서 자유 시장 시스템이 어떻게 작동하지 않고 농부와 가족 농장에 미치는 영향을 탐구하며, 시장에서의 가격 변동이 농업에 미치는 영향을 논의하는 글이다. 기업 경제에서는 '공급과 수요 사이의 균형'을 찾을 수 있음을 ①과 ② 다음 문장에서 진술하고 있고, 농업 경제에서는 그 균형을 찾기 어려움을 ③과 ④ 다음 문장에서 진술하고 있다. 주어진 문장은 '농업경제의 상황'에 대한 설명으로 시작하고 있다. 따라서 주어진 문장이 들어가기에 가장 적절한 곳은 ③이다.

해석

자유 시장은 농업에서 잘된 적이 없고 앞으로도 그럴 것이다. (①) 가족 농장의 경제학은 기업의 경제학과 매우 다르다; 가격이 하락하면, 그 기업은 사람들을 해고하고 공장을 놀릴 수 있다. (②) 결국 시장은 공급과 수요 사이에서 새로운 균형을 찾는다. (③ 하지만 음식에 대한 수요는 탄력적이지 않다; 사람들은 단지 음식이 싸다고 더 많이 먹지 않는다.) 그리고 농부를 해고하는 것은 공급을 줄이는 데 도움이 되지 않는다. (④) 당신은 나를 해고할 수는 있지만 나의 땅을 해고할 수는 없는 것은 현금 유동성이 더 필요하거나 내가 그러한 것보다 더 효율적이라고 생각하는 다른 농부가 와서 농사를 지을 것이기 때문이다.

어휘

- □ agriculture 농업
- □ lay off 해고하다
- □ idle (특히 일시적으로 공장·일꾼 등을) 놀리다, 빈둥거리다
- □ cash flow 현금 유동성

정답 ③

Chapter 04

14 주어진 문장이 들어갈 위치로 가장 적절한 것은?

2021. 국가직 9급

For example, the state archives of New Jersey hold more than 30,000 cubic feet of paper and 25,000 reels of microfilm.

Archives are a treasure trove of material: from audio to video to newspapers, magazines and printed material — which makes them indispensable to any History Detective investigation. While libraries and archives may appear the same, the differences are important. (①) An archive collection is almost always made up of primary sources, while a library contains secondary sources. (②) To learn more about the Korean War, you'd go to a library for a history book. If you wanted to read the government papers, or letters written by Korean War soldiers, you'd go to an archive. (③) If you're searching for information, chances are there's an archive out there for you. Many state and local archives store public records — which are an amazing, diverse resource. (④) An online search of your state's archives will quickly show you they contain much more than just the minutes of the legislature — there are detailed land grant information to be found, old town maps, criminal records and oddities such as peddler license applications.

* treasure trove 귀중한 발굴물(수집물)
* land grant (대학·철도 등을 위해) 정부가 주는

해설

역사 탐정을 위한 필수 자료의 보고인 기록 보관소에 대한 글이다. 주어진 문장에서 '예를 들어 (for example)'로 시작되면서 구체적인 사례로 뉴저지의 주 기록 보관소에서 보유하는 자료에 대한 내용을 설명하고 있으므로 ④ 이전에 'many state and local archives ~'로 시작하는 부분의 예시로 볼 수 있다. 따라서 주어진 문장이 들어갈 위치로 가장 적절한 것은 ④이다.

해석

기록 보관소는 자료의 귀중한 발굴물이다: 오디오에서 비디오, 신문, 잡지, 인쇄물에 이르기까지 — 이것은 어떠한 역사 탐정 수사에 있어서 그것들이 없어서는 안 되게 만든다. 도서관과 기록 보관소는 동일하게 보일 수 있지만 차이점은 중요하다. (①) 기록 보관소 소장품은 거의 항상 1차 자료로 구성되는 반면, 도서관은 2차 자료로 구성된다. (②) 한국 전쟁에 대해 더 배우기 위해, 여러분은 역사책을 찾기 위해 도서관에 갈 것이다. (③) 만약 여러분이 정부 문서나 한국 전쟁 군인들이 쓴 편지를 읽고 싶다면, 여러분은 기록 보관소로 갈 것이다. 만약 여러분이 정보를 찾고 있다면, 여러분을 위한 기록 보관소가 있을 것이다. 많은 주 및 지역 기록 보관소는 놀랍고 다양한 자료인 공공 기록을 저장한다. (④ 예를 들어, 뉴저지의 기록 보관소는 30,000입방피트 이상의 종이와 25,000릴의 마이크로필름을 보관하고 있다.) 당신의 주의 기록 보관소를 온라인으로 검색하면 의회 회의록뿐만 아니라 더 많은 자료를 포함하고 있음을 당신에게 빠르게 보여줄 것이다 — 자세한 토지 보조금 정보가 발견될 수 있으며, 오래된 도시 지도, 범죄 기록 그리고 행상인 면허 신청서와 같은 특이한 것들이 있다.

어휘

- ☐ archive 기록 보관소
- ☐ material 재료, 자료
- ☐ indispensable 없어서는 안 될, 필수적인
- ☐ investigation 수사, 조사, 연구
- ☐ primary source 1차 자료
- ☐ secondary source 2차 자료
- ☐ minutes 회의록
- ☐ legislature 입법부, 의회
- ☐ oddity 이상한 것, 특이한 것
- ☐ peddler 행상인
- ☐ application 지원서, 신청서, 응용, 적용

정답 ④

15 주어진 문장이 들어갈 위치로 가장 적절한 것은?

2021. 지방직 9급

And working offers more than financial security.

Why do workaholics enjoy their jobs so much? Mostly because working offers some important advantages. (①) It provides people with paychecks — a way to earn a living. (②) It provides people with self-confidence; they have a feeling of satisfaction when they've produced a challenging piece of work and are able to say, "I made that". (③) Psychologists claim that work also gives people an identity; they work so that they can get a sense of self and individualism. (④) In addition, most jobs provide people with a socially acceptable way to meet others. It could be said that working is a positive addiction; maybe workaholics are compulsive about their work, but their addiction seems to be a safe — even an advantageous — one.

해설

일 중독의 긍정적인 측면과 그 이유와 이점을 일 중독자의 심리적 요인을 중심으로 설명하고 있는 글이다. 일이 사람들에게 제공하는 것을 '급여, 자신감, 정체성, 사회적 관계'를 열거하고 있다. 따라서 주어진 문장은 급여 다음의 내용에 이어져야 한다. 따라서 주어진 문장이 들어갈 위치로 가장 적절한 것은 ②이다.

해석

왜 일 중독자들은 그들의 일을 그렇게 즐기는가? 주로 일하는 것이 몇 가지 중요한 이점을 제공하기 때문이다. (①) 그것은 사람들에게 생계를 유지하는 방법인 급여를 제공한다. (② 그리고 일하는 것은 재정적인 안정보다 더 많은 것을 제공한다.) 그것은 사람들에게 자신감을 준다; 그들은 도전적인 작품을 만들고 "내가 그것을 만들었다"고 말할 수 있을 때 만족감을 느낀다. (③) 심리학자들은 일이 사람들에게 주체성을 준다고 주장한다; 그들은 그들이 자아와 개성을 얻을 수 있도록 일을 한다. (④) 게다가, 대부분의 직업은 사람들에게 다른 사람들을 만날 수 있는 사회적으로 용인되는 방법을 제공한다. 일하는 것은 긍정적인 중독이라고 말할 수 있다; 아마도 일 중독자들은 그들의 일에 대해 강박적일 수 있지만, 그들의 중독은 안전하고 심지어 이로운 것처럼 보인다.

어휘

- □ workaholic 직장 중독자
- □ financial 재정의, 금융의
- □ paycheck 급여 수표
- □ self-confidence 자신감
- □ satisfaction 만족감, 충족
- □ challenging 힘든, 도전적인
- □ psychologist 심리학자
- □ identity 정체성, 신원
- □ individualism 개인주의
- □ acceptable 수용 가능한
- □ addiction 중독
- □ compulsive 강박적인, 강제적인
- □ advantageous 유리한, 이로운

정답 ②

16 주어진 문장이 들어갈 위치로 가장 적절한 것은?

2020. 국가직 9급

It was then he remembered his experience with the glass flask, and just as quickly, he imagined that a special coating might be applied to a glass windshield to keep it from shattering.

In 1903 the French chemist, Edouard Benedictus, dropped a glass flask one day on a hard floor and broke it. (①) However, to the astonishment of the chemist, the flask did not shatter, but still retained most of its original shape. (②) When he examined the flask he found that it contained a film coating inside, a residue remaining from a solution of collodion that the flask had contained. (③) He made a note of this unusual phenomenon, but thought no more of it until several weeks later when he read stories in the newspapers about people in automobile accidents who were badly hurt by flying windshield glass. (④) Not long thereafter, he succeeded in producing the world's first sheet of safety glass.

해설

프랑스의 화학자 Edouard Benedictus가 안전유리를 만든 과정을 설명하는 글이다. 주어진 문장에서 'It was then he remembered his experience~' 부분에서 바로 그때에 경험을 떠올렸다고 했으므로 이전까지는 기억하지 못했음을 알 수 있다. ③ 다음 문장에서 그는 유리 플라

Chapter 04

스크의 내용을 기록했지만 잊어버렸다고 했고, ④ 다음 문장에서 그가 안전유리를 만드는 데 성공했다고 진술하고 있으므로, 주어진 문장이 들어갈 위치로 가장 적절한 것은 ④이다.

해석

1903년 Edouard Benedictus라는 프랑스 화학자가 어느 날 유리 플라스크를 딱딱한 바닥에 떨어뜨려 그것을 깨뜨렸다. (①) 그러나 그 화학자가 놀랍게도, 플라스크는 산산조각이 나지 않았고, 여전히 원래의 모양을 유지하고 있었다. (②) 그가 플라스크를 조사했을 때, 그는 플라스크에 담겨있던 콜로디온 용액에서 남아 있는 잔여물인 필름 코팅이 내부에 들어 있었다는 것을 발견했다. (③) 그는 이 특이한 현상을 노트에 적었지만, 몇 주 뒤에 자동차 사고에서 날아오는 자동차 앞 유리에 의해 심하게 다친 사람들에 대한 기사를 신문에서 읽었을 때까지만 해도 더 이상 그것에 대해 생각하지 않았다. (④ 그때 그는 유리 플라스크에 대한 그의 경험을 기억했고, 그는 그렇게 빠르게 그것이 산산조각이 나지 않도록 차량 앞 유리에 특수한 코팅이 적용될지도 모른다고 생각했다.) 그 후로 얼마 지나지 않아, 그는 세계 최초의 안전 유리를 만드는 데 성공했다.

어휘

- ☐ special 특수한, 특별한
- ☐ apply to 적용되다
- ☐ shatter 산산이 부서지다, 산산조각 나다
- ☐ retain 유지하다, 보유하다
- ☐ original 원래의, 본래의, 원본
- ☐ residue 나머지, 잔여물
- ☐ solution 용액
- ☐ collodion 콜로디온(활성화된 셀룰로오스를 주성분으로 하는 약품)
- ☐ unusual 특이한, 드문, 색다른
- ☐ phenomenon 현상
- ☐ windshield (자동차의) 앞 유리
- ☐ thereafter 그 후에

정답 ④

17 주어진 문장이 들어갈 위치로 가장 적절한 것은?

2020. 지방직 9급

But there is also clear evidence that millennials, born between 1981 and 1996, are saving more aggressively for retirement than Generation X did at the same ages, 22 ~ 37.

Millennials are often labeled the poorest, most financially burdened generation in modern times. Many of them graduated from college into one of the worst labor markets the United States has ever seen, with a staggering load of student debt to boot. (①) Not surprisingly, millennials have accumulated less wealth than Generation X did at a similar stage in life, primarily because fewer of them own homes. (②) But newly available data providing the most detailed picture to date about what Americans of different generations save complicates that assessment. (③) Yes, Gen Xers, those born between 1965 and 1980, have a higher net worth. (④) And that might put them in better financial shape than many assume.

해설

밀레니얼 세대를 주제로 한 글로, 주어진 문장은 밀레니얼 세대의 긍정적인 측면이다. 따라서 긍정적인 내용으로 이어지는 진술 앞에 위치해야 한다. 그 긍정적인 진술은 '그리고 그것은 그들은 많은 이들이 추정하는 것보다 더 나은 재정적 상태에 놓일 수 있다'는 내용의 앞에 나와야 한다. 따라서 주어진 문장이 들어갈 위치로 가장 적절한 것은 ④이다.

해석

밀레니얼 세대는 종종 현대에서 가장 가난하고 경제적으로 부담이 큰 세대로 분류된다. 그들 중 다수가 대학을 졸업하여 학자금 대출이라는 해결해야 할 충격적인 짐을 진 채, 미국이 지금까지 목격해왔던 것들 중에서 최악의 노동 시장 중 하나에 진입했다. (①) 당연히, 밀레니얼 세대는 삶의 비슷한 단계에서 X세대보다 적은 자산을 축적했는데, 주로 그들 중 더 적은 수가 집을 소유하지 못했기 때문이다. (②) 그러나 서로 다른 세대의 미국인들이 무엇을 아끼는지에 대한 가장 상세한 그림을 제공하는 새로운 데이터는 그러한 평가를 더 복잡하게 만든다. (③) 그렇다, 1965년에서 1980년 사이에 태어난 X세대는 순자산이 더 높다. (④ 그러나 1981년과 1996년 사이에 태어난 밀레니얼 세대가 같은 나이인 22~37세대에 비해 X세대들이 했던 것보다 은퇴를 위해 더 적극적으로 저축하고 있다는 명백한 증거도 있다.) 그리고 그것은 많은 사람들이 추정하는 것보다 그들을 더 나은 재정적 상태에 이르게 할 수도 있다.

어휘

□ evidence 증거
□ aggressively 적극적으로, 공격적으로
□ retirement 은퇴, 퇴직
□ label 분류하다, 라벨을 붙이다
□ staggering 충격적인, 믿기 어려운
□ accumulate 모으다, 축적하다
□ detailed 상세한
□ complicate 복잡하게 하다, 복잡한
□ assessment 평가, 판단
□ net worth 순자산
□ financial 금융의, 재정의

정답 ④

18 글의 흐름으로 보아 아래 문장이 들어가기에 가장 적절한 곳은?

2020. 법원직 9급

The great news is that this is true whether or not we remember our dreams.

Some believe there is no value to dreams, but it is wrong to dismiss these nocturnal dramas as irrelevant. There is something to be gained in remembering. (①) We can feel more connected, more complete, and more on track. We can receive inspiration, information, and comfort. Albert Einstein stated that his theory of relativity was inspired by a dream. (②) In fact, he claimed that dreams were responsible for many of his discoveries. (③) Asking why we dream makes as much sense as questioning why we breathe. Dreaming is an integral part of a healthy life. (④) Many people report being inspired with a new approach for a problem upon awakening, even though they don't remember the specific dream.

해설

(자면서 꾸는) 꿈의 중요성을 강조하며, 꿈이 우리에게 영감, 연결, 정보, 그리고 희망을 제공함을 설명하고 있는 글이다. 주어진 문장의 'this'가 지칭하는 것은 ③ 다음 문장의 '꿈은 건강한 삶의 필수적인 부분이다'의 내용이다. 그리고 글쓴이가 강조하는 부분이며, 이에 대한 부연설명을 하고 있는 ④ 다음 문장과 자연스럽게 연결된다. 따라서 아래 문장이 들어가기에 가장 적절한 곳은 ④이다.

해석

어떤 사람들은 꿈이 가치가 없다고 믿지만, 밤에 일어나는 이러한 드라마들을 무관하다고 치부하는 것은 잘못된 것이다. 기억하는 것에서 얻을 수 있는 것이 있다. (①) 우리는 더 연결되고, 더 완전하고, 더 제대로 진행되고 있다고 느낄 수 있다. 우리는 영감, 정보, 그리고 편안함을 받을 수 있다. Albert Einstein은 그의 상대성 이론이 꿈에 의해 영감을 받았다고 말했다. (②) 사실, 그는 꿈들이 그의 많은 발견의 원인이 되었다고 주장했다. (③) 꿈을 꾸는 이유를 묻는 것은 우리가 왜 숨을 쉬는지 의문을 제기하는 것만큼 타당한 질문이다. 꿈을 꾸는 것은 건강한 삶의 필수적인 부분이다. (④ 좋은 소식은 우리가 꿈을 기억하든 안하든 이것이 사실이라는 것이다.) 많은 사람들이 구체적인 꿈을 기억하지 못할지라도, 깨어났을 때 어떤 문제에 대한 새로운 접근법에 영감을 얻는다고 말한다.

어휘

□ nocturnal 밤에 일어나는, 야행성의
□ irrelevant 무관한, 상관없는
□ on track 제대로 진행되고 있는
□ inspiration 영감
□ make sense 이해하다, 타당하다
□ questioning 질문, 의문, 심문
□ integral 필수적인, 완전한
□ discovery 발견

정답 ④

19 주어진 문장이 들어갈 위치로 가장 적절한 것은?

2019. 국가직 9급

Some of these ailments are short-lived; others may be long-lasting.

For centuries, humans have looked up at the sky and wondered what exists beyond the realm of our planet. (①) Ancient astronomers examined the night sky hoping to learn more about the universe. More recently, some movies explored the possibility of sustaining human life in outer space, while other films have questioned whether extraterrestrial life forms may have visited our planet. (②) Since astronaut Yuri Gagarin became the first man to travel in space in 1961, scientists have researched what conditions are like beyond the Earth's atmosphere, and what effects space travel has on the human body. (③) Although most astronauts do not spend more than a few months in space, many experience physiological and psychological problems when they return to the Earth. (④) More than two-thirds of all astronauts suffer from motion sickness while traveling in space. In the gravity-free environment, the body cannot differentiate up from down. The body's internal balance system sends confusing signals to the brain, which can result in nausea lasting as long as a few days.

해설

우주여행과 인간의 생리적 영향을 주제로, 연구된 우주여행의 역사와, 지구 대기권 너머의 환경과 우주여행이 인간의 몸에 미치는 생리적 영향에 관한 내용을 다루는 글이다. 주어진 문장에서의 '이러한 질병들 (these ailments)'에 대한 내용이 ③ 다음 문장에서 언급되고, 구체적인 예시가 ④ 다음 문장에서 이어지고 있다. 따라서 주어진 문장이 들어갈 위치로 가장 적절한 것은 ④이다.

해석

수세기 동안, 인간은 하늘을 쳐다보았고 우리 행성의 영역 너머에 무엇이 존재하는지 궁금해했다. (①) 고대 천문학자들은 우주에 대해 더 많은 것을 배우기를 바라며 밤하늘을 조사했다. 더 최근에는, 몇몇 영화들은 우주 공간에서 인간의 생명을 유지할 수 있는 가능성을 탐구했고, 반면에 다른 영화들은 외계 생명체가 우리 행성을 방문했을지에 대해 의문을 가졌다. (②) 1961년 우주 비행사 Yuri Gagarin이 우주여행을 한 최초의 인간이 된 이후로, 과학자들은 지구 대기권 너머의 상태가 어떤지, 우주여행이 인체에 어떤 영향을 미치는지 연구해 왔다. (③) 대부분의 우주 비행사들이 우주에서 몇 달 이상을 보내지는 않지만, 그들이 지구로 돌아올 때 많은 사람들이 생리적, 심리적 문제를 겪는다. (④ <u>이러한 질병들 중 일부는 일시적이지만, 다른 것들은 장기적일 수 있다.</u> 우주 비행사들의 3분의 2 이상이 우주여행을 하는 동안 멀미로 고통받는다. 무중력 환경에서, 신체는 위와 아래를 구별할 수 없다. 신체의 내부 균형 시스템은 혼란스러운 신호를 뇌에 보내며, 이것은 며칠 동안 오래 지속되는 메스꺼움을 초래할 수 있다.

어휘

- □ ailment 질병
- □ realm 영역, 범위, 왕국
- □ astronomer 천문학자
- □ explore 탐구하다, 분석하다
- □ extraterrestrial 외계의
- □ astronaut 우주 비행사
- □ effect 영향, 결과, 효과
- □ physiological 생리적인
- □ psychological 심리적인, 정신적인
- □ gravity-free 무중력
- □ differentiate 구별하다, 구분 짓다
- □ result in 결과를 초래하다
- □ nausea 메스꺼움
- □ lasting 영속적인, 지속적인

정답 ④

20 주어진 문장이 들어갈 위치로 가장 적절한 것은?

2019. 지방직 9급

The same thinking can be applied to any number of goals, like improving performance at work.

The happy brain tends to focus on the short term. (①) That being the case, it's a good idea to consider what short-term goals we can accomplish that will eventually lead to accomplishing long-term goals. (②) For instance, if you want to lose thirty pounds in six months, what short-term goals can you associate with losing the smaller increments of weight that will get you there? (③) Maybe it's something as simple as rewarding yourself each week that you lose two pounds. (④) By breaking the overall goal into smaller, shorter-term parts, we can focus on incremental accomplishments instead of being overwhelmed by the enormity of the goal in our profession.

해설

단기목표 설정의 중요성과 행복한 뇌의 집중력에 대한 글로, 긍정적인 뇌의 특성을 기반으로, 단기 목표를 통한 집중과 성취를 통해 장기적인 목표를 이루는 방법에 대해 설명하고 있다. 주어진 문장에 'the same thing'이라는 대명사가 있으며, 본문의 내용은 '예시 → 예시 → 결론'으로 이어지고 있으며, 그 예시는 '살을 빼는 것'으로 ②와 ③ 다음 문장에서 설명하고 있으므로 주어진 문장이 들어갈 위치로 가장 적절한 것은 ④이다.

해석

행복한 뇌는 단기간에 집중하는 경향이 있다. (①) 그것이 사실이라면, 궁극적으로 장기 목표를 달성하는 데에 어떤 단기 목표를 달성할 수 있을 지를 생각해 보는 것이 좋다. (②) 예를 들어, 만약 여러분이 6개월 안에 30파운드를 빼기를 원한다면, 여러분은 어떤 단기 목표를 여러분을 거기에 도달하게 할 더 작은 무게의 증가량을 빼는 것과 연관 지을 수 있는가? (③) 아마 2파운드를 빼는 걸 매주 스스로에게 보람 있는 것만큼 간단한 일일 것이다. (④ 그 동일한 생각은 업무에서 성과 향상하는 것과 같은 다양한 목표에도 적용될 수 있다.) 전체적인 목표를 더 작고 단기적인 부분으로 나눔으로써, 우리는 직업에서 목표의 엄청남에 압도되는 대신에 우리는 점진적인 성취에 초점을 맞출 수 있다.

어휘

- □ apply to ~에 적용되다
- □ improve 나아지다, 향상시키다
- □ performance 성과
- □ short term 단기
- □ accomplish 완수하다, 달성하다
- □ associate 연상하다, 연관짓다
- □ increment 증가, 임금 인상
- □ weight 체중
- □ rewarding 보람 있는
- □ incremental 점진적인, 증가하는
- □ accomplishment 성취, 업적
- □ overwhelm 압도하다
- □ enormity 엄청남, 막대함, 심각함
- □ profession 직업, 직종

정답 ④

21 〈보기〉의 문장이 들어갈 위치로 가장 적절한 것은?

2019. 서울시 9급

보 기

In this situation, we would expect to find less movement of individuals from one job to another because of the individual's social obligations toward the work organization to which he or she belongs and to the people comprising that organization.

Cultural differences in the meaning of work can manifest themselves in other aspects as well. (①) For example, in American culture, it is easy to think of work simply as a means to accumulate money and make a living. (②) In other cultures, especially collectivistic ones, work may be seen more as fulfilling an obligation to a larger group. (③) In individualistic cultures, it is easier to consider leaving one job and going to another because it is easier to separate jobs from the self. (④) A different job will just as easily accomplish the same goals.

해설

문화적 다양성과 직업 이동에 대한 글로, 직업에 관한 인식이 문화에 따라 어떻게 달라질 수 있는지를 설명하는 글로, '미국의 문화', '집단주의적 문화', 그리고 '개인주의적 문화'라는 세 가지 범주에서 차이점을 설명하고 있다. 이때, 보기의 문장에서 언급하는 '이러한 상황에서 (In this situation)'는 어떠한 문화를 가리키고 있는지를 찾은 것이 문제 풀이의 핵심이 된다.

보기의 문장에서 직장 조직과 그 조직 내 사람들에 대한 책임을 강조하고 있으므로 '집단적인 문화'에 대해 진술하고 있으므로 ② 다음 문장 뒤에 오는 것이 자연스럽고, ③ 다음 문장에는 '개인적인 문화'에 대한 내용이 진술되고 있다. 따라서 보기의 문장이 들어갈 위치로 가장 적절한 것은 ③이다.

해석

직업의 의미에서의 문화적 다양성은 또한 다른 면에서도 그것들 자체를 드러나게 된다. (①) 예를 들어 미국 문화에서는 직업을 단순히 돈을 모으고 생계를 꾸리기 위한 수단으로 쉽게 생각한다. (②) 다른 문화에서는, 특히 집단주의적 문화의 경우 직업은 오히려 더 큰 집단에 대한 의무를 이행하는 것으로 여겨질 수 있다. (③ 이러한 상황에서 우리는 그 또는 그녀가 속한 직장 조직에 대한, 그리고 그 조직을 구성하고 있는 사람들에 대한 개인의 사회적 책임으로 인하여 개개인이 하나의 직업에서 또 다른 직업으로 더 적게 이동할 것임을 기대하게 된다.) 개인주의적 문화의 경우, 한 직업을 떠나 다른 직업으로 이동하는 것이 더 쉽게 여겨질 수 있는데 왜냐하면 직업을 개인으로부터 더욱 쉽게 분리할 수 있기 때문이다. (④) 다른 직업도 그만큼 쉽게 동일한 목표를 달성할 수 있을 것이다.

어휘

- □ obligation 의무, 책임, 책무
- □ comprise 구성하다
- □ accumulate 모으다, 축적하다
- □ make a living 생계를 꾸리다
- □ collectivistic 집단주의의
- □ fulfill 이행하다, 달성하다
- □ accomplish 완수하다, 달성하다

정답 ③

22 글의 흐름으로 보아, 주어진 문장이 들어가기에 가장 적절한 곳은?

2019. 법원직 9급

"Soft power" on the contrary is "the ability to achieve goals through attraction and persuasion, rather than coercion or fee."

The concept of "soft power" was formed in the early 1990s by the American political scientist, deputy defense of the Clinton's administration, Joseph Nye, Jr. The ideas of the American Professor J. Nye allowed to take a fresh look at the interpretation of the concept of "power," provoked scientific debate and stimulated the practical side of international politics. (①) In his works he identifies two types of power: "hard power" and "soft power." (②) He defines "hard power" as "the ability to get others to act in ways that contradict their initial preferences and strategies." (③) The "soft power" of the state is its ability to "charm" other participants in the world political process, to demonstrate the attractiveness of its own culture (in a context it is attractive to others), political values and foreign policy (if considered legitimate and morally justified). (④) The main components of "soft power" are culture, political values and foreign policy.

* contradict 부인하다, 모순되다

해설

'하드 파워'에 상대가 되는 '소프트 파워'의 개념을 소개하고, 이것이 권력과 정치에 새로운 시각을 제공하는 방식을 다루고 있는 글이다. ② 다음 문장에서 '하드 파워'에 대한 설명을 하고 있고, ③ 다음 문장부터는 '소프트 파워'에 대한 설명을 하고 있다. 주어진 문장은 접속부사 '반대로 (on the contrary)'로 시작하여 '소프트 파워'에 대한 진술을 시작하고 있다. 따라서 주어진 문장이 들어가기에 가장 적절한 곳은 ③이다.

해석

"소프트 파워"의 개념은 1990년대 초에 클린턴 행정부의 부대변인인 미국의 정치학자 Joseph Nye, Jr에 의해 형성되었다. 미국의 J. Nye 교수의 아이디어는 "파워"의 개념에 대한 해석을 새롭게 보도록 했고, 과학적 논쟁을 불러일으켰고, 국제정치의 실용적인 측면을 자극했다. (①) 그의 연구에서 그는 "하드 파워"와 "소프트 파워"라는 두 가지 힘의 유형을 발견한다. (②) 그는 "하드 파워"를

"다른 사람들이 그들의 초기 선호와 전략에 모순되는 방식으로 행동하도록 하는 능력"이라고 정의한다. (③ "소프트 파워"는 반대로 "강요나 수수료가 아닌 유인과 설득을 통해 목표를 달성하는 능력"이다.) 국가의 "소프트 파워"는 세계 정치 과정에서 다른 참가자들을 "매혹시키고" 하고, 자국 문화의 매력을 (다른 사람들에게 매력적인) 보여주고, 정치적 가치와 외교 정책(합법적이고 도덕적으로 정당하다고 여겨진다면)의 보여주는 능력이다. (④) "소프트 파워"의 주요 구성요소는 문화, 정치적 가치와 외교 정책이다.

어휘

- □ on the contrary 그와는 반대로
- □ persuasion 설득, 신념
- □ coercion 강제, 강압, 강요
- □ administration 집행, 행정직, 행정부
- □ interpretation 해석, 이해, 설명
- □ strategy 전략, 작전
- □ charm 매력
- □ demonstrate 입증하다, 설명하다, 보여주다
- □ attractiveness 매력, 매혹
- □ context 맥락, 상황
- □ legitimate 합법적인, 정당한, 타당한
- □ component 구성 요소
- □ morally 도덕적으로
- □ justitied 정당한, 당연한

정답 ③

23 주어진 문장이 들어갈 위치로 가장 적절한 것은?

2018. 국가직 9급

Some remain intensely proud of their original accent and dialect words, phrases and gestures, while others accommodate rapidly to a new environment by changing their speech habits, so that they no longer "stand out in the crowd."

Our perceptions and production of speech change with time. (①) If we were to leave our native place for an extended period, our perception that the new accents around us were strange would only be temporary. (②) Gradually, we will lose the sense that others have an accent and we will begin to fit in to accommodate our speech patterns to the new norm. (③) Not all people do this to the same degree. (④) Whether they do this consciously or not is open to debate and may differ from individual to individual, but like most processes that have to do with language, the change probably happens before we are aware of it and probably couldn't happen if we were.

해설

언어와 인식의 변화에 대한 글로, 시간이 지나면서 우리의 인식과 언어 생산은 변화하는데, 특히 새로운 환경에 적응하며 언어 습관과 방언이 변화하며, 이는 논란의 여지가 있으나 의식적이든 아니든 변화가 일어날 수 있음을 보여주는 글이다. 주어진 문장에서 'some'과 'others'는 세부사항의 대조의 관계를 나타낸다. 따라서 일반적인 진술이 끝난 다음에 나와야 한다. ③ 다음 문장에 '모든 사람들이 같은 정도로 이렇게 하는 것은 아니다'는 일반적인 진술 다음에 오는 것이 자연스럽다. 따라서 주어진 문장이 들어갈 위치로 가장 적절한 것은 ④이다.

해석

말투에 대한 우리의 인식과 생산은 시간이 지나면서 변한다. (①) 만약 우리가 장기간 동안 우리의 고향을 떠나게 된다면 우리 주변의 새로운 억양이 이상하다는 우리의 인식은 단지 일시적일 뿐이다. (②) 서서히 우리는 다른 사람들이 억양을 가지고 있다는 느낌을 잃을 것이고 우리는 새로운 기준에 우리의 말하는 패턴을 맞추기 위해 적응하기 시작할 것이다. (③) 모든 사람들이 같은 정도로 이렇게 하는 것은 아니다. (④ 어떤 사람들은 원래의 억양과 방언 어휘들, 구절들과 몸짓들에 대해 몹시 자랑스러워하는 반면, 다른 사람들은 그들이 더 이상 "군중에서 두드러지지" 않도록 말하기 습관을 바꿈으로써 새로운 환경에 빠르게 적응한다.) 그들이 의식적으로 이

것을 하는지 아닌지는 논쟁의 여지가 있고 개개인에 따라 다를 수 있지만, 언어와 관련된 대부분의 과정들처럼, 변화는 아마도 우리가 그것들을 인식하기 전에 일어날 것이고, 아마도 우리가 인식한다면 아마 일어나지 못할 것이다.

어휘

- □accent 억양, 말씨, 악센트, 강세
- □dialect 방언, 사투리
- □phrase 표현, 어구
- □accommodate 적응하다, 조정하다, 수용하다
- □stand out 두드러지다
- □perception 지각, 인식
- □with time 시간이 흐름에 따라, 마침내
- □temporary 일시적인, 임시의
- □fit in 적응하다, 어울리다
- □norm 규범, 표준
- □consciously 의식적으로
- □be open to ~의 여지가 있다
- □debate 논쟁, 논란, 토론

정답 ④

24 주어진 문장이 들어갈 위치로 가장 적절한 것은?

2018. 지방직 9급

If neither surrendered, the two exchanged blows until one was knocked out.

The ancient Olympics provided athletes an opportunity to prove their fitness and superiority, just like our modern games. (①) The ancient Olympic events were designed to eliminate the weak and glorify the strong. Winners were pushed to the brink. (②) Just as in modern times, people loved extreme sports. One of the favorite events was added in the 33rd Olympiad. This was the pankration, or an extreme mix of wrestling and boxing. The Greek word pankration means "total power." The men wore leather straps with metal studs, which could make a terrible mess of their opponents. (③) The dangerous form of wrestling had no time or weight limits. In this event, only two rules applied. First, wrestlers were not allowed to gouge eyes with their thumbs. Secondly, they could not bite. Anything else was considered fair play. The contest was decided in the same manner as a boxing match. Contenders continued until one of the two collapsed. (④) Only the strongest and most determined athletes attempted this event. Imagine wrestling "Mr. Fingertips," who earned his nickname by breaking his opponents' fingers!

해설

고대 올림픽과 그 안의 극한 스포츠에 대한 글로, 올림픽의 성격과 그 안에서 벌어진 극한 스포츠 활동을 설명하고 있다. '만약 둘 다 항복하지 않는다면, 그 둘은 한 사람이 쓰러질 때까지 주먹을 교환할 것이다'는 진술은, 주어진 문장에서 언급된 '그 두 사람(the two)'에 대한 언급이 된 다음 문장에 와야 자연스럽다. ③ 다음 문장에 두 사람이 언급되어 있다. 따라서 주어진 문장이 들어갈 위치로 가장 적절한 것은 ④이다.

해석

고대 올림픽은 우리의 현대 경기와 같이, 운동선수들에게 그들의 건강과 우월성을 증명하는 기회를 제공했다. (①) 고대 올림픽 경기들은 약자를 없애고 강자를 미화하기 위해 고안되었다. 승자들은 벼랑 끝으로 내몰렸다. (②) 현대와 같이, 사람들은 익스트림 스포츠를 사랑했다. 가장 좋아하는 경기들 중 하나는 33번째 올림픽에서

추가되었다. 이것은 판크라티온, 즉 레슬링과 복싱의 극단적인 혼합이었다. 그리스어의 판크라티온은 "총력"을 의미한다. 그 남자들은 상대방을 엉망으로 만들 수 있는 금속 징이 달린 가죽 끈을 착용했다. (③) 그 위험한 형태의 레슬링은 시간이나 무게 제한이 없었다. 이 경기에서는, 단지 두 가지 규칙이 적용되었다. 첫 번째로, 레슬링 선수들은 그들의 엄지손가락으로 눈을 찌르는 것이 허용되지 않았다. 두 번째로, 그들은 물 수 없었다. 그 외의 다른 것은 정당한 행위로 여겨졌다. 그 경기는 복싱 경기와 같은 방식으로 결정되었다. 경쟁자들은 그 둘 중 한 명이 쓰러질 때까지 계속되었다. (④ 만약 둘 다 항복하지 않는다면, 그 둘은 한 사람이 쓰러질 때까지 주먹을 교환할 것이다.) 오직 가장 강하고 굳게 결심한 운동선수들만 이 경기를 시도했다. 경쟁자의 손가락을 부러뜨려서 그의 별명을 얻은 레슬링 "Mr. Fingertips"를 상상해 보라!

어휘

- □ surrender 항복하다, 굴복하다
- □ superiority 우월성
- □ glorify 미화하다, 칭찬하다
- □ gouge 찌르다
- □ contender 경쟁자, 도전자
- □ determined 굳게 결심한, 단호한

정답 ④

25 주어진 문장이 들어갈 위치로 가장 적절한 곳은?

2017. 국가직 9급

This inequality is corrected by their getting in their turn better portions from kills by other people.

Let us examine a situation of simple distribution such as occurs when an animal is killed in a hunt. One might expect to find the animal portioned out according to the amount of work done by each hunter to obtain it. (①) To some extent this principle is followed, but other people have their rights as well. (②) Each person in the camp gets a share depending upon his or her relation to the hunters. (③) When a kangaroo is killed, for example, the hunters have to give its main parts to their kinfolk and the worst parts may even be kept by the hunters themselves. (④) The net result in the long run is substantially the same to each person, but through this system the principles of kinship obligation and the morality of sharing food have been emphasized.

해설

사냥을 통한 동물 분배와 사회적 상호작용의 원칙에 대한 글로, 사냥을 통해 얻은 동물의 분배를 예로 들어, 사회적인 상호작용과 도덕성을 강조하는 방식으로 사냥꾼들 간의 자원 분배와 친족 의무에 대한 원칙을 설명하고 있다. ④ 앞 문장에 이런 불균형의 예시가 나오고 ④ 다음 문장에 불균형을 수정함으로써 그에 대한 결과를 진술하고 있다. 따라서 주어진 문장이 들어갈 위치로 가장 적절한 곳은 ④이다.

해석

사냥을 통해 동물을 죽였을 때, 발생하는 이런 단순한 분배 상황을 검토해 보자. 사람들은 그 동물을 얻는 데 각 사냥꾼들의 행해진 일의 양에 따라 그 동물이 분배될 것으로 기대할지 모른다. (①) 어느 정도까지는 이 원칙이 따라지나, 다른 사람들 역시 그들의 권리를 갖는다. (②) 그 진영의 각각의 사람은 자기와 사냥꾼들과의 관계에 따라 몫을 받는다. (③) 예를 들어 한 마리의 캥거루가 사냥되었을 때, 사냥꾼들은 그들의 친척들에게 그것의 주요 부분을 줘야 하고 심지어 최악의 부분을 사냥꾼들 자신이 가질 수 있다. (④ 이런 불평등은 그들이 다른 사람들의 사냥감으로부터 더 좋은 몫을 자신들의 차례에서 받음으로써 수정될 수 있다.) 각 사람들에게 장기적으로 순수한 결과는 실질적으로는 똑같으나, 이런 시스템을 통해서 친족의 의무라는 원칙과 음식을 공유하는 도덕성이 강조되어져 왔다.

어휘

- □ inequality 불균형, 불평등
- □ kill 죽이다, 사냥감
- □ distribution 분배, 분포, 유통
- □ portion 분배하다, 나누다
- □ kinfolk 친척, 친족
- □ substantially 상당히, 실질적으로
- □ principle 원리, 원칙
- □ kinship 친족, 연대감
- □ obligation 의무
- □ morality 도덕성
- □ emphasize 강조하다, 두드러지게 하다

정답 ④

26 주어진 문장이 들어갈 위치로 가장 적절한 곳은?

2017. 국가직 9급 하반기

Only New Zealand, New Caledonia and a few small islands peek above the waves.

Lurking beneath New Zealand is a long-hidden continent called Zealandia, geologists say. But since nobody is in charge of officially designating a new continent, individual scientists will ultimately have to judge for themselves. (①) A team of geologists pitches the scientific case for the new continent, arguing that Zealandia is a continuous expanse of continental crust covering around 4.9 million square kilometers. (②) That's about the size of the Indian subcontinent. Unlike the other mostly dry continents, around 94 percent of Zealandia hides beneath the ocean. (③) Except those tiny areas, all parts of Zealandia submerge under the ocean. "If we could pull the plug on the world's oceans, it would be quite clear that Zealandia stands out about 3,000 meters above the surrounding ocean crust," says a geologist. (④) "If it wasn't for the ocean level, long ago we'd have recognized Zealandia for what it was—a continent."

해설

새로운 대륙이 있다는 주장과 그 대륙의 특징에 대한 이 글은 뉴질랜드 아래에 숨겨져 있는 Zealandia라는 미확인 대륙에 대한 지질학자들의 주장과 관련된 내용을 다루고 있으며, 대륙의 크기, 바다 아래의 비중, 그리고 대양의 없음에 따른 특징 등을 설명하고 있다. 주어진 문장에서 언급한 '뉴질랜드, 뉴칼레도니아 및 일부 작은 섬(New Zealand, New Caledonia and a few small islands)'을 ③ 다음 문장의 '이러한 소수 지역들(Except those tiny areas)을 제외하고'와 연결되고 있다. 따라서 주어진 문장이 들어갈 위치로 가장 적절한 곳은 ③이다.

해석

뉴질랜드 아래에 길고 숨겨져 있는 Zealandis라고 불리는 대륙이 있다고 지질학자들을 말한다. 그러나 어떠한 사람도 공식적으로 새로운 대륙을 지정하지 않았기 때문에 개인적인 지질학자들은 궁극적으로 스스로 판단을 해야 할 것이다. (①) 지질학자 팀이 Zealndia가 약 490만 평방 킬로미터를 덮는 대륙지각의 연속적인 확장이라고 주장하면서 신대륙에 대한 과학적 주장을 했다. (②) 그것은 대략 인도의 아대륙의 크기이다. 다른 대부분의 건조한 대륙과는 달리, 뉴질랜드의 약 94%가 바다 밑에 숨어 있다. (③ 오로지 뉴질랜드, 뉴칼레도니아 및 일부 작은 섬만이 파도 위에 보인다.) 이러한 소수 지역들만 제외하고, 모든 Zealandia의 부분들은 물속에 잠겨있다. "우리가 세계의 바다를 모두 제거할 수 있다면, Zealandia가 대양 지각에서 3000미터 가량 위로 튀어나온 것이 분명히 보일 것이다." 라고 지질학자는 말한다. (④) "만약 해수면이 없었다면, 우리는 오래 전에 Zealandia를 그것의 원래 존재인 대륙으로 인식했을 것이다."

어휘

- □ beneath 아래에, 밑에
- □ continent 대륙
- □ geologist 지질학자
- □ designate 지정하다, 지명하다
- □ pitch 던지다, 제시하다
- □ case 경우, 사건, 사실, 주장
- □ subcontinent 아(亞)대륙
- □ pull the plug on 제거하다, 생명 유지 장치를 떼어 내다
- □ stand out 튀어나오다, 두드러지다

정답 ③

27 주어진 문장이 들어갈 위치로 가장 적절한 것은?

2017. 지방직 9급

Fortunately, however, the heavy supper she had eaten caused her to become tired and ready to fall asleep.

Various duties awaited me on my arrival. I had to sit with the girls during their hour of study. (①) Then it was my turn to read prayers; to see them to bed. Afterwards I ate with the other teachers. (②) Even when we finally retired for the night, the inevitable Miss Gryce was still my companion. We had only a short end of candle in our candlestick, and I dreaded lest she should talk till it was all burnt out. (③) She was already snoring before I had finished undressing. There still remained an inch of candle. (④) I now took out my letter; the seal was an initial F. I broke it; the contents were brief.

해설

바쁜 일상에서의 여러 가지 일들에 대한 글로, 여러 가지 해야 할 일들로 인해 바쁜 일상을 겪으면서 주인공의 경험과 감정을 풍부하게 묘사하고 있다. 그녀가 먹은 많은 식사가 그녀를 피곤하게 해서 잠에 빠지게 할 준비가 되게 하였다는 주어진 문장이 원인이 되고, 그 결과 그녀는 코를 골고 있었다(잠을 자고 있었다)가 원인의 결과가 된다. 따라서 주어진 문장이 들어갈 위치로 가장 적절한 것은 ③이다.

해석

> 내가 도착하자마자 다양한 의무들이 나를 기다리고 있었다. 나는 소녀들이 공부하는 시간에 함께 앉아 있어야 했다. (①) 그때가 내가 기도문을 읽을 차례였고 나는 그들이 잠자리에 드는 것을 보았다. 그 이후에 나는 다른 선생님들과 식사를 했다. (②) 우리가 드디어 잠을 자기 위해 물러났을 때조차도 Miss Gryce는 변함없이 여전히 나의 벗이었다. 촛대의 초가 아주 조금 밖에 남지 않아서 그것이 모두 타버릴 때까지 그녀가 말을 걸지 않을까 나는 두려웠다. (③ 그러나 다행히 그녀가 먹은 많은 양의 저녁식사가 그녀를 피곤하게 하여 잠에 빠질 준비가 되게 하였다.) 그녀는 내가 옷을 벗기도 전에 이미 코를 골고 있었다. 단지 일 인치의 초가 남아 있었다. (④) 나는 그때 나의 편지를 꺼냈고, 인장은 이니셜 F였다. 나는 그 봉인을 부수어 편지를 뜯었고, 그 내용은 간결했다.

어휘

- ☐ supper 저녁식사
- ☐ see to bed 잠자리로 보내다
- ☐ afterward 나중에
- ☐ inevitable 피할 수 없는
- ☐ companion 동반자, 동행
- ☐ dread 두려워하다
- ☐ lest ~하지 않기 위해서
- ☐ snoring 코를 고는
- ☐ take out 꺼내다
- ☐ seal 인장
- ☐ brief 간단한, 간결한, 짧은

정답 ③

28 주어진 문장이 들어갈 위치로 가장 적절한 곳은?

2017. 지방직 9급 하반기

> However, should understanding not occur, you will find yourself soon becoming drowsy.

> Dictionaries are your most reliable resources for the study of words. Yet the habit of using them needs to be cultivated. Of course, it can feel like an annoying interruption to stop your reading and look up a word. You might tell yourself that if you keep going, you would eventually understand it from the context. (①) Indeed, reading study guides often advise just that. (②) Often it's not the need for sleep that is occurring but a gradual loss of consciousness. (③) The knack here is to recognize the early signs of word confusion before drowsiness takes over when it is easier to exert sufficient willpower to grab a dictionary for word study. (④) Although this special effort is needed, once the meaning is clarified, the perceptible sense of relief makes the effort worthwhile.

해설

사전 활용의 중요성과 장애요소에 대한 글로, 사전은 신뢰할 수 있는 단어 학습 출처이지만 사용 습관을 개발하는 것이 중요하며, 단어 찾기가 번거로워서 학습에 방해가 될 수 있음을 설명하고 있다. 주어진 문장은 단어 학습에 대한 부정적인 진술이며, 이것을 보충 설명하는 문장이 ② 다음 문장에 진술되고 있다. 따라서 주어진 문장이 들어갈 위치로 가장 적절한 곳은 ②이다.

해석

> 사전은 단어 연구를 위한 당신의 가장 신뢰할 수 있는 자원이다. 그러나 그것들을 사용하는 습관은 길러질 필요가 있다. 물론, 읽기를 멈추고 단어를 찾아보는 것은 성가신 방해처럼 느껴질 수 있다. 당신은 계속하면 결국 맥락에서 그것을 이해하게 될 것이라고 스스로에게 말할 수 있다. (①) 사실, 학습지도서에서도 종종 그것을 조언을 한다. (② 그러나, 이해를 하는 것이 발생하지 않는다면, 당신은 당신 자신이 졸고 있는 것을 발견하게 될 것이다.) 종종 이것은 잠을 필요로 하는 것이 아니라 점진적으로 의식을 잃어가는 것이다. (③) 여기에서 요령은 노곤함이 발생하기 전에 단어 공부를 위해 사전을 잡는 충분한 의지를 발휘하는 것이 쉬울 때를 인지하는 것이다. (④) 이러한 특별한 노력이 필요함에도 불구하고, 의미가 명확해지면 인지할 수 있는 안도감이 그 노력을 가치 있게 만들 것이다.

어휘

□ drowsy 졸리는, 나른하게 만드는
□ reliable 신뢰할 수 있는
□ cultivate 기르다, 경작하다
□ annoying 짜증나는
□ interruption 방해
□ look up 찾아보다
□ gradual 점진적인
□ consciousness 의식
□ knack 요령
□ confusion 혼란
□ exert 발휘하다, 가하다, 힘쓰다
□ sufficient 충분한
□ willpower 의지
□ clarified 명확해진
□ perceptible 인지할 수 있는
□ relief 안도감
□ worthwhile 가치 있는

정답 ②

29 다음 주어진 문장이 들어갈 가장 적절한 곳은?

2017. 서울시 9급

Instead, these employees spoke first of the sincerity of the relationships at work, that their work culture felt like an extension of home, and that their colleagues were supportive.

(①) There is a clear link between job satisfaction and productivity. However, job satisfaction also depends on the service culture of an organization. (②) This culture comprises the things that make a business distinctive and make the people who work there proud to do so. (③) When employees of the Top 10 Best Companies to Work For were asked by Fortune magazine why they loved working for these companies, it was notable that they didn't mention pay, reward schemes, or advancing to a more senior position. (④)

해설

직무 만족도와 조직 문화의 관계에 대한 글로, 직무 만족도와 생산성 사이의 연관성뿐만 아니라 조직의 서비스 문화가 직무 만족도에 미치는 영향을 다루며, 일하기 좋은 회사의 특징과 관련하여 사원들의 의견을 소개하고 있다. 주어진 문장에서 '대신에(instead)'는 'instead of 동명사'의 표현으로 문맥의 의미상 '대신(그들이 월급, 보상제도 혹은 상급직으로의 승진 같은 것들을 언급하는 것 대신에)'의 의미가 된다. '월급, 보상제도, 혹은 상급직으로의 승진'이 언급된 마지막 문장 다음에 위치해야 한다. 따라서 주어진 문장이 들어갈 가장 적절한 곳은 ④이다.

해석

(①) 직무 만족도와 생산성 사이에 명백한 연관성이 있다. 그러나 직무 만족도는 또한 조직의 서비스 문화에 따라 다르다. (②) 이러한 문화는 한 기업을 뚜렷이 구별되게 만들어 주며 그곳에서 일하는 사람들이 그렇게 하는 것을 자랑스러워하게 만드는 것들로 구성되어 있다. (③) 일하기 좋은 10대 회사의 사원들에게 Fortune 잡지에서 왜 그들이 이러한 회사들에서 일하기를 좋아하느냐고 질문을 받았을 때, 그들이 월급, 보상 제도 혹은 상급직으로의 승진 같은 것들을 언급하지 않은 것이 주목할 만하다. (④ 대신에, 이러한 직원들은 직장에서의 관계의 진실성을 먼저 언급했으며, 그들의 직장 문화가 가정의 연장처럼 느끼며, 그들의 동료들이 서로 지원을 아끼지 않는다.)

어휘

□ instead 대신에
□ sincerity 진심, 진실성
□ extension 확장
□ colleague 동료
□ job satisfaction 직무 만족도
□ comprise 구성되다, 이뤄지다
□ distinctive 독특한
□ scheme 계획, 제도, 책략
□ advance 진전, 발전, 출세를 돕다
□ senior position 고위직

정답 ④

04 문장 삽입 유형 기출 독해 어휘 복습 TEST 정답

정답

1	controversial	논란이 많은	21	negotiation	협상, 절충
2	messy	지저분한, 엉망인, 골치 아픈	22	outlook	전망, 관점
3	strenuous	격렬한, 몹시 힘든, 완강한, 불굴의	23	variability	변동성, 가변성
4	commitment	헌신, 약속, 전념	24	ultimate	궁극적인, 최후의
5	federal	연방 정부의, 연방제의	25	circulate	순환하다, 유포하다
6	suspend	부유시키다, 매달다, 중지하다, 연기하다	26	localized	국부적인, 국지적인
7	amendment	개정, 수정	27	momentary	순간적인, 잠깐의
8	inhabit	거주하다, 살다	28	horizontal	수평의, 가로의
9	preserve	보존하다, 지키다, 전유물	29	analogy	비유, 유추
10	reveal	드러내다, 밝히다	30	structure	구조, 체계
11	cabin	선실, 오두막	31	dissimilar	같지 않은, 다른
12	startle	깜짝 놀라게 하다	32	reverse	(정)반대, 뒤바꾸다
13	reform	개혁, 개선, 개혁하다, 개선하다	33	relaxed	편안한, 여유 있는
14	resolve	결의, 결심, 결심하다, 해결하다	34	lay off	해고하다
15	deputy	대리인, 의원, 보안관	35	material	재료, 자료
16	come by	잠깐 들르다, 얻다	36	application	지원서, 신청서, 응용, 적용
17	objective	목적, 목표, 객관적인	37	indispensable	없어서는 안 될, 필수적인
18	subjectively	주관적으로	38	peddler	행상인
19	unverified	검증되지 않은	39	financial	재정의, 금융의
20	escalate	확대되다, 증가되다	40	satisfaction	만족감, 충족

04 문장 삽입 유형 기출 독해 어휘 복습 TEST 정답

정답

41	addiction	중독	61	coercion	강제, 강압, 강요
42	compulsive	강박적인, 강제적인	62	dialect	방언, 사투리
43	advantageous	이로운, 유리한	63	fit in	적응하다, 어울리다
44	shatter	산산이 부서지다, 산산조각 나다	64	be open to	~의 여지가 있다
45	retain	유지하다, 보유하다	65	debate	논쟁, 논란, 토론
46	residue	나머지, 잔여물	66	superiority	우월성
47	retirement	은퇴, 퇴직	67	glorify	미화하다, 칭찬하다
48	staggering	충격적인, 믿기 어려운	68	contender	경쟁자, 도전자
49	inspiration	영감	69	distribution	분배, 분포, 유통
50	integral	필수적인, 완전한	70	portion	분배하다, 나누다
51	realm	영역, 범위, 왕국	71	kinfolk	친척, 친족
52	astronomer	천문학자	72	beneath	아래에, 밑에
53	result in	결과를 초래하다	73	continent	대륙
54	lasting	영속적인, 지속적인	74	stand out	튀어나오다, 두드러지다
55	accomplish	완수하다, 달성하다	75	afterward	나중에
56	incremental	점진적인, 증가하는	76	companion	동반자, 동행
57	overwhelm	압도하다	77	brief	간단한, 간결한, 짧은
58	obligation	의무, 책임, 책무	78	drowsy	졸리는, 나른하게 만드는
59	on the contrary	그와는 반대로	79	worthwhile	가치 있는
60	persuasion	설득, 신념	80	sincerity	진심, 진실성

chapter 05

순서 배열 유형 정답 및 해설

ANSWER

01 ③	02 ②	03 ②	04 ③	05 ③
06 ②	07 ②	08 ④	09 ②	10 ③
11 ③	12 ③	13 ④	14 ①	15 ③
16 ①	17 ②	18 ②	19 ③	20 ②
21 ③	22 ③	23 ①	24 ①	25 ③
26 ③	27 ④	28 ②	29 ③	30 ②
31 ②	32 ②	33 ④	34 ③	

01 주어진 글 다음에 이어질 글의 순서로 가장 적절한 것은?

2025. 출제 기조 전환 2차

Nick started a fire with some chunks of pine he got with the ax from a stump. Over the fire he stuck a wire grill, pushing the four legs down into the ground with his boot.

(A) They began to bubble, making little bubbles that rose with difficulty to the surface. There was a good smell. Nick got out a bottle of tomato ketchup and cut four slices of bread.

(B) The little bubbles were coming faster now. Nick sat down beside the fire and lifted the frying pan off.

(C) Nick put the frying pan on the grill over the flames. He was hungrier. The beans and spaghetti warmed. He stirred them and mixed them together.

① (B) − (A) − (C)　② (B) − (C) − (A)
③ (C) − (A) − (B)　④ (C) − (B) − (A)

해설

Nick이 캠핑을 할 때 요리하는 장면을 묘사하는 글이다. 소나무 조각으로 불을 피우고, 철망 그릴을 설치했다는 제시문 다음에는 Nick이 그릴 위에 프라이팬을 올리고 음식을 데우는 과정이 자연스럽게 이어진다. 먼저 (C)에서 프라이팬을 그릴 위에 올리고, (A)에서는 기포가 생기는 모습을 설명하며, 마지막으로 (B)에서 작은 기포들이 더 빨리 올라오고 있는 모습과 함께 글이 마무리된다. 따라서 글의 순서로 가장 적절한 것은 ③이다.

해석

Nick은 그루터기에서 도끼로 얻은 소나무 조각으로 불을 피우기 시작했다. 그는 불 위에 철망 그릴을 얹고, 네 개의 다리를 부츠로 땅에 눌러 고정했다.

(C) Nick은 불꽃 위에 그릴에 프라이팬을 올렸다. 그는 더 배가 고팠다. 콩과 스파게티가 데워졌다. 그는 그것들을 저어 섞었다.

(A) 그것들은 기포가 생기기 시작했고, 작은 기포들이 힘겹게 표면으로 올라왔다. 좋은 냄새가 났다. Nick은 토마토케첩 병을 꺼내고 빵 네 조각을 잘랐다.

(B) 작은 기포들이 이제 더 빨리 올라오고 있었다. Nick은 불 옆에 앉아 프라이팬을 들어 올렸다.

어휘

- □ pine 소나무, 솔
- □ stump (나무의) 그루터기, 남은 부분
- □ surface 표면, 지면
- □ beside 옆에, ~에 비해
- □ lift 들어 올리다, 올라가다
- □ flame 불꽃, 불길, 활활 타오르다
- □ warm 데워지다, 따뜻해지다, 따뜻한
- □ stir 섞다, 젓다, 흔들리다, 동요, 충격, 젓기

정답 ③

02 주어진 글 다음에 이어질 글의 순서로 가장 적절한 것은?

2025. 출제 기조 전환 1차

Before anyone could witness what had happened, I shoved the loaves of bread up under my shirt, wrapped the hunting jacket tightly about me, and walked swiftly away.

(A) When I dropped them on the table, my sister's hands reached to tear off a chunk, but I made her sit, forced my mother to join us at the table, and poured warm tea.
(B) The heat of the bread burned into my skin, but I clutched it tighter, clinging to life. By the time I reached home, the loaves had cooled somewhat, but the insides were still warm.
(C) I sliced the bread. We ate an entire loaf, slice by slice. It was good hearty bread, filled with raisins and nuts.

① (A) − (B) − (C) ② (B) − (A) − (C)
③ (B) − (C) − (A) ④ (C) − (A) − (B)

해설

어려운 상황에서 빵을 집에 가져가 필사적으로 노력하는 가족들과 함께 식사를 즐기고 있는 내용의 이야기이다. 첫 문장에서 주인공이 빵을 몰래 가져가는 상황이 기술되어 있다. 그 후에 이어질 글에서는 그 빵을 가지고 어떻게 행동했는지에 관한 내용이 나와야 하므로 빵을 가지고 집으로 돌아가는 동안의 상황을 묘사한 (B)가 먼저 나오고, 여동생과 어머니를 식탁에 앉게 하는 (A)의 내용이 이어진 다음, 빵을 같이 먹는 (C)의 상황으로 글이 마무리가 되어야 한다. 따라서 글의 순서로 적절한 것은 ②이다.

해석

누군가가 무슨 일이 일어났는지 목격하기 전에 나는 빵 덩어리들을 내 셔츠 아래로 아무렇게나 넣고 헌팅 재킷을 몸에 꽉 감싸 입고 신속하게 걸어 나갔다.
(B) 빵의 열기가 내 피부 안을 태웠지만, 나는 그것을 더 단단히 꽉 움켜잡고 삶에 매달렸다. 집에 도착할 때쯤, 빵 덩어리들은 약간 식었지만 속은 여전히 따뜻했다.
(A) 내가 그것들을 식탁에 떨어뜨릴 때, 내 누나의 손이 다가와 한 덩어리를 찢으려고 했지만 나는 그녀를 앉히고 식탁에 어머니께서 우리와 함께 하도록 했고, 따뜻한 차를 따랐다.
(C) 나는 빵을 잘랐다. 우리는 한 조각 한 조각씩, 빵 한 덩이 전체를 먹었다. 그것은 건포도와 견과류로 가득찬 좋은 푸짐한 빵이었다.

어휘

- □ witness 목격하다, 목격자, 증인
- □ shove 아무렇게나 넣다, 밀치다
- □ tightly 꽉, 단단히, 빽빽이
- □ swiftly 신속하게, 재빠르게
- □ burn 태우다, 불에 타다, 화상을 입히다
- □ clutch (꽉) 움켜잡다
- □ cling to 매달리다, 고수하다
- □ by the time ~할 때쯤, ~할 때까지
- □ tear off 찢어내다, 떼어내다, ~을 벗기다
- □ chunk 덩어리
- □ pour (음료를) 따르다[따라 주다], 붓다
- □ slice 자르다, 썰다, 조각, 부분
- □ entire 전체의, 전부의
- □ hearty 푸짐한, 원기 왕성한, 애정어린, 친절한
- □ filled with ~으 가득찬
- □ raisin 건포도
- □ nut 견과

정답 ②

03 주어진 글 다음에 이어질 글의 순서로 적절한 것은?

2024. 국가직 9급

Interest in movie and sports stars goes beyond their performances on the screen and in the arena.

(A) The doings of skilled baseball, football, and basketball players out of uniform similarly attract public attention.
(B) Newspaper columns, specialized magazines, television programs, and Web sites record the personal lives of celebrated Hollywood actors, sometimes accurately.
(C) Both industries actively promote such attention, which expands audiences and thus increases revenues. But a fundamental difference divides them: What sports stars do for a living is authentic in a way that what movie stars do is not.

① (A) − (C) − (B) ② (B) − (A) − (C)
③ (B) − (C) − (A) ④ (C) − (A) − (B)

해설

영화배우와 스포츠 스타에 대한 관심은 그들의 활약을 넘어 개인적인 측면까지 이어진다. 양쪽 모두 이러한 관심을 촉진하지만, 그들의 진정성과 일하는 방식에 근본적인 차이가 있음을 설명하는 글이다. 영화와 스포츠

스타에 대한 관심에 대한 언급을 한 제시문 다음에 '영화스타'에 대한 언급을 하는 (B)로 연결되며, '스포츠스타'에 대한 언급을 하는 (A)로 이어져야 하며, 마지막으로 '영화스타'와 '스포츠스타'에 차이에 대한 설명을 하는 (C)로 이어져야 한다. 따라서 글의 순서로 적절한 것은 ②이다.

해석

영화와 스포츠 스타에 대한 관심은 화면과 경기장에서의 활약을 넘어선다.
(B) 신문 칼럼, 전문 잡지, 텔레비전 프로그램, 웹사이트는 유명한 할리우드 배우들의 사생활들을 때로는 정확하게 기록한다.
(A) 유니폼에서 벗어난 숙련된 야구, 축구, 농구 선수들의 행동들은 마찬가지로 비슷하게 대중의 관심을 끈다.
(C) 두 산업 모두 이러한 관심을 적극적으로 장려하는데 이것은 관객을 확대하고 따라서 수입을 증가시킨다. 그러나 근본적인 차이가 그들을 나눈다: 스포츠 스타들이 생계를 위해 하는 것은 영화 스타들이 하는 것과는 다른 방식으로 진정성이 있다는 것이다.

어휘

- □ arena 경기장, 투기장
- □ celebrated 유명한, 축하받는
- □ accurately 정확하게
- □ promote 촉진하다, 홍보하다
- □ expand 확장하다, 넓히다
- □ fundamental 기본적인, 근본적인
- □ authentic 진정한, 진짜의

정답 ②

04 주어진 글 다음에 이어질 글의 순서로 적절한 것은?

2024. 지방직 9급

Computer assisted language learning (CALL) is both exciting and frustrating as a field of research and practice.

(A) Yet the technology changes so rapidly that CALL knowledge and skills must be constantly renewed to stay apace of the field.

(B) It is exciting because it is complex, dynamic and quickly changing — and it is frustrating for the same reasons.

(C) Technology adds dimensions to the domain of language learning, requiring new knowledge and skills for those who wish to apply it into their professional practice.

① (A) − (C) − (B)　　② (B) − (A) − (C)

③ (B) − (C) − (A)　　④ (C) − (B) − (A)

해설

컴퓨터 보조 언어 학습(CALL)의 특성에 대한 글이다. 컴퓨터 보조 언어 학습(CALL)의 장점과 단점에 대한 제시문 다음에 이러한 장점과 단점의 이유에 대한 진술인 (B)로 이어져야 하며, 기술에 대한 진술인 나머지 문장들은 강조의 역할을 하는 접속부사(Yet)를 기준으로 '새로운 지식과 기술을 요한다'는 내용의 (C) 다음에, 기술들이 너무 빠르게 변해서 그 분야에서 더 나아가기 위해서는 끊임없이 갱신되어야 한다는 결론의 (A)가 이어져야 한다. 따라서 글의 순서로 적절한 것은 ③이다.

해석

컴퓨터 보조 언어 학습(CALL)은 연구와 실행의 분야로서 흥미롭지만 좌절감을 주기도 한다.
(B) 그것은 복잡하고 역동적이며 빠르게 변화하기 때문에 흥미롭지만, 같은 이유로 인해 좌절감을 준다.
(C) 기술은 언어 학습 영역에 새로운 차원을 더하며, 이를 전문적인 실행에 적용하려는 사람들에게 새로운 지식과 기술을 요구한다.
(A) 그러나 기술이 너무 빠르게 변화하기 때문에, CALL 지식과 기술은 그 분야에서 더 나아가기 위해 끊임없이 갱신되어야 한다.

어휘

- □ practice 실행, 실천, 관행, 관례
- □ renew 갱신하다, 재개하다
- □ rapidly 빠르게
- □ complex 복잡한, (건물) 단지
- □ dynamic 역동적인, 활발한, 역학
- □ dimension 차원, 관점, 규모, 크기
- □ domain 영역, 범위, 소유지[영토]
- □ professional 전문적인, 전문가의

정답 ③

05 주어진 글 다음에 이어질 글의 순서로 알맞은 것은?

2023. 국가직 9급

All civilizations rely on government administration. Perhaps no civilization better exemplifies this than ancient Rome.

(A) To rule an area that large, the Romans, based in what is now central Italy, needed an effective system of government administration.
(B) Actually, the word "civilization" itself comes from the Latin word civis, meaning "citizen."
(C) Latin was the language of ancient Rome, whose territory stretched from the Mediterranean basin all the way to parts of Great Britain in the north and the Black Sea to the east.

① (A) − (B) − (C)　② (B) − (A) − (C)
③ (B) − (C) − (A)　④ (C) − (A) − (B)

해설

고대 로마를 예로 들면서 정부 행정의 중요성을 강조하는 글로, 고대 로마는 라틴어에 기초한 효과적인 행정 체계를 가지고 있었고, 그들은 대영제국에서 흑해에 이르는 광대한 영토를 통치할 수 있었음을 설명하고 있는 글이다.
제시문에서 언급한 문명에 대한 추가적인 설명을 (B)에서, 'civilization'이 'citizen'이라는 라틴어 단어에서 비롯됨을 언급하고, 이어서 (C)에서는 로마의 지리적 범위와 로마어의 중요성에 대해 언급하며, 마지막 (A)에서는 로마가 광범위한 지역을 효과적으로 통치하기 위해 행정시스템 필요함을 이야기 한다. 따라서 글의 순서로 알맞은 것은 ③이다.

해석

모든 문명은 정부의 행정에 의존한다. 아마도 고대 로마보다 이것의 전형적인 예가 되는 문명은 없을 것이다.
(B) 실제로, "문명"이라는 단어 자체는 "시민"을 의미하는 라틴어 civis에서 왔다.
(C) 라틴어는 고대 로마의 언어인데, 로마의 영토는 지중해 분지에서 북쪽의 그레이트브리튼섬 일부와 동쪽의 흑해까지 뻗어 있었다.
(A) 이처럼 넓은 지역을 통치하기 위해서는 현재 이탈리아 중부에 기반을 둔 로마인들은 효과적인 행정 체계가 필요했다.

어휘

□ administration 행정, 관리, 집행
□ civilization 문명
□ exemplity 전형적인 예가 되다, 예를 들다
□ rule 통치하다, 지배하다
□ effective 효과적인
□ territory 영토, 지역, 영역
□ Mediterranean 지중해
□ basin 분지, 유역
□ the Black Sea 흑해

정답 ③

06 주어진 글 다음에 이어질 글의 순서로 가장 적절한 것은?

2023. 지방직 9급

Just a few years ago, every conversation about artificial intelligence (AI) seemed to end with an apocalyptic prediction.

(A) More recently, however, Things have begun to change. AI has gone from being a scary black box to something people can use for a variety of use cases.
(B) In 2014, an expert in the field said that, with AI, we are summoning the demon, while a Nobel Prize winning physicist said that AI could spell the end of the human race.
(C) This shift is because these technologies are finally being explored at scale in the industry, particularly for market opportunities.

① (A) − (B) − (C)　② (B) − (A) − (C)
③ (B) − (C) − (A)　④ (C) − (A) − (B)

해설

인공지능의 변화를 주제로 하는 글로, AI에 대한 예전의 종말론적인 대화와 달리, 최근에는 AI가 더 이상 무서운 존재가 아니라 다양한 용도로 활용될 수 있는 기술로 변화하고 있으며, 이는 산업에서 큰 관심을 받고 있기 때문임을 보여주는 글이다. 부정적인 제시문에서 또 다른 부정적인 '인류의 종말'을 언급하는 (B)의 진술로 이어져야 하며, 긍정적인 AI에 대한 인식에 대해 진술이 '그러나 (however)' 다음에 이어져야 하며, 그리고 긍정적인 진술로서의 '이러한 변화(This shift)'가 이어져야 한다. 따라서 글의 순서로 알맞은 것은 ②이다.

해석

몇 년 전만 해도, 인공지능(AI)에 관한 모든 대화가 종말론적인 예측으로 끝나는 것처럼 보였다.
(B) 2014년에는 해당 분야의 전문가가 AI로 인해 우리가 악마를 소환하고 있다고 말했고, 노벨상 수상자인 한 물리학자는 AI가 인류의 종말을 가져올 수 있다고 말했다.

(A) 최근에는 그러나 상황이 변하기 시작했다. AI는 무서운 블랙박스에서 사람들이 다양한 경우에 활용할 수 있는 것으로 변해갔다.
(C) 이러한 변화는 이러한 기술들이 마침내 산업에서, 특히 시장 기회에 충분한 양으로 연구되고 있기 때문이다.

어휘

- □ artificial intelligence (AI) 인공지능
- □ apocalyptic 종말론적, 세상에 종말이 온 듯한
- □ prediction 예측, 예견
- □ summon 소환하다, 부르다
- □ physicist 물리학자
- □ demon 악마, 악령
- □ spell 가져오다, 의미하다
- □ human race 인류
- □ scale 규모, 범위, 등급
- □ explore 탐구하다, 분석하다

정답 ②

07 주어진 글 다음에 이어질 글의 순서로 가장 적절한 것은?

2023. 법원직 9급

Sports fan depression is a real phenomenon that affects many avid sports fans, especially during times of disappointment or defeat.

(A) Fans may experience a decrease in mood, appetite, and sleep quality, as well as an increase in stress levels and a heightened risk of developing anxiety or depression. There are many factors that can contribute to sports fan depression, including personal investment in a team's success, social pressures to support a particular team, and the intense media coverage and scrutiny that often accompanies high-profile sports events.

(B) For many fans, their emotional investment in their favorite teams or athletes can be so intense that losing or failing to meet expectations can lead to feelings of sadness, frustration, and even depression. Research has shown that sports fan depression can have a range of negative effects on both mental and physical health.

(C) To mitigate the negative effects of sports fan depression, it's important for fans to maintain a healthy perspective on sports and remember that they are ultimately just games. Engaging in self-care activities such as exercise, spending time with loved ones, and seeking support from a mental health professional can also be helpful.

* avid 열심인

① (A) − (C) − (B)　② (B) − (A) − (C)
③ (B) − (C) − (A)　④ (C) − (B) − (A)

해설

스포츠팬들의 우울증에 대한 글로, 이 글은 스포츠팬들이 스포츠에서의 패배나 실망으로 인해 경험하는 우울증에 대해 다루고 있으며, 이 현상이 정신 건강과 신체 건강에 미치는 부정적인 영향과 해결책을 제시하는 글이다. 제시문에서 스포츠팬들의 우울증에 대해 언급 후, '스포츠팬 우울증의 원인과 영향'에 대한 진술인 (B)로 연결되며, '스포츠팬 우울증의 기타 원인들'에 대한 (A)로 연결된 다음, '스포츠 우울증의 해결책'을 제시하는 (C)로 연결되어야 한다. 따라서 글의 순서로 적절한 것은 ②이다.

해석

스포츠 팬의 우울증은 많은 열렬한 스포츠팬들에게 영향을 미치는 실제 현상으로, 특히 실망이나 패배의 시기에 더욱 그렇다.
(B) 많은 팬들에게 그들이 가장 좋아하는 팀이나 운동선수들에 대한 그들의 감정적 투자는 너무 강렬해서 기대를 잃거나 충족시키지 못하는 것은 슬픔, 좌절감 그리고 심지어 우울증으로 이어질 수 있다. 연구에 따르면 스포츠팬의 우울증은 정신적 그리고 신체적 건강 모두에 다양한 부정적인 영향을 미칠 수 있다.
(A) 팬들은 스트레스 수준의 증가와 불안 또는 우울증에 걸릴 위험성의 증가뿐만 아니라 기분, 식욕, 그리고 수면의 질의 감소를 경험할 수 있다. 한 팀의 성공에 대한 개인적인 투자, 특정한 팀을 지원하라는 사회적인 압력, 그리고 종종 세간의 이목을 끄는 스포츠 경기에 수반되는 강력한 언론 보도와 정밀 조사를 포함하여, 스포츠 팬 우울증을 유발할 수 있는 많은 요인들이 있다.
(C) 스포츠 팬의 우울증의 부정적인 영향을 완화하기 위해서는 팬들이 스포츠에 대한 건강한 관점을 유지하고 궁극적으로 단순한 게임이라는 것을 기억하는 것이 중요하다. 운동과 같은 자기 관리 활동에 참여하고, 사랑하는 사람들과 시간을 보내고, 정신 건강 전문가에게 지원을 구하는 것도 도움이 될 수 있다.

어휘

- □ defeat 패배
- □ mood 기분, 분위기
- □ appetite 식욕
- □ stress level 스트레스 수준
- □ anxiety 불안, 염려, 걱정거리
- □ depression 우울증, 불경기
- □ scrutiny 정밀 조사, 철저한 검토
- □ sadness 슬픔, 슬픈 일
- □ frustration 좌절, 불안
- □ mitigate 완화시키다, 경감시키다
- □ perspective 시각, 관점
- □ engage in 참여하다, 관여하다

정답 ②

08 주어진 글 다음에 이어질 글의 순서로 가장 적절한 것은?

2023. 법원직 9급

On the human level, a cow seems simple. You feed it grass, and it pays you back with milk. It's a trick whose secret is limited to cows and a few other mammals (most can't digest grass).

(A) A cow's complexity is even greater. In particular, a cow (plus a bull) can make a new generation of baby cows. This is a simple thing on a human level, but inexpressibly complex on a microscopic level.
(B) Seen through a microscope, though, it all gets more complicated. And the closer you look, the more complicated it gets. Milk is not a single substance, but a mixture of many. Grass is so complex that we still don't fully understand it.
(C) You don't need to understand the details to exploit the process: it's a straightforward transformation from grass into milk, more like chemistry — or alchemy — than biology. It is, in its way, magic, but it's rational magic that works reliably. All you need is some grass, a cow and several generations of practical knowhow.

* alchemy 연금술

① (B) − (A) − (C)　② (B) − (C) − (A)
③ (C) − (A) − (B)　④ (C) − (B) − (A)

해설

소와 우유 생산의 복잡성에 대해 다루고 있으며, 이것이 인간 눈에는 단순해 보이지만 미시적인 차원에서는 굉장히 복잡하다는 점을 강조하고 있는 글이다. 첫 번째 문장으로 우유로 만드는 과정이 '단순하다'는 (C)로 이어져야 하는데, 그 이유는 그 과정이 '복잡하다'는 진술의 (B)와 대조를 이루기 때문이다. 마지막으로 '그 복잡성이 더 커진다'는 (A)로 이어져야 한다. 따라서 글의 순서로 가장 적절한 것은 ④이다.

해석

인간의 수준에서, 소는 단순해 보인다. 당신이 풀을 먹이면 당신에게 소는 우유로 보답한다. 그것은 비밀이 소와 몇몇 다른 포유동물(대부분은 풀을 소화할 수 없음)에 국한된 특징이다.
(C) 당신은 그 과정을 이용하기 위해 세부적인 것들을 이해할 필요

가 없다. 이것은 풀에서 우유로의 변환으로, 생물학보다는 화학이나 연금술과 더 닮은 간단한 변화이다. 그것은, 나름대로 마술이지만, 확실하게 작동하는 것은 이성적인 마술이다. 필요한 것은 잔디와 소 한 마리, 그리고 몇 세대에 걸친 실용적인 노하우뿐이다.

(B) 하지만 현미경으로 보면, 모든 것이 더 복잡해진다. 자세히 들여다보면 볼수록 더 복잡해진다. 우유는 하나의 물질이 아니라 많은 물질의 혼합물이다. 잔디는 너무 복잡해서 우리는 아직도 풀을 완전히 이해하지 못한다.

(A) 소의 복잡성은 훨씬 더 크다. 특히, 암소 (또한 황소도)는 새로운 세대의 젖소를 만들 수 있다. 이것은 인간적인 차원에서는 단순하지만, 미시적인 차원에서는 표현할 수 없을 정도로 복잡하다.

어휘

- □ trick 특징, 묘기, 재주, 속임수
- □ complexity 복잡성
- □ mammal 포유류
- □ digest 소화하다
- □ microscopic 미시적인, 미세한
- □ mixture 혼합물
- □ exploit 이용하다, 착취하다
- □ transformation 변화, 변신
- □ rational 합리적인, 이성적인
- □ reliably 확실하게, 믿을 수 있게
- □ practical 실용적인, 현실적인

정답 ④

09 주어진 글 다음에 이어질 글의 순서로 가장 적절한 것은?

2023. 법원직 9급

At the level of lawmaking, there is no reason why tech giants should have such an ironclad grip on technological resources and innovation.

(A) As the Daily Wire's Matt Walsh has pointed out, for example, if you don't buy your kid a smartphone, he won't have one. There is no need to put in his hand a device that enables him to indulge his every impulse without supervision.

(B) At the private and personal level, there's no reason why they should have control of your life, either. In policy, politics, and our personal lives, it should not be taken as "inevitable" that our data will be sold to the highest bidder, our children will be addicted to online games, and our lives will be lived in the metaverse.

(C) As a free people, we are entitled to exert absolute control over which kinds of digital products we consume, and in what quantities. Most especially, parents should control what tech products go to their kids.

① (B) − (A) − (C)　　② (B) − (C) − (A)
③ (C) − (A) − (B)　　④ (C) − (B) − (A)

해설

주어진 문장에서 입법 수준에서는 기술 대기업들이 기술 자원들과 혁신에 대해 그렇게 변경할 수 없는 통제를 가져야 할 이유는 없다고 언급하고 있다. (B)에서 사적이고 개인적인 차원에서도 그들이 당신의 삶을 통제해야 할 이유가 없다고 언급하고 있다. 이어서 (C)에서 우리는 우리가 소비하는 디지털 제품들의 종류들과 양에 대해 절대적인 통제권을 행사할 자격이 있으며 특히 부모는 자녀에게 제공되는 기술 제품을 통제해야 한다고 이야기하고 있다. 뒤이어 (A)에서 그 예시로, 당신이 자녀에게 스마트폰을 사주지 않으면 그는 스마트폰을 갖지 못할 것이라고 설명하고 있다. 따라서 글의 순서로 가장 적절한 것은 ②이다.

해석

입법 수준에서, 기술 대기업들이 기술 자원들과 혁신에 대해 그렇게 변경할 수 없는 통제를 가져야 할 이유는 없다.

(B) 사적이며 개인적인 수준에서도, 그들이 당신들의 삶을 통제해야 할 이유 또한 없다. 정책, 정치, 그리고 우리의 사생활에서 우리의 데이터가 최고 응찰자에게 팔릴 것이고, 우리의 아이들

이 온라인 게임에 중독될 것이며, 우리의 삶들이 메타버스에서 살 것이라는 것을 "불가피한" 것으로 받아들여서는 안 된다.

(C) 자유로운 국민으로서, 우리는 우리가 소비하는 디지털 제품들의 종류들과 양들에 대해 절대적인 통제권을 행사할 권리가 있다. 특히, 부모들은 어떤 기술 제품들이 자녀에게 가는지 통제해야 한다.

(A) Daily Wire의 Matt Walsh가 지적했듯이, 예를 들어, 만약 당신의 아이에게 스마트폰을 사주지 않으면 그는 그것을 가질 수 없다. 관리없이 그의 모든 충동을 충족시킬 있게 하는 장치를 그의 손에 넣어줄 필요는 없다.

어휘

□ lawmaking 입법
□ ironclad 변경할 수 없는, 이의를 제기할 수 없는
□ grip 통제, 지배, 꽉 붙잡음, 움켜쥠
□ innovation 혁신, 쇄신
□ point 지적하다, 지시하다, 가리키다
□ indulge 충족시키다, 채우다
□ supervision 관리, 감독, 지도, 지휘
□ inevitable 불가피한, 필연적인
□ bidder 응찰자, 가격 제시자
□ entitle 권리[자격]를 주다
□ addict 중독되게 하다, 중독자
□ exert 행사하다, 가하다, 분투하다
□ absolute 절대적인, 완전한, 확실한

정답 ②

10 주어진 글 다음에 이어질 글의 순서로 가장 적절한 것은?

2022. 국가직 9급

Today, Lamarck is unfairly remembered in large part for his mistaken explanation of how adaptations evolve. He proposed that by using or not using certain body parts, an organism develops certain characteristics.

(A) There is no evidence that this happens. Still, it is important to note that Lamarck proposed that evolution occurs when organisms adapt to their environments. This idea helped set the stage for Darwin.

(B) Lamarck thought that these characteristics would be passed on to the offspring. Lamarck called this idea *inheritance of acquired characteristics*.

(C) For example, Lamarck might explain that a kangaroo's powerful hind legs were the result of ancestors strengthening their legs by jumping and then passing that acquired leg strength on to the offspring. However, an acquired characteristic would have to somehow modify the DNA of specific genes in order to be inherited.

① (A) − (C) − (B)　② (B) − (A) − (C)
③ (B) − (C) − (A)　④ (C) − (A) − (B)

해설

Lamarck의 후천적 특성 이론과 진화론에 대한 오해에 대해 설명하는 글이다. 첫 번째 문장에서 특정한 형질들(특징들)을 발전시킨다고 언급하고 있고, 이 형질들(특징들)에 대한 설명을 (B)에서 하고 있다. 이 특징들을 '획득형질의 유전'이라고 칭하고 나서 그에 따른 구체적인 예시로 (C)가 이어져야 한다. (C)에서는 특정한 형질이 유전되기 위해서는 DNA를 변형시켜야 한다고 말하고 있다. 마지막 문장 (A)에서는 이러한 유전적 변형이 이루어져 있다는 증가가 없다고 진술하고 있다. 따라서 글의 순서로 가장 적절한 것은 ③이다.

해석

오늘날, Lamarck는 적응이 어떻게 진화하는지에 대한 잘못된 설명으로 인해 불공평하게 기억되고 있다. 그는 특정 신체 부위를 사용하거나 사용하지 않음으로써 유기체가 특정한 특징들을 발달시킬 것이라고 제안했다.

(B) Lamarck는 이러한 특징들이 자손들에게 전달될 것이라고 생각했다. Lamarck는 이 생각을 후천적 특징의 계승이라고 불렀다.
(C) 예를 들어, Lamarck는 캥거루의 강력한 뒷다리가 선조들이 점프를 해서 다리를 튼튼하게 하고 그 후에 다리의 힘을 자손들에게 물려준 결과라고 설명할 수도 있다. 그러나 후천적 특징이 기위해서는 특정 유전자의 DNA를 어떻게든 수정해야 할 것이다.
(A) 이런 일이 일어난다는 증거는 없다. 그럼에도 불구하고, Lamarck는 유기체가 그들의 환경에 적응할 때 진화가 일어난다고 제안했다는 것에 주목해야 한다. 이 생각은 Darwin의 기초를 닦을 수 있도록 도움이 되었다.

어휘
□ adaptation 적응, 적응력
□ evolve 진화하다, 발달하다
□ organism 생물체
□ characteristic 특징, 특성
□ inheritance 유전, 상속
□ offspring 자손, 자식
□ mistaken 잘못된, 틀린
□ proposal 제안
□ environment 환경
□ ancestor 조상
□ strengthen 강화하다, 강력해지다
□ hind leg 뒷다리
□ modify 수정하다, 변경하다
□ gene 유전자

정답 ③

11 주어진 글 다음에 이어질 글의 순서로 가장 적절한 것은?

2022. 지방직 9급

For people who are blind, everyday tasks such as sorting through the mail or doing a load of laundry present a challenge.

(A) That's the thinking behind Aira, a new service that enables its thousands of users to stream live video of their surroundings to an on-demand agent, using either a smartphone or Aira's proprietary glasses.
(B) But what if they could "borrow" the eyes of someone who could see?
(C) The Aira agents, who are available 24/7, can then answer questions, describe objects or guide users through a location.

① (A) − (B) − (C)　② (A) − (C) − (B)
③ (B) − (A) − (C)　④ (C) − (A) − (B)

해설

시각 장애인을 위한 새로운 서비스 'Aira'에 대한 글이다. 시각 장애인들이 일상생활에서 마주하는 어려움에 대한 언급 다음에 문제의 해결책을 제시하는 (B)가 이어져야 하며, (A)에서는 이러한 문제를 해결하기 위한 새로운 서비스 'Aira'에 대해 언급한 다음 마지막으로 (C)에서 이 서비스에 대한 추가적인 설명이 이어져야 한다. 따라서 글의 순서로 가장 적절한 것은 ③이다.

해석

시각 장애인들에게, 우편물을 분류하거나 세탁을 많이 하는 것과 같은 일상적인 일들은 어려움을 안겨준다.
(B) 하지만 그들이 볼 수 있는 누군가의 눈을 "빌릴" 수 있다면 어떨까?
(A) 그것은 수천 명의 사용자들이 스마트폰 또는 Aira의 전용 안경을 사용하면서, 그들의 주변 환경의 생중계 비디오를 온-디맨드 에이전트에게 스트리밍할 수 있게 해주는 새로운 서비스인 Aira의 기반이 되는 생각이다.
(C) 1년 내내 이용할 수 있는 Aira 에이전트들은 질문에 답변하고, 물체를 설명하거나, 사용자에게 위치를 안내할 수 있다.

어휘
□ blind 시각 장애인
□ task 일, 과업, 과제
□ sort 종류, 유형, 분류하다, 구분하다
□ laundry 세탁
□ challenge 도전, 어려움
□ borrow 빌리다, 대여하다
□ surroundings 주변 환경
□ proprietary 전용의, 사유의, 독점의
□ 24/7 1년 내내, 언제나

정답 ③

12 주어진 글 다음에 이어질 글의 순서로 가장 적절한 것은?

2022. 법원직 9급

Once they leave their mother, primates have to keep on making decisions about whether new foods they encounter are safe and worth collecting.

(A) By the same token, if the sampler feels fine, it will reenter the tree in a few days, eat a little more, then wait again, building up to a large dose slowly. Finally, if the monkey remains healthy, the other members figure this is OK, and they adopt the new food.

(B) If the plant harbors a particularly strong toxin, the sampler's system will try to break it down, usually making the monkey sick in the process. "I've seen this happen," says Glander. "The other members of the troop are watching with great interest — if the animal gets sick, no other animal will go into that tree. There's a cue being given — a social cue."

(C) Using themselves as experiment tools is one option, but social primates have found a better way. Kenneth Glander calls it "sampling." When howler monkeys move into a new habitat, one member of the troop will go to a tree, eat a few leaves, then wait a day.

① (A) − (B) − (C)　② (B) − (A) − (C)
③ (C) − (B) − (A)　④ (C) − (A) − (B)

해설

영장류의 먹이 선택과 사회적 행동에 대한 글로, 영장류가 새로운 먹이를 선택할 때 샘플링 하는 방법을 통해 음식안정성을 확인한다는 것을 원숭이의 예를 통해 설명하고 있는 글이다. 첫 번째 문장은 음식을 안정성을 확인하는 '샘플링'에 대해 설명하는 (C)가 나와야 하며, 그 샘플링의 부정적인 상황의 (B)의 경우와 그 샘플링이 긍정적인 상황인 (A)로 이어져야 한다. 따라서 글의 순서로 가장 적절한 것은 ③이다.

해석

일단 그들이 자신의 어미를 떠나면, 영장류들은 그들이 마주치는 새로운 먹이가 안전한지 그리고 모을 가치가 있는지에 관해 계속 결정을 내려야 한다.

(C) 그들 자신을 실험 도구로 사용하는 것은 하나의 선택이지만, 사회적 영장류들은 더 나은 방법을 발견했다. Kenneth Glander는 그것을 "샘플링"이라고 부른다. 짖는원숭이들은 새로운 서식지로 이동할 때, 그 무리의 한 구성원이 한 나무에 가서, 몇 개의 잎들을 먹고, 그러고 나서 하루를 기다린다.

(B) 만약 그 식물이 특히 강한 독소를 숨기고 있다면, 시식자의 몸은 그것을 분해하려고 할 것이며, 대개 그 과정에서 그 원숭이를 병이 들게 만든다. "나는 이런 일이 일어나는 것을 본 적이 있습니다,"라고 Glander는 말한다. "그 무리의 다른 구성원들은 큰 관심을 갖고 지켜보고 있어요 — 만약 그 동물이 병이 들게 된다면, 다른 어떠한 동물도 그 나무에 들어가지 않을 것입니다. 주어지고 있는 신호 즉 사회적 신호가 있습니다."

(A) 같은 이유로, 만약 시식자가 괜찮으면, 그 시식자는 며칠 뒤에 그 나무에 다시 들어갈 것이고, 조금 더 먹고, 그러고 나서 다시 기다리며, 천천히 많은 분량으로 커진다. 마침내 만약 그 원숭이가 건강을 유지한다면, 다른 구성원들은 이것이 괜찮다고 생각하고, 그들은 그 새로운 먹이를 채택한다.

어휘

- □ primate 영장류
- □ encounter 마주치다
- □ reenter 다시 들어가다
- □ toxin 독소
- □ breakdown 분해, 고장, 붕괴
- □ adopt 채택하다, 입양하다
- □ harbor 숨기다, 숨겨 주다
- □ process 과정, 절차, 처리하다
- □ experiment 실험
- □ habitat 서식지
- □ troop 무리, 부대

정답 ③

13 주어진 글 다음에 이어질 글의 순서로 가장 적절한 것은?

2022. 법원직 9급

The historical evolution of Conflict Resolution gained momentum in the 1950s and 1960s, at the height of the Cold War, when the development of nuclear weapons and conflict between the superpowers seemed to threaten human survival.

(A) The combination of analysis and practice implicit in the new ideas was not easy to reconcile with traditional scholarly institutions or the traditions of practitioners such as diplomats and politicians.

(B) However, they were not taken seriously by some. The international relations profession had its own understanding of international conflict and did not see value in the new approaches as proposed.

(C) A group of pioneers from different disciplines saw the value of studying conflict as a general phenomenon, with similar properties, whether it occurs in international relations, domestic politics, industrial relations, communities, or between individuals.

① (B) − (A) − (C)　② (B) − (C) − (A)
③ (C) − (A) − (B)　④ (C) − (B) − (A)

해설

갈등 해결의 진화에 대해 다루며, 새로운 아이디어와 전문분야의 선구자들에 대한 연구와 이와 반대의 상황에 대해 설명하고 있는 글이다. 글의 소재인 '갈등 해결의 역사적 진화'에 대한 '갈등연구의 가치'를 아는 선구자들의 설명을 하는 (C)가 첫 번째 문장이 되어야 하고, '갈등연구의 가치'를 인정하지 않는 (B)로 이어지고, 마지막으로 이에 대한 이유를 설명하는 (A)로 이어져야 한다. 따라서 글의 순서로 가장 적절한 것은 ④이다.

해석

갈등 해결의 역사적 진화는 냉전의 최고조였던 1950년대와 1960년대에 활기를 찾았는데, 그 당시 초강대국들 사이에 핵무기의 개발과 갈등이 인류의 생존을 위협하는 것처럼 보였다.

(C) 서로 다른 지식 분야에서 온 한 그룹의 선구자들은, 갈등이 국제 관계에서 발생하든, 국내 정치에서, 산업 관계에서, 지역사회에서 또는 개인들 간에 발생하든, 비슷한 특성을 가진 일반적인 현상으로서 갈등을 연구하는 그 가치를 알았다.

(B) 하지만 그들은 일부 사람들에게는 진지하게 받아들여지지 않았다. 국제 관계 종사자들은 국제 갈등에 대해 자신만의 이해를 가지고 있었고, 제안된 바와 같은 새로운 접근법에서 가치를 보지 않았다.

(A) 새로운 아이디어에 내포된 분석과 실행의 결합은, 전통적인 학술 기관이나 외교관과 정치인 같은 전문직 종사자들의 관례와 조화를 이루기가 쉽지 않았다.

어휘

- □ conflict 갈등, 충돌, 분쟁
- □ resolution 해결
- □ gain momentum 활기를 찾다, 번성하다
- □ the Cold War 냉전
- □ superpower 초강대국
- □ threaten 위협하다, 협박하다
- □ combination 결합, 조합
- □ reconcile 조화시키다, 받아들이다
- □ traditional 전통적인
- □ scholarly 학문적인, 학술적인
- □ institution 기관, 단체, 협회
- □ practitioner 실무자
- □ diplomat 외교관
- □ approach 접근법
- □ pioneer 개척자
- □ discipline 규율, 훈육, 지식 분야
- □ property 재산, 자산, 토지, 특성, 속성
- □ domestic 국내의, 가정의

정답 ④

14 주어진 글 다음에 이어질 글의 순서로 가장 적절한 것은?

2022. 법원직 9급

Ambiguity is so uncomfortable that it can even turn good news into bad. You go to your doctor with a persistent stomachache. Your doctor can't figure out what the reason is, so she sends you to the lab for tests.

(A) And what happens? Your immediate relief may be replaced by a weird sense of discomfort. You still don't know what the pain was! There's got to be an explanation somewhere.
(B) A week later you're called back to hear the results. When you finally get into her office, your doctor smiles and tells you the tests were all negative.
(C) Maybe it is cancer and they've just missed it. Maybe it's worse. Surely they should be able to find a cause. You feel frustrated by the lack of a definitive answer.

① (B) − (A) − (C) ② (B) − (C) − (A)
③ (C) − (A) − (B) ④ (C) − (B) − (A)

해설

애매모호함에 대한 부정적인 면을 복통을 호소하는 환자의 예를 통해서 설명하고 있는 글이다. 주어진 글 다음에 첫 번째 문장인 검사실로 보낸 결과가 일주일 뒤에 나온다는 내용인 (B)가 나와야 하며, 검사의 결과를 듣고 안도감이 불안감 대체된다는 내용인 (A)로 이어지고, 정확한 원인을 몰라 좌절감을 느낀다는 (C)로 이어져야 한다. 따라서 글의 순서로 가장 적절한 것은 ①이다.

해석

애매모호함은 너무나 불편해서 그것은 심지어 좋은 소식을 나쁜 것으로 바꿀 수 있다. 당신이 지속되는 복통으로 의사에게 간다. 당신의 의사는 그 이유가 무엇인지 알아내지 못하고, 그래서 그녀는 테스트를 위해 당신을 검사실로 보낸다.
(B) 일주일 후에 당신은 결과를 듣도록 다시 호출된다. 당신이 마침내 그녀의 진료실에 도착할 때, 당신의 의사는 웃으면서, 당신에게 테스트가 모든 음성이라고 말해준다.
(A) 그리고 무슨 일이 일어나는가? 당신의 즉각적인 안도는 이상한 불안감으로 대체될 수 있다. 당신은 여전히 그 통증이 무엇이었는지 알지 못한다. 틀림없이 어딘가에 설명이 있을 것이다.
(C) 아마 그것은 암이고 그들이 그것을 놓쳤을지도 모른다. 아마 더 나쁠지도 모른다. 분명히 그들은 원인을 찾을 수 있어야 한다. 당신은 확실한 대답의 부족으로 좌절감을 느낀다.

어휘

- □ ambiguity 애매모호함
- □ uncomfortable 불편한
- □ stomachache 복통
- □ figure out 파악하다
- □ lab 실험실
- □ immediate 즉각적인, 즉시의
- □ relief 안도, 안심, 경감
- □ weird 이상한, 기이한, 기괴한
- □ discomfort 불편, 불안
- □ negative 부정적인, 소극적인
- □ frustrated 좌절감을 느끼는, 불만스러워 하는
- □ definitive 확실한, 최종적인

정답 ①

15 주어진 글 다음에 이어질 글의 순서로 가장 적절한 것은?

2021. 국가직 9급

To be sure, human language stands out from the decidedly restricted vocalizations of monkeys and apes. Moreover, it exhibits a degree of sophistication that far exceeds any other form of animal communication.

(A) That said, many species, while falling far short of human language, do nevertheless exhibit impressively complex communication systems in natural settings.
(B) And they can be taught far more complex systems in artificial contexts, as when raised alongside humans.
(C) Even our closest primate cousins seem incapable of acquiring anything more than a rudimentary communicative system, even after intensive training over several years. The complexity that is language is surely a species-specific trait.

① (A) − (B) − (C) ② (B) − (C) − (A)
③ (C) − (A) − (B) ④ (C) − (B) − (A)

해설

영장류의 의사소통과 언어와의 비교를 하면서 언어와 특징과 영장류들의 의사소통에 대해서 설명하는 글이다. 주어진 글은 인간의 언어가 다른 동물들보다 뛰어나다는 내용이며 (C) 앞부분 역시 인간 언어가 더 뛰어나다는 내용이므로 다음에 이어질 내용으로 가장 적절하고 (A) 앞부분은 (C) 내용과 같은 내용이지만, nevertheless를 통해 동물들의 복잡한 의사소통

시스템의 내용으로 바뀌었다. (B)는 (A)의 복잡한 의사소통 다음 내용으로 연결된다. 따라서 글의 순서로 가장 적절한 것은 ③이다.

해석

확실히, 인간의 언어는 원숭이와 유인원의 분명히 제한된 발성으로부터 눈에 띄게 차이가 난다. 게다가, 그것은 어떤 다른 형태의 동물적 의사소통을 훨씬 능가하는 정교화의 정도를 보여준다.
(C) 심지어 우리의 가장 가까운 영장류 종자들조차도 몇 년 동안 집중적인 훈련을 받은 후에도 기본적인 의사소통 시스템 이상의 것을 습득할 수 없는 것처럼 보인다. 언어라는 복잡성은 확실히 종의 특유한 특성이다.
(A) 그렇긴 하지만, 많은 종들은 인간의 언어에는 크게 미치지 못하더라도, 자연 환경에서 인상적인 복잡한 의사소통 체계를 보여준다.
(B) 그리고 그들은 인간과 함께 자랐을 때처럼 인공적인 맥락에서 훨씬 더 복잡한 시스템을 배울 수 있다.

어휘

- □ to be sure 분명히, 확실히
- □ that said 그렇긴 하지만
- □ stand out 눈에 띄다, 뚜렷하게 나타나다
- □ decidedly 확실히, 분명히
- □ restricted 제한된
- □ vocalization 발성
- □ ape 유인원
- □ sophistication 정교화
- □ fall short 부족해지다
- □ nevertheless 그럼에도 불구하고
- □ setting 환경, 배경
- □ alongside 함께, 동시에
- □ primate 영장류
- □ cousin 사촌, 친척, 종자
- □ incapable of ~할 수 없는
- □ acquire 습득하다, 획득하다
- □ rudimentary 기본적인, 기초적인
- □ intensive 집중적인

정답 ③

16 주어진 글 다음에 이어질 글의 순서로 가장 적절한 것은?

2021. 지방직 9급

Growing concern about global climate change has motivated activists to organize not only campaigns against fossil fuel extraction consumption, but also campaigns to support renewable energy.

(A) This solar cooperative produces enough energy to power 1,400 homes, making it the first large-scale solar farm cooperative in the country and, in the words of its members, a visible reminder that solar power represents "a new era of sustainable and 'democratic' energy supply that enables ordinary people to produce clean power, not only on their rooftops, but also at utility scale."

(B) Similarly, renewable energy enthusiasts from the United States have founded the Clean Energy Collective, a company that has pioneered "the model of delivering clean power-generation through medium-scale facilities that are collectively owned by participating utility customers."

(C) Environmental activists frustrated with the UK government's inability to rapidly accelerate the growth of renewable energy industries have formed the Westmill Wind Farm Co-operative, a community-owned organization with more than 2,000 members who own an onshore wind farm estimated to produce as much electricity in a year as that used by 2,500 homes. The Westmill Wind Farm Co-operative has inspired local citizens to form the Westmill Solar Co-operative.

① (C) − (A) − (B) ② (A) − (C) − (B)
③ (B) − (C) − (A) ④ (C) − (B) − (A)

해설

지속 가능한 에너지 공급을 위한 지역공동체 조직들의 활동들을 여러 회사들의 예를 통해서 설명하는 글이다. 주어진 글의 마지막 부분에 신재생 에너지를 지지하는 캠페인에 대한 내용이 더 강조되고 있다는 것을 알 수 있고 이후의 이어지는 내용은 신재생 에너지를 지지하는 캠페인의 구체적인 예의 내용이 나와야한다. (C)에서 영국의 신재생 에너지 운동을 소개하는 예시가 나오고 (A)에서 태양 발전 회사에 대한 설명을 하고 나서, (B)에서 비슷한 미국의 신재생 에너지 단체까지 소개하는 것이 올바르다. 따라서 글의 순서로 가장 적절한 것은 ①이다.

해석

지구 기후 변화에 대한 증가하는 걱정은 화석 연료 추출 소비에 대한 캠페인뿐만 아니라 신재생 에너지를 지지할 수 있는 캠페인을 조직하는 활동에도 동기를 부여해왔다.

(C) 영국 정부가 재생 에너지 산업의 성장을 빠르게 가속화하지 못하는 것에 좌절한 환경 운동가들은 2500개 가정에 의해 사용되는 연간 전력만큼을 생산하는 걸로 추정되는 내륙의 풍력 발전 단지를 소유한, 2000명 이상의 지역공동체가 소유하는 조직인 Westmill Wind Farm 주식회사를 설립했다. Westmill Wind Farm 주식회사는 지역의 시민들이 Westmill Solar 주식회사를 설립하도록 영감을 주었다.

(A) 이 태양 발전 협동조합은 1,400가구에 전력을 공급할 수 있는 충분한 에너지를 생산하는 국내 최초의 대규모 태양 발전 회사이며, 구성원들의 말로 볼 때, 태양 발전이 "그들의 지붕 위에뿐 아니라 공익 시설의 규모로 평범한 사람들이 청정에너지를 생산할 수 있도록 하는 지속 가능하고 '민주적인' 에너지 공급의 새로운 시대"를 대표한다는 것을 가시적으로 상기시키는 것이다.

(B) 이와 비슷하게 미국의 재생에너지 지지자들은 "참여 전력회사 고객이 집단적으로 소유한 중규모 설비를 통해 청정발전을 전달하는 모델"을 개척한 기업 Clean Energy Collecive를 설립했다.

어휘

□ fossil fuel 화석 연료
□ renewable 재생 가능한
□ solar 태양의
□ cooperative 협동조합
□ sustainable 지속 가능한
□ democratic 민주적인
□ utility 유용, 공익 시설
□ medium 중간의
□ onshore 육지의, 내륙의
□ wind farm 풍력 발전소
□ organization 조직
□ electricity 전기

정답 ①

17 주어진 글 다음에 이어질 글의 순서로 가장 적절한 것은?

2021. 법원직 9급

Religion can certainly bring out the best in a person, but it is not the only phenomenon with that property.

(A) People who would otherwise be self-absorbed or shallow or crude or simply quitters are often ennobled by their religion, given a perspective on life that helps them make the hard decisions that we all would be proud to make.

(B) Having a child often has a wonderfully maturing effect on a person. Wartime, famously, gives people an abundance of occasions to rise to, as do natural disasters like floods and hurricanes.

(C) But for day-in, day-out lifelong bracing, there is probably nothing so effective as religion: it makes powerful and talented people more humble and patient, it makes average people rise above themselves, it provides sturdy support for many people who desperately need help staying away from drink or drugs or crime.

① (B) − (A) − (C)　　② (B) − (C) − (A)
③ (C) − (A) − (B)　　④ (C) − (B) − (A)

해설

종교와 긍정적인 역할에 대한 글로, 종교가 인내와 성장을 촉진하고 어려움을 극복하는 데 어떤 역할을 하는지를 강조하는 글이다. 종교외에도 사람에게 영향을 미치는 '아이를 갖는 것, 전쟁, 자연재해'들에 대한 언급을 한 (B) 다음에는 다시 '종교가 평생 동안의 준비에 가장 큰 영향을 미친다'는 (C)가 이어져야 하며, 종교가 없다면 '자기만족하거나, 천박하거나, 조잡하거나, 단순히 포기하는 사람'들이 '자랑스러워 할 어려운 결정'을 돕는 역할을 종교가 한다는 (A)로 이어져야 한다. 따라서 글의 순서로 가장 적절한 것은 ②이다.

해석

종교는 확실히 사람에게서 최고를 이끌어낼 수 있지만, 그 속성이 가진 유일한 현상은 아니다.

(B) 아이를 갖는 것은 종종 사람에게 놀랄 만큼 성숙한 영향을 미친다. 유명한 말이지만, 전쟁은 홍수나 허리케인과 같은 자연재해와 마찬가지로 사람들에게 일어날 수 있는 많은 기회를 준다.

(C) 그러나 하루하루 빠짐없이 평생 동안의 준비에는 아마도 종교만큼 효과적인 것이 없을 것이다. 그것은 강력하고 재능 있는 사람들을 더 겸손하고 인내심 있게 만들고, 보통 사람들을 그들 자신보다 성장하게 하며, 음주 또는 마약이나 범죄로부터 벗어나는데 필사적으로 도움을 필요로 하는 많은 사람들에게 견고한 지원을 제공한다.

(A) 그렇지 않으면 자기 만족적이거나, 천박하거나, 조잡하거나, 단순히 그만두는 사람이 될 수도 있는 사람들은 우리 모두가 자랑스러워 할 어려운 결정을 내리는 데 도움을 주는 삶에 대한 관점을 고려한다면, 그들의 종교에 의해 종종 기품 있게 된다.

어휘

- □ ennoble 품위를 높이다, 기품 있게 하다
- □ perspective 관점, 시각
- □ maturing 성장, 성숙
- □ abundance 풍부, 충만, 다수, 대량
- □ lifelong 일생일대의
- □ bracing 격렬한, 힘찬
- □ humble 겸손한, 낮은
- □ patient 인내심 있는, 환자
- □ sturdy 튼튼한, 강인한
- □ desperately 필사적으로, 절박하게

정답 ②

18 주어진 글 다음에 이어질 글의 순서로 가장 적절한 것은?

2021. 법원직 9급

More people require more resources, which means that as the population increases, the Earth's resources deplete more rapidly.

(A) Population growth also results in increased greenhouse gases, mostly from CO_2 emissions. For visualization, during that same 20th century that saw fourfold population growth, CO_2 emissions increased twelvefold.

(B) The result of this depletion is deforestation and loss of biodiversity as humans strip the Earth of resources to accommodate rising population numbers.

(C) As greenhouse gases increase, so do climate patterns, ultimately resulting in the long-term pattern called climate change.

* deplete 고갈시키다, 대폭 감소시키다

① (A) − (B) − (C)　　② (B) − (A) − (C)
③ (B) − (C) − (A)　　④ (C) − (A) − (B)

해설

인구 증가와 자원 고갈 사이의 관계를 다루며, 이로 인해 발생하는 환경 문제들을 나열하는 글이다. 자원고갈에 대한 결과에 대한 진술을 하는 (B)가 먼저 나와야 하며, 인구증가로 인한 이산화 탄소배출에 대한 (A)로 이어지고, 마지막으로 '장기적인 기후변화'에 대한 (C)로 이어져야 한다. 따라서 글의 순서로 가장 적절한 것은 ②이다.

해석

더 많은 사람들이 더 많은 자원을 필요로 하는데, 이는 인구가 증가함에 따라 지구의 자원이 더 빠르게 고갈된다는 것을 의미한다.

(B) 이 고갈의 결과는 인간이 증가하는 인구수를 수용하기 위해 자원을 지구에서 제거함에 따라 삼림 벌채와 생물 다양성의 손실이다.

(A) 인구 증가 또한 대부분 이산화탄소 배출로 인한 온실가스를 증가시킨다. 시각화해보면, 4배의 인구 증가를 보인 20세기 동안 이 산화탄소 배출량은 12배 증가했다.

(C) 온실가스가 증가함에 따라 기후 패턴도 증가하여 궁극적으로 기후 변화라고 불리는 장기적인 패턴을 초래한다.

어휘

- □ emission 배출, 방출
- □ deforestation 산림 파괴
- □ biodiversity 생물 다양성
- □ accommodate 수용하다, 공간을 제공하다
- □ greenhouse gas 온실 가스
- □ long term 장기적인

정답 ②

19 주어진 글 다음에 이어질 글의 순서로 가장 적절한 것은?

2021. 법원직 9급

Sequoya (1760?-1843) was born in eastern Tennessee, into a prestigious family that was highly regarded for its knowledge of Cherokee tribal traditions and religion.

(A) Recognizing the possibilities writing had for his people, Sequoya invented a Cherokee alphabet in 1821. With this system of writing, Sequoya was able to record ancient tribal customs.
(B) More important, his alphabet helped the Cherokee nation develop a publishing industry so that newspapers and books could be printed. School-age children were thus able to learn about Cherokee culture and traditions in their own language.
(C) As a child, Sequoya learned the Cherokee oral tradition; then, as an adult, he was introduced to Euro-American culture. In his letters, Sequoya mentions how he became fascinated with the writing methods European Americans used to communicate.

① (B) − (A) − (C)　② (B) − (C) − (A)
③ (C) − (A) − (B)　④ (C) − (B) − (A)

해설

Sequoya와 체로키 자모가 어떻게 체로키 문화와 전통을 보존하는 데 기여했는지를 시간순으로 설명하고 있는 글이다. 글쓰기를 배웠다는 (C)가 Sequoya의 탄생 내용의 다음으로 이어져야 하고, 체로키 자모를 발명했다는 (A) 다음에 '출판 산업이 발전하도록 도왔다'는 (B)로 이어져야 한다. 따라서 글의 순서로 가장 적절한 것은 ③이다.

해석

Sequoya(1760?-1843)는 테네시 주 동부에서 태어났고, 체로키 인디언 부족의 전통과 종교에 대한 지식으로 높이 평가받는 명성 있는 가문에서 태어났다.
(C) 어렸을 때, Sequoya는 체로키 인디언의 구전을 배웠고, 어른이 되면서 그는 유럽계 미국인 문화를 접하게 되었다. 그의 편지에서 Sequoya는 어떻게 유럽계 미국인들이 의사소통을 하기 위해 사용했던 글쓰기 방법에 매료되었는지 언급한다.
(A) 그의 백성들을 위해 글쓰기가 가진 가능성을 인식한 Sequoya는 1821년에 체로키 자모를 발명했다. 이 글쓰기 체계로, Sequoya는 고대 부족의 관습을 기록할 수 있었다.
(B) 더욱 중요한 것은, 그의 알파벳이 체로키 국가가 신문과 책을 인쇄할 수 있도록 출판 산업을 발전시킬 수 있도록 도왔다는 것이다. 취학 연령의 아이들은 그들의 언어로 체로키 문화와 전통에 대해 배울 수 있었다.

어휘

□ prestigious 훌륭한, 명성 있는
□ tribal 부족의, 종족의
□ religion 종교
□ custom 관습, 풍습
□ publishing industry 출판 산업
□ oral tradition 구전
□ mention 언급하다, 말하다

정답 ③

20 주어진 글 다음에 이어질 글의 순서로 가장 적절한 것은?

2021. 소방직 9급

There are hundreds of gas stations around San Francisco in the California Bay Area. One might think that gas stations would spread out to serve local neighborhoods.

(A) The phenomenon is partly due to population clustering. Gas stations will be more common where demand is high, like in a city, rather than in sparsely populated areas like cornfields.
(B) But this idea is contradicted by a common observation. Whenever you visit a gas station, there is almost always another in the vicinity, often just across the street. In general, gas stations are highly clustered.
(C) Moreover, there are many factors at play. Locating a gas station is an optimization problem involving demand, real estate prices, estimates of population growth, and supply considerations such as the ease of refueling.

① (A) − (C) − (B)　② (B) − (A) − (C)
③ (C) − (A) − (B)　④ (C) − (B) − (A)

해설

캘리포니아 만 지역의 주유소 밀집 현상과 주유소 위치 결정에 대해 다룬 글이다. 주어진 글에는 주유소가 지역 주민들에게 서비스를 제공하기 위한 것이라고 생각한다고 통념을 제시하고 있다. (B)에 이러한 통념은 모순이라며 잘못되었음을 말하고 주유소가 일반적으로 밀집도가 높다고 하고 있고, (A)에 밀집도가 높은 이유를 보여주고 있고, 마지막으로 (C)에 이유를 추가적으로 진술하고 있다. 따라서 글의 순서로 가장 적절한 것은 ②이다.

해석

캘리포니아 만 지역의 샌프란시스코 주변에는 수백 개의 주유소가 있다. 누군가는 주유소가 지역 주민들에게 서비스를 제공하기 위해 퍼져 나갈 것이라고 생각할지도 모른다.
(B) 그러나 이 생각은 일반적인 관찰에 의해 모순된다. 당신이 주유소를 방문할 때마다, 거의 항상 근처에 다른 주유소가 있는데, 종종 바로 길 건너편에 있다. 일반적으로 주유소는 밀집도가 높다.
(A) 이러한 현상은 부분적으로 인구 집단에 기인한다. 주유소는 옥수수 밭처럼 인구가 적은 지역보다는 도시처럼 수요가 많은 곳에서 더 흔할 것이다.
(C) 게다가 여러 가지 요인이 작용하고 있다. 주유소의 입지는 수요, 부동산 가격, 인구 증가 추정, 주유의 용이성 등의 공급 고려 등이 수반되는 최적화 문제이다.

어휘

- □ phenomenon 현상
- □ population 인구
- □ cluster 집단, 무리
- □ demand 수요
- □ sparsely 드문드문, 성기게
- □ cornfield 옥수수밭
- □ contradict 반박하다, 부정하다
- □ vicinity 주변, 근처
- □ clustered 집결한, 모여 있는
- □ optimization 최적화
- □ real estate 부동산

정답 ②

21 주어진 글 다음에 이어질 글의 순서로 가장 적절한 것은?

2020. 국가직 9급

Past research has shown that experiencing frequent psychological stress can be a significant risk factor for cardiovascular disease, a condition that affects almost half of those aged 20 years and older in the United States.

(A) Does this mean, though, that people who drive on a daily basis are set to develop heart problems, or is there a simple way of easing the stress of driving?
(B) According to a new study, there is. The researchers noted that listening to music while driving helps relieve the stress that affects heart health.
(C) One source of frequent stress is driving, either due to the stressors associated with heavy traffic or the anxiety that often accompanies inexperienced drivers.

① (A) − (C) − (B)　　② (B) − (A) − (C)
③ (C) − (A) − (B)　　④ (C) − (B) − (A)

해설

스트레스가 심혈관 질환의 중요한 위험이 될 수 있다고 설명하는 글이다. (C)에서 스트레스의 한 원인으로 운전을 예로 들며, 이 내용을 (A)의 this로 이어 받아서 운전의 스트레스를 줄일 수 있는 방법이 있는 것인지 묻고 있다. 그리고 (B)에서 새로운 연구에 따르면 운전 중 음악을 듣는 방법이 효과적이라고 진술하고 있다. 따라서 글의 순서로 가장 적절한 것은 ③이다.

해석

과거의 연구는 빈번한 심리적 스트레스를 경험하는 것이 심혈관 질환의 중대한 위험 요인이 될 수 있다는 것을 보여 주는데, 이것은 미국에서 20세 이상인 사람들의 거의 절반에게 발생하는 질환이다.
(C) 빈번한 스트레스의 한 가지 원인은 운전인데, 이는 교통 체증과 관련된 스트레스 요인이나 미숙한 운전자들에게 종종 동반하는 불안감 때문이다.
(A) 하지만, 이것은 매일 운전하는 사람들이 심장 질환이 생기도록 되어 있다는 것을 의미하는가, 아니면 운전의 스트레스를 완화시킬 수 있는 간단한 방법이 있는가?
(B) 새로운 연구에 따르면, 그것은 있다. 연구원들은 운전하는 동안에 음악을 듣는 것이 심장 건강에 영향을 미치는 스트레스를 완화하는 데 도움이 된다고 언급했다.

어휘

- □ psychological 심리적인, 정신의
- □ cardiovascular 심혈관의
- □ risk factor 위험 요소
- □ note 언급하다, 말하다
- □ heavy traffic 교통체증
- □ anxiety 불안, 염려, 걱정거리
- □ relieve 완화시키다, 줄이다

정답 ③

22 주어진 글 다음에 이어질 글의 순서로 가장 적절한 것은?

2020. 지방직 9급

Nowadays the clock dominates our lives so much that it is hard to imagine life without it. Before industrialization, most societies used the sun or the moon to tell the time.

(A) For the growing network of railroads, the fact that there were no time standards was a disaster. Often, stations just some miles apart set their clocks at different times. There was a lot of confusion for travelers.

(B) When mechanical clocks first appeared, they were immediately popular. It was fashionable to have a clock or a watch. People invented the expression "of the clock" or "o'clock" to refer to this new way to tell the time.

(C) These clocks were decorative, but not always useful. This was because towns, provinces, and even neighboring villages had different ways to tell the time. Travelers had to reset their clocks repeatedly when they moved from one place to another. In the United States, there were about 70 different time zones in the 1860s.

① (A) − (B) − (C)　　② (B) − (A) − (C)
③ (B) − (C) − (A)　　④ (C) − (A) − (B)

해설

시간을 말하기 위해 해와 달을 사용했었던 산업화 이전의 시기에 말하고 있는 글이다. 주어진 문장의 산업화 이전의 시기는 (B)에서 When mechanical clocks first appeared로 이어질 수 있고, 시계가 처음 생겨서 시계를 갖는 것이 fashionable하게 여겨졌다는 내용은 (C) these clocks were decorative로 이어진다. (C)에서 마을마다 different ways to tell the time을 가지고 있었기 때문에 문제점이 생겼다고 설명하고 이에 대한 예로 (A)의 첫 부분에서 이러한 서로 다른 표준시간대가 혼란을 야기한다는 내용이 나오고 있다. 특히 '시계'에 대한 설명은 these라는 지시형용사를 통해 (B)에서 (C)로 이어짐을 알 수 있고, 'time zone'에 대한 설명이 (C)에서 (A)로 이어지므로 있음을 알 수 있다. 따라서 글의 순서로 가장 적절한 것은 ③이다.

해석

오늘날 시계는 우리의 삶을 너무 많이 지배하고 있어서 시계가 없는 삶은 상상하기 어렵다. 산업화 이전에, 대부분의 사회는 태양이나 달을 사용하여 시간을 알 수 있었다.

(B) 기계식 시계가 처음 등장했을 때, 그것들은 즉시 인기가 있었다. 시계나 손목시계를 갖는 것은 유행이었다. 사람들은 "시계의" 또는 "시계"라는 표현을 이 새로운 시간 측정 방법을 언급하기 위해 발명하기도 했다.

(C) 이 시계들은 장식적이었지만, 항상 유용하지는 않았다. 마을, 지방, 심지어 이웃 마을에서도 시간을 알 수 있는 방법이 달랐기 때문이다. 여행자들은 한 장소에서 다른 장소로 이동할 때 반복적으로 시계를 다시 맞춰야 했다. 미국에는 1860년대에 약 70개의 다른 시간대가 있었다.

(A) 철도망이 발달하면서 시간 기준이 없다는 사실이 재앙이었다. 종종, 단지 몇 마일 떨어져 있는 역들은 그들의 시계를 다른 시간에 맞춘다. 여행자들에게 많은 혼란이 있었다.

어휘

- □ dominate 지배하다
- □ railroad 철로
- □ confusion 혼란, 혼동, 당혹
- □ mechanical clock 기계식 시계
- □ fashionable 유행인
- □ refer to 언급하다, 참고하다
- □ province 주, 지방, 분야
- □ reset 재설정하다

정답 ③

23 주어진 글 다음에 이어질 글의 순서로 가장 적절한 것은?

2020. 법원직 9급

As cars are becoming less dependent on people, the means and circumstances in which the product is used by consumers are also likely to undergo significant changes, with higher rates of participation in car sharing and short-term leasing programs.

(A) In the not-too-distant future, a driverless car could come to you when you need it, and when you are done with it, it could then drive away without any need for a parking space. Increases in car sharing and short-term leasing are also likely to be associated with a corresponding decrease in the importance of exterior car design.

(B) As a result, the symbolic meanings derived from cars and their relationship to consumer self-identity and status are likely to change in turn.

(C) Rather than serving as a medium for personalization and self-identity, car exteriors might increasingly come to represent a channel for advertising and other promotional activities, including brand ambassador programs, such as those offered by Free Car Media.

① (A) − (C) − (B)　　② (B) − (C) − (A)
③ (C) − (A) − (B)　　④ (C) − (B) − (A)

해설

자동차 공유와 단기 임대 프로그램이 증가함에 따라 자동차 제품 사용 및 환경에 어떤 변화가 일어날 수 있는지 다루고 있는 글이다. 자동차의 의존도가 낮아면서 나타나는 변화들에 언급하고 있는 제시문 다음에 미래에 대한 전망을 하는 (A)가 나와야 하며, 자동차가 개인화와 자아정체성에 대한 것으로서 보다는 브랜드 홍보와 광고 및 홍보채널로 역할을 한다는 (C)가 이어져야 하며, 그로 인한 결과에 대한 설명을 하는 (B)로 이어져야 한다. 따라서 글의 순서로 가장 적절한 것은 ①이다.

해석

자동차가 사람에 대한 의존도가 낮아지고 있는 만큼 자동차 공유와 단기 임대 프로그램 참여율이 높아지는 등 소비자가 제품을 사용하는 수단과 상황도 큰 변화를 겪을 가능성이 높다.

(A) 멀지 않은 미래에 운전자가 없는 자동차가 당신이 필요할 때 당신에게 올 수 있고, 그것을 끝냈을 때, 그것은 주차 공간 없이 운전해서 갈 수 있다. 자동차 공유의 증가와 단기 임대 또한 상응하는 외장 자동차 디자인의 중요성 감소와 관련이 있을 것으로 보인다.

(C) 자동차 외부는 개인화와 자아 정체성을 위한 매개체 역할을 하기 보다는 점점 더 자유로운 자동차 미디어가 제공하는 것과 같은 브랜드 홍보 프로그램을 포함한 광고 및 기타 홍보 활동을 위한 채널을 제시하게 될 것이다.

(B) 그 결과, 자동차에서 파생되는 상징적 의미와 소비자의 자아 정체성 및 지위와의 관계가 차례로 변화할 가능성이 높다.

어휘

□ dependent 의존적인
□ significant 중요한, 상당한
□ participation 참여
□ short term 단기
□ leasing 임대, 대여
□ driverless car 무인 자동차
□ exterior 외부, 겉
□ symbolic 상징적
□ meaning 의미
□ self identity 자아 정체성
□ status 지위, 상태
□ represent 제시하다, 보여주다, 나타내다, 대표하다
□ advertising 광고
□ promotional 홍보의

정답 ①

24 주어진 글 다음에 이어질 글의 순서로 가장 적절한 것은?

2020. 법원직 9급

There is a wonderful story of a group of American car executives who went to Japan to see a Japanese assembly line. At the end of the line, the doors were put on the hinges, the same as in America.

(A) But something was missing. In the United States, a line worker would take a rubber mallet and tap the edges of the door to ensure that it fit perfectly. In Japan, that job didn't seem to exist.

(B) Confused, the American auto executives asked at what point they made sure the door fit perfectly. Their Japanese guide looked at them and smiled sheepishly. "We make sure it fits when we design it."

(C) In the Japanese auto plant, they didn't examine the problem and accumulate data to figure out the best solution — they engineered the outcome they wanted from the beginning. If they didn't achieve their desired outcome, they understood it was because of a decision they made at the start of the process.

① (A) − (B) − (C)　② (A) − (C) − (B)
③ (B) − (A) − (C)　④ (B) − (C) − (A)

해설

일본의 자동차 조립 라인에서의 접근 방식을 미국에서의 상황과 비교하는 글이다. 이 글에서의 핵심적인 질문은 '왜 문이 꼭 맞는 것을 확인하지 않는지'이다. 제시문 다음에 처음 나와야 할 것은 '미국과 일본에서의 차이점'을 언급하고 있는 (A)의 '뭔가 빠져 있었다'이다. 그리고 그러한 이유를 물어보는 (B)로 이어져야 하며, 추가적인 설명을 하는 (C)로 이어져야 한다. 따라서 글의 순서로 가장 적절한 것은 ①이다.

해석

일본 조립라인을 보러 일본에 간 미국 자동차 임원들의 멋진 사연이 있다. 줄의 끝에는 미국처럼 문짝에 경첩에 달았다

(A) 그런데 뭔가 빠져 있었다. 미국에서는 라인 노동자가 고무망치를 가지고 문 가장자리를 두드려서 그것이 완벽하게 맞는지 확인하곤 했다. 일본에서는 그런 일이 존재하지 않는 것 같았다

(B) 당황한 미국 자동차 임원들은 어느 시점에 문이 꼭 맞는 것 을 확인하는지 물었다. 그들의 일본인 안내원이 그들을 바라보며 열없게 웃었다. "애초에 디자인할 때 꼭 맞도록 한다"고 말했다

(C) 일본 자동차 공장에서 그들은 문제를 조사하지 않고 데이터를 축적하여 최상의 해결책을 찾아내지 않았다 — 그들은 처음부터 그들이 원하는 결과를 설계했다. 만약 그들이 원하는 결과를 얻지 못했다면, 그들은 그것이 그 과정의 시작에서 내린 결정 때문이라고 이해했다.

어휘

- □ executive 경영진, 임원
- □ assembly 조립, 집회, 의회
- □ hinge 경첩, 경첩을 달다
- □ tap 가볍게 치다
- □ ensure 확실히 하다
- □ confused 당황한, 혼란스러운
- □ outcome 결과

정답 ①

25 주어진 글 다음에 이어질 글의 순서로 가장 적절한 것은?

2020. 소방직 9급

In World War II, Japan joined forces with Germany and Italy. So there were now two fronts, the European battle zone and the islands in the Pacific Ocean.

(A) Three days later, the United States dropped bombs on another city of Nagasaki. Japan soon surrendered, and World War II finally ended.

(B) In late 1941, the United States, Britain and France participated in a fight against Germany and Japan; the U.S. troops were sent to both battlefronts.

(C) At 8:15 a.m. on August 6, 1945, a U.S. military plane dropped an atomic bomb over Hiroshima, Japan. In an instant, 80,000 people were killed. Hiroshima simply ceased to exist. The people at the center of the explosion evaporated. All that remained was their charred shadows on the walls of buildings.

① (A) − (B) − (C)　② (B) − (A) − (C)
③ (B) − (C) − (A)　④ (C) − (A) − (B)

해설

히로시마와 나가사키에 떨어진 원자 폭탄의 파괴적인 영향과 일본의 항복에 대해 다루고 있는 글이다. 강조하는 문장은 "1945년 8월 6일 오전 8시 15분, 미군 전투기는 일본, 히로시마에 원자 폭탄을 떨어트렸다. 즉시 8만 명의 사람이 죽었다."이다. 이 문장을 바탕으로 사건의 시간의 흐름과, 제시문에서 제시하는 '두개의 전선'에 대한 설명을 바탕으로 올바른 순서를 정할 수 있다. 첫 번째 문장은 두개의 최전선을 언급하는 (B)가 나와야 하며, 히로시마에 원자 폭탄을 투하한 (C)로 이어져야 하며, 삼일 후에 일본이 항복했다는 (A)로 이어져야 한다. 따라서 글의 순서로 가장 적절한 것은 ③이다.

해석

세계 2차 대전에서 일본은 독일과 이탈리아와 함께 참전했다. 그래서 지금 유럽 전쟁 지대와 태평양에 있는 두 개의 전선이 있었다.

(B) 1941년 후반에, 미국과 영국, 프랑스는 독일과 일본에 대항하는 전쟁에 참여했다. 미국 군대는 두 최선으로 보내졌다.

(C) 1945년 8월 6일 오전 8시 15분, 미군 전투기는 일본, 히로시마에 원자 폭탄을 떨어트렸다. 즉시 8만 명의 사람이 죽었다. 히로시마는 바로 사라졌다. 그 폭발의 중심부에 있던 사람들은 사라졌다. 남은 것이라곤 건물의 벽에 까맣게 그을린 그림자가 전부였다.

(A) 3일 후에 미국은 나가사키의 또 다른 도시에 폭탄을 떨어뜨렸다. 일본은 바로 항복하였고, 세계 2차 대전은 마침내 끝이 났다.

어휘

- □ drop 떨어뜨리다
- □ surrender 항복하다, 포기하다
- □ participate 참가하다
- □ instant 순간, 즉각적인
- □ cease 그치다, 중단되다
- □ evaporate 증발하다, 사라지다
- □ remain 남다
- □ charred 타버린, 탄 색의

정답 ③

26 주어진 글 다음에 이어질 글의 순서로 가장 적절한 것은?

2020. 소방직 9급

Trivial things such as air conditioners or coolers with fresh water, flexible schedules and good relationships with colleagues, as well as many other factors, impact employees' productivity and quality of work.

(A) At the same time, there are many bosses who not only manage to maintain their staff's productivity at high levels, but also treat them nicely and are pleasant to work with.

(B) In this regard, one of the most important factors is the manager, or the boss, who directs the working process.

(C) It is not a secret that bosses are often a category of people difficult to deal with: many of them are unfairly demanding, prone to shifting their responsibilities to other workers, and so on.

① (A) − (B) − (C) ② (B) − (A) − (C)
③ (B) − (C) − (A) ④ (C) − (B) − (A)

해설

상사가 직원의 생산성과 일의 질에 어떤 영향을 미치는지에 대해 설명하고 있는 글로, '상사가 대하기 어려운 사람의 부류라는 것은 비밀이 아니다'가 글의 주제이다. 주어진 글에 대한 언급을 하는 (B)로 시작해야 하며, 이러한 상사의 부정적인 언급을 하는 (C)로 이어져야 하고, '동시에 즐거운 상사'에 대해 언급을 하는 (A)로 이어져야 한다. 따라서 글의 순서로 가장 적절한 것은 ③이다.

해석

많은 다른 요소들뿐만 아니라 에어컨과 신선한 물이 있는 냉장고, 유연한 일정과 동료들과의 좋은 관계와 같은 사소한 것들은 직원들의 생산성과 일(노동)의 질에 영향을 미친다.

(B) 이와 관련하여 가장 중요한 요소 중의 하나는 일의 처리 과정을 지시하는 관리자 또는 상사이다.

(C) 상사가 대하기 어려운 사람의 부류라는 것은 비밀이 아니다. 그들의 다수는 부당하게 많은 것을 요구하고, 그들의 책임을 다른 직원들에게 돌리는 등의 경향이 있다.

(A) 동시에 그들의 직원의 생산성을 높이도록 관리할 뿐만 아니라 직원들을 친절하게 대하고 함께 일하는 것이 즐거운 상사들도 많이 있다.

어휘

□ flexible 유명한, 융통성 있는
□ impact 영향을 미치다
□ maintain 유지하다
□ treat 대하다, 처우하다
□ pleasant 즐거운, 기분좋은
□ direct 지시하다, 관리하다
□ demanding 요구가 많은, 힘든
□ prone to ~하는 경향이 있는, ~하기 쉬운
□ shift 옮기다, 전환하다

정답 ③

27 주어진 문장 다음에 이어질 글의 순서로 가장 적절한 것은?

2019. 국가직 9급

South Korea boasts of being the most wired nation on earth.

(A) This addiction has become a national issue in Korea in recent years, as users started dropping dead from exhaustion after playing online games for days on end. A growing number of students have skipped school to stay online, shockingly self-destructive behavior in this intensely competitive society.
(B) In fact, perhaps no other country has so fully embraced the Internet.
(C) But such ready access to the Web has come at a price as legions of obsessed users find that they cannot tear themselves away from their computer screens.

① (A) − (B) − (C)
② (A) − (C) − (B)
③ (B) − (A) − (C)
④ (B) − (C) − (A)

해설

한국의 인터넷 문제와 중독 현상에 대한 글로, 한국의 뛰어난 인터넷 접속 환경은 중독과 학교 결석과 같은 부정적 영향을 가져오며, 이에 대한 문제가 국가적으로 논의되고 있는 상황을 다루고 있다. 주어진 글에 대한 재진술로 어떤 다른 국가도 인터넷을 포용하지 못한다는 (B)가 와야하고, 그러한 포용에는 상당한 대가를 치른다는 역접의 내용으로 (C)가 오고, 상당한 대가를 (A)의 이러한 중독 이라고 받는 것이 자연스럽다. 따라서 글의 순서로 가장 적절한 것은 ④이다.

해석

한국은 지구상에서 가장 인터넷 연결이 잘 되어 있는 나라라고 자랑한다.
(B) 사실, 아마도 어떤 다른 나라도 그렇게 완전히 인터넷을 수용하고 있지 않다.
(C) 그러나 웹에 대한 그런 재빠른 접근은 다수의 집착하는 사용자들이 그들의 컴퓨터 화면으로부터 그들이 자기 자신을 떼어 놓을 수 없다는 것을 알게 되면서 대가가 따랐다.
(A) 이 중독은 최근 몇 년 동안 한국에서 국가적 문제가 되고 있는데, 사용자들이 여러 날 동안 계속해서 온라인 게임을 한 후 피로로 급사하기 시작했기 때문이다. 점점 더 많은 학생들이 온라인에 접속해 있기 위해 학교를 빼먹고 있고, 이것은 몹시 경쟁적인 사회에서 충격적일 정도로 자멸적인 행동이다.

어휘

□ boast 자랑하다
□ wired nation 인터넷에 연결된 국가
□ addiction 중독
□ national 국가의, 전국적인
□ exhaustion 피로, 고갈
□ days on end 연속으로 며칠 동안
□ intensely 극심한, 강렬한
□ competitive 경쟁을 하는, 경쟁력 있는
□ embrace 받아들이다
□ obsessed 빠져있는, 집착하는

정답 ④

28 주어진 글 다음에 이어질 글의 순서로 가장 적절한 것은?

2019. 지방직 9급

There is a thought that can haunt us: since everything probably affects everything else, how can we ever make sense of the social world? If we are weighed down by that worry, though, we won't ever make progress.

(A) Every discipline that I am familiar with draws caricatures of the world in order to make sense of it. The modern economist does this by building models, which are deliberately stripped down representations of the phenomena out there.

(B) The economist John Maynard Keynes described our subject thus: "Economics is a science of thinking in terms of models joined to the art of choosing models which are relevant to the contemporary world."

(C) When I say "stripped down," I really mean stripped down. It isn't uncommon among us economists to focus on one or two causal factors, exclude everything else, hoping that this will enable us to understand how just those aspects of reality work and interact.

① (A) − (B) − (C)　　② (A) − (C) − (B)
③ (B) − (C) − (A)　　④ (B) − (A) − (C)

해설

사회 세계의 복잡성과 이해에 대한 글로, 글은 사회 현상의 복잡성과 이해에 대한 고민과 경제학자들의 접근 방식을 다루고 있다. 주어진 문장의 make sense of the social world를 받아 (A)에서 make sense of it을 위한 방법에 대한 내용을 다루고 있다. 이어 stripped down 이라는 말을 처음으로 언급한 후, When I say "stripped down," 이라는 말로 풀어 설명하는 것으로 (C)가 뒤따름을 알 수 있다. (B)에서 경제학자의 말을 인용해 이런 현상에 대한 설명을 마무리 짓는 것을 thus를 통해 알 수 있다. 따라서 글의 순서로 가장 적절한 것은 ②이다.

해석

우리를 괴롭힐 수 있는 생각이 하나 있다: 아마 모든 것이 다른 모든 것에 영향을 미치므로, 어떻게 우리가 사회 세계를 이해할 수 있을까? 하지만 우리가 그 걱정에 짓눌린다면, 우리는 결코 나아갈 수 없을 것이다.

(A) 내가 익숙한 모든 규율은 그것을 이해하기 위해 세상에 대한 캐리커처를 그린다. 현대 경제학자는 의도적으로 저 밖에서 일어난 현상들의 묘사를 벗겨내려고 하는 '모형'을 만듦으로써 이런 일을 한다.

(C) 내가 "벗겨졌다"라고 하면 정말로 벗겨졌다는 걸 의미한다. 이것이 현실의 그런 측면들이 어떻게 작용하고 상호 작용하는지 이해할 수 있게 해주기를 바라면서 우리 사이에서 경제학자들이 한두 가지 인과적 요인들에 초점을 맞추고 다른 모든 것은 배제하는 것이 흔한 일은 아니다.

(B) 경제학자인 John Maynard Keynes는 우리 주제를 이렇게 묘사했다: "경제학은 현 시대와 관련된 모형을 고르는 예술에 결합된 모형들의 관점에서 생각하는 과학이다."

어휘

- □ haunt 출몰하다, 나타나다
- □ make sense of 이해하다, 의미를 파악하다
- □ weigh down 무겁게 누르다, 짓누르다
- □ discipline 규율, 훈육, 지식 분야
- □ stripped down 불필요한 것을 모두 뺀, 가장 기본적인 것만 남긴
- □ representation 표현, 묘사
- □ phenomena 현상, 사건
- □ relevant 관련된, 적절한
- □ contemporary 동시대의, 현대의
- □ causal 인과의
- □ exclude 제외하다
- □ aspect 측면, 관점

정답 ②

29 주어진 문장 다음에 이어질 글의 순서로 가장 적절한 것은?

2018. 국가직 9급

A technique that enables an individual to gain some voluntary control over autonomic, or involuntary, body functions by observing electronic measurements of those functions is known as biofeedback.

(A) When such a variable moves in the desired direction (for example, blood pressure down), it triggers visual or audible displays feedback on equipment such as television sets, gauges, or lights.
(B) Electronic sensors are attached to various parts of the body to measure such variables as heart rate, blood pressure, and skin temperature.
(C) Biofeedback training teaches one to produce a desired response by reproducing thought patterns or actions that triggered the displays.

① (A) − (B) − (C) ② (B) − (C) − (A)
③ (B) − (A) − (C) ④ (C) − (A) − (B)

해설

'생체 자기 제어' 기술과 자발적인 통제력를 주제로 하는 글로, '생체 자기 제어' 기술에 대한 설명으로, 전자센서를 이용해 몸의 심박 수, 혈압, 피부 온도 등의 변수를 측정하고 시각·청각적인 디스플레이로 해당 변수를 피드백하며 개인이 몸의 기능을 통제할 수 있음을 설명하고 있다. (A)의 그러한 변수는 (B)의 심박수, 혈압, 그리고 피부 온도와 같은 변수들에서 나온 것이고, 추가적으로 (C)에 생체 자기 제어에 대한 추가 설명이 이어져야 한다. 따라서 글의 순서로 가장 적절한 것은 ③이다.

해석

개인이 자동적, 또는 무의식적인 몸의 기능에 대한 일부 자발적인 통제력을, 그러한 기능들을 전자적으로 측정한 것들을 관찰함으로써 일부 자발적인 통제력을 얻을 수 있도록 하는 기술은 생체 자기 제어로 알려져 있다.
(B) 전자센서가 심박 수, 혈압, 피부 온도 등의 변수를 측정하기 위해 몸의 다양한 부분에 부착된다.
(A) 그러한 변수들이 바라는 방향으로 움직일 때 (예를 들면, 혈압이 내려간다), 이것은 시각적이고 청각적인 디스플레이 피드백을 텔레비전세트나, 장치들 혹은 빛과 같은 기기들에 나타나게 한다.
(C) 생체 자기 제어 훈련은 사람이 그 디스플레이를 촉발시켰던 생각 패턴 또는 행동들을 재생하여 원하는 반응을 얻어낼 수 있도록 가르친다.

어휘

- □ gain 얻다, 획득하다
- □ biofeedback 생체 자기 제어
- □ sensor 센서, 감지기
- □ blood pressure 혈압
- □ trigger 촉발시키다, 일으키다, 방아쇠
- □ equipment 장비, 기기
- □ attach 붙이다, 첨부하다
- □ variable 변수, 변동이 심한
- □ reproduce 재생하다, 복사[복제]하다

정답 ③

30 주어진 문장 다음에 이어질 글의 순서로 가장 적절한 것은?

2018. 지방직 9급

Devices that monitor and track your health are becoming more popular among all age populations.

(A) For example, falls are a leading cause of death for adults 65 and older. Fall alerts are a popular gerotechnology that has been around for many years but have now improved.
(B) However, for seniors aging in place, especially those without a caretaker in the home, these technologies can be lifesaving.
(C) This simple technology can automatically alert 911 of a close family member the moment a senior has fallen.

*gerotechnology 노인을 위한 양로 기술

① (B) − (C) − (A) ② (B) − (A) − (C)
③ (C) − (A) − (B) ④ (C) − (B) − (A)

해설

건강 추적 기술의 중요성과 노인들을 위한 생명 보호를 주제로 하는 글로, 건강 추적 기술의 인기 상승과 노인들을 위한 생명 보호를 위한 기술의 중요성을 설명하고 있다. 노인들과 특별한 환경에서 살아가는 사람들을 위한 기술의 중요성에 대해 소개하는 (B)부터 시작해야 하고, (A)의 'a popular gerotechnology'에서 (C)의 'this technology'로 이어진다. 따라서 글의 순서로 가장 적절한 것은 ②이다.

해석

당신의 건강을 감시하고 추적하는 장비들이 모든 연령층에서 인기를 얻어가고 있다.
(B) 그러나, 노인들, 특히 집에 돌보는 사람들이 없는 사람들에게는, 이러한 기술들은 생명을 살릴 수 있다.
(A) 예를 들어, 낙상은 65세 이상의 성인들의 주요한 죽음의 원인이다. 낙상 경보는 대중적인 노인을 위한 양로 기술로 수년간 우리 주변에 있었지만, 최근에 개선되었다.
(C) 이러한 단순한 기술들은 노인이 쓰러지는 그 순간 자동적으로 가까운 가족 구성원의 911에 경보를 울린다.

어휘

□ device 기기, 장치
□ monitor 모니터하다, 감시하다
□ track 추적하다
□ fall 낙상, 떨어짐, 넘어지다, 떨어지다
□ leading 주요한, 선도적인
□ cause 원인
□ improve 개선하다
□ senior 노인
□ caretaker 간병인
□ lifesaving 생명을 구하는

정답 ②

31 주어진 글 다음에 이어질 글의 순서로 가장 적절한 것은?

2017. 국가직 9급

The most innovative of the group therapy approaches was psychodrama, the brainchild of Jacob L. Moreno. Psychodrama as a form of group therapy started with premises that were quite alien to the Freudian worldview that mental illness essentially occurs within the psyche or mind.

(A) But he also believed that creativity is rarely a solitary process but something brought out by social interactions. He relied heavily on theatrical techniques, including role-playing and improvisation, as a means to promote creativity and general social trust.
(B) Despite his theoretical difference from the mainstream viewpoint, Moreno's influence in shaping psychological consciousness in the twentieth century was considerable. He believed that the nature of human beings is to be creative and that living a creative life is the key to human health and well-being.
(C) His most important theatrical tool was what he called role reversal — asking participants to take on another's persona. The act of pretending "as if" one were in another's skin was designed to help bring out the empathic impulse and to develop it to higher levels of expression.

① (A) − (C) − (B)　　② (B) − (A) − (C)
③ (B) − (C) − (A)　　④ (C) − (B) − (A)

해설

주어진 글에서는 집단요법의 혁신적 접근법인 Jacob L. Moreno의 심리드라마에 대한 내용이 소개되고 있고, 그 다음에는 'Moreno의 이론적인 관점과 영향력'에 설명하는 (B)로 이어져야 하며, 그가 사회적 상호작용을 통해 창의성을 발현하도록 돕기 위해 연극적 기법을 사용했음을 언급하는 (A)로 이어져야 하고, 마지막으로 그가 가장 중요하게 여겼던 연극적 도구 중 하나인 '역할 바꾸기'에 진술인 (C)로 이어져야 한다. 따라서 글의 순서로 가장 적절한 것은 ②이다.

해석

가장 혁신적인 집단 치료 접근법은 Jacob L. Moreno의 독창적인 생각인 사이코드라마 집단 치료의 한 형태로써 사이코드라마는 정신병은 본질적으로 정신 또는 마음 안에서 발생한다는 프로이드의 세계관과는 상당히 다른 전제 조건으로 시작되었다.

(B) 주류 관점과는 다른 그의 이론적 차이에도 불구하고, 20세기에 정신적 의식을 형성하는 데 있어 Moreno의 영향력은 상당했다. 그는 인간의 본질은 창조하는 것이고, 창조적인 생활이 인간의 건강과 행복의 핵심이라고 믿었다.

(A) 그러나 그는 창조성이 거의 유일한 과정이 아니라 사회적인 상호관계에 의해 발생된 무엇이라고 또한 믿었다. 그는 창조성과 일반적인 사회적 신뢰를 증대하는 수단으로서 역할극과 즉흥극을 포함한 연극적 기법에 상당히 의존했다.

(C) 그의 가장 중요한 연극적 도구는 그가 역할 바꾸기라고 부르는 즉, 참가자들에게 다른 사람의 모습을 하도록 요구하는 것이었다. 마치 한 사람이 다른 사람의 가죽을 쓴 것인 양 하는 행동은 동정적 충동을 이끌어내는 데 도움을 주고 그것을 더 높은 수준의 표현으로 발전시키기 위해 고안되었다.

어휘

- □ innovative 혁신적인
- □ group therapy 집단 치료
- □ psychodrama 사이코드라마, 심리극
- □ brainchild 독창적인 생각, 창작품
- □ premise 전제
- □ alien 다른, 이질적인, 외국의
- □ psyche 정신, 마음
- □ solitary 유일한, 고독한
- □ bring out ~을 꺼내다, 이끌다
- □ improvisation 즉흥(극)
- □ means 수단, 수입
- □ consciousness 의식
- □ considerable 상당한
- □ reversal 전환
- □ persona 모습
- □ pretend ~인 체하다, 가장하다
- □ empathic 감정이입의
- □ impulse 자극, 욕망

정답 ②

32 주어진 글 다음에 이어질 글의 순서로 가장 적절한 것은?

2017. 국가직 9급 하반기

Through the ages, industrious individuals have continuously created conveniences to make life easier. From the invention of the wheel to the lightbulb, inventions have propelled society forward.

(A) In addition, interactive media can be used to question a lecturer or exchange opinions with other students via e-mail. Such computerized lectures give students access to knowledge that was previously unavailable.

(B) One recent modern invention is the computer, which has improved many aspects of people's lives. This is especially true in the field of education. One important effect of computer technology on higher education is the availability of lectures.

(C) As a result of the development of computer networks, students can obtain lectures from many universities in real time. They are now able to sit down in front of a digital screen and listen to a lecture being given at another university.

① (A) − (B) − (C) ② (B) − (C) − (A)
③ (C) − (A) − (B) ④ (C) − (B) − (A)

해설

컴퓨터 기술과 교육의 현대적인 발전에 대한 글이다. 제시문에서 언급하고 있는 '현대까지 이르는 발명품' 다음에 '컴퓨터'를 언급하는 (B)로 이어져야 하며, 컴퓨터 네트워크에 대한 진술의 (C)로 이어져야 하며, 그 다음에는 강의 접근성에 대한 진술의 (A)로 이어져야 한다. 따라서 글의 순서로 가장 적절한 것은 ②이다.

해석

세대를 통해, 근면한 개인들은 삶을 더 쉽게 만들기 위해 계속적으로 편리한 것들을 만들어 왔다. 바퀴의 발명부터 전구에 이르기까지 발명품들은 사회를 더욱 앞으로 나아가게 했다.

(B) 하나의 최근의 현대식 발명품은 컴퓨터다, 그리고 그것은 사람들의 삶의 많은 측면을 향상 시켜왔다. 이것은 교육의 분야에서 더욱이 사실이다. 고등교육에서 컴퓨터 기술의 하나의 중요한 영향은 강의의 이용성이다.

(C) 컴퓨터 네트워크의 발전의 결과로써, 학생들은 많은 대학들에서 실시간으로 강의를 받을 수 있다. 그들은 이제 디지털화면 앞에 앉아, 또 다른 대학에서 강의되어지는 강의를 듣는 것이 가능하다.
(A) 게다가, 상호적인 매체들은 강의에 대해 질문하거나, 또는 e-mail을 통해 다른 학생들과 의견을 교환하기 위해 사용되어질 수 있다. 그러한 컴퓨터화 된 강의들은 학생들에게 전에는 사용할 수 없었던 지식에 대한 접근성을 주었다.

어휘

- ☐ interactive 상호작용하는
- ☐ access 접근, 입장, 접근하다, 이용하다
- ☐ previously 이전에
- ☐ unavailable 이용 불가능한
- ☐ availability 이용 가능성
- ☐ lecture 강의, 강연, 강의하다
- ☐ via 경유하여, 거쳐, 통하여
- ☐ obtain 얻다, 구하다
- ☐ real time 실시간

정답 ②

33 주어진 글 다음에 이어질 글의 순서로 가장 적절한 것은?

2017. 지방직 9급

I remember the day Lewis discovered the falls. They left their camp at sunrise and a few hours later they came upon a beautiful plain and on the plain were more buffalo than they had ever seen before in one place.

(A) A nice thing happened that afternoon, they went fishing below the falls and caught half a dozen trout, good ones, too, from sixteen to twenty-three inches long.
(B) After a while the sound was tremendous and they were at the great falls of the Missouri River. It was about noon when they got there.
(C) They kept on going until they heard the faraway sound of a waterfall and saw a distant column of spray rising and disappearing. They followed the sound as it got louder and louder.

① (A) − (B) − (C)　② (B) − (C) − (A)
③ (C) − (A) − (B)　④ (C) − (B) − (A)

해설

미지의 폭포를 발견하는 경험에 대한 글로, 필자가 Lewis와 함께한 여정에서 폭포 발견과 송어 낚시의 특별한 순간을 회상하는 글이다. 과거의 하나의 일화를 바탕으로 한 글이다. 따라서 사건의 시간의 흐름을 찾아야 한다. 제시문의 시점은 '새벽'이고, 폭포 소리와 관련된 표현은 멀리서 들리는 소리 (C)와 그 소리 (B)이다. 그리고 마지막에 오후에 있었던 진술인 (A)로 이어져야 한다. 따라서 글의 순서로 가장 적절한 것은 ④이다.

해석

나는 Lewis가 그 폭포들을 발견했던 그 날을 기억한다. 그들은 그들의 야영지를 해가 뜰 때 떠났고 몇 시간 후에 그들은 아름다운 평야를 만났으며, 그 평야에 그들이 전에 한 장소에서 본 것보다 더 많은 들소들이 있었다.
(C) 그들은 멀리서 들리는 폭포의 소리를 들을 때까지 계속해 갔고 멀리서 솟아났다가 사라지는 물보라의 기둥을 발견했다. 그들은 그 소리가 점점 더 커질 때까지 그 소리를 따라갔다.
(B) 잠시 후에 그 소리는 엄청났다. 그리고 그들은 Missouri강의 거대한 폭포들에 있었다. 그들이 거기에 도착한 것은 정오 즈음이였다.
(A) 그날 오후에 한 기분 좋은 일이 일어났다. 그들은 폭포 아래로 낚시하러 갔다가 송어 여섯 마리를 잡았는데, 좋은 송어들이였고, 16인치에서 23인치 길이였다.

어휘

- ☐ plain 평야
- ☐ tremendous 엄청난, 대단한
- ☐ fall 폭포
- ☐ distant 먼
- ☐ column 기둥
- ☐ camp 야영지, 캠프장
- ☐ faraway 멀리 떨어진
- ☐ trout 송어

정답 ④

34 주어진 글 다음에 이어질 글의 순서로 가장 적절한 것은?

2016. 국가직 9급

All animals have the same kind of brain activation during sleep as humans. Whether or not they dream is another question, which can be answered only by posing another one: Do animals have consciousness?

(A) These are three of the key aspects of consciousness, and they could be experienced whether or not an animal had verbal language as we do. When the animal's brain is activated during sleep, why not assume that the animal has some sort of perceptual, emotional, and memory experience?

(B) Many scientists today feel that animals probably do have a limited form of consciousness, quite different from ours in that it lacks language and the capacity for propositional or symbolic thought.

(C) Animals certainly can't report dreams even if they do have them. But which pet owner would doubt that his or her favourite animal friend has perception, memory, and emotion

① (A) − (B) − (C)　　② (A) − (C) − (B)
③ (B) − (C) − (A)　　④ (C) − (B) − (A)

해설

주어진 제시문에 마지막 문장에서 질문을 던지고 있다. 이 경우 이에 대한 대답이 와야 할 것이다. (B)는 이에 대한 대답으로 제일 먼저 와야 한다. (A)와 (C)의 경우, (C)의 마지막에서 언급한 perception, memory, and emotion이 (A)의 three of the key aspects와 연결되므로 (C)가 오고 (A)로 이어져야 한다. 따라서 주어진 글의 순서로 가장 적절한 것은 ③이다.

해석

모든 동물들은 수면시간 동안 인간과 동일한 두뇌 활동을 보여준다. 그들이 꿈을 꾸느냐, 마느냐는, 다음의 질문을 제기함에 의해서만이 대답할 수 있는 또 다른 문제이다: 동물들은 지각능력이 있는가?

(B) 오늘날 많은 과학자들은 동물들은 아마도 제한된 형태의 지각능력을, 즉 언어, 그리고 명제적이거나 상징적인 사고에 대한 능력이 부재한다는 점에서 우리 인간의 것과는 다른 지각능력을 가지고 있다고 생각한다.

(C) 동물들은 분명 비록 그들이 꿈을 꾸더라도 꿈에 대해 이야기해 줄 수 없다. 그러나 대체 어떤 애완동물 주인이 그, 혹은 그녀가 사랑하는 동물 친구가 지각력과 기억, 그리고 감정을 갖고 있다는 것을 의심하겠는가?

(A) 이것이 바로 지각능력의 세 가지 중요한 요소이다. 그리고 동물들이 우리와 같은 음성언어를 가지고 있는지 없는지와 상관없이 이러한 것들은 경험되어질 수 있는 것이다. 동물의 두뇌가 수면시간 동안 활동한다면, 동물들이 어떤 인식적이고 감정적인, 그리고 기억과 관련된 종류의 활동을 한다고 가정하지 않을 이유가 무엇이겠는가?

어휘

- □ activation 활동, 활성화
- □ pose (질문을) 제기하다
- □ aspect 요소, 면
- □ consciousness 의식
- □ perceptual 인식의
- □ lack 부족하다
- □ capacity 공간, 능력
- □ propositional 명제적인
- □ even if ~일지라도
- □ perception 지각, 자각, 인식, 의식

정답 ③

05 순서 배열 유형 기출 독해 어휘 복습 TEST 정답

정답

1	surface	표면, 지면	21	rational	합리적인, 이성적인
2	beside	옆에, ~에 비해	22	practical	실용적인, 현실적인
3	stir	섞다, 젓다, 흔들리다, 동요, 충격, 젓기	23	indulge	충족시키다, 채우다
4	witness	목격하다, 목격자, 증인	24	exert	행사하다, 가하다, 분투하다
5	tear off	찢어내다, 떼어내다, ~을 벗기다	25	evolve	진화하다, 발달하다
6	hearty	푸짐한, 원기 왕성한, 애정어린, 친절한	26	inheritance	유전, 상속
7	promote	촉진하다, 홍보하다	27	offspring	자손, 자식
8	expand	확장하다, 넓히다	28	mistaken	잘못된, 틀린
9	authentic	진정한, 진짜의	29	surroundings	주변 환경
10	renew	갱신하다, 재개하다	30	proprietary	전용의, 사유의, 독점의
11	dimension	차원, 관점, 규모, 크기	31	breakdown	분해, 고장, 붕괴
12	administration	행정, 관리, 집행	32	adopt	채택하다, 입양하다
13	exemplify	전형적인 예가 되다, 예를 들다	33	harbor	숨기다, 숨겨 주다
14	territory	영토, 지역, 영역	34	reconcile	조화시키다, 받아들이다
15	prediction	예측, 예견	35	institution	기관, 단체, 협회
16	summon	불러내다, 소환하다	36	diplomat	외교관
17	depression	우울증, 불경기	37	property	특성, 속성
18	scrutiny	정밀 조사, 철저한 검토	38	immediate	즉각적인
19	mitigate	완화시키다, 경감시키다	39	weird	이상한, 기이한, 기괴한
20	mammal	포유류	40	definitive	확실한, 최종적인

05 순서 배열 유형 기출 독해 어휘 복습 TEST 정답

정답

41	fall short	부족해지다	61	executive	경영진, 임원
42	rudimentary	기본적인, 기초적인	62	assembly	조립, 집회, 의회
43	intensive	집중적인	63	outcome	결과
44	utility	유용, 공익 시설	64	surrender	항복하다, 포기하다
45	medium	중간의	65	participate	참가하다
46	abundance	풍부, 충만, 다수, 대량	66	cease	그치다, 중단되다
47	humble	겸손한, 낮은	67	evaporate	증발하다, 사라지다
48	sturdy	튼튼한, 강인한	68	flexible	유연한, 융통성 있는
49	deplete	고갈시키다, 대폭 감소시키다	69	demanding	요구가 많은, 힘든
50	accommodate	수용하다, 공간을 제공하다	70	prone to	~하는 경향이 있는, ~하기 쉬운
51	prestigious	훌륭한, 명성 있는	71	exhaustion	피로, 고갈
52	tribal	부족의, 종족의	72	days on end	연속으로 며칠 동안
53	sparsely	드문드문, 성기게	73	obsessed	빠져있는, 집착하는
54	cardiovascular	심혈관의	74	make sense of	이해하다, 의미를 파악하다
55	confusion	혼란, 혼동, 당혹	75	representation	표현, 묘사
56	refer to	언급하다, 참고하다	76	attach	붙이다, 첨부하다
57	province	주, 지방, 분야	77	variable	변수, 변동이 심한
58	exterior	외부, 겉	78	solitary	유일한, 고독한
59	represent	제시하다, 보여주다, 나타내다, 대표하다	79	pretend	~인 체하다, 가장하다
60	promotional	홍보의	80	tremendous	엄청난, 대단한

chapter 06 빈칸 추론 유형 정답 및 해설

ANSWER

01 ④	02 ③	03 ①	04 ③	05 ②
06 ①	07 ①	08 ①	09 ②	10 ①
11 ①	12 ③	13 ①	14 ③	15 ④
16 ②	17 ②	18 ④	19 ③	20 ①
21 ②	22 ④	23 ①	24 ①	25 ①
26 ②	27 ③	28 ①	29 ②	30 ③
31 ③	32 ①	33 ②	34 ④	35 ②
36 ②	37 ①	38 ②	39 ①	40 ④
41 ②	42 ①	43 ②	44 ④	45 ①
46 ③	47 ②	48 ③		

01 밑줄 친 부분에 들어갈 말로 가장 적절한 것은?

2025. 출제 기조 전환 2차

Technological progress can destroy jobs in a single industry such as textiles. However, historical evidence shows that technological progress does not produce unemployment in a country as a whole. Technological progress increases productivity and incomes in the overall economy, and higher incomes lead to higher demand for goods and thus ______________________. As a result, workers who lose jobs in one industry will be able to find jobs in others, although for many of them this might take time and some of them, like the Luddites, will end up with lower wages in their new jobs.

① increased job losses
② delayed promotion at work
③ greater work satisfaction
④ higher demand for labor

해설

'기술 발전과 고용과의 관계'에 대한 글로, 기술 발전은 특정 산업의 일자리를 파괴할 수 있지만, 역사적 증거는 오히려 경제의 생산성과 소득을 증가시켜 노동 수요를 높일 수 있음을 강조하는 글이다. 따라서 상품에 대한 수요 증가로 인해 노동에 대한 수요도 증가하게 되어, 이로 인해 실직한 노동자들이 다른 산업에서 일자리를 찾을 수 있는 가능성이 높아진다. 따라서 밑줄 친 부분에 들어갈 말로 가장 적절한 것은 ④이다.

해석

기술 발달은 섬유와 같은 특정 산업에서 일자리를 파괴할 수 있다. 그러나 역사적 증거는 기술 발전이 국가 전체에서 실업을 초래하지 않는다는 것을 보여준다. 기술 발전은 전체 경제의 생산성과 소득을 증가시키며, 높은 소득은 상품에 대한 수요를 증가시키고, 따라서 노동력에 대한 높은 수요도 증가한다. 결과적으로 한 산업에서 일자리를 잃은 근로자들은 다른 산업에서 일자리를 찾을 수 있을 거지만, 그들 중 많은 사람들은 이것이 시간이 걸릴 수 있고, 러다이트(the Luddites)와 같은 그들 중 일부는 그들의 새로운 일자리에서 결국 더 낮은 임금을 받게 될 것이다.

① 증가하는 실직
② 직장에서의 승진 지연
③ 직장의 만족도 향상
④ 노동력에 대한 높은 수요

어휘

- ☐progress 발달, 진보, 전진, 진행. 나아가다, 진행하다
- ☐textile 섬유 산업, 직물, 옷감
- ☐unemployment 실업(률)
- ☐overall 전체의, 종합[전반]적인
- ☐income 소득, 수입
- ☐be able to ~할 수 있다, ~이 가능하다
- ☐end up 결국 ~하게 되다
- ☐wage 임금, 급료

정답 ④

02 밑줄 친 부분에 들어갈 말로 가장 적절한 것은?

2025. 출제 기조 전환 2차

> There is no substitute for oil, which is one reason ____________________, taking the global economy along with it. While we can generate electricity through coal or natural gas, nuclear or renewables — switching from source to source, according to price — oil remains by far the predominant fuel for transportation. When the global economy heats up, demand for oil rises, boosting the price and encouraging producers to pump more. Inevitably, those high prices eat into economic growth and reduce demand just as suppliers are overproducing. Prices crash, and the cycle starts all over again. That's bad for producers, who can be left holding the bag when prices plummet, and it hurts consumers and industries uncertain about future energy prices. Low oil prices in the 1990s lulled U.S. auto companies into disastrous complacency; they had few efficient models available when oil turned expensive.

① the automobile industry thrives
② it creates disruptions between borders
③ it is prone to big booms and deep busts
④ the research on renewable energy is limited

해설

석유의 경제적 영향과 대체 에너지의 한계에 대한 글로, 석유는 세계 경제에 큰 영향을 미치며, 가격 변동이 경제 성장과 생산자에 미치는 부정적인 영향이 큼을 세 번째 문장을 중심으로 설명하고 있다. 따라서 밑줄 친 부분에 들어갈 말로 가장 적절한 것은 ③이다.

해석

> 석유를 대체할 수 있는 것은 없으며, <u>이것은 큰 호황과 깊은 불황에 빠지기 쉬운</u> 이유 중 하나로, 그로 인해 세계 경제도 영향을 받는다. 우리는 석탄이나 천연가스, 원자력 또는 신재생 에너지를 통해 전기를 생성할 수 있지만, 가격에 따라 에너지원에서 에너지원으로 전환하더라도 석유는 여전히 운송을 위한 가장 주요한 연료이다. 세계 경제가 활기를 띨 때, 석유에 대한 수요가 증가하고, 가격이 상승하며 생산자들이 더 많은 석유를 퍼내도록 자극한다. 필연적으로 이러한 높은 가격은 경제 성장을 저해하고 공급자들이 과잉 생산을 하고 있을 때 수요를 줄인다. 가격이 급락하면 사이클이 다시 시작된다. 이는 가격이 급락할 때 빈손이 될 수 있는 생산자들에게 나쁘며, 미래의 에너지 가격이 불확실한 소비자와 산업에도 피해를 준다. 1990년대의 낮은 석유 가격은 미국 자동차 회사들을 안심시켜 처참한 안일함에 빠지게 했다. 석유가 비싸졌을 때 사용할 수 있는 효율적인 모델이 거의 없었기 때문이다.

① 자동차 산업이 번창하는
② 이것은 국경 간의 혼란을 초래하는
③ 이것은 큰 호황과 깊은 불황에 빠지기 쉬운
④ 재생 에너지에 대한 연구가 제한적인

어휘

- □ substitute 대체하다, 대신하다, 대체물, 대리자
- □ generate 생성하다, 만들어 내다, 발생시키다
- □ coal 석탄
- □ renewables 재생 가능 에너지, 신재생 에너지
- □ bust 불황, 실패, 파산
- □ predominant 주요한, 우세한, 지배적인, 두드러진, 뚜렷한
- □ inevitably 필연적으로, 불가피하게
- □ supplier 공급자, 공급 회사
- □ overproduce 과잉 생산하다
- □ plummet 급락하다, 곤두박질치다
- □ lull into ~를 안심시켜 ~하게 만들다
- □ disastrous 처참한, 재앙의, 불길한
- □ complacency 안주, 안일

정답 ③

03 밑줄 친 부분에 들어갈 말로 가장 적절한 것은?

2025. 출제 기조 전환 1차

> Falling fertility rates are projected to result in shrinking populations for nearly every country by the end of the century. The global fertility rate was 4.7 in 1950, but it dropped by nearly half to 2.4 in 2017. It is expected to fall below 1.7 by 2100. As a result, some researchers predict that the number of people on the planet would peak at 9.7 billion around 2064 before falling down to 8.8 billion by the century's end. This transition will also lead to a significant aging of populations, with as many people reaching 80 years old as there are being born. Such a demographic shift ________________, including taxation, healthcare for the elderly, caregiving responsibilities, and retirement. To ensure a "soft landing" into a new demographic landscape, researchers emphasize the need for careful management of the transition.

① raises concerns about future challenges
② mitigates the inverted age structure phenomenon
③ compensates for the reduced marriage rate issue
④ provides immediate solutions to resolve the problems

해설

21세기 말까지 거의 모든 국가에서 낮아지는 출산율은 인구 감소로 이어지며, 이 변화로 인해 고령화가 급증하며 미래의 과제로 세금, 노인 건강관리, 양육 책임, 퇴직 등이 우려되고 있음을 설명하고 있다. 빈칸의 내용은 '세금, 노인 건강관리, 돌봄 책임 및 은퇴를 포함한 문제'들을 포괄하는 '인구 감소로 말미암은 문제점'에 대해 나와야 한다. 따라서 밑줄 친 부분에 들어갈 말로 적절한 것은 ①이다.

해석

떨어지는 출산율이 세기말까지 거의 모든 국가의 인구 감소를 야기할 것으로 예상된다. 세계 출산율은 1950년에 4.7명이었지만 2017년에는 거의 절반인 2.4명으로 감소했다. 2100년에는 1.7명 아래로 떨어질 것으로 예상된다. 결과적으로, 일부 연구원들은 지구상의 사람들의 수가 세기말에는 88억 명으로 떨어지기 전에 2064년에 97억 명으로 절정에 달할 것으로 예측한다. 이 전환은 태어나는 수만큼 많은 사람들이 80세에 도달하며 또한 인구의 상당한 고령화로 이어질 것이다. 이러한 인구학적 변화는 세금, 노인 건강관리, 돌봄 책임 및 은퇴를 포함한 미래의 문제에 대한 우려를 제기한다. 새로운 인구의 지형으로의 "부드러운 착륙"을 보장하기 위해 연구원들은 전환의 신중한 관리의 필요성을 강조한다.

① 미래의 문제에 대한 우려를 제기한다
② 뒤집힌 연령 구조 현상을 완화한다
③ 감소한 결혼율 문제를 보상한다
④ 문제 해결을 위한 즉각적인 해결책을 제공한다

어휘

□ fertility rate 출산율, 출생률
□ project 예상하다, 추정하다, 계획하다, 계획, 과제
□ shrink 줄어들다, 오그라들다
□ population 인구, 주민
□ nearly 거의, 대략
□ lead to ~로 이어지다
□ aging 고령화, 노령화, 노화
□ demographic 인구 통계학적인, 인구학의, 인구의
□ taxation 조세
□ elderly 노인, 어르신들, 나이가 지긋한
□ caregiving 돌봄, 부양
□ management 관리, 경영, 운영
□ mitigate 완화하다, 진정시키다

정답 ①

04 밑줄 친 부분에 들어갈 말로 가장 적절한 것은?

2025. 출제 기조 전환 1차

Many listeners blame a speaker for their inattention by thinking to themselves: "Who could listen to such a character? Will he ever stop reading from his notes?" The good listener reacts differently. He may well look at the speaker and think, "This man is incompetent. Seems like almost anyone would be able to talk better than that." But from this initial similarity he moves on to a different conclusion, thinking "But wait a minute. I'm not interested in his personality or delivery. I want to find out what he knows. Does this man know some things that I need to know?" Essentially, we "listen with our own experience." Is the speaker to be held responsible because we are poorly equipped to comprehend his message? We cannot understand everything we hear, but one sure way to raise the level of our understanding is to ______________.

① ignore what the speaker knows
② analyze the character of a speaker
③ assume the responsibility which is inherently ours
④ focus on the speaker's competency of speech delivery

해설

청취자의 역할과 책임을 강조하는 글로, 이 글은 나쁜 청취자와 좋은 청취자 간의 차이를 강조하며, 좋은 청취자는 발표자의 외모나 말하는 방식이 아닌 정보에 집중하며, 우리가 듣는 것을 이해하기 위한 확실한 방법은 우리에게 내재된 책임을 떠맡는 것이라 설명하고 있다. 추론의 근거로 다섯 번째 문장의 진술을 통해서 '우리의 책임'을 표현하는 선택지를 고르면 된다. 따라서 밑줄 친 부분에 들어갈 말로 적절한 것은 ③이다.

해석

많은 청자들은 "누가 그런 등장인물의 말을 들을 수 있을까? 그가 그의 메모들로부터 읽는 것을 언제 멈출 수 있을까?"라고 혼자 생각함으로써 그들의 부주의에 대해 화자를 비난한다. 좋은 청자는 다르게 반응한다. 그는 화자를 보고 "이 남자는 무능하다. 거의 누구나 그것보다 더 잘 말할 수 있을 것 같다"고 생각할 것이다. 그러나 이러한 초기의 유사성으로부터 그는 다른 결론으로 넘어가면서 생각한다. "하지만 잠시만. 나는 그의 성격이나 전달력에 관심이 없어. 나는 그가 무엇을 알고 있는지 알고 싶어. 이 남자는 내가 알아야 할 것들을 알고 있나?" 근본적으로, 우리는 "우리 자신의 경험으로 듣는다." 우리가 그의 메시지를 이해할 수 있는 능력이 잘못 갖춰져 있기 때문에 화자에게 책임이 있는가? 우리가 듣는 모든 것을 이해

할 수는 없지만, 우리의 이해 수준을 높일 수 있는 한 가지 확실한 방법은 본질적으로 우리의 것인 책임을 지는 것이다.

① 화자가 알고 있는 것을 무시하다
② 화자의 성격을 분석하다
③ 본질적으로 우리의 것인 책임을 지다
④ 화자의 말 전달 능력에 집중한다

어휘

□ blame 비난하다, ~을 탓하다, 비난, 책임
□ inattention 부주의, 태만, 무관심
□ initial 초기의, 처음의
□ personality 성격, 인격, 개성
□ find out ~을 알아내다, 알게 되다
□ speaker 화자, 발표자, 연설가
□ responsible ~에 대해 책임이 있는, ~의 원인이 되는
□ equip 갖추다, 차려입게 하다
□ comprehend 이해하다, 파악하다, 포함하다, 의미하다
□ assume (책임을) 지다, (권력을) 쥐다, (역할을) 맡다, 추정하다
□ inherently 본질적으로, 선천적으로

정답 ③

05 밑줄 친 부분에 들어갈 말로 적절한 것은?

2024. 국가직 9급

____________________________________. Nearly every major politician hires media consultants and political experts to provide advice on how to appeal to the public. Virtually every major business and special-interest group has hired a lobbyist to take its concerns to Congress or to state and local governments. In nearly every community, activists try to persuade their fellow citizens on important policy issues. The workplace, too, has always been fertile ground for office politics and persuasion. One study estimates that general managers spend upwards of 80 % of their time in verbal communication — most of it with the intent of persuading their fellow employees. With the advent of the photocopying machine, a whole new medium for office persuasion was invented — the photocopied memo. The Pentagon alone copies an average of 350,000 pages a day, the equivalent of 1,000 novels.

① Business people should have good persuasion skills
② Persuasion shows up in almost every walk of life
③ You will encounter countless billboards and posters
④ Mass media campaigns are useful for the government

해설

정치인, 기업, 사회 활동가, 직장 등의 모든 분야에서 설득이 중요한 역할을 함을 강조하는 글이다. 첫 번째 문장이 글의 주제문으로 두 번째 문장 이하의 '주요 정치인', '주요 산업과 특별 이익 집단', '거의 모드 지역 단체의 운동가', '직장인들'의 구체적인 사례를 통해서 '설득'을 하려한다는 것을 설명하고 있다. 추가적으로 의사소통의 시간 80 퍼센트가 설득을 목적으로 사용된다는 구체적인 연구결과를 통해서 밑줄 친 부분에 들어갈 말로 가장 적절한 것은 ②이다.

해석

설득은 인생의 거의 모든 분야에서 나타난다. 거의 모든 주요 정치인들은 대중에게 호소할 방법에 대한 조언을 제공할 미디어 컨설턴트와 정치 전문가들을 고용한다. 사실상 모든 주요 기업과 특수 이익 단체들은 그것의 우려들을 의회나 주 정부 또는 지방 정부에 전달하기 위해 로비스트를 고용한다. 거의 모든 지역사회에서 활동가들은 중요한 정책 문제에 대해 동료 시민들을 설득하려고 노력한다. 직장 역시 항상 사무실 정치와 설득을 위한 비옥한 장소였다. 한 연구는 일반 관리자들이 그들의 시간의 80% 이상을 언어적 의사소통에-그 중 대부분은 동료 직원들을 설득하기 위한 목적으로 소비한다고 추정한다. 복사기의 등장으로, 사무실 내 설득을 위한 완전히 새로운 매체인 복사된 메모가 발명되었다. 미 국방부에서만 하루에 평균 35만 페이지를 복사하는데, 이는 소설 1,000권에 상당하는 것이다.

① 사업가들은 좋은 설득 능력들을 가져야 한다
② 설득은 인생의 거의 모든 분야에서 나타난다
③ 당신은 수많은 광고판과 포스터를 접하게 될 것이다
④ 대중 매체 캠페인들은 정부에 유용하다

어휘

□ appeal 매력, 호소
□ virtually 사실상, 거의
□ special-interest group 이해관계 단체
□ lobbyist 로비스트, 목회가
□ persuasion 설득, 강요
□ verbal 말로 된, 언어의
□ equivalent 동등한, 상당한

정답 ②

06 밑줄 친 부분에 들어갈 말로 적절한 것은?

2024. 국가직 9급

It is important to note that for adults, social interaction mainly occurs through the medium of language. Few native-speaker adults are willing to devote time to interacting with someone who does not speak the language, with the result that the adult foreigner will have little opportunity to engage in meaningful and extended language exchanges. In contrast, the young child is often readily accepted by other children, and even adults. For young children, language is not as essential to social interaction. So-called 'parallel play', for example, is common among young children. They can be content just to sit in each other's company speaking only occasionally and playing on their own. Adults rarely find themselves in situations where ________________________________.

① language does not play a crucial role in social interaction
② their opinions are readily accepted by their colleagues
③ they are asked to speak another language
④ communication skills are highly required

해설

성인은 주로 언어를 통해 사회적 상호 작용을 하지만, 어린이는 언어 없이도 쉽게 상호 작용할 수 있음을 강조하는 글이다. 따라서 밑줄 친 부분에 들어갈 말로 가장 적절한 것은 ①이다.

해석

성인에게 사회적 상호 작용은 주로 언어라는 수단을 통해 발생한다는 점에 주목하는 것이 중요하다. 모국어를 사용하는 성인들은 그 언어를 사용하지 않는 누군가와 상호 작용하는 것에 시간을 거의 바치지 않고, 그 결과 성인 외국인은 의미 있고 확장된 언어 교환에 참여할 기회를 거의 갖지 못할 것이다. 그에 반해 어린아이는 종종 다른 아이들, 심지어 성인에게도 쉽게 받아들여진다. 어린아이들에게 언어는 사회적 상호 작용에 있어서는 필수적이지 않다. 예를 들어, 이른바 '병행 놀이'는 어린아이들 사이에서 흔하다. 그들은 단지 서로 함께 있는 사람들과 앉아서 가끔씩만 말을 하고 혼자서 노는 것만으로도 만족할 수 있다. 어른들은 사회적 상호 작용에서 언어가 중요한 역할을 하지 않는 상황에 있는 그들 자신을 거의 발견하지 못한다.

① 사회적 상호 작용에서 언어가 중요한 역할을 하지 않는다
② 그들의 의견은 동료들에게 쉽게 받아들여진다
③ 그들은 다른 언어를 사용하라고 요청받는다
④ 의사소통 능력이 매우 요구된다

어휘

□ medium 매체, 수단
□ devote 헌신하다, 전념하다
□ readily 즉시, 기꺼이
□ parallel play 병렬 놀이 (어린이들이 함께 있으면서 각자의 활동을 하는 것)
□ occasionally 가끔, 때때로

정답 ①

07 밑줄 친 부분에 들어갈 말로 적절한 것은?

2024. 지방직 9급

Javelin Research noticed that not all Millennials are currently in the same stage of life. While all Millennials were born around the turn of the century, some of them are still in early adulthood, wrestling with new careers and settling down. On the other hand, the older Millennials have a home and are building a family. You can imagine how having a child might change your interests and priorities, so for marketing purposes, it's useful to split this generation into Gen Y.1 and Gen Y.2. Not only are the two groups culturally different, but they're in vastly different phases of their financial life. The younger group is financial beginners, just starting to show their buying power. The latter group has a credit history, may have their first mortgage and is raising young children. The __________ in priorities and needs between Gen Y.1 and Gen Y.2 is vast.

① contrast　② reduction
③ repetition　④ ability

해설

밀레니얼 세대들의 문화적 재정적 차이를 주제로 하는 글이다. 특히 여섯 번째 문장의 진술을 통해서 '1세대'와 '2세대'의 문화적, 재정적인 차이가 있음을 나타내고 있으므로, 마지막 문장에서 'Gen Y.I'과 'Gen Y.2'의 우선순위들과 필요성에 있어서의 '차이'를 나타내는 단어가 정답이 된다. 따라서 밑줄 친 부분에 들어갈 말로 적절한 것은 ①이다.

해석

Javelin Research는 모든 밀레니얼 세대가 현재 동일한 생애 단계에 있지 않다는 것을 알아냈다. 모든 밀레니얼은 모두 세기가 바뀌는 시기쯤에 태어났지만, 그들 중 일부는 여전히 초기 성인기에 있어 새로운 직업에 대응하고 자리 잡는 중이다. 반면에, 더 나이가 많은 밀레니얼 세대는 이미 집을 가지고 가족을 이루고 있다. 자녀를 가지는 것이 어떻게 여러분의 관심사와 우선순위를 바꿀 수 있는지 상상해 볼 수 있다. 그래서 마케팅 목적으로 이 세대를 Gen Y.1과 Gen Y.2로 나누는 것이 유용하다. 이 두 그룹은 문화적으로 다를 뿐만 아니라 금융 생활의 단계에서도 매우 다르다. 젊은 그룹은 금융 초보자로서 구매력을 보이기 시작한 것입니다. 반면에 후자 그룹은 신용 기록이 있고 첫 대출을 가진 사람들이자 어린 자녀를 기르고 있습니다. Gen Y.1과 Gen Y.2 사이의 우선순위와 요구 사항의 대조는 광범위하다.

① 대조
② 감소
③ 반복
④ 능력

어휘

☐ Millennials 밀레니얼 세대
☐ century 세기, 100년
☐ adulthood 성인, 성년
☐ settle down 안정을 찾다
☐ priority 우선 사항, 우선 순위
☐ financial 금융의, 재정의
☐ mortgage 대출(금), 융자(금), 저당 잡히다

정답 ①

08 밑줄 친 부분에 들어갈 말로 적절한 것은?

2024. 지방직 9급

Cost pressures in liberalized markets have different effects on existing and future hydropower schemes. Because of the cost structure, existing hydropower plants will always be able to earn a profit. Because the planning and construction of future hydropower schemes is not a short-term process, it is not a popular investment, in spite of low electricity generation costs. Most private investors would prefer to finance ____________________, leading to the paradoxical situation that although an existing hydropower plant seems to be a cash cow, nobody wants to invest in a new one. Where public shareholders/owners (states, cities, municipalities) are involved, the situation looks very different because they can see the importance of the security of supply and also appreciate long-term investments.

① more short-term technologies
② all high technology industries
③ the promotion of the public interest
④ the enhancement of electricity supply

해설

단기적인 이윤을 추구하는 자유화된 시장에서의 수력발전 가치에 대한 글이다. 수력발전에 있어서의 자본시장에서의 '비용 압박(Cost Pressures)'으로 말미암아, 투자가에게 '단기적인 과정이 아닌(not a short-term process)' 것이 인기가 있는 투자 (a popular investment)가 되지 못함을 빈칸 앞에서 진술하고 있으므로 대부분의 개인 투자자들이 선호하는 것은 '더 단기적인 것'이 되어야 한다. 따라서 밑줄 친 부분에 들어갈 말로 적절한 것은 ①이다.

해석

자유화된 시장에서의 비용 압박은 기존과 미래의 수력발전 계획에 서로 다른 영향을 미친다. 비용 구조 때문에 기존의 수력발전소는 항상 수익을 낼 수 있다. 그러나 미래의 수력발전 계획의 기획과 건설은 단기적인 과정이 아니기 때문에, 전력 생산 비용이 낮더라도 인기가 있는 투자 대상은 아니다. 대부분의 민간 투자자들은 더 단기적인 기술들에 자금을 지원하기를 선호하여, 기존의 수력 발전소는 고수익 사업으로 보이지만 새로운 수력 발전소에는 아무도 투자하고 싶어하지 않는 역설적인 상황이 발생한다. 공공 주주/소유주(국가, 도시, 지방 자치 단체)가 관련된 경우에는 그들은 공급 안정성의 중요성을 알 수 있고 장기적인 투자도 높이 평가하기 때문에 상황이 매우 다르게 나타난다.

① 더 단기적인 기술들
② 모든 첨단 기술 산업들
③ 공익 증진
④ 전기 공급 강화

어휘

□ liberalize 자유화하다, 완화하다
□ existing 기존의, 현재 사용되는
□ scheme 계획, 방안, 책략을 꾸미다
□ hydropower plant 수력 발전소
□ paradoxical 역설적인
□ cash cow 고수익 사업[상품]
□ shareholder 주주
□ municipality 지방 자치제
□ supply 공급, 공급[제공]하다

정답 ①

09 밑줄 친 부분에 들어갈 말로 알맞은 것은? 2023. 국가직 9급

In recent years, the increased popularity of online marketing and social media sharing has boosted the need for advertising standardization for global brands. Most big marketing and advertising campaigns include a large online presence. Connected consumers can now zip easily across borders via the internet and social media, making it difficult for advertisers to roll out adapted campaigns in a controlled, orderly fashion. As a result, most global consumer brands coordinate their digital sites internationally. For example, Coca-Cola web and social media sites around the world, from Australia and Argentina to France, Romania, and Russia, are surprisingly ___________. All feature splashes of familiar Coke red, iconic Coke bottle shapes, and Coca-Cola's music and "Taste the Feeling" themes.

① experimental ② uniform
③ localized ④ diverse

해설

글로벌 브랜드 광고의 표준화 필요성 증대를 주제로 하는 글로, 글로벌 브랜드들은 온라인 마케팅과 소셜 미디어의 인기 상승으로 인해 '광고 표준화'를 필요로 하며, 국경을 넘나들기 쉬운 소비자들을 위해 캠페인을 전개하기 어렵기 때문에 전 세계적으로 디지털 사이트를 조정하고 있음을 설명하고 있다. 첫 번째 문장이 이 글의 주제문으로 '표준화(standardization)'를 한다는 것은 '획일적'으로 한다는 것을 의미한다. 따라서 밑줄 친 부분에 들어갈 말로 알맞은 것은 ②이다.

해석

최근 몇 년 동안 온라인 마케팅과 소셜 미디어 공유의 인기 상승으로 인해 글로벌 브랜드들의 광고 표준화에 대한 필요성이 증가하고 있다. 대부분의 대형 마케팅 및 광고 캠페인에는 대규모의 온라인 참여가 포함된다. 연결된 소비자들은 이제 인터넷과 소셜 미디어를 통해 쉽게 국경을 넘나들 수 있으며, 이로 인해 광고주들이 통제되고 정돈된 방식으로 적합한 캠페인을 시작하는 것이 어려워지고 있다. 그 결과, 대부분의 글로벌 소비자 브랜드들은 국제적으로 디지털 사이트를 동등하게 한다. 예를 들어, 전 세계적으로 호주와 아르헨티나부터 프랑스, 루마니아, 러시아에 이르기까지 코카-콜라 웹과 소셜 미디어 사이트들은 놀랍도록 획일적이다. 전부 친숙한 빨간색 코카콜라의 튀기는 소리, 상징적인 코카콜라 병 모양과 코카콜라의 음악과 "Taste the Feeling" 테마를 특징으로 한다.

① 실험적인
② 획일적인
③ 국지적인
④ 다양한

어휘

□ popularity 인기
□ standardization 표준화, 규격화, 통일, 획일
□ presence 있음, 존재, 실재, 참석
□ roll out 출시하다, 시작하다, 밀어서 펴다
□ orderly 정돈된, 질서 있는
□ coordinate 조정[조화]하다, 동등하게 하다
□ feature 특징, 특징을 가지다
□ splash 튀기는 소리, 얼룩
□ iconic 대표적인, 상징적인
□ uniform 획일적인, 균일한
□ feature ~의 특징을 이루다

정답 ②

10 밑줄 친 부분에 들어갈 말로 알맞은 것은? 2023. 국가직 9급

Over the last fifty years, all major subdisciplines in psychology have become more and more isolated from each other as training becomes increasingly specialized and narrow in focus. As some psychologists have long argued, if the field of psychology is to mature and advance scientifically, its disparate parts (for example, neuroscience, developmental, cognitive, personality, and social) must become whole and integrated again. Science advances when distinct topics become theoretically and empirically integrated under simplifying theoretical frameworks. Psychology of science will encourage collaboration among psychologists from various sub-areas, helping the field achieve coherence rather than continued fragmentation. In this way, psychology of science might act as a template for psychology as a whole by integrating under one discipline all of the major fractions/factions within the field. It would be no small feat and of no small import if the psychology of science could become a model for the parent discipline on how to combine resources and study science ______________________.

① from a unified perspective
② in dynamic aspects
③ throughout history
④ with accurate evidence

해설

과학심리학의 발전과 분야 간 협력의 중요성을 강조하는 글로, 심리학이 과학적으로 성숙하고 발전하려면, 이질적인 부분이 완전해지고 다시 통합되어야 한다는 것을 강조하는 글이다. 문제점에 대한 해결책을 제시하고 그 근거를 제시하는 구조를 가진 글로, 두 번째 문장에서 "심리학 분야가 과학적으로 성숙하고 발전하려면, 그것의 이질적인 부분(예를 들어, 신경과학, 발달, 인지, 성격, 그리고 사회)이 완전해지고 다시 통합되어야 한다"는 진술을 통해서 밑줄 친 부분에 들어갈 말로 알맞은 것은 ①이다.

해석

지난 50년 동안, 훈련이 점점 더 전문화되고 초점이 좁혀짐에 따라 심리학의 모든 주요 하위 학문들은 서로 점점 더 고립되어 왔다. 일부 심리학자들이 오랫동안 주장해 온 것처럼, 심리학 분야가 과학적으로 성숙하고 발전하려면, 그것의 이질적인 부분(예를 들어, 신경과학, 발달, 인지, 성격, 그리고 사회)이 완전해지고 다시 통합되어야 한다. 과학은 서로 다른 주제가 이론적, 경험적으로 단순화된 이론적 틀 아래 통합될 때 발전한다. 과학 심리학은 다양한 하위 영역의 심리학자들 간의 협업을 장려하여 지속적인 분열이 아닌 일관성을 달성하는 데 도움이 될 것이다. 이렇게 함으로써, 과학 심리학은 분야 내의 모든 주요 파벌을 하나의 학문으로 통합함으로써 심리학 전체에 대한 본보기로 역할을 할지도 모른다. 과학 심리학이 어떻게 자원을 결합하고 <u>통일된 관점에서</u> 과학을 공부할 것인가에 대한 모 학문의 모델이 될 수 있다면 그것은 작지 않은 위업이자 작지 않은 중요성이 될 것이다.

① 통일된 관점에서
② 역동적인 측면에서
③ 역사 전반에 걸쳐서
④ 정확한 증거와 함께

어휘

- □ subdiscipline 학문 분야의 하위 구분
- □ mature 성숙하다, 성숙한, 다 자란
- □ disparate 서로 전혀 다른, 이질적인
- □ neuroscience 신경 과학
- □ cognitive 인지의
- □ integrate 통합하다
- □ empirical 경험에 의거한, 실증적인
- □ simplify 간소화하다
- □ coherence 일관성
- □ fragmentation 분열
- □ fraction 파벌, 분할, 분수
- □ parent discipline 모 학문
- □ unified 통합된, 통일된

정답 ①

11 밑줄 친 부분에 들어갈 말로 가장 적절한 것은?

2023. 지방직 9급

We live in the age of anxiety. Because being anxious can be an uncomfortable and scary experience, we resort to conscious or unconscious strategies that help reduce anxiety in the moment — watching a movie or TV show, eating, video-game playing, and overworking. In addition, smartphones also provide a distraction any time of the day or night. Psychological research has shown that distractions serve as a common anxiety avoidance strategy. ____________, however, these avoidance strategies make anxiety worse in the long run. Being anxious is like getting into quicksand — the more you fight it, the deeper you sink. Indeed, research strongly supports a well-known phase that "what you resist, persists."

① Paradoxically ② Fortunately
③ Neutrally ④ Creatively

해설

불안을 피하기 위한 전략의 역설에 대한 글로, 우리는 불안한 시대에 살며 불안을 줄이기 위해 다양한 전략을 사용하지만, 이러한 회피 전략은 장기적으로 불안을 더 심해지게 한다는 것을 강조하고 있다. 빈칸 문장에서 문제 해결을 위해 불안 회피 전략이 결국 도움이 되지 않는다고 진술하고 있다. 따라서 밑줄 친 부분에 들어갈 말로 가장 적절한 것은 ①이다.

해석

우리는 불안의 시대에 살고 있다. 불안한 것은 불편하고 무서운 경험이 될 수 있기 때문에, 우리는 순간의 불안을 줄이는 데 도움이 되는 의식적이거나 무의식적인 전략들에 의지한다 — 영화나 TV 쇼 시청하기, 먹기, 비디오 게임 플레이하기, 과로하기. 게다가 스마트폰은 낮이나 밤이나 언제든지 주의 산만을 만든다. 심리학적 연구에 따르면, 주의 산만은 흔한 불안 회피 전략으로 역할한다. 그러나 역설적으로, 이러한 회피 전략은 장기적으로 불안을 더 악화시킨다. 불안한 것은 유사에 빠지는 것과 같은 것이다 — 더 많이 그것과 싸우수록 더 깊이 가라앉는다. 실제로, 연구는 잘 알려진 구절인 "당신이 저항하는 것은 지속된다"를 강력하게 지지한다.

① 역설적으로
② 다행히도
③ 중립적으로
④ 창조적으로

어휘

□ anxiety 불안
□ uncomfortable 불편한, 불안한
□ resort to 의지하다, 의존하다
□ conscious 의식적인
□ unconscious 무의식적인
□ strategy 전략, 방법
□ overwork 과로하다, 혹사하다
□ distraction 주의 산만, 방해
□ quicksand 유사(바람이나 물에 의해 아래로 흘러내리는 모래), 헤어나기 힘든 상황
□ sink 가라앉다
□ phase 단계
□ resist 저항하다
□ persist 지속되다, 집요하게 계속하다

정답 ①

12 밑줄 친 부분에 들어갈 말로 가장 적절한 것은?

2023. 지방직 9급

How many different ways do you get information? Some people might have six different kinds of communications to answer — test messages, voice mails, paper documents, regular mail, blog posts, messages on different online services. Each of these is type of in-box, and each must be processed on a continuous basis. It's an endless process, but it doesn't have to be exhausting or stressful. Getting your information management down to a more manageable level and into a productive zone starts by ______________________. Every place you have to go to check your messages or to read your incoming information is an in-box, and the more you have, the harder it is to manage everything. Cut the number of in-boxes you have down to the smallest number possible for you still to function in the ways you need to.

① setting several goals at once
② immersing yourself in incoming information
③ minimizing the number of in-boxes you have
④ choosing information you are passionate about

해설

효율적인 정보 관리를 주제로 하는 글로, 효율적인 정보 관리를 위해 미결 서류함의 수를 최소화하여 스트레스를 줄이고 생산적으로 일할 수 있다. 미결 서류함은 모든 메시지와 수신 정보를 처리해야 할 장소로, 미결 서류함의 수가 적을수록 관리가 용이해짐을 마지막 문장에서 강조하고 있다. 따라서 밑줄 친 부분에 들어갈 말로 가장 적절한 것은 ③이다.

해석

당신은 얼마나 다양한 방식으로 정보를 받아들이는가? 어떤 사람들은 답장해야 할 여섯 가지 종류의 커뮤니케이션을 가지고 있을 수도 있다 — 텍스트 메시지, 음성 메일, 종이 문서, 일반 우편, 블로그 글, 다른 온라인 서비스의 메시지 등. 각각은 하나의 인박스 유형이며, 지속적으로 처리되어야 한다. 이는 끝없는 프로세스지만, 지치거나 스트레스 받을 필요는 없다. 정보 관리를 더 관리하기 쉬운 수준으로 낮추고 생산적인 영역으로 이동시키기 위해서는 당신이 가지고 있는 미결 서류함의 수를 최소화함으로써 시작해야 한다. 메시지를 확인하거나 수신 정보를 읽기 위해 가야 할 모든 장소는 미결 서류함이며, 가지고 있는 미결 서류함이 많을수록 모든 것을 관리하기가 더 어려워진다. 필요한 방식으로 여전히 기능을 수행할 수 있도록 당신이 가진 미결 서류함의 수를 최소한으로 줄여라.

① 동시에 여러 목표를 설정하는 것
② 들어오는 정보에 몰두하는 것
③ 당신이 가지고 있는 미결 서류함의 수를 최소화하는 것
④ 당신이 열정적인 정보를 선택하는 것

어휘

□ in-box 미결 서류함, 받은 편지함
□ process 처리하다
□ continuous 연속적인
□ exhausting 지치게 하는, 소모적인
□ management 관리
□ immerse 담그다, 몰두하다, 몰두하게 만들다
□ minimize 최소화하다, 축소하다
□ at once 즉시, 동시에[한꺼번에]

정답 ③

13 다음 빈칸에 들어갈 말로 가장 적절한 것은?

2023. 법원직 9급

As global temperatures rise, so do sea levels, threatening coastal communities around the world. Surprisingly, even small organisms like oysters ____________________. Oysters are keystone species with *ripple effects on the health of their ecosystems and its inhabitants. Just one adult oyster can filter up to fifty gallons of water in a single day, making waterways cleaner. Healthy oyster reefs also provide a home for hundreds of other marine organisms, promoting biodiversity and ecosystem balance. As rising sea levels lead to pervasive flooding, oyster reefs act as walls to buffer storms and protect against further coastal erosion.

* ripple effect 파급효과

① can come to our defense
② can be the food for emergency
③ may be contaminated by microplastics
④ can increase the income of local residents

해설

해수면 상승 대비를 위한 굴의 역할에 대한 글로, 굴과 같은 작은 생물체도 환경을 보호하고 생태계 균형을 유지하는데 중요한 역할을 할 수 있으며, 굴이 여러 가지 환경적 이점을 제공하고 있다고 설명한다. 4번째 문장에서 "성체 굴 한 마리가 하루에 최대 50갤런의 물을 여과할 수 있어서 수로가 더 깨끗해진다"는 진술을 통해서 빈칸에 들어갈 말로 가장 적절한 것은 ①이다.

해석

지구 기온이 상승함에 따라 해수면도 상승하여 전 세계 연안 지역 공동체를 위협하고 있다. 놀랍게도, 굴과 같은 작은 유기체들도 우리의 방어물이 될 수 있다. 굴은 생태계와 주민들의 건강에 파급효과를 미치는 핵심종이다. 성체 굴 한 마리가 하루에 최대 50갤런의 물을 여과할 수 있어서 수로가 더 깨끗해진다. 건강한 굴 암초는 또한 생물 다양성과 생태계 균형을 촉진하면서 수백 개의 다른 해양 생물들에게 집을 제공한다. 해수면 상승으로 인해 홍수가 만연하게 발생하면 굴 암초는 폭풍을 완화시키고 더 많은 해안 침식으로부터 보호하는 벽 역할을 한다.

① 우리의 방어물이 될 수 있다
② 비상식량이 될 수 있다
③ 미세 플라스틱에 의해 오염될지도 모른다
④ 지역 주민들의 수입을 증가시킬 수 있다

어휘

□ sea level 해수면
□ coastal community 연안 지역 공동체
□ organism 유기체, 생물체
□ oyster 굴
□ keystone 핵심, 쐐기돌
□ reef 암초
□ biodiversity 생물 다양성
□ ecosystem 생태계
□ pervasive 만연하는
□ buffer 완화하다, 보호하다, 완충제
□ come to ~이 되다, 의식을 회복하다
□ defence 방어[물], 수비, 옹호

정답 ①

14 다음 빈칸에 들어갈 말로 가장 적절한 것은?

2023. 법원직 9급

Lewis Pugh is a British endurance swimmer, who is best known for his long-distance swims in cold and open waters. He swims in cold places as a way to draw attention to the urgent need to protect the world's oceans and waterways from the effects of climate change and pollution. In 2019, Pugh decided to swim in Lake Imja, which is located in the Khumbu region of Nepal, near Mount Everest. After a failed first attempt, Lewis had a *debrief to discuss the best way to swim at 5,300 meters above sea level. He is usually very aggressive when he swims because he wants to finish quickly and get out of the cold water. But this time he showed ____________ and swam slowly.

* debrief 평가회의

① grief ② anger
③ humility ④ confidence

해설

기후 변화와 오염으로부터 세계의 바다와 수로를 보호하기 위한 긴급한 필요성을 강조하기 위해 차가운 열린 물에서의 장거리 수영을 하는 Lewis Pugh에 대한 글이다. 빈칸이 들어갈 문장은 5번째 문장과 6번째 문장의 "그는 보통 수영을 할 때 매우 공격적입니다. 왜냐하면 그는 빨리 끝내고 차가운 물에서 벗어나고 싶기 때문입니다"의 진술과는 반대가 되는 진술이 나와야 한다. 따라서 빈칸에 들어갈 말로 가장 적절한 것은 ③이다.

해석

Lewis Pugh는 영국의 지구력 수영 선수로, 차갑고 탁 트인 바다에서 장거리 수영을 하는 것으로 가장 잘 알려져 있다. 그는 기후 변화와 오염의 영향으로부터 세계의 바다와 수로를 보호해야 하는 긴급한 필요성에 관심을 끌기 위한 방법으로 추운 곳에서 수영을 한다. 2019년에 Pugh는 에베레스트 산 근처의 네팔 Khumbu 지역에 위치한 Imja 호수에서 수영하기로 결정했다. 첫 번째 시도가 실패한 후, Lewis는 해발 5,300 미터에서 수영하는 가장 좋은 방법에 대해 논의하기 위한 평가회의를 가졌다. 그는 보통 수영을 할 때 매우 공격적이다. 왜냐하면 그는 빨리 끝내고 차가운 물에서 벗어나고 싶기 때문이다. 하지만 이번에 그는 겸손을 보여주었고 천천히 수영했다.

① 비통
② 분노
③ 겸손
④ 자신감

어휘

□ endurance 지구력, 내구성, 인내
□ long-distance 장거리
□ urgent 긴급한, 시급한
□ waterway 수로, 항로
□ pollution 오염
□ aggressive 공격적인

정답 ③

15 밑줄 친 부분에 들어갈 말로 가장 적절한 것은?

2022. 국가직 9급

Scientists have long known that higher air temperatures are contributing to the surface melting on Greenland's ice sheet. But a new study has found another threat that has begun attacking the ice from below: Warm ocean water moving underneath the vast glaciers is causing them to melt even more quickly. The findings were published in the journal Nature Geoscience by researchers who studied one of the many "ice tongues" of the Nioghalvfjerdsfjorden Glacier in northeast Greenland. An ice tongue is a strip of ice that floats on the water without breaking off from the ice on land. The massive one these scientists studied is nearly 50 miles long. The survey revealed an underwater current more than a mile wide where warm water from the Atlantic Ocean is able to flow directly towards the glacier, bringing large amounts of heat into contact with the ice and ____________ the glacier's melting.

① separating ② delaying
③ preventing ④ accelerating

해설

물속에서 위협이 되는 그린란드의 거대 빙하에 대한 글이다. 주제문에 해당되는 2번째 문장에서 아래에서부터의 공격으로 인해 빙산이 녹는다고 진술하고 있다. 그리고 마지막 문장을 통해서도 많은 양의 열은 빙하가 녹는 것을 가속화하는 논리가 타당함을 알 수 있다. 따라서 밑줄 친 부분에 들어갈 말로 가장 적절한 것은 ④이다.

해석

과학자들은 더 높은 대기 온도가 그린란드의 빙상 표면을 녹이는 원인이 되고 있다는 것을 오랫동안 알고 있었다. 그러나 새로운 연구는 얼음을 아래에서부터 공격하기 시작한 또 다른 위협을 발견했다: 거대한 빙하 아래로 이동하는 따뜻한 바닷물이 빙하를 훨씬 더 빨리 녹게 하고 있다. 이 연구 결과는 그린란드 북동부에 있는 Nioghalvfjerdsfjorden 빙하의 많은 "빙설" 중 하나를 연구한 연구원들에 의해 학술지 Nature Geoscience에 발표되었다. 빙설은 육지의 얼음과 분리되지 않고 물 위에 떠 있는 얼음 조각이다. 이 과학자들이 연구한 거대한 것은 길이가 거의 50마일이다. 이 조사는 대서양의 따뜻한 물이 빙하를 향해 직접 흐를 수 있는 폭이 1마일 이상인 수중 해류가 많은 양의 열을 얼음과 접촉시켜서 빙하가 녹는 것을 가속화하는 것을 밝혀냈다.

① 분리시키는 것
② 지연시키는 것
③ 막는 것
④ 가속화하는 것

어휘

□contribute ~한 원인이 되다
□ice sheet 빙산
□underneath 아래에, 밑면에
□glacier 빙하
□journal 저널 학술지
□ice tongue 빙설
□northeast 북동쪽의
□float 떠다니다
□break off 분리되다, 떨어지다
□massive 거대한, 심각한
□reveal 드러내다, 밝히다
□underwater current 수중 해류
□Atlantic Ocean 대서양
□accelerate 가속화하다, 촉진하다

정답 ④

16 밑줄 친 부분에 들어갈 말로 가장 적절한 것은?

2022. 지방직 9급

One of the most frequently used propaganda techniques is to convince the public that the propagandist's views reflect those of the common person and that he or she is working in their best interests. A politician speaking to a blue-collar audience may roll up his sleeves, undo his tie, and attempt to use the specific idioms of the crowd. He may even use language incorrectly on purpose to give the impression that he is "just one of the folks." This technique usually also employs the use of glittering generalities to give the impression that the politician's views are the same as those of the crowd being addressed. Labor leaders, businesspeople, ministers, educators, and advertisers have used this technique to win our confidence by appearing to be ________________.

① beyond glittering generalities
② just plain folks like ourselves
③ something different from others
④ better educated than the crowd

해설

이 글은 노동 지도자들, 사업가들, 장관들, 교육자들, 그리고 광고주들 같은 유명인들이 대중의 신뢰를 얻기 위한 선전 기법을 주제로 하는 글이다. 구체적인 예시들을 통해서 청중들에게 자신도 평범한 사람 중 하나라는 인상을 주기 위해 노력한다는 내용이 이어지고 있다. 따라서 밑줄 친 부분에 들어갈 말로 가장 적절한 것은 ②이다.

해석

가장 자주 사용되는 선전 기법 중 하나는 대중들에게 선전가의 견해가 일반인의 견해를 반영하고 있으며 그들의 최선의 이익을 위해 일하고 있다고 확신시키는 것이다. 육체노동자 청중에게 말하는 정치인은 소매를 걷어붙이고, 넥타이를 풀고, 군중의 특정 관용구를 사용하려고 시도할 수 있다. 그는 심지어 자신이 "그냥 사람들 중 한 명"이라는 인상을 주기 위해 의도적으로 언어를 잘못 사용할 수도 있다. 이 기법은 일반적으로 정치인의 견해가 연설되는 군중의 견해와 같다는 인상을 주기 위해 화려한 추상어를 사용하기도 한다. 노동 지도자들, 사업가들, 장관들, 교육자들, 그리고 광고주들은 우리와 같은 그저 평범한 사람들처럼 보임으로써 우리의 신뢰를 얻기 위해 이 기술을 사용해왔다.

① 화려한 추상어를 뛰어 넘는
② 우리와 같은 그저 평범한 사람들
③ 다른 사람들과 다른 무언가
④ 대중보다 더 잘 교육받은

어휘

□propaganda 선전
□interest 이해관계, 이익, 관심, 흥미
□blue-collar 육체노동자의
□undo 풀다, 원상태로 돌리다
□idiom 관용구, 숙어
□incorrectly 부적절하게
□on purpose 의도적으로, 고의로
□glittering generality 화려한 추상어, 미사어구
□businesspeople 사업가들
□minister 장관, 성직자, 목사
□confidence 신뢰, 자신, 확신
□plain 평범한, 보통의, 평원, 평지
□folk 사람들

정답 ②

17 밑줄 친 부분에 들어갈 말로 가장 적절한 것은?

2022. 지방직 9급

As a roller coaster climbs the first lift hill of its track, it is building potential energy — the higher it gets above the earth, the stronger the pull of gravity will be. When the coaster crests the lift hill and begins its descent, its potential energy becomes kinetic energy, or the energy of movement. A common misperception is that a coaster loses energy along the track. An important law of physics, however, called the law of conservation of energy, is that energy can never be created nor destroyed. It simply changes from one form to another. Whenever a track rises back uphill, the cars' momentum — their kinetic energy — will carry them upward, which builds potential energy, and roller coasters repeatedly convert potential energy to kinetic energy and back again. At the end of a ride, coaster cars are slowed down by brake mechanisms that create ____________ between two surfaces. This motion makes them hot, meaning kinetic energy is changed to heat energy during braking. Riders may mistakenly think coasters lose energy at the end of the track, but the energy just changes to and from different forms.

① gravity ② friction
③ vacuum ④ acceleration

해설

에너지 보존의 법칙을 롤러코스터를 통해 보여주는 글이다. 롤러코스터의 상하의 움직임과 에너지 변환에 대한 설명을 하면서, 위치 에너지와 운동 에너지를 설명하고 하고, 마지막에는 브레이크를 통해 운동 에너지가 열 에너지로 변환되는 것을 언급하고 있다. 따라서 열 에너지를 유발시키는 것은 브레이크와 선로의 마찰임을 쉽게 추론할 수 있다. 따라서 밑줄 친 부분에 들어갈 말로 가장 적절한 것은 ②이다.

해석

롤러코스터가 트랙의 최초의 리프트 언덕을 오르면서, 이 롤러코스터는 위치 에너지를 만들어 내고 있다 — 더 높이 이것이 지구 위로 올라가면 올라갈수록, 그만큼 중력의 당기는 힘이 더 강해질 것이다. 롤러코스터가 리프트 언덕을 넘어 하강하기 시작할 때, 그것의 위치 에너지는 운동 에너지, 즉 이동 에너지가 된다. 일반적인 오해는 롤러코스터가 트랙을 따라 에너지를 잃는다는 것이다. 그러나, 에너지 보존의 법칙이라고 불리는 물리학의 중요한 법칙은 에너지가 결코 생성되거나 파괴될 수 없다는 것이다. 그것은 단순히 한 형태에서 다른 형태로 변할 뿐이다. 트랙이 다시 오르막길로 올라갈 때마다 그 차량들의 가속도 — 자신의 운동 에너지 — 는 그것들을 위로 옮기고 그것은 위치 에너지를 만들어 롤러코스터는 반복적으로 잠재 에너지를 운동 에너지로 전환하였다 다시 되돌아온다. 놀이기구가 끝날 때, 롤러코스터 자동차는 두 표면 사이에 마찰을 일으키는 브레이크 장치에 의해 속도를 늦춘다. 이 운동은 그것들을 뜨겁게 만들며, 이는 제동 중에 운동 에너지가 열 에너지로 바뀐다는 것을 의미한다. 탑승자들은 트랙의 끝에서 에너지를 잃는다고 잘못 생각할 수 있다, 그러나 그 에너지는 단지 다른 형태로 혹은 다른 형태에서 바뀔 뿐이다.

① 중력
② 마찰
③ 진공
④ 가속

어휘

□lift hill 리프트 언덕
□potential energy 위치 에너지
□gravity 중력
□kinetic energy 운동 에너지
□misperception 오해
□law of conservation of energy 에너지 보존의 법칙
□momentum 탄력, 가속도, 운동량
□rider 승객

정답 ②

18 다음 빈칸에 들어갈 말로 가장 적절한 것은?

2022. 법원직 9급

There are a few jobs where people have had to ________________________. We see referees and umpires using their arms and hands to signal directions to the players — as in cricket, where a single finger upwards means that the batsman is out and has to leave the wicket. Orchestra conductors control the musicians through their movements. People working at a distance from each other have to invent special signals if they want to communicate. So do people working in a noisy environment, such as in a factory where the machines are very loud, or lifeguards around a swimming pool full of school children.

* wicket (크리켓에서) 삼주문

① support their parents and children
② adapt to an entirely new work style
③ fight in court for basic human rights
④ develop their signing a bit more fully

해설

이 글은 특정 직업에서 수화가 어떻게 사용되고 있으며, 앞으로 더 발전될 필요성이 있음을 설명하고 있다. 4번째 문장에서 '서로 좀 떨어져서 일하는 사람들은, 만약 그들이 소통하기를 원한다면, 특별한 신호를 고안해야 한다'의 진술을 통해서 빈칸에 들어갈 말로 가장 적절한 것은 ④이다.

해석

사람들이 그들의 손짓 언어를 조금 더 완전하게 발전시켜야 하는 몇몇 직업들이 있다. 우리는 심판들과 심판들이 선수들에게 지시를 전달하기 위해 팔과 손을 사용하는 것을 본다 — 크리켓처럼 손가락 하나를 위로 향하게 하면 타자가 아웃되어 삼주문을 떠나야 한다는 것을 의미한다. 오케스트라 지휘자는 자신의 움직임을 통해 음악가들을 통제한다. 서로 좀 떨어져서 일하는 사람들은, 만약 그들이 소통하기를 원한다면, 특별한 신호를 고안해야 한다. 기계들이 매우 큰 소리를 내는 공장과 같은 시끄러운 환경에서 일하는 사람들이나, 초등학생들로 가득 찬 수영장 주변의 인명 구조원들도 마찬가지이다.

① 그들의 부모들과 아이들을 지지한다
② 완전히 새로운 업무 방식에 적응한다
③ 기본적인 인권을 위해 법정에서 싸운다
④ 그들의 손짓 언어를 조금 더 완전하게 발전시켜야 한다

어휘

□ referee 심판
□ umpire 심판
□ cricket 크리켓(스포츠)
□ conductor 지휘자
□ noisy 시끄러운, 떠들썩한
□ lifeguard 인명 구조원, 안전 요원
□ entirely 전적으로, 완전히
□ fully 완전히, 충분히
□ signing 손짓 언어, 수화

정답 ④

19 다음 빈칸에 들어갈 말로 가장 적절한 것은?

2022. 법원직 9급

Water and civilization go hand-in-hand. The idea of a "*hydraulic civilization" argues that water is the unifying context and justification for many large-scale civilizations throughout history. For example, the various multi-century Chinese empires survived as long as they did in part by controlling floods along the Yellow River. One interpretation of the hydraulic theory is that the justification for gathering populations into large cities is to manage water. Another interpretation suggests that large water projects enable the rise of big cities. The Romans understood the connections between water and power, as the Roman Empire built a vast network of **aqueducts throughout land they controlled, many of which remain intact. For example, Pont du Gard in southern France stands today as a testament to humanity's investment in its water infrastructure. Roman governors built roads, bridges, and water systems as a way of ________________________.

* hydraulic 수력학의
** aqueduct 송수로

① focusing on educating young people
② prohibiting free trade in local markets
③ concentrating and strengthening their authority
④ giving up their properties to other countries

해설

수력학의 문명과 물의 관계에 대한 글로, 6번째 문장에서 '로마 제국은 그들이 지배했던 땅 전체에 걸쳐 광대한 송수로 망을 건설했기 때문에, 로마인들은 물과 권력 사이의 관련성을 이해했는데, 그것들 중 많은 것들이 손상되지 않은 채 있다'의 진술을 통해서 빈칸에 들어갈 말로 가장 적절한 것은 ③이다.

해석

물과 문명은 밀접한 관련이 있다. "수력학의 문명"이라는 아이디어는, 물이 역사를 통틀어 많은 대규모 문명에 대한 통합적 배경과 타당한 이유라고, 주장한다. 예컨대, 여러 세기 동안 존속된 다양한 중국 제국들은 부분적으로 황허 강을 따라 홍수를 통제함으로써 그들이 그랬던 만큼 오랫동안 살아남았다. 수력 이론의 한 가지 해석은, 인구를 대도시로 모은 타당한 이유가 물을 관리하기 위한 것이라는 점이다. 또 다른 해석은 대규모 치수 사업이 대도시의 출현을 가능하게 한다고 말한다. 로마 제국은 그들이 지배했던 땅 전체에 걸쳐 광대한 송수로 망을 건설했기 때문에, 로마인들은 물과 권력 사이의 관련성을 이해했는데, 그것들 중 많은 것들이 손상되지 않은 채 있다. 예컨대, 프랑스 남부에 있는 Pont du Gard는 오늘날 수력 공공 기반 시설에 대한 인류의 투자의 증거로서 세워져 있다. 로마 통치자들은 그들의 권한을 집중하고 강화하는 방법으로 도로, 다리 그리고 수계(水系)를 건설했다.

① 젊은이들을 교육하는 것에 집중하는
② 지역 시장에서 자유로운 거래를 금지하는
③ 그들의 권한을 집중하고 강화하는
④ 그들의 토지를 다른 나라에 넘겨주는

어휘

☐civilization 문명
☐go hand in hand 밀접한 관련이 있다
☐justification 정당화
☐Yellow River 황하
☐interpretation 해석
☐intact 손상되지 않은, 온전한, 그대로의
☐infrastructure 기반 시설
☐testament 증거
☐governor 통치가, 지배자
☐authority 권위, 권한
☐property 재산, 자산, 토지, 특성, 속성
☐give up to (~에게) ~을 넘겨주다

정답 ③

20 밑줄 친 부분에 들어갈 말로 가장 적절한 것은?

2021. 국가직 9급

Social media, magazines and shop windows bombard people daily with things to buy, and British consumers are buying more clothes and shoes than ever before. Online shopping means it is easy for customers to buy without thinking, while major brands offer such cheap clothes that they can be treated like disposable items — worn two or three times and then thrown away. In Britain, the average person spends more than £ 1,000 on new clothes a year, which is around four percent of their income. That might not sound like much, but that figure hides two far more worrying trends for society and for the environment. First, a lot of that consumer spending is via credit cards. British people currently owe approximately £ 670 per adult to credit card companies. That's 66 percent of the average wardrobe budget. Also, not only are people spending money they don't have, they're using it to buy things ______________________. Britain throws away 300,000 tons of clothing a year, most of which goes into landfill sites.

① they don't need
② that are daily necessities
③ that will be soon recycled
④ they can hand down to others

해설

영국인들의 과소비로 인한 사회와 환경의 문제를 주제로 하는 글이다. 본문의 마지막 문장에서 연간 30만 톤의 옷을 버리고 있다고 언급하고 2번째 문장에서는 한두 번 입고 버릴 만큼 많은 옷을 사고 있다고 언급하고 있으므로 빈칸에는 필요하지 않은 옷을 구입하는 데 돈을 쓰고 있다는 내용이 들어가야 올바르다. 따라서 밑줄 친 부분에 들어갈 말로 가장 적절한 것은 ①이다.

해석

소셜 미디어, 잡지, 상품 진열장은 매일 사람들에게 살 것들을 쏟아붓고, 영국 소비자들은 그 어느 때 보다 더 많은 옷과 신발을 사고 있다. 온라인 쇼핑은 고객들이 아무 생각 없이 사는 것이 쉽고, 한편, 주요 브랜드들은 그들이 두세 번 입고 버려지는 일회용품처럼 취급될 정도로 그렇게 싼 옷을 제공하는 것을 의미한다. 영국에서 보통 사람들은 1년에 새 옷에 1,000파운드 이상을 소비하는데, 이것은 그들의 수입의 약 4%에 해당한다. 그것은 별것 아닌 것처럼 들릴 수도 있지만, 그 수치는 사회와 환경을 위해 훨씬 더 걱정스러운 두 가지 추세를 숨기고 있다. 첫째, 소비자 지출의 상당 부분은 신용카드를 통해 이루어진다. 영국인들은 현재 신용카드 회사에 성인 1인당 약 670파운드를 빚지고 있다. 이는 평균 의상 예산의 66%에 해당하는 금액이다. 또한, 사람들은 그들이 가지고 있지 않은 돈을 쓸 뿐만 아니라, <u>그들이 필요하지 않은</u> 것을 사기 위해 그것을 사용하고 있다. 영국은 매년 30만 톤의 옷을 버리며, 그 중 대부분은 매립지로 들어간다.

① 그들은 필요하지 않다
② 일상 필수품이다
③ 곧 재활용될 것이다
④ 다른 사람들에게 건네줄 수 있다

어휘

□ bombard 쏟아 붓다, 퍼붓다
□ disposable item 일회용품
□ throw away 버리다, 없애다
□ figure 수치, 인물, 모양
□ spending 지출
□ wardrobe 옷장, 옷
□ budget 예산, 비용
□ via 경유하여, 거쳐, 통하여
□ landfill 매립지
□ necessity 필수품
□ hand down ~을 물려주다

정답 ①

21 밑줄 친 부분에 들어갈 말로 가장 적절한 것은?

2021. 국가직 9급

Excellence is the absolute prerequisite in fine dining because the prices charged are necessarily high. An operator may do everything possible to make the restaurant efficient, but the guests still expect careful, personal service: food prepared to order by highly skilled chefs and delivered by expert servers. Because this service is, quite literally, manual labor, only marginal improvements in productivity are possible. For example, a cook, server, or bartender can move only so much faster before she or he reaches the limits of human performance. Thus, only moderate savings are possible through improved efficiency, which makes an escalation of prices ____________. (It is an axiom of economics that as prices rise, consumers become more discriminating.) Thus, the clientele of the fine-dining restaurant expects, demands, and is willing to pay for excellence.

① ludicrous
② inevitable
③ preposterous
④ inconceivable

해설

고급 식당의 고객들은 식당의 우수성을 기대하고 기꺼이 높은 가격을 지불하려고 한다는 내용을 설명하는 글이다. 빈칸의 앞 내용은 레스토랑의 서비스 향상에 대한 내용이고 빈칸의 뒤에서 비용을 기꺼이 지불한다고 하였으므로 밑줄 친 부분에 들어갈 말로 가장 적절한 것은 ②이다.

해석

우수성은 고급 식사에서 절대적인 전제조건인데, 그 이유는 부과된 요금이 매우 비싸기 때문이다. 운영자는 식당을 효율적으로 만들기 위해 가능한 모든 것을 할 수 있지만, 손님들은 여전히 신중하고 개인적인 서비스, 즉 매우 숙련된 요리사가 주문하도록 준비되고 능숙한 종업원에 의해 전달되는 음식을 기대한다. 이 서비스는 말 그대로 육체노동이기 때문에 생산성에 있어 약간 개선만이 가능하다. 예를 들어, 요리사, 서빙하는 사람 또는 바텐더가 인간 수행의 한계에 도달하기 전에는 훨씬 더 빨리 움직일 수 있다. 따라서 효율성 향상을 통한 오직 보통의 절약만 가능하므로 가격 상승은 <u>불가피하다.</u> (가격이 오르면 소비자들이 더 안목이 있다는 것은 경제학의 공리이다.) 따라서 이 고급 레스토랑의 손님은 우수성을 기대하고, 요구하며, 기꺼이 비용을 지불한다.

① 터무니없는, 우스꽝스러운
② 불가피한
③ 말도 안 되는, 터무니없는
④ 상상할 수 없는

어휘

□excellence 뛰어남, 우수함
□absolute 절대적인
□prerequisite 전제 조건
□fine dining 고급 식당
□operator 경영자, 운영자
□efficient 효율적인
□manual labor 육체노동, 수작업
□marginal 미미한, 중요하지 않은, 주변적인
□productivity 생산성
□moderate 보통의, 적당한
□escalation 상승
□axiom of economic 경제학의 공리
□discriminate 구별하다, 식별하다, 차별하다
□discriminating 안목 있는
□clientele 손님, 고객

정답 ②

22 밑줄 친 부분에 들어갈 말로 가장 적절한 것은?

2021. 지방직 9급

As more and more leaders work remotely or with teams scattered around the nation or the globe, as well as with consultants and freelancers, you'll have to give them more ____________. The more trust you bestow, the more others trust you. I am convinced that there is a direct correlation between job satisfaction and how empowered people are to fully execute their job without someone shadowing them every step of the way. Giving away responsibility to those you trust can not only make your organization run more smoothly but also free up more of your time so you can focus on larger issues.

① work
② rewards
③ restrictions
④ autonomy

해설

멀리 떨어진 팀과의 협업을 위한 신뢰와 자율성의 중요성을 강조하는 글이다. 3번째 문장과 4번째 문장에서 '권한을 부여받는', '신뢰할 수 있는 사람에게 책임을 넘기는 것'은 자율성을 주는 것을 의미한다. 따라서 밑줄 친 부분에 들어갈 말로 가장 적절한 것은 ④이다.

해석

점점 더 많은 지도자들이 컨설턴트나 프리랜서뿐만 아니라 국내나 전 세계에 흩어져 있는 팀들과 함께 멀리서 작업하고 있기 때문에 당신은 그들에게 더 많은 <u>자율성</u>을 부여해야 할 것이다. 당신이 더 많은 신뢰를 줄수록, 다른 사람들은 당신을 더 신뢰한다. 나는 직무 만족도와 사람들이 매 순간마다 자신들을 따라다니는 사람 없이 일을 완벽히 수행하기 위해 얼마나 권한을 부여 받는지 사이에는 직접적인 상관관계가 있다고 확신한다. 신뢰할 수 있는 사람에게 책임을 넘기는 것은 조직이 보다 원활하게 운영되도록 할 뿐만 아니라 당신이 더 중요한 사안들에 집중하도록 더 많은 시간을 마련해 줄 수도 있다.

① 일
② 보상들
③ 제한들
④ 자율성

어휘

□remotely 원격으로
□scattered 산발적인, 흩어져 있는, 드문드문 있는
□autonomy 자율성, 자주성
□correlation 상관관계, 연관성
□job satisfaction 직무 만족도
□empower 권한을 부여하다
□execute 실행하다, 수행하다
□give away 나누어주다, 내주다
□smoothly 원활하게
□organization 조직, 단체

정답 ④

23 다음 빈칸에 들어갈 말로 가장 적절한 것은?

2021. 법원직 9급

Beeches, oaks, spruce and pines produce new growth all the time, and have to get rid of the old. The most obvious change happens every autumn. The leaves have served their purpose: they are now worn out and riddled with insect damage. Before the trees bid them adieu, they pump waste products into them. You could say they are taking this opportunity to relieve themselves. Then they grow a layer of weak tissue to separate each leaf from the twig it's growing on, and the leaves tumble to the ground in the next breeze. The rustling leaves that now blanket the ground — and make such a satisfying scrunching sound when you scuffle through them — are basically ____________________.

① tree toilet paper ② the plant kitchen
③ lungs of the tree ④ parents of insect

해설

이 글은 가을의 나뭇잎이 자연의 순환과 새로운 성장을 위한 과정에서 어떤 역할을 하는지를 설명하고 있다. 이 문제를 해결하기 위해서는 글 전체의 맥락을 파악해야한다. 자작나무, 참나무, 전나무, 소나무 등은 항상 새로운 성장을 하며 오래된 것을 제거해야 하며, 이것은 가을마다 잎이 떨어지는 것을 통해 나타냄을 파악해야 한다. 즉 나무가 폐기물을 제거하고 오래된 잎을 떨어뜨리는 이러한 역할을 하는 것을 비유적인 표현으로 빈칸에 들어갈 말로 가장 적절한 것은 ①이다.

해석

너도밤나무, 떡갈나무, 가문비나무, 소나무는 항상 새로운 성장을 하고, 오래된 것을 없애야 한다. 가장 분명한 변화는 매년 가을에 일어난다. 잎은 그들의 목적에 부합해 왔다. 잎들은 이제 닳아서 곤충들의 손상으로 가득 차 있다. 나무들이 그들에게 작별을 고하기 전에, 그들[나무]은 폐기물들을 그들[나뭇잎]에게 퍼 붓는다. 당신은 그들이 스스로를 구제하기 위해 이 기회를 잡고 있다고 말할 수 있다. 그리고 나서, 그들은 그것이 자라고 있는 나뭇가지로부터 각각의 잎을 분리하기 위해 약한 조직의 층을 기른다. 그리고 잎들은 다음번 산들 바람에 땅으로 굴러 떨어진다. 이제 땅을 덮고 당신이 그것들[낙엽들] 사이로 애써 나아갈 때 그렇게 만족스러운 소리를 내는 바스락거리는 나뭇잎들은 기본적으로 나무 화장지이다.

① 나무 화장지
② 식물 부엌
③ 나무의 폐
④ 곤충의 부모

어휘

□ beech 너도밤나무
□ oak 떡갈나무
□ spruce 가문비나무
□ autumn 가을
□ pine 소나무
□ get rid of ~을 제거하다
□ obvious 분명한, 명백한
□ waste product 폐기물
□ separate 분리되다, 갈라지다
□ twig 잔가지
□ tumble 굴러 떨어지다, 크게 추락하다
□ breeze 산들바람
□ rustling 바스락거리는 소리

정답 ①

24 다음 빈칸에 들어갈 말로 가장 적절한 것은?

2021. 법원직 9급

The seeds of willows and poplars are so minuscule that you can just make out two tiny dark dots in the fluffy flight hairs. One of these seeds weighs a mere 0.0001 grams. With such a meagre energy reserve, a seedling can grow only 1–2 millimetres before it runs out of steam and has to rely on food it makes for itself using its young leaves. But that only works in places where there's no competition to threaten the tiny sprouts. Other plants casting shade on it would extinguish the new life immediately. And so, if a fluffy little seed package like this falls in a spruce or beech forest, the seed's life is over before it's even begun. That's why willows and poplars ____________________.

* minuscule 아주 작은

① prefer settling in unoccupied territory
② have been chosen as food for herbivores
③ have evolved to avoid human intervention
④ wear their dead leaves far into the winter

해설

작은 씨앗의 생존과 그 조건에 대한 글로 작은 씨앗들이 어떻게 역경을 극복하며 생존하는지를 설명하며, 어떤 환경에서 씨앗의 생명이 위협받는지도 설명하고 있다. 6번째 문장에서 '만약 이런 솜털 같은 작은 씨앗 꾸러미가 가문비나무나 너도밤나무 숲에 떨어진다면, 씨앗의 삶은 시작하기 전에 끝난다'의 진술을 통해서 빈칸에는 이러한 작은 씨앗들이 생존하기 위해서는 다른 개체들이 없는 곳이 필요함을 알 수 있다. 따라서 빈칸에 들어갈 말로 가장 적절한 것은 ①이다.

해석

버드나무와 미루나무의 씨앗은 너무 작아서 솜털에서 두 개의 작고 어두운 점을 발견할 수 있다. 이 씨앗들 중 하나는 무게가 0.0001그램밖에 나가지 않는다. 이렇게 약한 에너지를 비축하면, 묘목은 수증기가 다 떨어지기 전에 겨우 1~2 밀리미터만 자랄 수 있고 어린 잎을 이용해 스스로 만든 음식에 의존해야 한다. 하지만 그것은 작은 새싹을 위협할 경쟁이 없는 곳에서만 효과가 있다. 그것에 그늘을 드리우는 다른 식물들은 새로운 생명을 즉시 소멸시킬 것이다. 그래서, 만약 이런 솜 털 같은 작은 씨앗 꾸러미가 가문비나무나 너도밤나무 숲에 떨어진다면, 씨앗의 삶은 시작도 하기 전에 끝난다. 그래서 버드나무와 미루나무들은 빈 지역에 정착하기를 선호한다.

① 빈 지역에 정착하기를 선호한다
② 초식동물의 먹이로 선정되다
③ 인간의 개입을 피하도록 진화해왔다
④ 먼 겨울까지 그들의 죽은 잎을 달다

어휘

□ willow 버드나무
□ poplar 미루나무
□ make out ~을 알아보다
□ fluffy 부드러운, 솜털의
□ seedling 묘목
□ run out of ~을 다 써버리다
□ sprout 싹
□ shade 그늘, 그늘지게 하다
□ beech 너도밤나무
□ unoccupied 비어있는, 점령되지 않은

정답 ①

25 밑줄 친 (A), (B)에 들어갈 말로 가장 적절한 것은?

2020. 국가직 9급

When an organism is alive, it takes in carbon dioxide from the air around it. Most of that carbon dioxide is made of carbon-12, but a tiny portion consists of carbon-14. So the living organism always contains a very small amount of radioactive carbon, carbon-14. A detector next to the living organism would record radiation given off by the carbon-14 in the organism. When the organism dies, it no longer takes in carbon dioxide. No new carbon-14 is added, and the old carbon-14 slowly decays into nitrogen. The amount of carbon-14 slowly ___(A)___ as time goes on. Over time, less and less radiation from carbon-14 is produced. The amount of carbon-14 radiation detected for an organism is a measure, therefore, of how long the organism has been ___(B)___. This method of determining the age of an organism is called carbon-14 dating. The decay of carbon-14 allows archaeologists to find the age of once-living materials. Measuring the amount of radiation remaining indicates the approximate age.

(A) …… (B)
① decreases …… dead
② increases …… alive
③ decreases …… productive
④ increases …… inactive

해설

'탄소-14 연대 측정법'을 주제로 하는 글이다. 이 측정법은 유기체가 사망한 후 탄소-14가 질량을 잃으며 붕괴하는 방식으로 연대를 측정하는 탄소-14 방식이다. (A)는 탄소-14가 사망한 후 시간이 지남에 따라 감소한다는 것을 나타내야 하므로 '감소하다(decreases)'가 들어가야 적절하고, (B)는 유기체가 살아있을 때 탄소-14의 방사선이 감지될 수 있으며, 탄소-14 농도는 유기체가 얼마나 오래 살아있었는지를 측정하는 것이라는 것을 나타내므로 '죽은(dead)'이 들어가야 적절하다.

해석

유기체가 살아있을 때, 그것은 주변의 공기에서 이산화탄소를 흡수한다. 이산화탄소의 대부분은 탄소-12로 이루어져 있지만, 일부분은 탄소-14로 이루어져 있다. 그래서 살아있는 유기체는 항상 아주 적은 양의 방사성 탄소인 탄소-14를 포함하고 있다. 살아있는 유기체

옆에 있는 검출기는 유기체에서 탄소-14에 의해 방출된 방사선을 기록할 것이다. 그 유기체가 죽으면 더 이상 이산화탄소를 흡수하지 않는다. 어떤 새로운 탄소-14도 추가되지 않고, 오래된 탄소-14는 천천히 질소로 분해된다. 탄소-14의 양은 시간이 지날수록 서서히 (A) 감소한다. 시간이 지남에 따라 탄소-14로부터의 방사선이 점점 더 적게 만들어진다. 그러므로 유기체에 대해 검출된 탄소-14 방사선의 양은 유기체가 (B) 죽은 지 얼마나 됐는지에 대한 측정법이다. 유기체의 연대를 결정하는 이 방법은 탄소-14 연대 측정이라고 불린다. 탄소-14의 부패는 고고학자들이 한 때 살았던 물질의 연대를 알아낼 수 있게 해준다. 남아 있는 방사선량을 측정하는 것은 대략적인 연대를 나타낸다.

(A) (B)
① 감소한다 …… 죽은
② 증가한다 …… 살아있는
③ 감소한다 …… 생산적인
④ 증가한다 …… 소극적인

어휘

□ organism 생물체
□ carbon dioxide 이산화탄소
□ radioactive 방사성의
□ radiation 방사선
□ nitrogen 질소
□ determine 결정하다, 알아내다, 밝히다
□ decay 부패, 부식, 부패하다, 썩다
□ measure 측정하다, 재다
□ archaeologist 고고학자
□ remaining 남은, 남아 있는
□ approximate 대략적인, 근사치인

정답 ①

26 밑줄 친 부분에 들어갈 말로 가장 적절한 것은?

2020. 국가직 9급

All creatures, past and present, either have gone or will go extinct. Yet, as each species vanished over the past 3.8-billion-year history of life on Earth, new ones inevitably appeared to replace them or to exploit newly emerging resources. From only a few very simple organisms, a great number of complex, multicellular forms evolved over this immense period. The origin of new species, which the nineteenth-century English naturalist Charles Darwin once referred to as "the mystery of mysteries," is the natural process of speciation responsible for generating this remarkable ______________ with whom humans share the planet. Although taxonomists presently recognize some 1.5 million living species, the actual number is possibly closer to 10 million. Recognizing the biological status of this multitude requires a clear understanding of what constitutes a species, which is no easy task given that evolutionary biologists have yet to agree on a universally acceptable definition.

① technique of biologists
② diversity of living creatures
③ inventory of extinct organisms
④ collection of endangered species

해설

생명체의 멸종과 진화를 주제로 하는 글로, 빈칸이 있는 문장 다음에 150만 종과 천만 종의 생물들을 진술하고 있다. 따라서 밑줄 친 부분에 들어갈 말로 가장 적절한 것은 ②이다.

해석

과거와 현재의 모든 생명체는 사라졌거나 혹은 멸종될 것이다. 그러나, 각 종들이 지난 38억 년의 지구 생명의 역사 동안 사라지면서, 새로운 종들이 그것들을 대체하기 위해 혹은 신생의 자원들을 이용하기 위해 필연적으로 나타났다. 소수의 아주 단순한 유기체로부터 다수의 복잡한 다세포 형태가 이 거대한 기간에 걸쳐 진화했다. 19세기 영국 박물학자 Charles Darwin이 "미스터리 중의 미스터리"라고 한때 언급했던 새로운 종의 기원은 인간이 지구를 함께 공유하는 이 놀라운 생물체들의 다양성을 만들어내는 데 책임이 있는 자연적인 종분화 과정이다. 비록 분류학자들은 현재 약 150만 개의 살아있는 종을 인정하지만, 실제 숫자는 아마도 천만 종에 가까울 것이다. 이 다수의 생물학적 지위를 인정하는 것은 무엇이 하나의 종을 구성하고 있는지에 대한 명확한 이해를 요구하며, 이것은 진화 생물학자들이 아직 보편적으로 받아들여지는 정의에 합의하지 못했다는 점을 고려하면 쉬운 일이 아니다.

① 생물학자들의 기술
② 생물들의 다양성
③ 멸종된 유기체들의 목록
④ 멸종 위기 종의 수집

어휘

- ☐vanish 사라지다
- ☐creature 생물
- ☐extinct 멸종된, 사라진
- ☐species 종
- ☐multicellular 다세포의
- ☐evolve 진화하다
- ☐speciation 종 분화
- ☐taxonomist 분류학자
- ☐constitute 구성하다, 이루다
- ☐universally 보편적으로
- ☐diversity 다양성
- ☐inventory 목록

정답 ②

27 밑줄 친 부분에 들어갈 말로 가장 적절한 것은?

2020. 지방직 9급

All of us inherit something: in some cases, it may be money, property or some object — a family heirloom such as a grandmother's wedding dress or a father's set of tools. But beyond that, all of us inherit something else, something ____________________, something we may not even be fully aware of. It may be a way of doing a daily task, or the way we solve a particular problem or decide a moral issue for ourselves. It may be a special way of keeping a holiday or a tradition to have a picnic on a certain date. It may be something important or central to our thinking, or something minor that we have long accepted quite casually.

① quite unrelated to our everyday life
② against our moral standards
③ much less concrete and tangible
④ of great monetary value

해설

'우리가 완전히 알지 못하는 것, 우리의 날마다의 일을 하는 것, 특정한 문제를 해결하는 것, 도덕적인 문제들, 생각들' 등이 빈칸에 대한 예시들로 예시들을 일반화할 수 있는 표현으로 밑줄 친 부분에 들어갈 말로 가장 적절한 것은 ③이다.

해석

우리 모두는 어떤 것을 물려받는다. 어떤 경우에는, 그것은 돈, 재산 또는 할머니의 웨딩드레스나 아버지의 도구 세트와 같은 가족의 가보와 같은 어떤 물건일 수 있다. 하지만 그 외에도, 우리 모두는 다른 것을 물려받는다, <u>훨씬 덜 구체적이고 유형적인</u> 것, 심지어 우리가 완전히 알지 못할 수도 있는 것도 말이다. 그것은 일상적인 일을 하는 방법일 수도 있고, 우리가 특정한 문제를 해결하거나 우리 자신을 위한 도덕적 문제를 결정하는 방법일 수도 있다. 그것은 휴일이나 특정한 날짜에 소풍을 가는 전통을 지키는 특별한 방식일 수도 있다. 그것은 우리의 사고에 중요하거나 중심적인 것일 수도 있고, 우리가 오랫동안 무심코 받아들인 사소한 것일 수도 있다.

① 우리 일상생활과 관련이 거의 없는
② 우리 도덕적 기준에 반하는
③ 훨씬 덜 구체적이고 유형적인
④ 거대한 큰 금전적 가치를 가진

어휘

- ☐inherit 물려받다
- ☐property 재산, 자산, 토지, 특성, 속성
- ☐heirloom 가보, 세습자산
- ☐daily task 일상적인 일
- ☐particular 특정한
- ☐moral 도덕적인
- ☐minor 중요하지 않은
- ☐casually 일상적으로, 무의식적으로
- ☐concrete 구체적인, 사실에 의거한
- ☐tangible 유형의, 만질[감지할] 수 있는
- ☐monetary 금전의, 통화의

정답 ③

28 다음 빈칸에 들어갈 말로 가장 적절한 것은?

2020. 법원직 9급

> Impressionable youth are not the only ones subject to ______________. Most of us have probably had an experience of being pressured by a salesman. Have you ever had a sales rep try to sell you some "office solution" by telling you that 70 percent of your competitors are using their service, so why aren't you? But what if 70 percent of your competitors are idiots? Or what if that 70 percent were given so much value added or offered such a low price that they couldn't resist the opportunity? The practice is designed to do one thing and one thing only — to pressure you to buy. To make you feel you might be missing out on something or that everyone else knows but you.

① peer pressure ② impulse buying
③ bullying tactics ④ keen competition

해설

외부 영향과 동료압박에 대한 글로, 외부 압박과 경쟁에 대한 생각을 통해 사람들이 어떻게 영향을 받고 반응하는지를 구체적인 사례를 통해 설명하고 있다. 3번째 문장부터 6번째 문장까지가 구체적인 문장이고, 마지막 두개의 문장을 통해서 '압박'에 대한 목표에 대해 설명하고 있다. 따라서 빈칸에는 이들 일반화할 수 있는 표현으로 빈칸에 들어갈 말로 가장 적절한 것은 ①이다.

해석

> 감수성이 예민한 젊은이들만 동료 압박에 영향을 받기 쉬운 것은 아니다. 우리 대부분은 아마도 판매원에게 압력을 받은 경험이 있을 것이다. 당신은 지금까지 판매 대표가 당신에게 70%의 경쟁자들이 그들의 서비스를 사용하고 있으니, 당신은 왜 사용하지 않는가라고 말함으로 써 당신에게 '사무실용 서비스(office solution)'을 판매하려고 시도한 적이 있지 않은가? 하지만 경쟁자들 중 70%가 바보라면 어떻게 할 것인가? 아니면 그 70%에게 너무 많은 부가가치가 주어지거나 기회를 거절할 수 없을 정도로 낮은 가격을 제시한다면 어떻게 할 것인가? 이 관행은 오직 한 가지만 하기 위해 고안되었다. 당신이 무언가를 놓치고 있거나 다른 사람들이 당신만 알고 있다는 것을 느끼게 하기 위해서.

① 동료 압박
② 충동구매
③ 괴롭히기 직전
④ 치열한 경쟁

어휘

□ impressionable 감수성이 예민한, 쉽게 외부의 영향을 받는
□ youth 젊은이
□ subject to 영향을 받기 쉬운
□ salesman 판매원, 영업 사원
□ competitor 경쟁자, 참가자
□ idiot 바보
□ value added 부가 가치
□ keen 치열한, 열렬한, 예리한
□ miss out 놓치다, ~을 빠뜨리다

정답 ①

29 다음 빈칸에 들어갈 말로 가장 적절한 것은?

2020. 법원직 9급

> Much is now known about natural hazards and the negative impacts they have on people and their property. It would seem obvious that any logical person would avoid such potential impacts or at least modify their behavior or their property to minimize such impacts. However, humans are not always rational. Until someone has a personal experience or knows someone who has such an experience, most people subconsciously believe "It won't happen here" or "It won't happen to me." Even knowledgeable scientists who are aware of the hazards, the odds of their occurrence, and the costs of an event ______________________.

① refuse to remain silent
② do not always act appropriately
③ put the genetic factor at the top end
④ have difficulty in defining natural hazards

해설

자연적 위험에 대한 이해와 대처하는 사람들의 방식대한 글로, 사람들이 항상 이성적으로 대처하는 것은 아님을 것을 강조하고 있다. 빈칸에는 3번째 문장의 '그러나, 인간이 항상 이성적인 것은 아니다'의 진술과 맥락을 같이 하는 '항상 적절하게 행동하지는 않는다'가 들어가야 한다. 특히 첫 번째 문장의 '이러한 것을 잘 아는 과학자조차도 늘 피할 수 있는 것은 아니다'의 진술을 통해서 사람들이 항상 이성적인 것은 아니라는 것을 강조하고 있다. 따라서 빈칸에 들어갈 말로 가장 적절한 것은 ②이다.

해석

현재 자연적인 위험 요소들과 그것들이 사람들과 그것들의 재산에 미치는 부정적인 영향들에 대해 많은 것이 알려져 있다. 어떤 논리적인 사람이 그러한 잠재적인 영향을 피하거나 최소한 그러한 영향을 최소화하기 위해 그들의 행동이나 재산을 수정하는 것은 명백해 보일 것이다. 그러나, 인간이 항상 이성적인 것은 아니다. 누군가가 개인적인 경험을 하거나 그러한 경험을 가진 누군가를 알기 전까지, 대부분의 사람들은 무의식적으로 "여기서는 그런 일이 일어나지 않을 것이다" 또는 "나에게는 그런 일이 일어나지 않을 것이다"라고 믿는다. 위험 요소들, 그것들이 발생할 확률들, 그리고 사건의 비용에 대해 아는 것이 있는 과학자들조차 항상 적절하게 행동하지는 않는다.

① 침묵을 지키는 것을 거부하다
② 항상 적절하게 행동하지는 않는다
③ 유전적 요인을 가장 높은 목표로 둔다
④ 자연의 위험 요소를 정의하는 데 어려움을 겪다

어휘

□ hazard 위험 요소
□ negative 부정적인
□ obvious 분명한, 명백한
□ at least 적어도
□ rational 합리적인
□ modify 수정하다, 변경하다
□ subconscious 잠재의식적인, 무의식적인
□ occurrence 발생
□ appropriately 적절하게
□ property 재산, 자산, 토지, 특성, 속성
□ odds 가능성, 역경, 곤란

정답 ②

30 밑줄 친 부분에 들어갈 말로 가장 적절한 것은?

2019. 국가직 9급

Why bother with the history of everything? ___________________________________. In literature classes you don't learn about genes; in physics classes you don't learn about human evolution. So you get a partial view of the world. That makes it hard to find meaning in education. The French sociologist Emile Durkheim called this sense of disorientation and meaninglessness anomie, and he argued that it could lead to despair and even suicide. The German sociologist Max Weber talked of the "disenchantment" of the world. In the past, people had a unified vision of their world, a vision usually provided by the origin stories of their own religious traditions. That unified vision gave a sense of purpose, of meaning, even of enchantment to the world and to life. Today, though, many writers have argued that a sense of meaninglessness is inevitable in a world of science and rationality. Modernity, it seems, means meaninglessness.

① In the past, the study of history required disenchantment from science
② Recently, science has given us lots of clever tricks and meanings
③ Today, we teach and learn about our world in fragments
④ Lately, history has been divided into several categories

해설

지식의 단편화와 의미의 상실을 주제로 하는 글로, 현대 교육은 단편적인 지식으로 가득한 세계를 형성하며, 이로 인한 의미의 상실과 아노미에 대한 우려를 나타내는 글이다. 4번째 문장에서 '그리하여 당신은 부분적인 견해를 갖게 된다'의 진술을 통해서 밑줄 친 부분에 들어갈 말로 가장 적절한 것은 ③이다.

해석

왜 모든 것의 역사에 신경쓰는가? 오늘날, 우리는 단편적으로 우리의 세계에 대해 가르치고 배운다. 문학 수업에서는 유전자에 대해 배우지 않고; 물리학 수업에서는 인간의 진화에 대해 배우지 않는다. 그래서 당신은 부분적인 세계관을 가진다. 그것은 교육에서 의미를 찾는 것을 어렵게 만든다. 프랑스 사회학자 Emile Durkheim은 이 혼미감과 무의미감을 아노미라고 불렀고 그는 그것이 절망과 심지어 자살로 이어질 수 있다고 주장했다. 독일 사회학자 Max Weber는 세계의 "각성"에 관해 이야기했다. 과거에, 사람들은 그들의 세계에 대한 통일된 시각 즉, 보통 그들 자신의 종교적 전통의 기원 이야기들에 의해 제공된 시각을 가지고 있었다. 그 통일된 시각은 목적감, 의미감, 심지어 세상과 삶에 대한 황홀감을 주었다. 하지만, 오늘날, 많은 작가들은 과학과 합리성의 세계에서 무의미감은 불가피하다고 주장했다. 현대성은 무의미함을 의미하는 것 같다.

① 과거에 역사 연구는 과학으로부터의 각성을 필요로 했다
② 최근에 과학은 우리에게 많은 기발한 묘책과 의의를 주었다
③ 오늘날 우리는 우리 세계에 대해 단편적으로 가르치고 배운다
④ 최근에 역사는 몇 가지 분야로 나누어졌다

어휘

□bother 신경 쓰다, 귀찮게 하다
□gene 유전자
□evolution 진화
□partial view 부분적인 세계관
□disorientation 혼미, 방향 감각 상실
□meaninglessness 무의미함
□anomie 무질서, 사회적 불안
□despair 절망, 절망하다
□suicide 자살
□disenchantment 각성, 눈뜸, 환멸감
□unified 통일된, 통합된, 하나로 된
□inevitable 불가피한
□rationality 합리성
□modernity 현대성
□in fragments 단편적으로
□delve into 조사하다

정답 ③

31 밑줄 친 (A), (B)에 들어갈 말로 가장 적절한 것은?

2019. 지방직 9급

In the 1840s, the island of Ireland suffered famine. Because Ireland could not produce enough food to feed its population, about a million people died of __(A)__; they simply didn't have enough to eat to stay alive. The famine caused another 1.25 million people to __(B)__; many left their island home for the United States; the rest went to Canada, Australia, Chile, and other countries. Before the famine, the population of Ireland was approximately 6 million. After the great food shortage, it was about 4 million.

① dehydration − be deported
② trauma − immigrate
③ starvation − emigrate
④ fatigue − be detained

해설

1840년대 아일랜드 기근과 인구 변화에 대한 글로, 아일랜드의 기근으로 인해 약 백만 명의 사망과 약 4백만 명의 인구 변화가 발생했던 역사를 다루고 있다. (A) 뒤 문장에서 앞 문장을 보충 설명하는 구조인데, '그들은 살아남을 정도로 충분히 먹지 않았다'의 진술을 통해 '기아(starvation)'가 가장 적절하고, (B) 뒤 문장에서 '고향 섬에서 미국으로 떠났다'의 진술을 통해 '이주하다(emigrate)'가 가장 적절하다.

해석

1840년대에 아일랜드의 섬은 기근에 시달렸다. 아일랜드는 인구를 먹일 충분한 식량을 생산할 수 없었기 때문에, 약 백만 명의 사람들이 (A) 기아로 죽었다; 그들은 단지 살아남기 위해 먹기에 충분하지 않았다. 이 기근은 또 다른 125만 명의 사람들이 (B) 이주하도록 야기했다; 많은 사람들은 그들의 고향 섬에서 미국으로 떠났다; 나머지는 캐나다, 호주, 칠레, 그리고 다른 나라들로 갔다. 기근 전에 아일랜드의 인구는 약 6백만 명이었다. 그 엄청난 식량 부족 후에 그것은 약 4백만이었다.

	(A)	(B)
①	탈수	추방당하다
②	정신적 외상	이주해 오다
③	기아, 굶주림	이주하다
④	피로	구금되다

어휘

□suffer 시달리다, 고통을 받다
□famine 기근
□emigrate 이주하다
□leave for ~로 떠나다
□feed 먹이를 주다
□approximately 대략적으로
□shortage 부족

정답 ③

32 밑줄 친 부분에 들어갈 말로 가장 적절한 것은?

2019. 지방직 9급

Language proper is itself double-layered. Single noises are only occasionally meaningful: mostly, the various speech sounds convey coherent messages only when combined into an overlapping chain, like different colors of ice-cream melting into one another. In birdsong also, ____________________: the sequence is what matters. In both humans and birds, control of this specialized sound-system is exercised by one half of the brain, normally the left half, and the system is learned relatively early in life. And just as many human languages have dialects, so do some bird species: in California, the white-crowned sparrow has songs so different from area to area that Californians can supposedly tell where they are in the state by listening to these sparrows.

① individual notes are often of little value
② rhythmic sounds are important
③ dialects play a critical role
④ no sound-system exists

해설

언어의 이중성과 소리의 복잡성에 대한 글로, 언어와 소리는 중복되는 연결고리를 통해 의미를 전달하며, 인간과 새 모두에게 특화된 음성 체계가 뇌의 절반을 통해 학습되며 사용됨을 설명하고 있다. 빈칸 뒤에 이어지는 내용은 빈칸의 내용과 같은 재진술로 '배열순서가 중요하다'의 의미이므로 빈칸에 들어갈 말로 가장 적절한 것은 ①이다.

해석

엄밀한 의미의 언어는 그 자체로 두 개의 층을 이루고 있다. 개별적 소음들은 단지 가끔씩만 의미가 있다. 대부분의 경우 다채로운 말의 소리가 중복되는 연결고리를 통해 결합되었을 때에만 일관성 있는 메시지를 전달하게 되는데 이는 마치 다양한 색깔의 아이스크림이 녹아 서로 섞이는 것과 같다. 새소리에 있어서도 또한 개별적인 음들은 종종 거의 의미가 없다: 배열순서가 중요하다. 인간과 새 둘 다에게 있어 이러한 특화된 음성 체계를 조절하는 것은 뇌의 절반, 주로 왼쪽 절반에 의해 행하여지며 그 체계는 상대적으로 삶의 초기에 학습된다. 그리고 많은 인간의 언어가 방언을 가지고 있듯이 몇몇 종의 새들 역시 그러하다: 캘리포니아에서 흰줄무늬 참새는 지역마다 다른 노랫소리를 갖고 있어서 캘리포니아 사람들은 아마도 이러한 참새 소리를 들음으로써 자신이 그 주의 어디에 있는지를 구별할 수 있을 것이다.

① 개별적인 음들은 종종 거의 의미가 없다
② 주기적인 소리가 중요하다
③ 방언이 중요한 역할을 하다
④ 어떤 소리 체계도 존재하지 않다

어휘

□ layered 층이 있는, 층을 이룬
□ occasionally 가끔
□ meaningful 의미 있는
□ convey 전달하다
□ coherent 일관성 있는, 논리 정연한
□ overlapping 겹쳐진
□ sequence 순서, 차례
□ dialect 방언, 사투리
□ white-crowned sparrow 흰줄무늬 참새
□ area 지역
□ note 음, 음표, 메모, 주목[주의]하다
□ rhythmic 주기적인

정답 ①

33 밑줄 친 부분에 들어갈 말로 가장 적절한 것은?

2019. 지방직 9급

Nobel Prize-winning psychologist Daniel Kahneman changed the way the world thinks about economics, upending the notion that human beings are rational decision-makers. Along the way, his discipline-crossing influence has altered the way physicians make medical decisions and investors evaluate risk on Wall Street. In a paper, Kahneman and his colleagues outline a process for making big strategic decisions. Their suggested approach, labeled as "Mediating Assessments Protocol," or MAP, has a simple goal: To put off gut-based decision-making until a choice can be informed by a number of separate factors. "One of the essential purposes of MAP is basically to __________ intuition," Kahneman said in a recent interview with The Post. The structured process calls for analyzing a decision based on six to seven previously chosen attributes, discussing each of them separately and assigning them a relative percentile score, and finally, using those scores to make a holistic judgment.

① improve
② delay
③ possess
④ facilitate

해설

심리학자 Daniel Kahneman으로 말미암은 의사결정과 경제학의 패러다임 변화에 대한 글로, '인간은 이성적 의사결정자들이다'의 '통념'을 바탕으로, 이것을 논박하는 단락구조를 가지고 있다. 빈칸 앞에서 진술한 '하나의 선택이 다수의 개별적 요소들에 의해 설명될 때까지 배짱에 의거한 의사결정을 지연시키는 것이다'의 진술을 통해서 밑줄 친 부분에 들어갈 말로 가장 적절한 것은 ②이다.

해석

노벨상 수상자인 심리학자 Daniel Kahneman은 인간이 이성적 의사결정자라는 개념을 뒤집으며 경제학에 관한 세계의 사고방식을 변화시켰다. 그 과정에서 그의 학문 전체에 걸친 영향력은 의사들이 의학적 결정을 내리는 방식, 그리고 투자가들이 월 스트리트에서의 위험을 평가하는 방식을 변화시켰다. 한 논문에서 Kahneman과 그의 동료들은 큰 전략적 결정을 내리기 위한 과정에 대한 개요를 제시했다. '조정 평가 프로토콜', 혹은 MAP라고 부르는 그들이 제시한 접근법은 한 가지 간단한 목표를 갖는다: 하나의 선택이 다수의 개별적 요소들에 의해 설명될 때까지 직감에 의거한 의사결정을 연기하는 것이다. "MAP의 가장 중요한 목표 중에 하나는 기본적으로 직감을 미루는 것이다"라고 Kahneman은 최근 '포스트'와의 인터뷰에서 말했다. 이러한 구조화된 과정은 이전에 선택된 여섯 개에서 일곱 개의 요소들에 의거하여 하나의 결정을 분해하고 각각을 개별적으로 논의한 후, 이들에게 상대적인 백분점수를 부여하고 마지막으로 총체적 판단을 위해 그 점수를 사용할 것을 요구한다.

① 개선시키다
② 미루다
③ 소유하다
④ 용이하게 하다, 촉진하다

어휘

□ psychologist 심리학자
□ upend 철저한[근본적인] 영향을 주다, 거꾸로 세우다, 엎어놓다
□ rational 합리적인, 이성적인
□ discipline 훈육, 훈련, 학과
□ alter 변경하다, 바꾸다
□ evaluate 평가하다
□ outline 개요를 제시하다, 윤곽을 보여주다
□ label ~라고 부르다, 분류하다
□ gut 직감, 창자, 배짱
□ intuition 직감, 직관
□ call for 요구하다
□ attribute 특성, 탓으로 돌리다
□ holistic 전체적인, 종합적인

정답 ②

34 글의 흐름상 빈칸에 들어갈 말로 가장 적절한 것은?

2019. 서울시 9급

"Highly conscientious employees do a series of things better than the rest of us," says University of Illinois psychologist Brent Roberts, who studies conscientiousness. Roberts owes their success to "hygiene" factors. Conscientious people have a tendency to organize their lives well. A disorganized, unconscientious person might lose 20 or 30 minutes rooting through their files to find the right document, an inefficient experience conscientious folks tend to avoid. Basically, by being conscientious, people ________________ they'd otherwise create for themselves.

① deal with setbacks
② do thorough work
③ follow norms
④ sidestep stress

해설

양심, 생활위생 그리고 성공과의 관계를 주제로 하는 글로, 일반적으로 성실한 사람들은 생활을 잘 정돈하며 일을 효율적으로 처리함으로써 성공을 이루는 경향이 있다는 심리학적 연구 결과를 보여주는 글이다. 결국 성실하면 불성실과 무질서로 인해 초래되는 스트레스를 겪지 않아도 된다는 표현이 들어가야 한다. 따라서 빈칸에 들어갈 말로 가장 적절한 것은 ④이다.

해석

"매우 성실한 직원들은 나머지 우리들보다 일련의 업무를 더 잘한다."고 Illinois 대학 심리학자 Brent Roberts는 말하는데, 그는 성실함을 연구했다. Roberts는 그들의 성공을 "위생" 요인들에 돌렸다. 성실한 사람들은 그들의 생활을 잘 정돈하는 경향이 있다. 무질서한, 불성실한 사람은 그들의 파일들 사이에서 올바른 서류를 뽑아내기 위해 20분이나 30분을 허비할지도 모르는데, 이는 성실한 사람이라면 피하는 경향이 있는 비효율적인 경험이다. 기본적으로, 사람들은 성실함으로써, 자신들이 그렇지 않으면 만들어낼 스트레스를 회피한다.

① 방해들을 처리하다
② 철저히 일하다
③ 규범을 따르다
④ 스트레스를 회피하다

어휘

□ conscientious 양심적인, 성실한
□ a series of 일련의

□ psychologist 심리학자
□ hygiene 위생
□ tendency 경향, 동향, 성향
□ organize 조직하다, 정리하다
□ inefficient 비효율적인
□ otherwise 그렇지 않으면, 다른 방식으로
□ deal with 처리하다
□ setback 방해, 차질
□ thorough 철저한, 빈틈없는
□ norm 규범, 규준, 기준
□ sidestep 회피하다, 피하다

정답 ④

35 글의 흐름상 빈칸에 들어갈 말로 가장 적절한 것은?

2019. 서울시 9급

Climate change, deforestation, widespread pollution and the sixth mass extinction of biodiversity all define living in our world today — an era that has come to be known as "the Anthropocene". These crises are underpinned by production and consumption which greatly exceeds global ecological limits, but blame is far from evenly shared. The world's 42 wealthiest people own as much as the poorest 3.7 billion, and they generate far greater environmental impacts. Some have therefore proposed using the term "Capitalocene" to describe this era of ecological devastation and growing inequality, reflecting capitalism's logic of endless growth and ______________.

① the better world that is still within our reach
② the accumulation of wealth in fewer pockets
③ an effective response to climate change
④ a burning desire for a more viable future

해설

환경 파괴와 불평등의 시대를 주제로 하는 글로, 이 글은 기후 변화, 환경 파괴, 대량 멸종 등의 위기로 인한 현재의 지구 상황과 이로 인한 불평등을 강조하며, 'Capitalocene'이라는 용어를 제안하여 자본주의와 환경 파괴의 관련성을 강조하는 글이다. 빈칸 앞 문장에 세계에서 가장 부유한 40여 명이 최빈층 37억 명의 재산을 합한 만큼을 소유하며 환경에도 더 지대한 영향을 미치고 있다는 내용을 다루고 있다. 따라서 빈칸에 들어갈 말로 가장 적절한 것은 ②이다.

해석

기후 변화, 산림파괴, 널리 퍼진 오염, 그리고 생물의 다양성의 여섯 번째 대량 멸종 모두 오늘날 우리 세계에서의 모든 삶을 정의한다 — (즉) "인류세"로 알려지게 된 시대로 정의한다. 이러한 위기들은 세계적인 환경적인 한계들을 매우 초과하는 생산과 소비들에 의해 만들어 졌으나, 그러나 비난은 공평하게 공유되지 않는다. 세상의 42명의 가장 부자들이 가난한 37억 명의 부만큼을 가지고 있으며, 그들은 더 큰 환경적인 충격들을 만들어 낸다. 그래서, 몇몇 사람들은 끝없는 성장의 자본주의의 논리와 소수의 주머니로의 부의 축적이라는 자본주의의 논리를 반영하면서, 생태계의 파괴의 시대와 점점 커져가는 불평등을 묘사하기 위해서 "Capitalocene"이라는 용어를 사용하는 것을 제안해 왔다.

① 여전히 우리가 도달할 수 있는 더 좋은 세상
② 소수의 주머니로의 부의 축적
③ 기후변화에의 효과적인 대응
④ 더욱 성공할 수 있는 미래를 향한 불타는 욕망

어휘

□ deforestation 산림 파괴, 산림 벌채
□ mass 대규모의
□ widespread 널리 퍼진, 보편적인
□ extinction 멸종
□ biodiversity 생물 다양성
□ Anthropocene 인류세
□ underpin 뒷받침하다, 근거를 대다
□ ecological 생태계의
□ far from 전혀 ~이 아닌
□ generate 발생시키다, 만들어내다
□ impact 영향, 충격
□ evenly 균등하게
□ devastation 황폐화, 대대적인 파괴
□ inequality 불평등
□ reflect 반영하다
□ viable 성공[실행] 가능한

정답 ②

36 다음 빈칸에 들어갈 말로 가장 적절한 것은?

2019. 법원직 9급

With the present plummeting demand market for office buildings, resulting in many vacant properties, we need to develop plans that will enable some future exchange between residential and commercial or office functions. This vacancy has reached a historic level; at present the major towns in the Netherlands have some five million square metres of unoccupied office space, while there is a shortage of 160,000 homes. At least a million of those square metres can be expected to stay vacant, according to the association of Dutch property developers. There is a real threat of 'ghost towns' of empty office buildings springing up around the major cities. In spite of this forecast, office building activities are continuing at full tilt, as these were planned during a period of high returns. Therefore, it is now essential that ______________________.

① a new design be adopted to reduce costs for the maintenance of buildings
② a number of plans for office buildings be redeveloped for housing
③ residential buildings be converted into commercial buildings
④ we design and deliver as many shops as possible

해설

도시 공간의 활용의 일환으로 오피스 빌딩을 주거용으로 재개발하는 것을 주제로 하는 글로, 현재 사무용 건물 공석과 주택 부족 문제를 해결하기 위해 오피스 빌딩을 주거용으로 재개발해야 하는 필요성을 강조하고 있다. 따라서 빈칸에 들어갈 말로 가장 적절한 것은 ②이다.

해석

현재 사무실용 건물의 수요 시장이 폭락하여 많은 비어있는 건물이 발생함에 따라, 우리는 주거용과 상업용 또는 사무용 기능의 교환이 가능한 계획을 개발할 필요가 있다. 이 빈자리는 역사적인 수준에 도달했다. 현재 네덜란드의 주요 도시들은 약 5백만 평방미터의 사무실 공간을 가지고 있는 반면 16만 채의 집이 부족하다. 네덜란드 부동산 개발 협회에 따르면 이 평방미터 중 적어도 100만미터는 공석이 될 것으로 예상된다고 한다. 주요 도시 주변에는 빈 사무실용 건물들로 이루어진 '유령 도시'의 위협이 현실화되고 있다. 이러한 전망에도 불구하고, 사무실용 건물 활동은 고수익의 기간 동안 계획되었던 것처럼 완전히 기울어져 계속되고 있다. 그러므로, 사무실용 건물에 대한 많은 계획이 주택을 위한 것으로 재개발되어야 하는 것이 필수적이다.

① 건물의 유지관리 비용을 줄이기 위해 새로운 디자인이 채택되어야 한다
② 사무실용 건물에 대한 많은 계획이 주택을 위한 것으로 재개발되어야 한다
③ 주거용 건물 상업용 건물로 전환되어야 한다
④ 우리는 가능한 한 많은 가게를 설계하고 전달한다

어휘

□ plummet 급락하다, 곤두박질치다
□ vacant 비어 있는
□ property 재산, 자산, 토지, 특성, 속성
□ exchange 교환, 교환하다
□ unoccupied 비어있는, 점령되지 않은
□ shortage 부족
□ ghost town 유령 도시
□ high return 고소득, 고수익
□ convert 개조하다, 전환시키다

정답 ②

37 다음 빈칸에 들어갈 말로 가장 적절한 것은?

2019. 법원직 9급

Although we all possess the same physical organs for sensing the world — eyes for seeing, ears for hearing, noses for smelling, skin for feeling, and mouths for tasting — our perception of the world depends to a great extent on the language we speak, according to a famous hypothesis proposed by linguists Edward Sapir and Benjamin Lee Whorf. They hypothesized that language is like a pair of eyeglasses through which we "see" the world in a particular way. A classic example of the relationship between language and perception is the word snow. Eskimo languages have as many as 32 different words for snow. For instance, the Eskimos have different words for falling snow, snow on the ground, snow packed as hard as ice, slushy snow, wind-driven snow, and what we might call "cornmeal" snow. The ancient Aztec languages of Mexico, in contrast, used only one word to mean snow, cold, and ice. Thus, if the Sapir-Whorf hypothesis is correct and we can perceive only things that we have words for, the Aztecs perceived snow, cold, and ice as ______________________.

① one and the same phenomenon
② being distinct from one another
③ separate things with unique features
④ something sensed by a specific physical organ

해설

언어와 지각의 관계를 에스키모어와 아즈텍어의 비교를 통해서 설명하는 글로, 언어학자의 가설에 따르면, 언어에 따라 우리의 지각도 달라진다는 것이다. 빈칸에는 에스키모어는 눈에 대해 32가지 다른 단어를 가지고 있는 것과 대조를 이루는 내용이 나와야 하며, 아즈텍어는 눈, 추위, 얼음을 하나의 단어로 구분하지 않아서 '하나의 같은 현상'으로 인식함을 표현해야 한다. 따라서 빈칸에 들어갈 말로 가장 적절한 것은 ①이다.

해석

비록 우리 모두는 보는 눈, 듣는 귀, 냄새 맡는 코, 느끼는 피부, 맛보는 입과 같은 세상을 감지하는 동일한 신체적 기관을 가지고 있지만 언어학자 Edward Sapir와 Benjamin Lee Whorf에 의해 제안된 유명한 가설에 따르면, 세상에 대한 우리의 인식은 우리가 말하는 언어에 상당 부분 의존한다. 그들은 언어는 우리가 특정한 방식으로 세상을 "보는" 안경과 같다고 가설을 세웠다. 언어와 인식 사이의 관계에 대한 대표적인 예는 눈이라는 단어이다. 에스키모 언어들은 눈에 대한 32개의 다른 단어들을 가지고 있다. 예를 들어, 에스키모어들은 내리는 눈, 땅 위의 눈, 얼음처럼 단단하게 쌓인 눈, 미끄러운 눈, 바람이 불면 움직이는 눈, 그리고 우리가 "옥수수 가루"라고 부르는 눈에 대한 다른 단어들을 가지고 있다. 대조적으로, 멕시코의 고대 아즈텍 언어들은 눈, 추위, 그리고 얼음을 의미하는 단 하나의 단어만을 사용했다. 그러므로, 만일 Sapir-Whorf 가설이 맞고 우리가 단어를 가지고 있는 것들만 인식할 수 있다면, 아즈텍 사람들은 눈, 추위, 그리고 얼음을 <u>하나의 같은 현상</u>으로 인식했다.

① 하나의 같은 현상
② 서로 구별되는 것
③ 독특한 특징을 가진 별개의 것들
④ 특정한 신체 기관에 의해 감지되는 어떤 것

어휘

□perception 지각, 자각, 통찰력
□language 언어
□hypothesis 가설, 추정, 추측
□linguist 언어학자
□classic 전형적인, 대표적인
□perceive 감지하다, 인지하다, 인식하다
□phenomenon 현상
□separate 별개의, 구분된, 분리된, 서로 다른

정답 ①

38 밑줄 친 부분에 들어갈 말로 가장 적절한 것은?

2018. 국가직 9급

Kisha Padbhan, founder of Everonn Education, in Mumbai, looks at his business as nation-building. India's student-age population of 230 million (kindergarten to college) is one of the largest in the world. The government spends $83 billion on instruction, but there are serious gaps. "There aren't enough teachers and enough teacher-training institutes," says Kisha. "What children in remote parts of India lack is access to good teachers and exposure to good-quality content." Everonn's solution? The company uses a satellite network, with two-way video and audio ______________________. It reaches 1,800 colleges and 7,800 schools across 24 of India's 28 states. It offers everything from digitized school lessons to entrance exam prep for aspiring engineers and has training for job-seekers, too.

① to improve the quality of teacher training facilities
② to bridge the gap through virtual classrooms
③ to get students familiarized with digital technology
④ to locate qualified instructors across the nation

해설

인도의 교육 혁신을 이끄는 Everonn Education의 역할을 소재로 하는 글로, Everonn Education의 설립자 Kisha Padbhan은 인도의 대규모 교육 시스템을 향상시키기 위해 가상 교실과 강의를 활용하는 방법을 제시하며, 이를 통해 교사 부족과 교육 격차를 해소하려는 노력하고 있음을 진술하고 있다. 빈칸은 앞 문장에 제시한 'Everonn의 해결책'이 나와야 하며, 8번째 문장부터는 그 해결책으로 제시된 사례들을 진술하고 있다. 따라서 밑줄 친 부분에 들어갈 말로 가장 적절한 것은 ②이다.

해석

Mumbai시에 있는 Everonn Education의 설립자인 Kisha Padbhan는 그의 사업을 국가 건설로 본다. 인도의 2억 3천만 명(유치원부터 대학까지)의 학생 연령 인구는 세계에서 가장 큰 규모 중 하나이다. 정부는 8백 3십억 달러를 교육에 쓰지만, 심각한 격차가 존재한다. "교사와 교사 교육 기관이 충분하지 않다"라고 Kisha는 말한다. "인도 외딴 지역의 아이들에게 부족한 것은 좋은 교사와 양질의 내용에 대한 노출이다." Everonn의 해결책은 무엇인가? <u>가상 교실을 통해 그 격차를 메우기 위해</u> 이 회사는 양방향 비디오와 오디오를 활용한 위성 네트워크를 사용한다. 이것은 인도 28개 주 중 24개 주의 1800개 대학과 7800개 학교에 연결된다. 또한 이것은 디지털화된 수업부터 장차 엔지니어가 되기 위한 입학 시험 준비과정에 이르기까지 모든 것을 제공하고 구직자를 위한 훈련 과정도 있다.

① 교사 교육 시설의 질을 향상시키기 위해
② 가상교실을 통해 그 격차를 메우기 위해
③ 학생들을 디지털 기술에 익숙하게 하기 위해
④ 자질을 갖춘 교육자를 전국에 배치하기 위해

어휘

□ founder 창립자, 설립자
□ kindergarten 유치원
□ instruction 교육, 가르침, 명령, 지시
□ institute 기관, 단체, 협회
□ access 접근, 접근하다
□ exposure 노출, 경험
□ content 내용
□ satellite 위성
□ entrance 입장, 등장
□ prep 예습, 준비
□ aspiring 장차 ~가 되려는, 포부가 있는
□ job-seeker 구직자
□ familiarize 익숙하게 하다
□ two-way 양방향의

정답 ②

39 밑줄 친 부분에 들어갈 말로 가장 적절한 것은?

2018. 지방직 9급

In our time it is not only the law of the market which has its own life and rules over man, but also the development of science and technique. For a number of reasons, the problems and organization of science today are such that a scientist does not choose his problems; the problems force themselves upon the scientist. He solves one problem, and the result is not that he is more secure or certain, but that ten other new problems open up in place of the single solved one. They force him to solve them; he has to go ahead at an ever-quickening pace. The same holds true for industrial techniques. The pace of science forces the pace of technique. Theoretical physics forces atomic energy on us; the successful production of the fission bomb forces upon us the manufacture of the hydrogen bomb. We do not choose our problems, we do not choose our products; we are pushed, we are forced — by what? By a system which has no purpose and goal transcending it, and which ________________________.

① makes man its appendix
② creates a false sense of security
③ inspires man with creative challenges
④ empowers scientists to control the market laws

해설

과학과 기술의 발전에서 나타나는 지배력과 강제성에 대한 글로, 과학과 기술의 발전으로 인해 현대 사회에서 인간을 지배하고 강제하는 현상에 대해 설명하고 있다. 이 글은 세부적인 사항을 열거한 다음 주제문을 의문문과 그것에 대한 답변으로 제시하고 있다. 문제점의 원인을 '목적과 목표가 없고, 인간을 비인간화 시키는 것'으로 보고 있다. 따라서 밑줄 친 부분에 들어갈 말로 가장 적절한 것은 ①이다.

해석

우리의 시대에 자신의 생명력을 가지고 사람들을 지배하는 것은 시장법칙뿐만 아니라 과학과 기술의 발전 또한 그러하다. 수많은 이유들 때문에, 과학의 문제들과 조직은 오늘날 그러해서 과학자는 그의 문제를 선택하지 않다; 문제들이 그 과학자들을 강제한다. 그는 하나의 문제를 풀고, 그 결과는 그가 더 안전하고 확신하는 것이 아니라, 열 개의 다른 새로운 문제들이 하나의 문제가 있었던 곳에 열려있다. 그 문제들은 과학자가 그것들을 해결하게 강제한다; 그는 지금까지 보다 더 빠른 속도로 앞서 나가야 한다. 산업의 기술에게도 마찬가지이다. 과학의 속도는 기술의 속도를 강제한다. 이론 물리학은 우리에게 원자 에너지를 강제하고, 원자 폭탄의 성공적인 생산은 우리에게 수소 폭탄의 제조를 강제한다. 우리는 우리의 문제들을 선택하지 않고, 우리는 우리의 제품들을 선택하지 않는다; 우리는 강제 된다 — 무엇에 의해서 일까? 그것을 초월하는 목적과 목표가 없고, 인간을 그것의 부속물로 만드는 시스템에 의해서다.

① 인간을 그것의 부속물로 만든다
② 안전성의 잘못된 인식을 만든다
③ 창의적인 도전들로 사람에게 영감을 준다
④ 과학자들이 시장법을 통제하도록 권한을 부여한다

어휘

□ rule over 지배하다
□ fission bomb 원자 폭탄
□ manufacture 제조, 생산, 제조하다
□ hydrogen bomb 수소 폭탄
□ transcend 초월하다, 능가하다
□ appendix 부속물, 부록
□ empower 권한을 부여하다
□ secure 안전한, 확고한

정답 ①

40 밑줄 친 부분에 들어갈 말로 가장 적절한 것은?

2018. 지방직 9급

The secret of successful people is usually that they are able to concentrate totally on one thing. Even if they have a lot in their head, they have found a method that the many commitments don't impede each other, but instead they are brought into a good inner order. And this order is quite simple: ____________________. In theory, it seems to be quite clear, but in everyday life it seems rather different. You might have tried to decide on priorities, but you have failed because of everyday trivial matters and all the unforeseen distractions. Separate off disturbances, for example, by escaping into another office, and not allowing any distractions to get in the way. When you concentrate on the one task of your priorities, you will find you have energy that you didn't even know you had.

① the sooner, the better
② better late than never
③ out of sight, out of mind
④ the most important thing first

해설

성공한 사람들의 비밀인 집중의 힘에 대한 글로, 성공한 사람들이 하나에 집중하고 우선 순위를 설정하여 내적 질서로 이끌어내야함을 강조하고 있다. 빈칸에는 우선 순위를 의미하는 표현이 나와야 한다. 따라서 밑줄 친 부분에 들어갈 말로 가장 적절한 것은 ④이다.

해석

성공한 사람들의 비밀은 보통 그들이 한 가지 일에 완전히 집중할 수 있다는 것이다. 비록 그들의 머릿속에 많은 것이 있다 하더라도, 그들은 많은 약속들이 서로를 방해하지 않고, 대신 좋은 내적 순서로 이끌어내는 방법을 발견했다. 그리고 이 순서는 꽤 간단하다: 가장 중요한 일이 먼저다. 이론적으로, 그것은 꽤 명확해 보이지만, 일상생활에서 그것은 오히려 다르게 보인다. 당신은 우선순위를 결정하려고 노력했을지 모르지만, 매일의 사소한 문제들과 예측하지 못한 모든 방해들 때문에 실패했다. 예를 들어, 다른 사무실로 도망치고, 어떠한 방해도 받지 않도록 함으로써, 방해를 분리하라. 당신이 우선순위의 한 가지 일에 집중할 때, 당신은 당신이 가지고 있었는지도 몰랐던 에너지를 가지고 있다는 것을 발견할 것이다.

① 빠를수록 더 좋다
② 전혀 하지 않는 것보다 늦는 것이 더 낫다
③ 눈에서 멀어지면, 마음에서 멀어진다
④ 가장 중요한 일이 먼저다

어휘

□ concentrate 집중하다, 전념하다
□ commitment 약속, 전념, 헌신, 책무
□ impede 방해하다, 지연시키다
□ priority 우선순위
□ trivial 사소한, 하찮은
□ unforeseen 예측하지 못한, 뜻밖의
□ distraction 방해, 주의 산만
□ disturbance 방해, 소란, 장애
□ escape 도망하다, 달아나다
□ get in the way 방해되다

정답 ④

41 다음 글의 빈칸에 들어갈 말로 가장 적절한 것은?

2018. 법원직 9급

A great ad is a wonderful thing; it's why you love advertising. But what you're looking at is only half of what's there, and the part you can't see has more to do with that ad's success than the part you can. Before those surface features (the terrific headline or visual or storyline or characters or voiceover or whatever) can work their wonders, the ad has to have something to say, something that matters. Either it addresses real consumer motives and real consumer problems, or it speaks to no one. To make great ads, then, you have to start where they start: with ____________________.

① the effective tool
② the invisible part
③ the corporate needs
④ the surface features

해설

광고 성공의 보이지 않는 부분에 대한 글로, 광고의 성공에 있어 시각적인 표면 뒤의 숨겨진 요소 사이의 관계를 강조하는 글이다. 2번째 문장에서 '당신이 볼 수 없는 부분이 당신이 볼 수 있는 부분보다 광고의 성공과 더 관련이 있다'의 진술을 통해서 빈칸은 겉으로 드러나지 않는 부분을 의미하는 표현이 나와야 한다. 따라서 빈칸에 들어갈 말로 가장 적절한 것은 ②이다.

해석

훌륭한 광고는 멋진 것이다; 그래서 당신이 광고를 좋아하는 것이다. 하지만 당신이 보고 있는 것은 거기에 있는 것의 절반에 불과하고, 당신이 볼 수 없는 부분은 당신이 볼 수 있는 부분보다 그 광고의 성공과 더 많은 관련이 있다. 표면의 특징들(멋진 표제, 시각적인 것, 줄거리, 등장인물들, 해설 소리 또는 무엇이든)이 놀라운 효과를 발휘하기 전에, 광고는 중요한 할 말이 있어야 한다. 그것은 실제 소비자 동기나 실제 소비자 문제를 다루거나, 아무에게도 말하지 않는다. 그렇다면, 훌륭한 광고를 만들기 위해서는 광고가 시작하는 곳에서 시작해야 한다: 보이지 않는 부분에서 말이다.

① 효과적인 도구
② 보이지 않는 부분
③ 기업의 요구 사항들
④ 표면의 특징들

어휘

□ advertising 광고
□ surface 표면, 겉, 표면의, 피상적인
□ feature 특징, 특성
□ headline 표제, 주요 제목
□ visual 시각적인
□ voiceover (TV따위의 화면 밖의) 해설 소리
□ matter 문제, 상황, 중요하다, 문제되다
□ address 다루다, 연설하다
□ consumer 소비자
□ motive 동기, 이유
□ invisible 보이지 않는, 무형의
□ corporate 기업의, 회사의

정답 ②

42 빈칸 (A), (B)에 들어갈 말로 가장 적절한 것은?

2017. 국가직 9급

The amount of information gathered by the eyes as contrasted with the ears has not been precisely calculated. Such a calculation not only involves a translation process, but scientists have been handicapped by lack of knowledge of what to count. A general notion, however, of the relative complexities of the two systems can be obtained by ((A)) the size of the nerves connecting the eyes and the ears to the centers of the brain. Since the optic nerve contains roughly eighteen times as many neurons as the cochlear nerve, we assume it transmits at least that much more information. Actually, in normally alert subjects, it is probable that the eyes may be as much as a thousand times as effective as the ears in ((B)) information.

* cochlear 달팽이관의

	(A)	(B)
①	comparing	…… sweeping up
②	comparing	…… reducing
③	adding	…… disseminating
④	adding	…… clearing up

해설

눈과 귀의 정보 수집과 정보 처리의 차이를 주제로 하는 글로, 눈과 귀의 상대적인 복잡성과 신경 크기를 통해 정보 전달의 효율성을 서로 비교하고 있다.

(A) 4번째 문장에서 '시신경은 달팽이관 신경보다 약 18배 많다'는 진술을 통해서, '눈과 귀를 뇌의 중심에 연결하는 신경들의 크기'를 '추가하는(adding)' 것보다는 '비교하는(comparing)' 것이 가장 적절하다.

(B) '눈이 귀보다 정보를 무엇하는데 수천 배 더 효율적이다'라는 진술을 통해서, 눈으로 수집하는 정보의 양에 대한 글이므로 '모으다 (sweeping up)'가 가장 적절하다.

해석

눈에 의해 수집된 정보의 양은 귀와는 대조적으로 정확하게 계산되지 않았다. 그러한 계산은 번역 과정을 포함할 뿐만 아니라 과학자들은 무엇을 중요한지에 대한 지식 부족으로 인해 장애를 겪어 왔다. 그러나 두 체계의 상대적 복잡성에 대한 일반적인 개념은 눈과 귀 사이를 연결하는 신경들의 크기를 뇌의 중심과 (A) 비교함으로써 얻을 수 있다. 시신경은 달팽이관 신경보다 약 18배 많은 뉴런을 포함하고 있기 때문에 훨씬 더 많은 정보를 전달한다고 가정한다. 사실, 정상적으로 위험을 알리는 대상들에 있어서, 아마도 정보를 (B) 쓸어 모으는 데 있어 눈이 귀의 수천 배 더 효율적일 지도 모른다.

(A) (B)

① 비교하는 …… 쓸어 모으는 데
② 비교하는 …… 줄이는 데
③ 추가하는 …… 전파하는 데
④ 추가하는 …… 정리하는 데

어휘

□contrast with ~와 대조를 이루다
□precisely 정확하게, 신중하게
□calculate 계산하다, 산출하다
□translation 번역
□handicap 장애, 불리한 조건
□count 중요하다, 세다
□notion 개념, 생각
□complexity 복잡성
□optic nerve 시신경
□roughly 대략, 거의
□assume 가정하다, 추측하다
□transmit 전송하다, 보내다
□alert 기민한, 경계하는, (위험 등을)알리다
□sweep up 쓸다, 쓸어 담다
□disseminate 퍼뜨리다, 전파하다

정답 ①

43 밑줄 친 부분에 들어갈 말로 가장 적절한 것은?

2017. 국가직 9급

Why might people hovering near the poverty line be more likely to help their fellow humans? Part of it, Keltner thinks, is that poor people must often band together to make it through tough times — a process that probably makes them more socially astute. He says, "When you face uncertainty, it makes you orient to other people. You build up these strong social networks." When a poor young mother has a new baby, for instance, she may need help securing food, supplies, and childcare, and if she has healthy social times, members of her community will pitch in. But limited income is hardly a prerequisite for developing this kind of empathy and social responsiveness. Regardless of the size of our bank accounts, suffering becomes a conduit to altruism or heroism when our own pain compels us to be ______________ other people's needs and to intervene when we see someone in the clutches of the kind of suffering we know so well.

① more indifferent to
② more attentive to
③ less preoccupied with
④ less involved in

해설

빈곤선 근처에 있는 사람들이 왜 동료들을 더 도와주는지에 대한 이유를 설명하는 글이다. 첫 번째 문장(의문문)의 대답으로 가난한 사람들이 그들의 동료들을 더 잘 도와주는 경향이 있는 이유로 적절한 것을 선택해야 한다. 따라서 빈칸은 '고통이 있는 사람이 그 고통을 더 잘 알기에 고통이 있는 사람에 공감을 느끼고 도와주고 더 주의를 기울인다'는 진술로 이어져야 한다. 따라서 밑줄 친 부분에 들어갈 말로 가장 적절한 것은 ②이다.

해석

왜 빈곤선 근처에 맴도는 사람들이(가난에 가까운 사람들이) 동료들을 더 도와줄 가능성이 높은가? Keltner는 부분적으로는 가난한 사람들의 경우 힘든 시기들을 견뎌내기 위해 자주 함께 뭉쳐야만 한다고 생각한다 — 이것은 아마 그들을 좀 더 사회적으로 기민하게 만드는 과정이다. 그는 "만약 여러분이 불확실성에 직면한다면, 그것이 여러분으로 하여금 좀 더 다른 사람에게 적응시키도록 만들어 준다. 당신은 이와 같은 강력한 사회적 관계망을 형성하게 될 것이다"라고 말한다. 예를 들어, 만약 가난한 젊은 엄마에게 갓 태어난 아기가 있다면 그녀는 음식과 생필품, 그리고 육아를 확보하기 위한 도움이 필요할 수도 있을 것이고, 만약 그녀가 건강한 사회생활을 하고 있다면 그녀의 공동체 멤버들은 협력할 것이다. 그러나 제한된 수입은 이러한 공감과 사회적 반응성을 개발하는데 있어 거의 필수적인 조건은 아니다. 우리의 은행 계좌의 크기(잔액)와는 상관없이, 우리 자신의 고통이 다른 사람들의 필요에 더 주의를 기울이도록 강제하고 우리가 잘 알고 있는 그런 고통에 빠진 사람을 보고 개입할 때, 고통은 이타주의 혹은 영웅주의에 전달자가 된다.

① 더 무관심한
② 더 주의를 기울이는
③ 덜 사로잡혀 있는
④ 덜 관련되는

어휘

□hover 맴돌다
□poverty line 빈곤선(최저한도의 생활을 유지하는 데 필요한 수입 수준)
□band together 함께 뭉치다, 무리를 이루다
□tough 힘든, 어려운
□astute 교활한, 약삭빠른
□uncertainty 불확실성
□orient to ~에 적응시키다
□secure 안심하는, 안전한, 획득하다, 확보하다
□pitch in 협력하다
□prerequisite 전제 조건
□empathy 감정이입, 공감
□regardless of ~에 상관없이
□conduit 전달자

□ altruism 이타주의, 이타심
□ intervene 개입하다, 끼어들다
□ in the clutches 괴로운 상황에, 위기에 처해서

정답 ②

44 밑줄 친 부분에 들어갈 말로 가장 적절한 것은?

2017. 국가직 9급

The Soleil department store outlet in Shanghai would seem to have all the amenities necessary to succeed in modern Chinese retail: luxury brands and an exclusive location. Despite these advantages, however, the store's management thought it was still missing something to attract customers. So next week they're unveiling a gigantic, twisting, dragon-shaped slide that shoppers can use to drop from fifth-floor luxury boutiques to first-floor luxury boutiques in death-defying seconds. Social media users are wondering, half-jokingly, whether the slide will kill anyone. But Soleil has a different concern that Chinese shopping malls will go away completely. Chinese shoppers, once seemingly in endless supply, are no longer turning up at brick-and-mortar outlets because of the growing online shopping, and they still go abroad to buy luxury goods. So, repurposing these massive spaces for consumers who have other ways to spend their time and money is likely to require a lot of creativity. ________________________________.

① Luxury brands are thriving at Soleil
② Soleil has decided against making bold moves
③ Increasing the online customer base may be the last hope
④ A five-story dragon slide may not be a bad place to start

해설

상하이 Soleil 백화점 아웃렛의 독특한 시도에 대한 글로, 상하이의 Soleil 백화점 아웃렛이 고객 유치를 위한 창의적인 방법으로 대담한 미끄럼틀 도입을 시도하며, 오프라인 쇼핑의 어려움을 극복하고자 함을 설명하고 있다. 따라서 빈칸에는 이 글의 주제인 창의적인 방법의 하나의 사례인 5층의 미끄럼틀의 내용이 반드시 들어가야 한다. 따라서 밑줄 친 부분에 들어갈 말로 가장 적절한 것은 ④이다.

해석

상하이에 있는 Soleil 백화점 아웃렛은 고급 브랜드와 독점적인 위치 등 현대식 중국 소매업계에서 성공하기 위해 필요한 모든 편의 시설을 갖추고 있는 것으로 보인다. 그러나 이러한 장점에도 불구하고 매장 관리자들은 고객 유치를 위한 뭔가가 여전히 놓치고 생각했다. 그래서 다음 주에 그들은 쇼핑객들이 5층 럭셔리 부티크에서 1층 럭셔리 부티크까지 아슬아슬한 속도로 타고 내려올 수 있는 엄청나게 크고, 비틀린, 용 모양의 미끄럼틀을 발표한다. 소셜 미디어 사용자들은 농담 반 진담 반으로 그 미끄럼틀이 누군가를 죽이지 않을지 궁금해 한다. 그러나 Soleil은 중국 쇼핑몰이 완전히 사라질 우려가 있다는 다른 걱정을 하고 있다. 한때 겉보기에는 끝없는 공급을 이루어 오던 중국 구매자는 온라인 쇼핑이 증가함에 따라 더 이상 오프라인 매장에 나타나고 있지 않으며, 여전히 고급 상품들을 사러 해외로 나가고 있다. 따라서 그들의 시간과 돈을 쓰는 다른 방식을 가진 고객들을 위해 이 거대한 공간을 다른 목적으로 사용하도록 하는 것은 많은 창의성이 필요할 것이다. <u>5층짜리 미끄럼틀이 나쁜 시작은 아닐지도 모른다.</u>

① 명품 브랜드들이 Soleil에서 번성하고 있다
② Soleil는 대담한 조치에 반대하기로 결정했다
③ 온라인 고객 기반을 증가하는 것이 마지막 희망일지도 모른다
④ 5층짜리 용 미끄럼틀이 나쁜 시작은 아닐지도 모른다

어휘

□ amenity 생활 편의 시설
□ retail 소매, 유통, 소매하다
□ exclusive 독점적인, 배타적인
□ attract 끌어들이다
□ unveil 덮개를 벗기다, 발표하다
□ death-defying 아슬아슬한, 죽음에 도전하는
□ half-jokingly 농담 반 진담 반으로
□ concern 우려, 걱정
□ seemingly 겉보기에는, 외견상으로
□ turn up 나타나다
□ brick-and-mortar 소매의, 오프라인 거래의
□ repurpose 다른 목적에 맞게 만들다
□ massive 거대한, 엄청나게 큰
□ thrive 번창하다, 성장하다
□ bold 대담한, 용감한

정답 ④

45 밑줄 친 부분에 들어갈 말로 가장 적절한 것은?

2017. 국가직 9급

It is easy to devise numerous possible scenarios of future developments, each one, on the face of it, equally likely. The difficult task is to know which will actually take place. In hindsight, it usually seems obvious. When we look back in time, each event seems clearly and logically to follow from previous events. Before the event occurs, however, the number of possibilities seems endless. There are no methods for successful prediction, especially in areas involving complex social and technological changes, where many of the determining factors are not known and, in any event, are certainly not under any single group's control. Nonetheless, it is essential to ______________________. We do know that new technologies will bring both dividends and problems, especially human, social problems. The more we try to anticipate these problems, the better we can control them.

① work out reasonable scenarios for the future
② legitimize possible dividends from future changes
③ leave out various aspects of technological problems
④ consider what it would be like to focus on the present

해설

이 글은 미래에 대한 다양한 시나리오를 만드는 것의 중요성과 예측의 어려움을 강조하며, 불확실한 미래에 대비하기 위해 합리적인 시나리오를 고려하는 중요성을 다루고 있다. 이 미래 계획에 대한 의견은 빈칸 다음에 나오는데, 그 내용으로 'the 비교급' 구문으로 '우리가 이러한 문제들을 예측하려 노력하면 노력할수록, 우리는 그것들을 더 잘 통제할 수 있다'라는 진술을 통해, 미래 계획의 필요성에 대해서 이야기를 하고 있다. 따라서 밑줄 친 부분에 들어갈 말로 가장 적절한 것은 ①이다.

해석

미래발전에 대한 많은 가능한 시나리오들을 만드는 것은 쉽고, 각각의 시나리오는 외관상 동일하게 가능성이 있다. 어려운 일은 실제로 어떤 일이 발생할 것인지를 아는 것이다. 시간이 지나고 나서 보니까, 이것은 보통 명백하게 보인다. 시간이 지남에 따라 우리가 과거를 돌아볼 때, 각 사건은 명확하며 논리적으로 선행 사건으로부터 뒤따라 나온 것으로 보인다. 그러나 사건이 일어나기 전에 가능성의 수는 끝이 없는 것처럼 보인다. 특히 복잡한 사회 및 기술 변화를 포함하는 분야에서 성공적인 예측을 위한 방법은 없으며, 많은 결정 요인이 알려지지 않았으며, 어떤 경우에도 확실히 단일 그룹의 통제하에 있지 않다. 그럼에도 불구하고 미래를 위한 합리적인 시나리오를 만드는 것이 중요하다. 우리는 새로운 기술들이 이익들과 문제들 둘 다 가져올 것이라는 것을 알고 있고, 특별히 인간적이고 사회적인 문제들에서 그러하다. 더 많이 우리가 이러한 문제들을 예측하려 노력하면 노력할수록, 우리는 그것들을 더 잘 통제할 수 있다.

① 미래를 위한 합리적인 시나리오를 만드는
② 미래의 변화로 인해 가능한 이익 배당금을 정당화하는
③ 기술적 문제의 다양한 측면을 빠뜨리는
④ 현재에 초점을 맞추는 것이 어떤 것인지를 고려해보는

어휘

☐ devise 고안하다, 마련하다
☐ numerous 수많은, 다양한
☐ task 과제, 임무
☐ take place 발생하다
☐ in hindsight 지나고 나서 보니까
☐ prediction 예측, 예견
☐ involve 수반하다, 포함하다, 관련시키다
☐ dividend 이익, 배당금
☐ anticipate 기대하다, 예상하다
☐ legitimize 정당화하다, 합법화하다
☐ leave out 생략하다, 빼다, 무시하다

정답 ①

46 밑줄 친 부분에 들어갈 말로 가장 적절한 것은?

2017. 지방직 9급

One of the tricks our mind plays is to highlight evidence which confirms what we already believe. If we hear gossip about a rival, we tend to think "I knew he was a nasty piece of work"; if we hear the same about our best friend, we're more likely to say "that's just a rumour." Once you learn about this mental habit — called confirmation bias — you start seeing it everywhere. This matters when we want to make better decisions. Confirmation bias is OK as long as we're right, but all too often we're wrong, and we only pay attention to the deciding evidence when it's too late. How ______________________ depends on our awareness of why, psychologically, confirmation bias happens. There are two possible reasons. One is that we have a blind spot in our imagination and the other is we fail to ask questions about new information.

① we make our rivals believe us
② our blind spot helps us make better decisions
③ we can protect our decisions from confirmation bias
④ we develop exactly the same bias

해설

확증편향과 이것의 결정에 미치는 영향을 주제로 하는 글로, 확증편향으로부터 결정을 보호하고 상상력 약한 부분과 새로운 정보에 대한 질문의 중요성을 이해하는 것이 필요함을 강조하고 있다. 확증편향이라는 문제를 해결을 어떻게 하는지에 대한 해결책이 빈칸에 들어가야 한다. 따라서 밑줄 친 부분에 들어갈 말로 가장 적절한 것은 ③이다.

해석

우리의 마음이 하는 속임수들 중 하나는 우리가 이미 믿고 있는 것들을 확인하는 증거들을 강조하는 것이다. 만약 우리가 경쟁자에 대한 소문을 듣는 다면, 우리는 "그 녀석이 형편없는 사람인줄 알고 있었어"라고 생각하는 경향이 있다. 우리가 제일 친한 친구에 관한 똑같은 소문을 듣는다면 우리는 "그건 단지 뜬소문이야"라고 말할 가능성이 높다. 일단 당신이 이러한 마음의 습관 – 확증 편향이라 불리는 – 을 알게 되면 당신은 이것을 여러 곳에서 목격하기 시작할 것이다. 이것은 우리가 좀 더 훌륭한 결정을 내리기를 원할 때 중요하다. 우리가 생각하는 바가 맞는 한 확증 편향은 문제가 없다. 그러나 너무나 자주 우리는 틀리며, 너무 늦게야 결정을 내려주는 증거들에 주목하게 된다. 어떻게 우리가 확증 편향으로부터 우리의 결정을 보호할지는 어떤 이유에서 확증 편향이 심리적으로 발생하는지를 인지하는 것에 달려있다. 이에는 두 개의 가능성 있는 이유가 있다. 하나는 우리는 맹점을 가지고 있으며, 또 다른 하나는 우리가 새로운 정보에 대해 질문하는 것에 실패한다는 점이다.

① 우리의 경쟁자들이 우리를 믿게 만드는지
② 우리의 맹점이 우리로 하여금 더 나은 결정을 하도록 도와주는지
③ 우리가 확증 편향으로부터 우리의 결정들을 보호할지
④ 우리는 정확히 같은 편견을 형성하는지

어휘

□ trick 속임수, 장난
□ highlight 강조하다
□ evidence 증거
□ confirm 확인해주다, 확정하다
□ gossip 풍문, 소문
□ nasty 끔찍한, 형편없는, 못된
□ confirmation bias 확증 편향
□ psychologically 심리적으로, 정신적으로
□ blind spot 맹점, 약점

정답 ③

47 밑줄 친 부분에 들어갈 말로 가장 적절한 것은? 2017. 지방직 9급

For many big names in consumer product brands, exporting and producing overseas with local labor and for local tastes have been the right thing to do. In doing so, the companies found a way to improve their cost structure, to grow in the rapidly expanding consumer markets in emerging countries. But, Sweets Co. remains stuck in the domestic market. Even though its products are loaded with preservatives, which means they can endure long travel to distant markets, Sweets Co. ______________________, let alone produce overseas. The unwillingness or inability to update its business strategy and products for a changing world is clearly damaging to the company.

① is intent on importing
② does very little exporting
③ has decided to streamline operations
④ is expanding into emerging markets

해설

소비재 기업의 글로벌 전략과 도전에 대한 글로, 도전에 대한 해결책으로 수출 혹은 현지생산을 제시하고 있다. 빈칸에는 Sweets Co.가 겪는 문제에 대한 원인이 들어가야 한다. 글의 주제가 외국에서 생산과 판매(수출)하는 것이다. 스위스 회사가 성장하지 못한 이유는 외국에서 생산을 하지 않을 뿐만 아니라 수출도 하지 않기 때문이다. 따라서 밑줄 친 부분에 들어갈 말로 가장 적절한 것은 ②이다.

해석

소비재 제품 브랜드에서의 큰 회사들에게 있어, 외국으로 수출하는 것과 지역 노동력과 함께 지역의 취향을 목적으로 외국에서 생산하는 것은 해야 할 올바른 것이다. 그렇게 하는데 있어서, 기업들은 그들의 비용구조를 향상시키면서 신흥 국가들에의 빠르게 확장되는 소비자 시장에 있어 성장할 수 있는 방법을 찾았다. 그러나 Sweets Co.는 국내 시장에 머물러 있다. 회사의 제품들이 방부제들로 충분히 있어서 먼 시장으로의 긴 여행을 견딜 수 있다는 것을 의미하지만, Sweets Co. 회사는 해외에서의 생산은 말할 것도 없이 수출을 거의 하지 않는다. 변화하는 세계를 목표로 하는 사업전략과 제품들을 업데이트 하지 않는 꺼림과 무능력은 그 회사에게 분명히 타격을 주고 있다.

① 수입에 열중한다
② 수출을 거의 하지 않는다
③ 운영을 능률화하기로 결정하고 있다
④ 신흥 시장으로 확장하고 있는 중이다

어휘

□ be loaded with 충분히 있다
□ preservative 방부제
□ endure 견디다
□ let alone 말할 것도 없이, ~은 커녕
□ unwillingness 본의 아님, 자발적이 아님
□ inability 무능, 불능
□ import 수입, 수입하다
□ export 수출, 수출하다
□ streamline 간소화하다, 능률화하다

정답 ②

48 밑줄 친 부분에 들어갈 말로 가장 적절한 것은?

2017. 지방직 9급

London taxi drivers have to undertake years of intense training known as "the knowledge" to gain their operating license, including learning the layout of over twenty-five thousand of the city's streets. A researcher and her team investigated the taxi drivers and the ordinary people. The two groups were asked to watch videos of routes unfamiliar to them through a town in Ireland. They were then asked to take a test about the video that included sketching out routes, identifying landmarks, and estimating distances between places. Both groups did well on much of the test, but the taxi drivers did significantly better on identifying new routes. This result suggests that the taxi drivers' mastery can be ____________ to new and unknown areas. Their years of training and learning through deliberate practice prepare them to take on similar challenges even in places they do not know well or at all.

① confined
② devoted
③ generalized
④ contributed

해설

택시 운전기사들의 지식과 숙련도에 관한 연구를 주제로 하는 글로, 한 연구는 런던의 택시 운전기사들이 특별한 훈련을 통해 쌓은 지식과 숙련도가 새로운 길을 찾아내는 능력에 어떤 영향을 미치는지를 설명하고 있다. 연구의 실험결과로 택시 운전기사들이 새롭고 알지 못하는 환경에서도 잘해 낸다고 진술하고 있다. 따라서 밑줄 친 부분에 들어갈 말로 가장 적절한 것은 ③이다.

해석

런던의 택시 운전기사들은 자신들의 운행 허가를 얻기 위해 그 도시의 이만오천개가 넘는 길에 대한 배치도를 배우는 것을 포함하여 "지식"으로 알려진 강렬한 훈련을 몇 년간 받아야 할 의무를 진다. 한 연구자와 그녀의 팀은 택시 운전기사들과 일반인을 조사했다. 이 두 그룹은 아일랜드의 어떤 마을을 통과하는 그들에게 익숙하지 않은 길들의 비디오를 보도록 요청되었다. 그러고 나서 그들은 길을 그려내고, 주요 지형지물을 구별하고, 장소 사이의 거리를 추정하는 것이 포함된 테스트를 받도록 요청받았다. 이 두 그룹은 테스트의 대부분에서 잘 했으나, 택시 운전기사들은 새로운 길을 찾아내는 데 있어서는 상당히 더 잘 했다. 이 결과는 택시 운전기사들의 숙련도가 새롭고 알지 못하는 지역에도 일반화되는 것을 보여준다. 그들의 의도된 연습을 통한 수년간의 훈련과 학습이 그들이 유사한 도전들을 심지어 그들이 잘 알지 못하거나 전혀 알지 못하는 장소에서 조차 잘 수행할 수 있도록 준비시킨다.

① 한정되는
② 헌신하는
③ 일반화되는
④ 공헌하는

어휘

□ undertake 착수하다, 떠맡다, ~할 의무를 지다
□ intense 강렬한
□ operating license 운행 허가
□ route 길, 경로
□ layout 배치
□ investigate 조사하다
□ landmark 주요 지형지물
□ mastery 숙련도
□ deliberate 의도적인, 고의의, 사려 깊은

정답 ③

06 빈칸 추론 유형 기출 독해 어휘 복습 TEST 정답

정답

1	unemployment	실업(률)	21	standardization	표준화, 규격화, 통일, 획일
2	income	소득, 수입	22	roll out	출시하다, 시작하다, 밀어서 펴다
3	substitute	대체하다, 대신하다, 대체물, 대리자	23	uniform	획일적인, 균일한
4	predominant	주요한, 우세한, 지배적인, 두드러진, 뚜렷한	24	disparate	서로 전혀 다른, 이질적인
5	inevitably	필연적으로, 불가피하게	25	empirical	경험에 의거한, 실증적인
6	disastrous	처참한, 재앙의, 불길한	26	distraction	주의 산만, 방해
7	project	예상하다, 추정하다, 계획하다, 계획, 과제	27	persist	지속되다, 집요하게 계속 하다
8	population	인구, 주민	28	immerse	담그다, 몰두하다, 몰두하게 만들다
9	aging	고령화, 노령화, 노화	29	buffer	완화하다, 보호하다, 완충제
10	demographic	인구 통계학적인, 인구학의, 인구의	30	break off	분리되다, 떨어지다
11	elderly	노인, 어르신들, 나이가 지긋한	31	massive	거대한, 심각한
12	inattention	부주의, 태만, 무관심	32	propaganda	선전
13	comprehend	이해하다, 파악하다, 포함하다, 의미하다	33	plain	평범한, 보통의, 평원, 평지
14	appeal	매력, 호소	34	misperception	오해
15	persuasion	설득, 강요	35	interpretation	해석, 이해, 설명
16	devote	헌신하다, 전념하다	36	authority	권위, 권한
17	settle down	안정을 찾다, 정착하다	37	throw away	버리다, 없애다
18	mortgage	대출(금), 융자(금), 저당 잡히다	38	budget	예산, 비용
19	existing	기존의, 현재 사용되는	39	hand down	~을 물려주다
20	paradoxical	역설적인	40	prerequisite	전제 조건

06 빈칸 추론 유형 기출 독해 어휘 복습 TEST 정답

정답

41	discriminate	구별하다, 식별하다, 차별하다	61	outline	개요를 제시하다, 윤곽을 보여주다
42	scattered	산발적인, 흩어져 있는, 드문드문 있는	62	intuition	직감, 직관
43	autonomy	자율성, 자주성	63	conscientious	양심적인, 성실한
44	unoccupied	비어있는, 점령되지 않은	64	setback	방해, 차질
45	determine	결정하다, 알아내다, 밝히다	65	underpin	뒷받침하다, 근거를 대다
46	decay	부패, 부식, 부패하다, 썩다	66	plummet	급락하다, 곤두박질치다
47	measure	측정하다, 재다	67	hypothesis	가설, 추정, 추측
48	approximate	대략적인, 근사치인	68	entrance	입장, 등장
49	extinct	멸종된, 사라진	69	manufacture	제조, 생산, 제조하다
50	constitute	구성하다, 이루다	70	transcend	초월하다, 능가하다
51	concrete	구체적인, 사실에 의거한	71	impede	방해하다, 지연시키다
52	subject to	영향을 받기 쉬운	72	trivial	사소한, 하찮은
53	keen	치열한, 열렬한, 예리한	73	matter	문제, 상황, 중요하다, 문제되다
54	modify	수정하다, 변경하다	74	calculate	계산하다, 산출하다
55	subconscious	잠재의식적인, 무의식적인	75	alert	기민한, 경계하는, (위험 등을) 알리다
56	odds	가능성, 역경, 곤란	76	astute	교활한, 약삭빠른
57	bother	신경 쓰다, 귀찮게 하다	77	altruism	이타주의, 이타심
58	famine	기근	78	legitimize	정당화하다, 합법화하다
59	coherent	일관성 있는, 논리 정연한	79	nasty	끔찍한, 형편없는, 못된
60	sequence	순서, 차례	80	streamline	간소화하다, 능률화하다

MEMO

MEMO

MEMO

MEMO

MEMO

MEMO

진가영 영어

반한다 기출 독해

정답 및 해설

박문각 공무원
진가영 영어 온라인강의
www.pmg.co.kr

박문각 공무원
진가영 영어 연구소
cafe.naver.com/easyenglish7

박문각 북스파
수험교재 및 교양서 전문
온라인 서점

충남 교행 수석 영어 100점 – 김**

가영쌤의 커리는 기본적으로 반복을 거듭해서 확실하게 기억하고 또 여러 방향으로 적용하면서 어떤 식으로 문제로 변형되어 나와도 확실하게 캐치할 수 있게 만드는 방향으로 진행됩니다. 특히 여러 번 강조해서 배우는, 자주 출제되는 중요한 내용들은 계속 따로 자료를 만들고, 또 특강으로도 계속 또 반복해서 빠짐없이 떠 먹여 주기까지 합니다. 따라가려고 노력만 하면 보상을 받을 수 있는 그런 시간을 보낼 수 있는 강의라고 생각합니다. 가영쌤은 또, 더 재밌는 강의를 위해 매번 좀 웃긴 거를 많이 준비해 오시는 것 같은 모습이 보이는데 많은 정성과 노력을 기울이고 계시다는 걸 느낄 수 있는 시간들이었습니다.

우정직 수석 합격 영어 85점 – 박*태

영어 선생님을 고를 때 가영쌤을 추천하는 이유는 먼저 탄탄한 커리큘럼과 숙제 관리, 그리고 문법 교재가 너무너무 좋습니다! 콤팩트한 책에 있을 내용 다 있고, 문판왕이나 동형모의고사 등 문풀 수업과의 연계도 잘 되어있습니다. 그리고 매주 실강 수업 때 나오는 ox 숙제를 계속 반복해야 문법 출제 포인트가 무엇인지 익숙해집니다. 또한, 가영쌤의 어휘책 구성도 좋았고, 매 수업 전에 테스트를 하기 때문에 미리 공부해가야 하는 게 실력 향상에 도움이 되었습니다. 덕분에 이번 문제 풀이 소요시간, 24분, 동형 때는 달성해보지 못했던 최고기록입니다. 가영쌤 I cannot thank you enough!!

2024 일반행정직 영어 100점 – **선

영어 100점은 진짜 운이라고 생각했는데 선생님 만나고 나서 이게 진짜 실력으로 된다는 걸 알았어요. 단어 미친 반복으로 겨우 다 외우고 문법도 단판승 3시간 너무 좋았고 독해는 그 200제가 정말 좋았어요. 제가 국가직 영어 35분 걸려서 정말 선생님도 찾아뵈고 걱정 많이 했는데 이번 지방직은 20분 컷해서 정말 좋았어요. 언제나 감사합니다!!

2024 일반행정직 영어 95점 – **경

공시 시작하고 가영쌤을 만나서 영어 공부도 즐겁게 할 수 있었고 95점이라는 고득점도 해볼 수 있었고 항상 최선을 다하시는 모습을 보면서 많이 본받아야겠다 생각했습니다. 나태해질 때마다 쌤을 보면서 힘을 얻었고 앞으로도 제가 많이 존경하고 진심으로 응원할 영원한 제 1타 강사 가영쌤♥ 건강 잘 챙기시고 곧 태어날 아이와 가족들 또 주변 사람들과 행복한 순간만 앞으로 더 가득하시면 좋겠어요♥ 서울 가게 되면 인사드리러 꼭 갈게요!! 쌤이랑 함께한 시간들 항상 소중했어요♥ I cannot thank you enough♥

2024년 사회복지직 영어 95점 – **화

I cannot thank you enough♥ 시험을 준비하면서 나름의 소소한 목표 중 하나가 영어 시험을 잘 봐서 가영쌤한테 제가 먼저 올해 영어 잘 봤다고 연락드리는 거였는데, 드디어 그 목표를 이룰 수 있게 되어서 너무 기뻐요! 처음 박문각 와서 하프 들었을 때 3,4개 맞기도 하고 그랬던 적이 있었는데~ 쌤과 열심히 함께 달렸더니 95점이라는 이런 좋은 점수를 받았습니다. 영어는 제 발목을 잡는 과목 중 하나여서 처음부터 끝까지 긴장을 놓지 않고 제일 큰 비중을 두고 공부한 과목이었습니다. 이번 지방직에서 단어, 문법, 생활영어까지 쌤과 함께 공부했던 범위 내에서 계속 반복하며 공부했던 부분들이라 신속하고 정확하게 풀 수 있어 시간 절약을 했던 것 같아요! 다 가영쌤과 함께한 덕분이에요!

박문각 www.pmg.co.kr **교재문의** 02-6466-7202 **동영상강의 문의** 02-6466-7201

정가 23,000원

13740

9 791172 622084

ISBN 979-11-7262-208-4

2025년

신경향(New Trend)

보완 커리큘럼

합격을 위한 선택 과정

기초 이론	공무원 영어 시작, 입문
구문 독해	진(Real) 독해 기초 체력 다지기 / 신경향 독해 기본 실력 다지기
문풀 N제	신경향 마스터 시리즈 (독해, 문법, 어휘)
적중 특강	진(眞) 족보 마무리 특강 시리즈 (독해, 문법, 어휘, 생활영어)

★★★★★ 2024년 사회복지직 영어 95점 **화

I can not thank you enough♡♡♡
시험을 준비하면서 나름의 소소한 목표 중 하나가 영어 시험을 잘 봐서 가영쌤한테 제가 먼저 올해 영어 잘 봤다고 연락드리는 거였는데, 드디어 그 목표를 이룰 수 있게 되어서 너무 기뻐요! 처음 박문각 와서 하프 들었을 때 3,4개 맞기도 하고 그랬던 적이 있었는데~ **쌤과 열심히 함께 달렸더니 95점이라는 이런 좋은 점수를 받았습니다. 영어는 제 발목을 잡는 과목 중 하나여서 처음부터 끝까지 긴장을 놓지 않고 제일 큰 비중을 두고 공부한 과목이었습니다. 이번 지방직에서 단어, 문법, 생활영어까지 쌤과 함께 공부했던 범위 내에서 계속 반복하며 공부했던 부분들이라 신속하고 정확하게 풀 수 있어 시간 절약을 했던 것 같아요!** 다 가영쌤과 함께한 덕분이에요!

★★★★★ 2024 일방행정직 영어 95점 **경

공시 시작하고 가영쌤을 만나서 영어 공부도 즐겁게 할 수 있었고 95점이라는 고득점도 해볼 수 있었고 항상 최선을 다하시는 모습을 보면서 많이 본받아야겠다 생각했습니다. 나태해질 때마다 쌤을 보면서 힘을 얻었고 앞으로도 제가 많이 존경하고 진심으로 응원할 영원한 제 1타 강사 가영쌤♡ 건강 잘 챙기시고 곧 태어날 아이와 가족들 또 주변 사람들과 행복한 순간만 앞으로 더 가득하시면 좋겠어요♡서울 가게 되면 인사드리러 꼭 갈게요!! 쌤이랑 함께한 시간들 항상 소중했어요♡
I cannot thank you enough♡♡

★★★★★ 2024년 일반농업직 영어 100점 **주

3번 도전 끝에 마지막이라고 생각한 시험에서 다행히도 최종합격이라는 좋은 결과를 얻을 수 있었습니다. 제가 이번 **국가직에서 최종합격 할 수 있었던 이유는 진가영 선생님 덕분입니다!** 이번 국가직 영어가 어렵게 출제가 되었지만 **가영쌤을 믿고 따른 결과 100점이라는 성적을 거둘 수 있었습니다.** 혹시라도 영어 강의 선택을 앞두고 계신 분들이 있다면 무.조.건. 진.가.영. 영.어.를 선택하시길 바랍니다! 내년에 바뀌는 시험에서도 안전하게 여러분들을 합격까지 인도해주실 것입니다.

★★★★★ 2024 일방행정직 영어 95점 **선

영어 100점은 진짜 운이라고 생각했는데 선생님 만나고 나서 이게 진짜 실력으로 된다는 걸 알았어요. 단어 미친 반복으로 겨우 다 외우고 문법도 단판승 3시간 너무 좋았고 독해는 그 200제가 정말 좋았어요. 제가 국가직 영어 35분 걸려서 정말 선생님도 찾아뵈고 걱정 많이 했는데 이번 지방직은 20분 컷해서 정말 좋았어요. 언제나 감사합니다!!